結界師（けっかいし）
KEKKAISHI

32

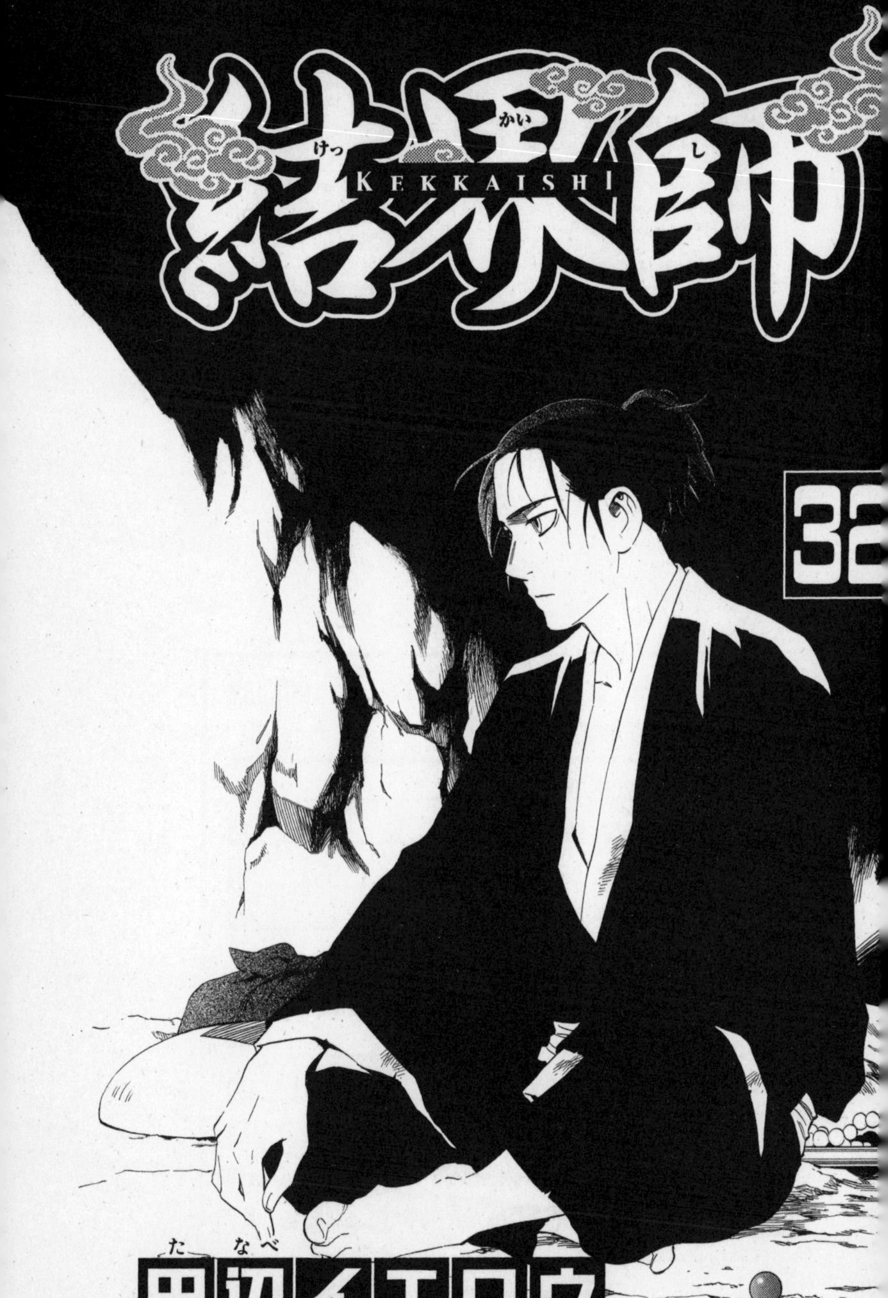

田辺（たなべ）イエロウ

YELLOW TANABE PRESENTS

The Story Thus Far

Yoshimori begins training with his mother's shikigami at an abandoned mountainside mansion to learn how to permanently seal away Lord Chushinmaru.

The man who appeared with the ayakashi Kumon to test Yoshimori's skill turned out to be Tokimori Hazama, the founder of the Hazama-style kekkai technique. Tokimori has been waiting 400 years for the opportunity to teach his new technique, Shinkai, to someone worthy of it...

Meanwhile, from the documents left by her beloved Michiru, Kakeru discovers the true nature of Nichinaga, the leader of the Shadow Organization—and vows revenge. Nichinaga has chosen Arashizaki Shrine, the home of the Ogi Family, as his next target. The time for a definitive battle draws near...!

KEKKAISHI   VOL. 32

TABLE OF CONTENTS

CHAPTER 306

TERRITORY

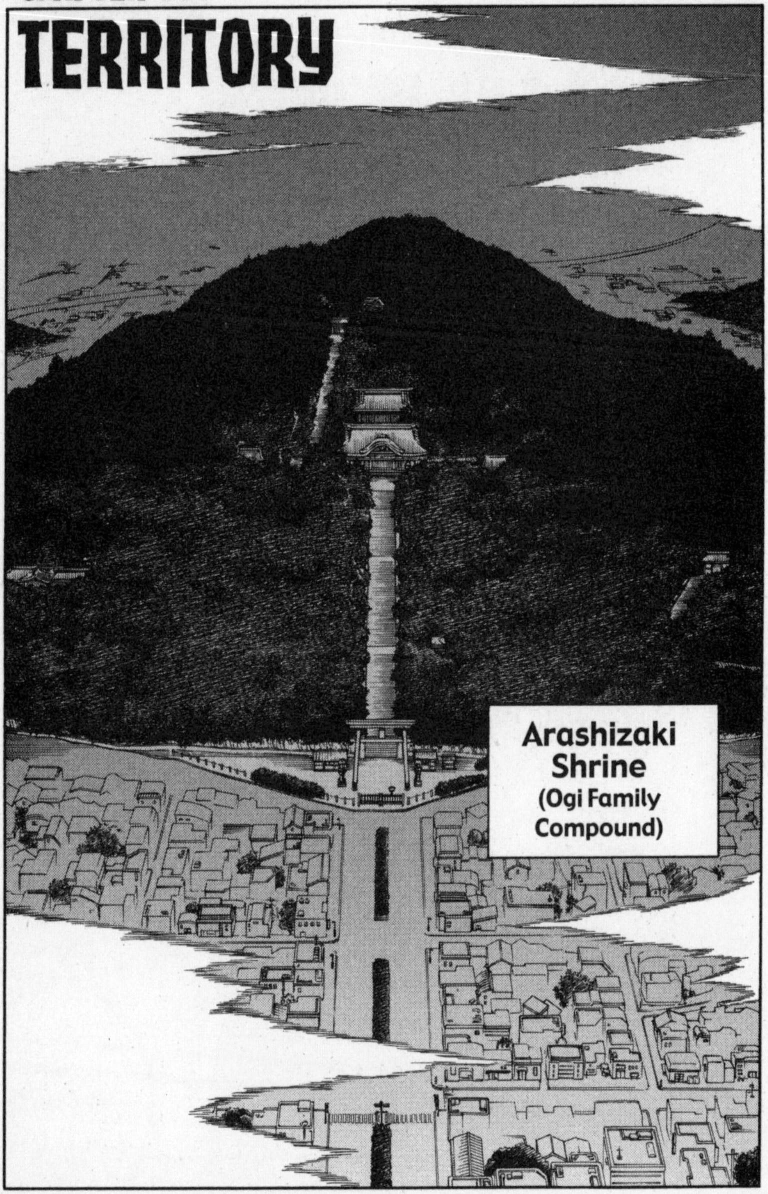
Arashizaki Shrine
(Ogi Family Compound)

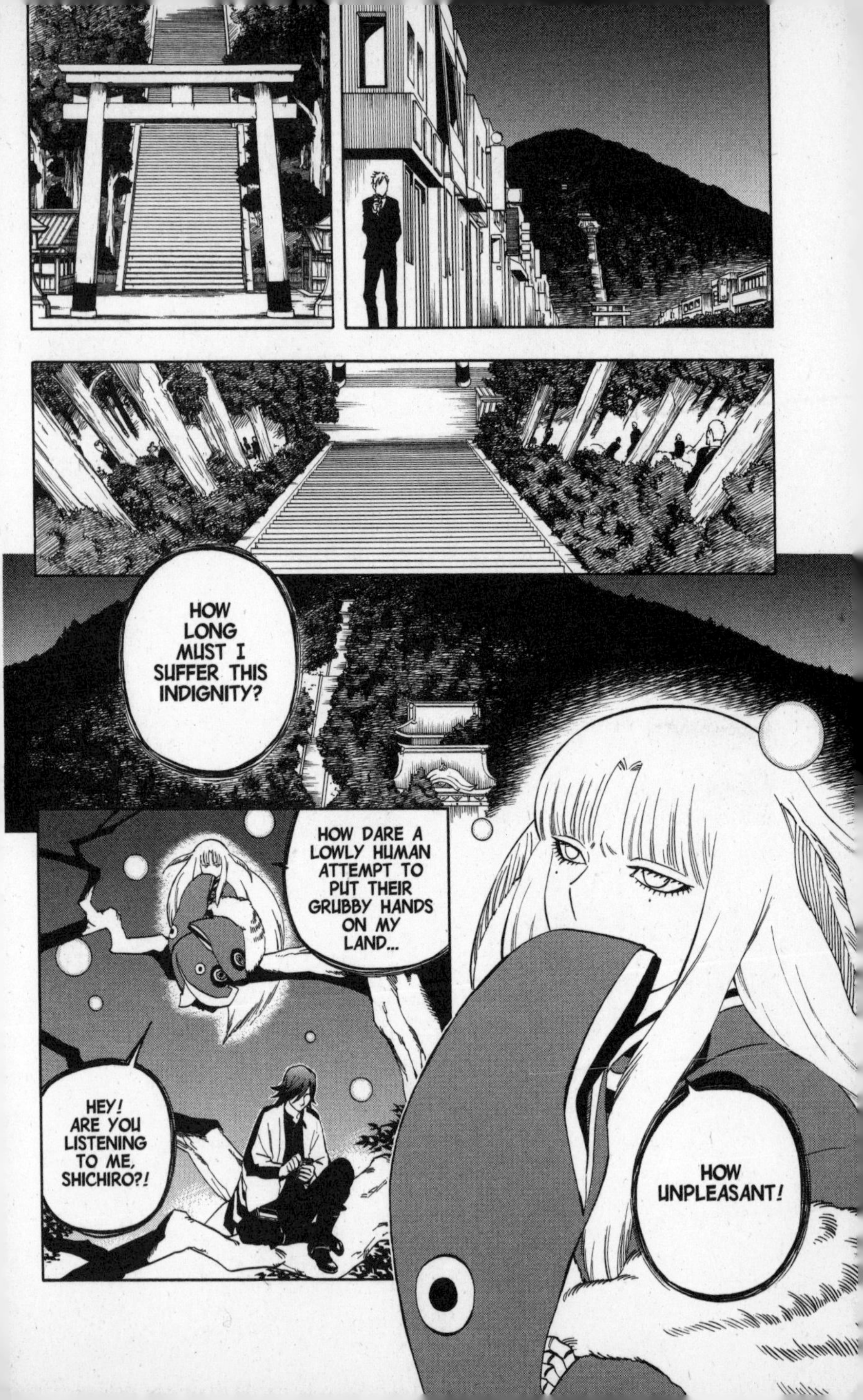
HOW LONG MUST I SUFFER THIS INDIGNITY?
HOW DARE A LOWLY HUMAN ATTEMPT TO PUT THEIR GRUBBY HANDS ON MY LAND...
HOW UNPLEASANT!
HEY! ARE YOU LISTENING TO ME, SHICHIRO?!

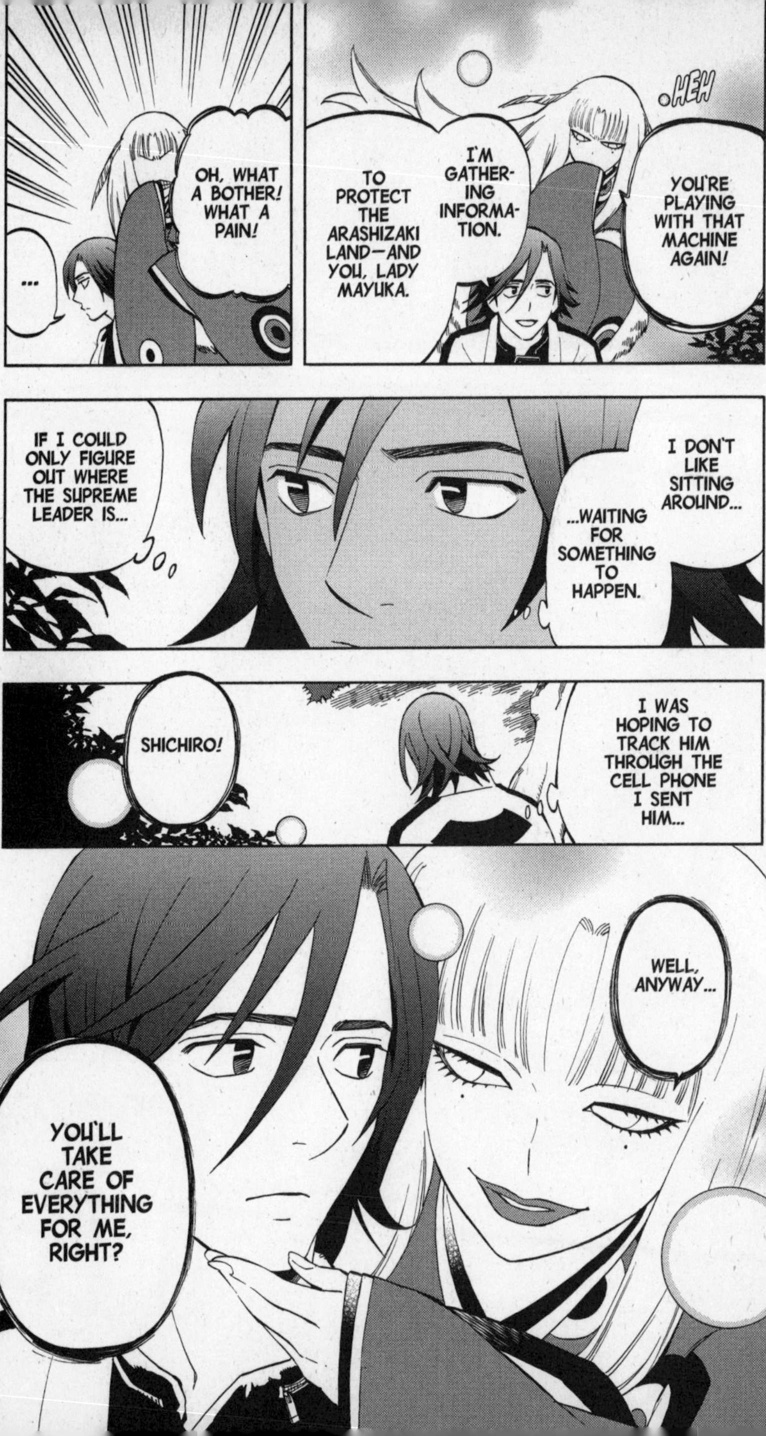
HEH
YOU'RE PLAYING WITH THAT MACHINE AGAIN!
I'M GATHERING INFORMATION.
TO PROTECT THE ARASHIZAKI LAND—AND YOU, LADY MAYUKA.
OH, WHAT A BOTHER! WHAT A PAIN!
...
I DON'T LIKE SITTING AROUND...
...WAITING FOR SOMETHING TO HAPPEN.
IF I COULD ONLY FIGURE OUT WHERE THE SUPREME LEADER IS...
I WAS HOPING TO TRACK HIM THROUGH THE CELL PHONE I SENT HIM...
SHICHIRO!
WELL, ANYWAY...
YOU'LL TAKE CARE OF EVERYTHING FOR ME, RIGHT?

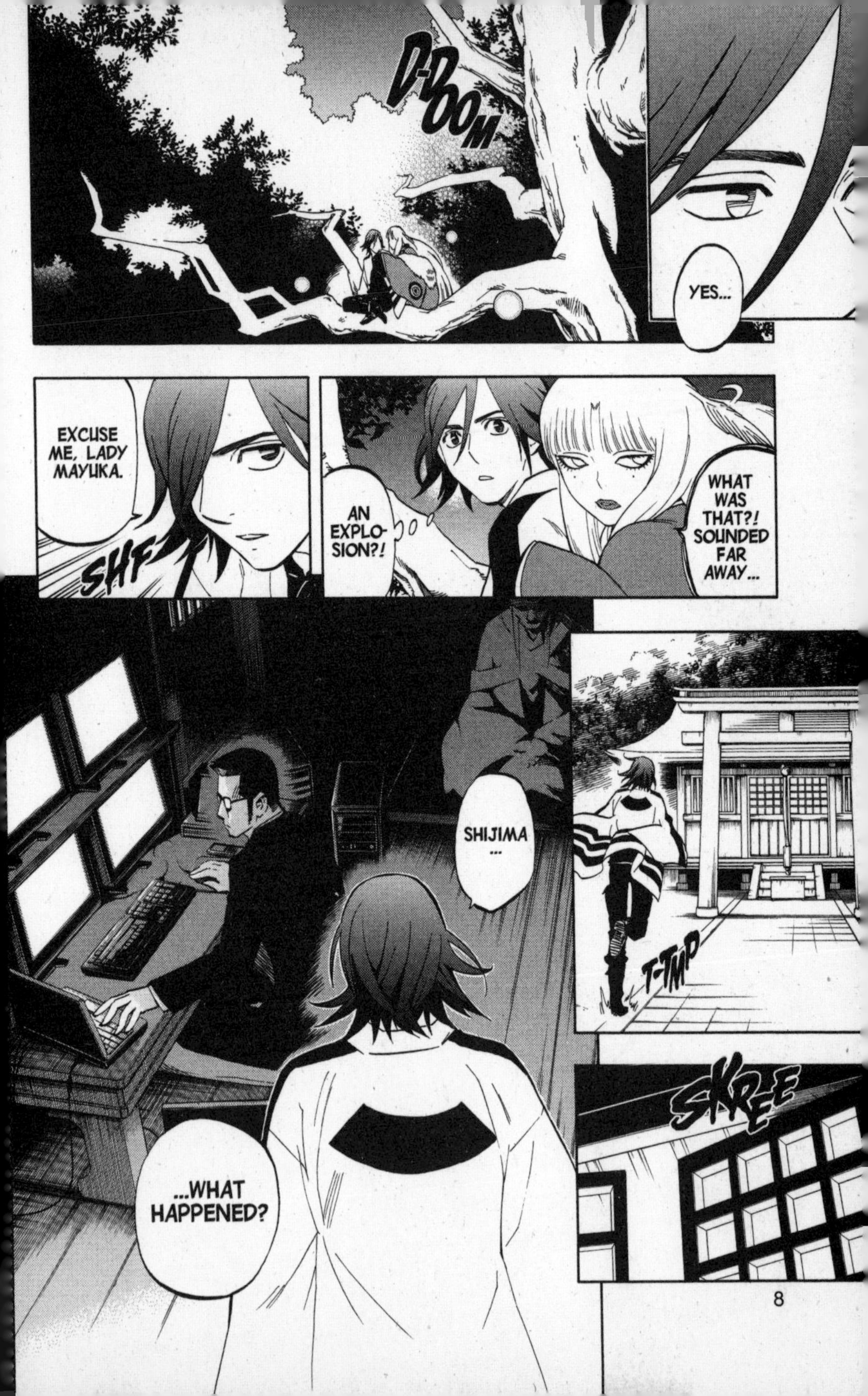
YES...
D-DOOM
WHAT WAS THAT?! SOUNDED FAR AWAY...
AN EXPLOSION?!
EXCUSE ME, LADY MAYUKA.
SHF
T-TMP
SKREE
SHIJIMA...
...WHAT HAPPENED?

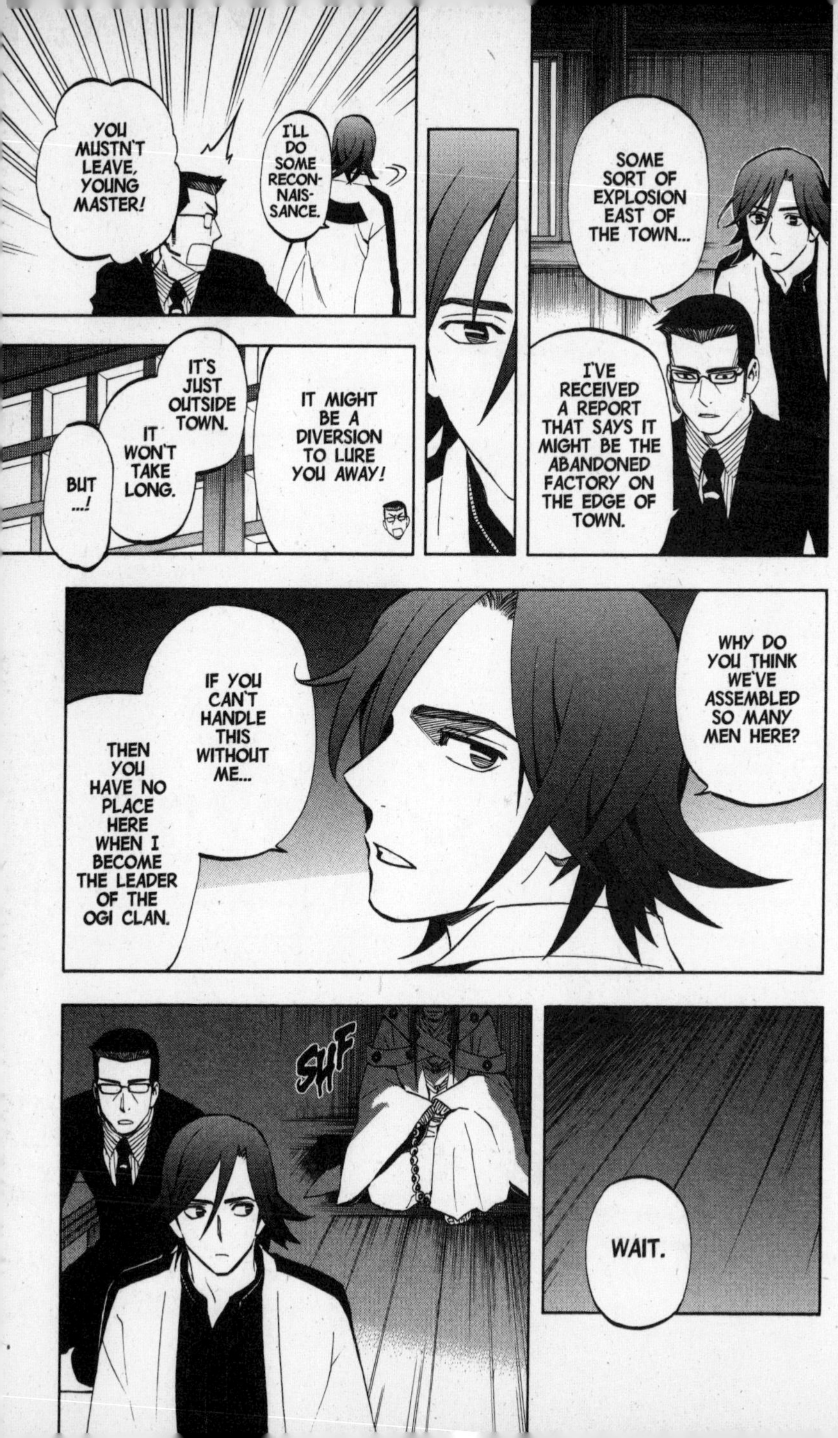
SOME SORT OF EXPLOSION EAST OF THE TOWN...
I'VE RECEIVED A REPORT THAT SAYS IT MIGHT BE THE ABANDONED FACTORY ON THE EDGE OF TOWN.
I'LL DO SOME RECONNAISSANCE.
YOU MUSTN'T LEAVE, YOUNG MASTER!
IT MIGHT BE A DIVERSION TO LURE YOU AWAY!
IT'S JUST OUTSIDE TOWN.
IT WON'T TAKE LONG.
BUT ...!
WHY DO YOU THINK WE'VE ASSEMBLED SO MANY MEN HERE?
IF YOU CAN'T HANDLE THIS WITHOUT ME...
THEN YOU HAVE NO PLACE HERE WHEN I BECOME THE LEADER OF THE OGI CLAN.
WAIT.
SHF

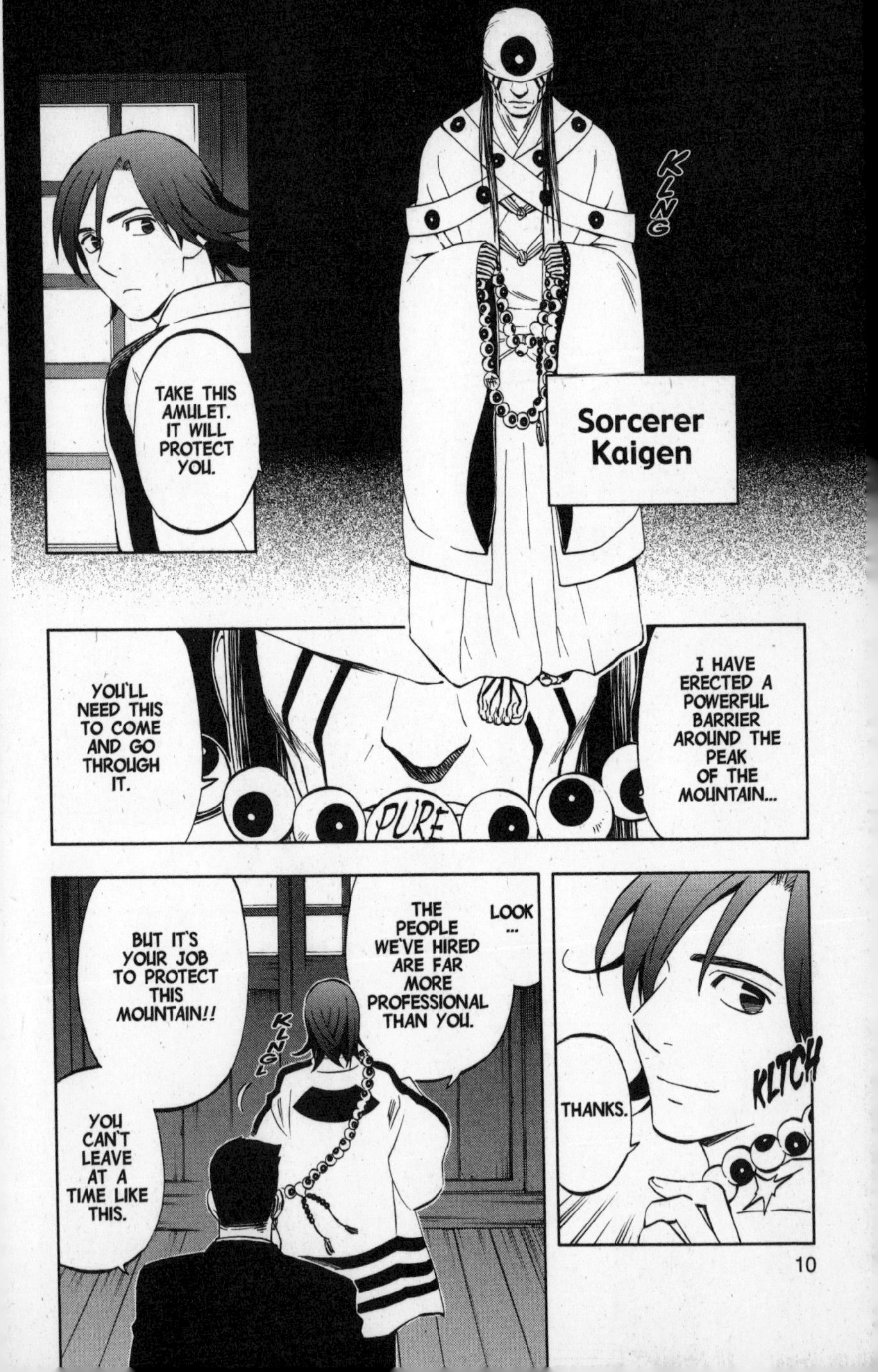
KLING
Sorcerer Kaigen
TAKE THIS AMULET. IT WILL PROTECT YOU.
I HAVE ERECTED A POWERFUL BARRIER AROUND THE PEAK OF THE MOUNTAIN...
YOU'LL NEED THIS TO COME AND GO THROUGH IT.
PURE
KLTCH
THANKS.
LOOK...
THE PEOPLE WE'VE HIRED ARE FAR MORE PROFESSIONAL THAN YOU.
BUT IT'S YOUR JOB TO PROTECT THIS MOUNTAIN!!
YOU CAN'T LEAVE AT A TIME LIKE THIS.
KLING

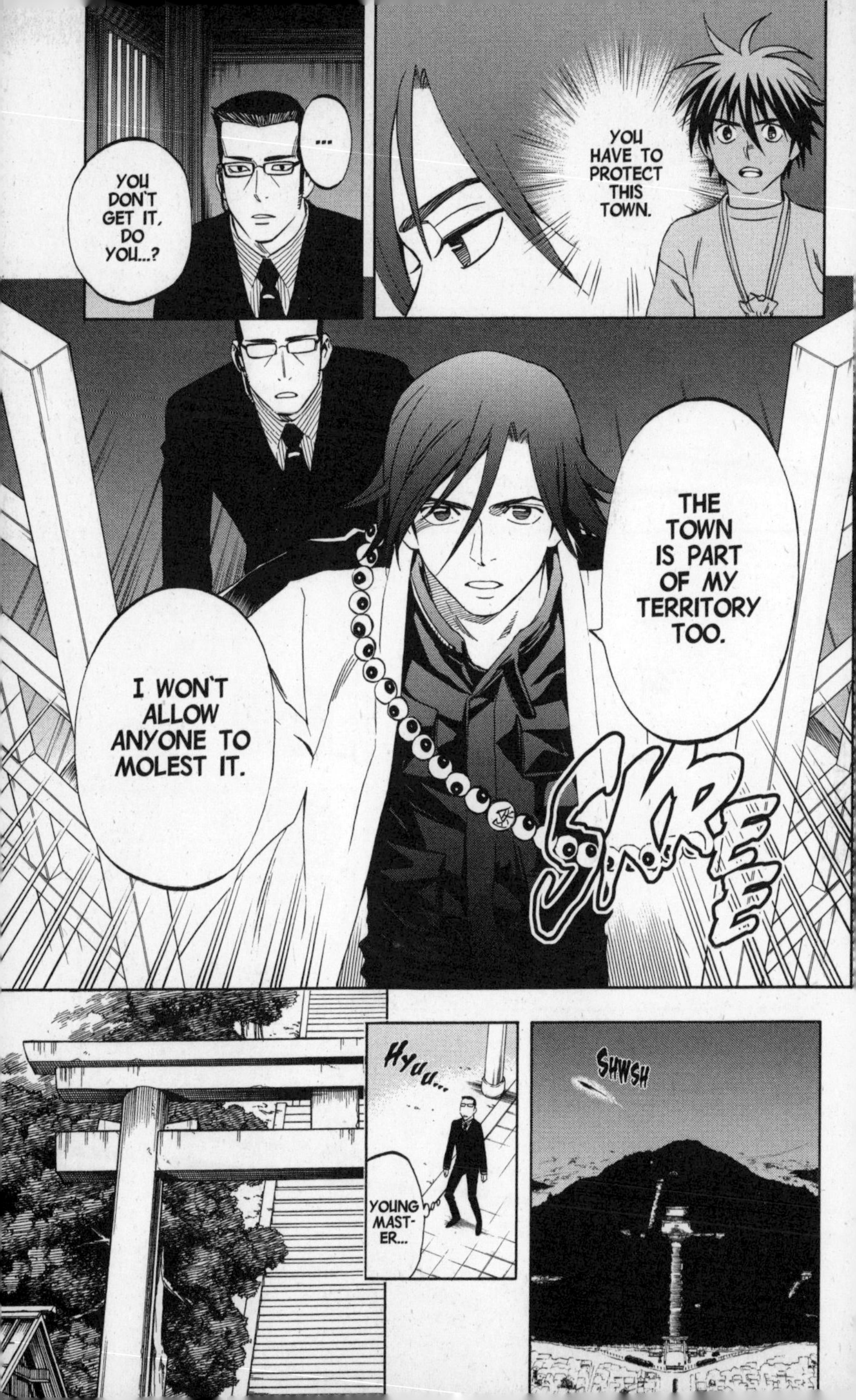
YOU HAVE TO PROTECT THIS TOWN.
...
YOU DON'T GET IT, DO YOU...?
THE TOWN IS PART OF MY TERRITORY TOO.
I WON'T ALLOW ANYONE TO MOLEST IT.
SHREE
SHWSH
HYUU...
YOUNG MAST-ER...

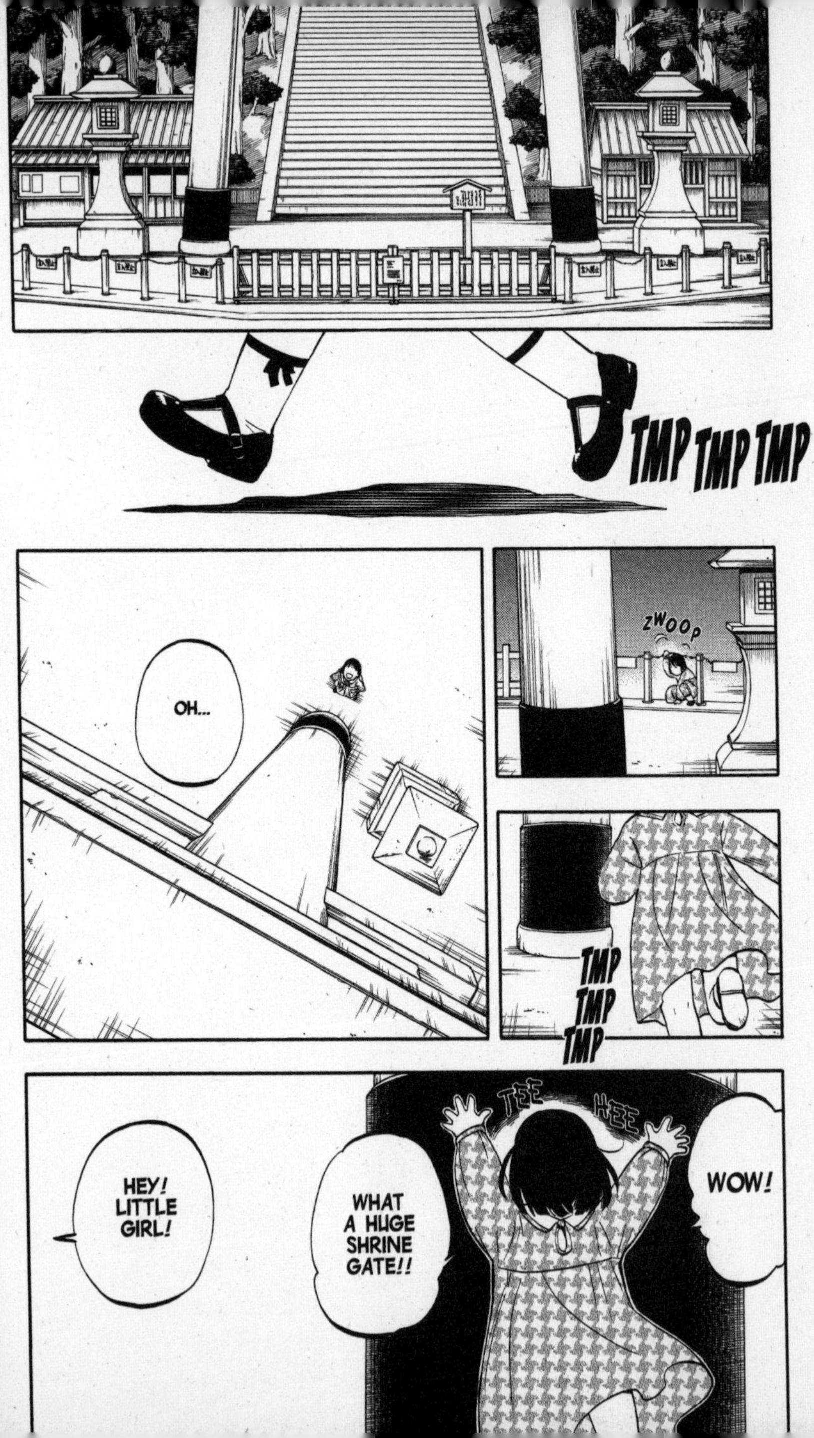
TMP TMP TMP
ZWOOP
TMP
TMP
TMP
OH...
WOW!
TEE HEE
WHAT A HUGE SHRINE GATE!!
HEY! LITTLE GIRL!

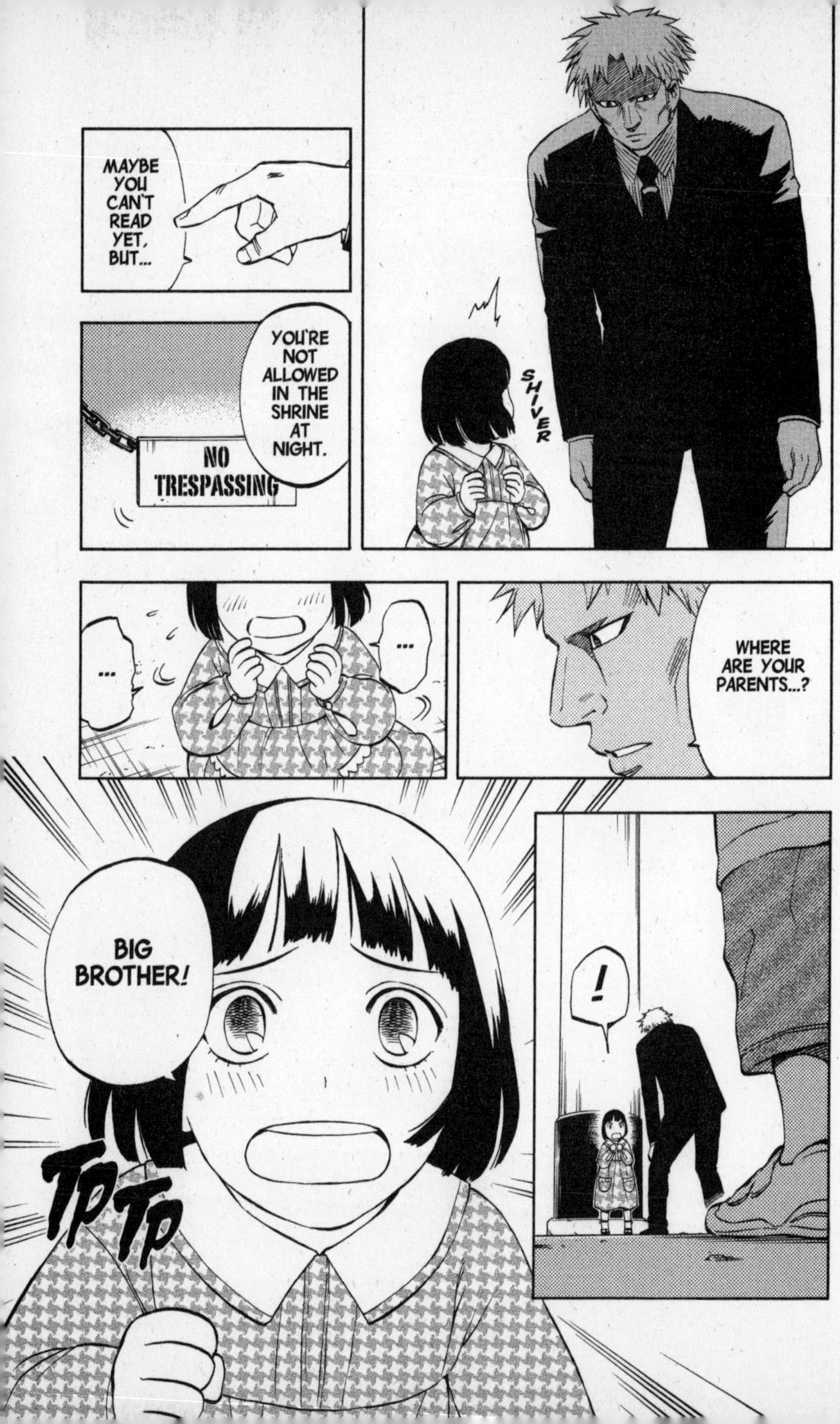
SHIVER
MAYBE YOU CAN'T READ YET, BUT...
YOU'RE NOT ALLOWED IN THE SHRINE AT NIGHT.
NO TRESPASSING
WHERE ARE YOUR PARENTS...?
...
...
!
BIG BROTHER!
TP TP

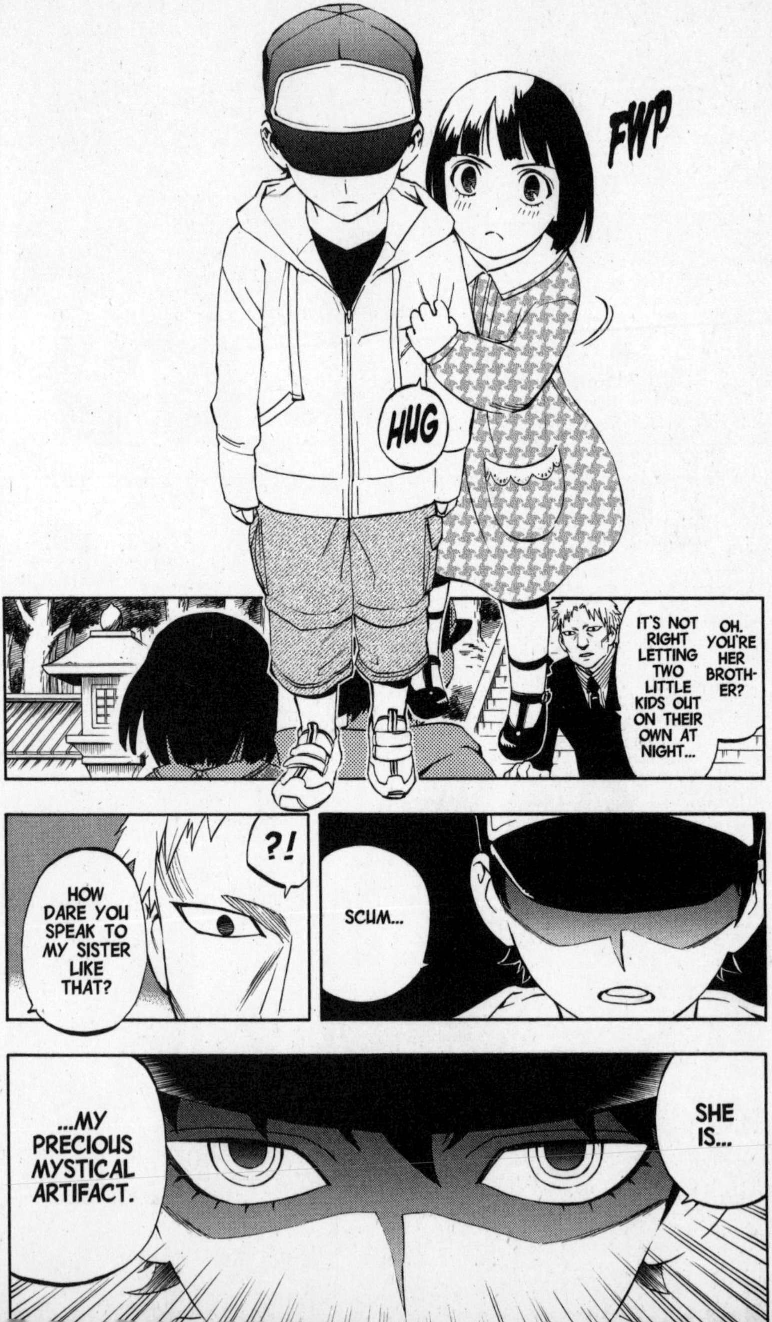
FWP
HUG
OH. YOU'RE HER BROTHER?
IT'S NOT RIGHT LETTING TWO LITTLE KIDS OUT ON THEIR OWN AT NIGHT...
SCUM...
?!
HOW DARE YOU SPEAK TO MY SISTER LIKE THAT?
SHE IS...
...MY PRECIOUS MYSTICAL ARTIFACT.

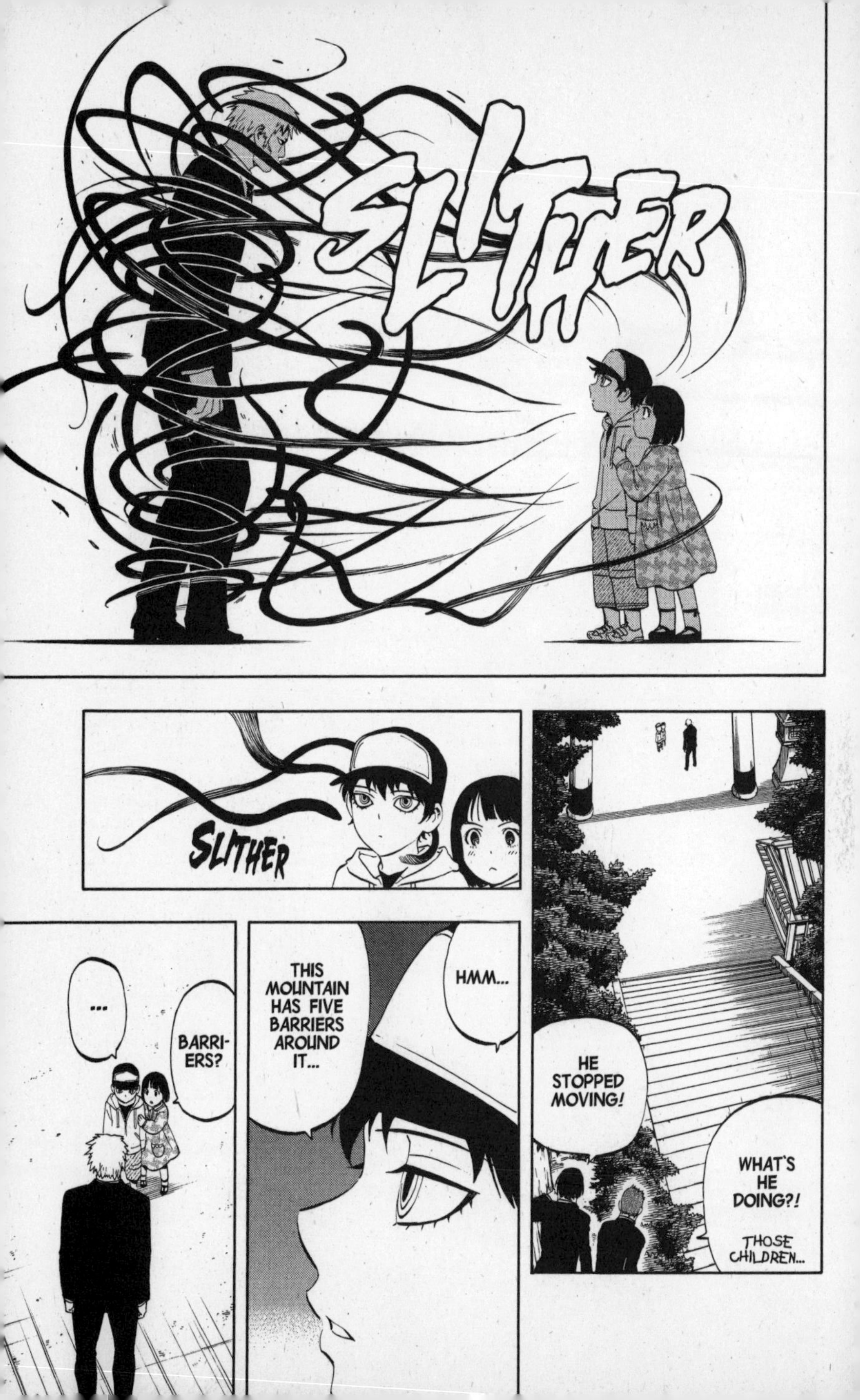
SLITHER
HE STOPPED MOVING!
WHAT'S HE DOING?!
THOSE CHILDREN...
SLITHER
HMM...
THIS MOUNTAIN HAS FIVE BARRIERS AROUND IT...
BARRI-ERS?
...

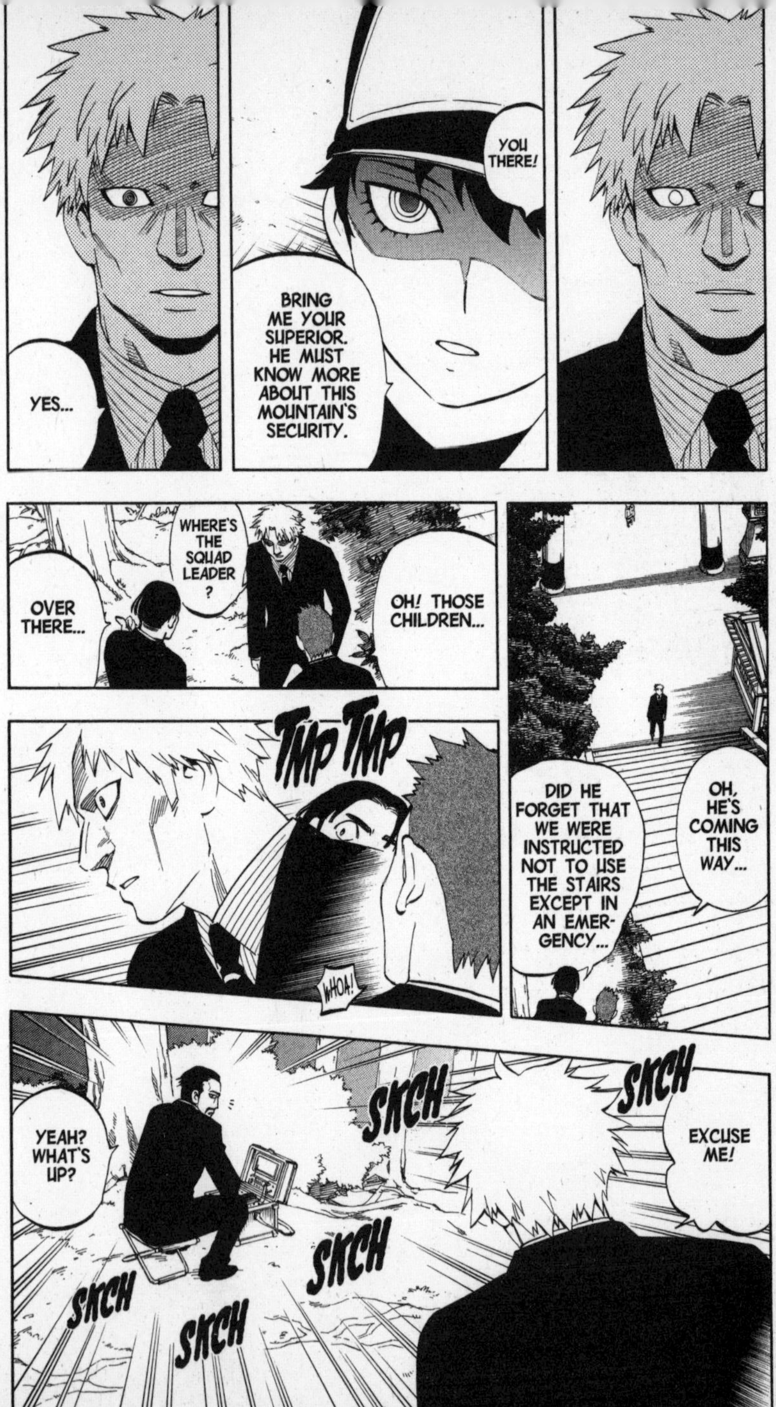
YOU THERE!
BRING ME YOUR SUPERIOR. HE MUST KNOW MORE ABOUT THIS MOUNTAIN'S SECURITY.
YES...
OH, HE'S COMING THIS WAY...
DID HE FORGET THAT WE WERE INSTRUCTED NOT TO USE THE STAIRS EXCEPT IN AN EMERGENCY...
OH! THOSE CHILDREN...
WHERE'S THE SQUAD LEADER?
OVER THERE...
TMP TMP
WHOA!
SKCH
EXCUSE ME!
SKCH
SKCH
YEAH? WHAT'S UP?
SKCH
SKCH

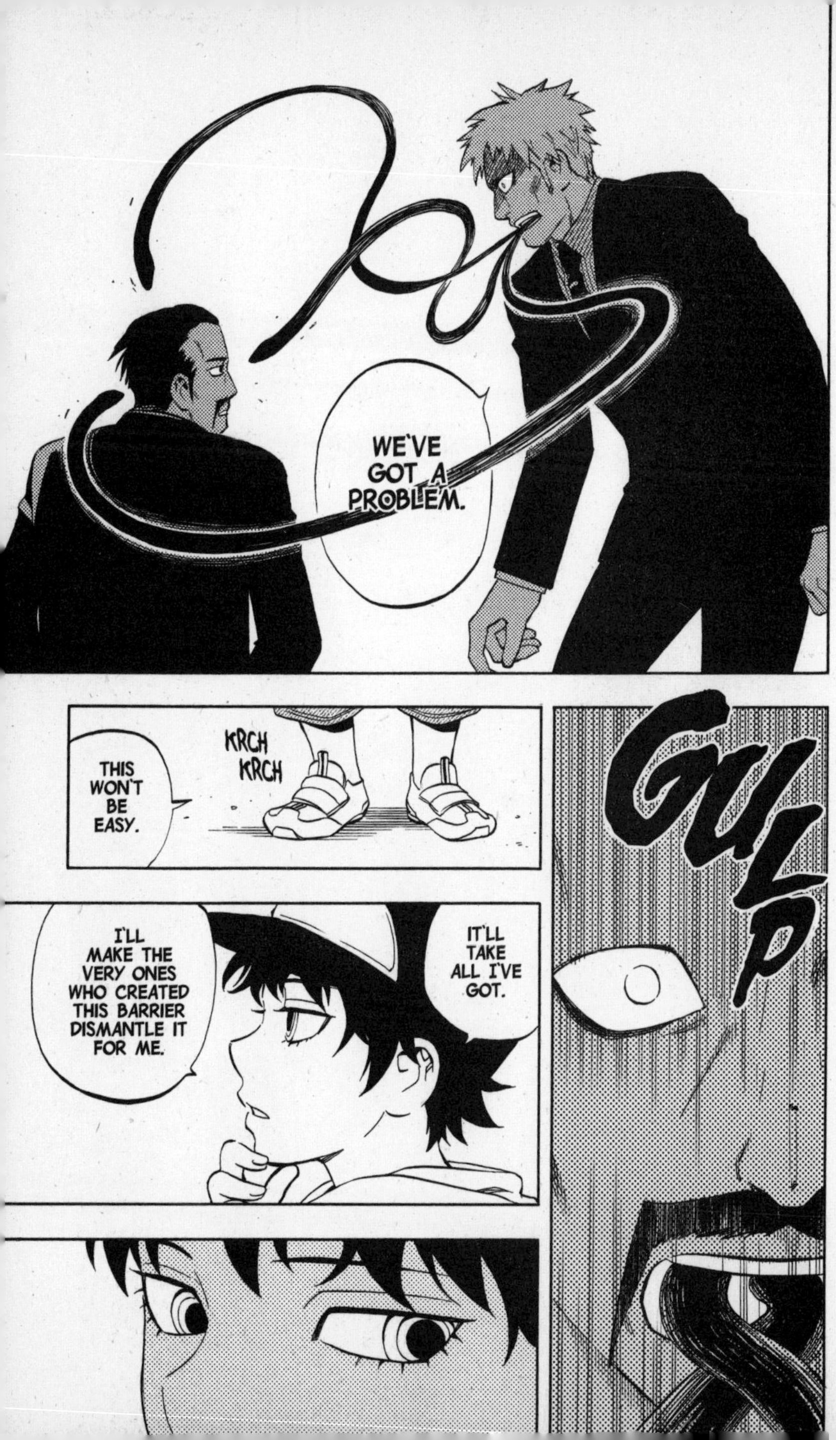
WE'VE GOT A PROBLEM.
GULP
KRCH KRCH
THIS WON'T BE EASY.
IT'LL TAKE ALL I'VE GOT.
I'LL MAKE THE VERY ONES WHO CREATED THIS BARRIER DISMANTLE IT FOR ME.

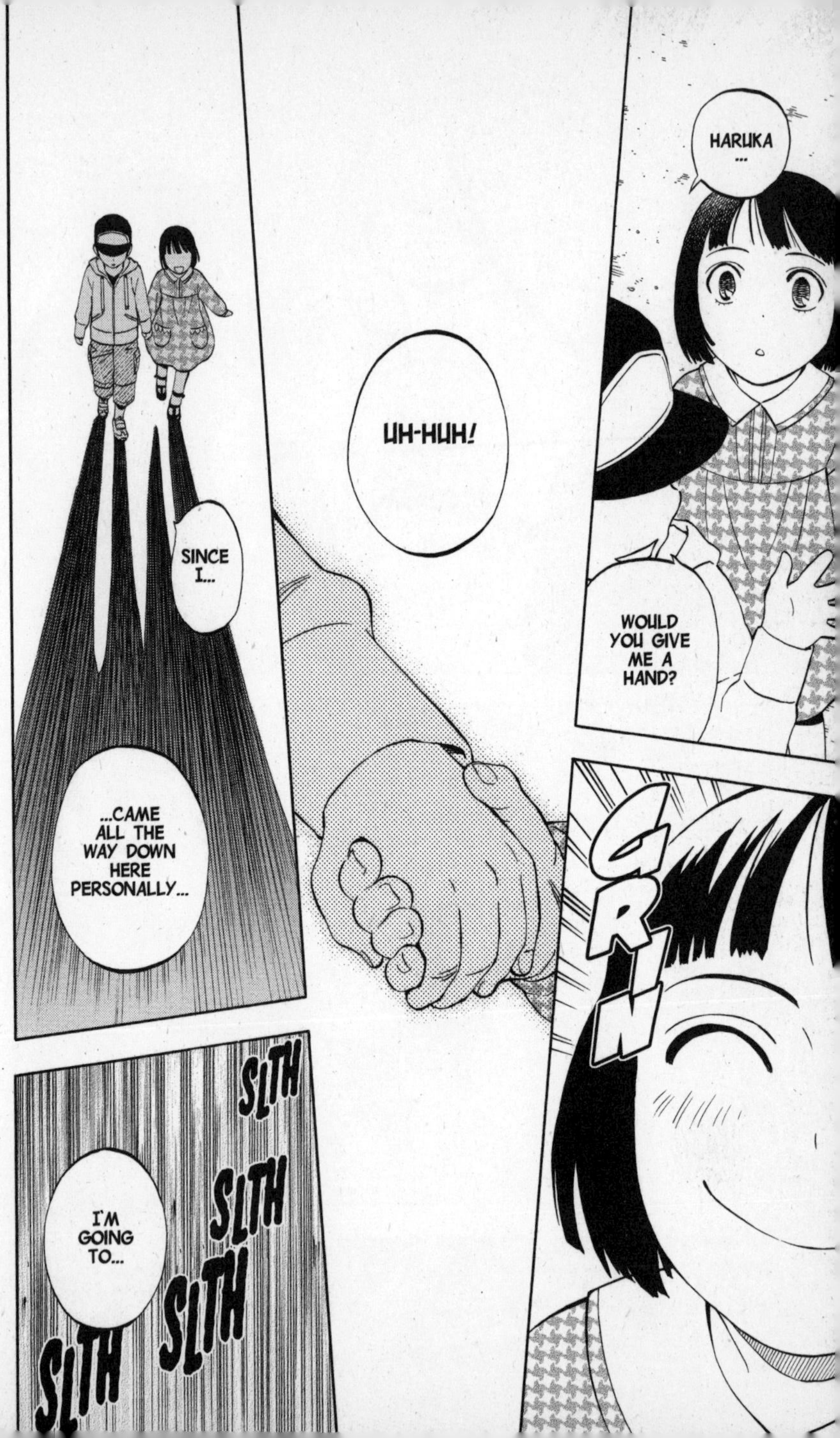
HARUKA ...
WOULD YOU GIVE ME A HAND?
GRIN
UH-HUH!
SINCE I...
...CAME ALL THE WAY DOWN HERE PERSONALLY...
I'M GOING TO...
SLTH SLTH SLTH SLTH SLTH

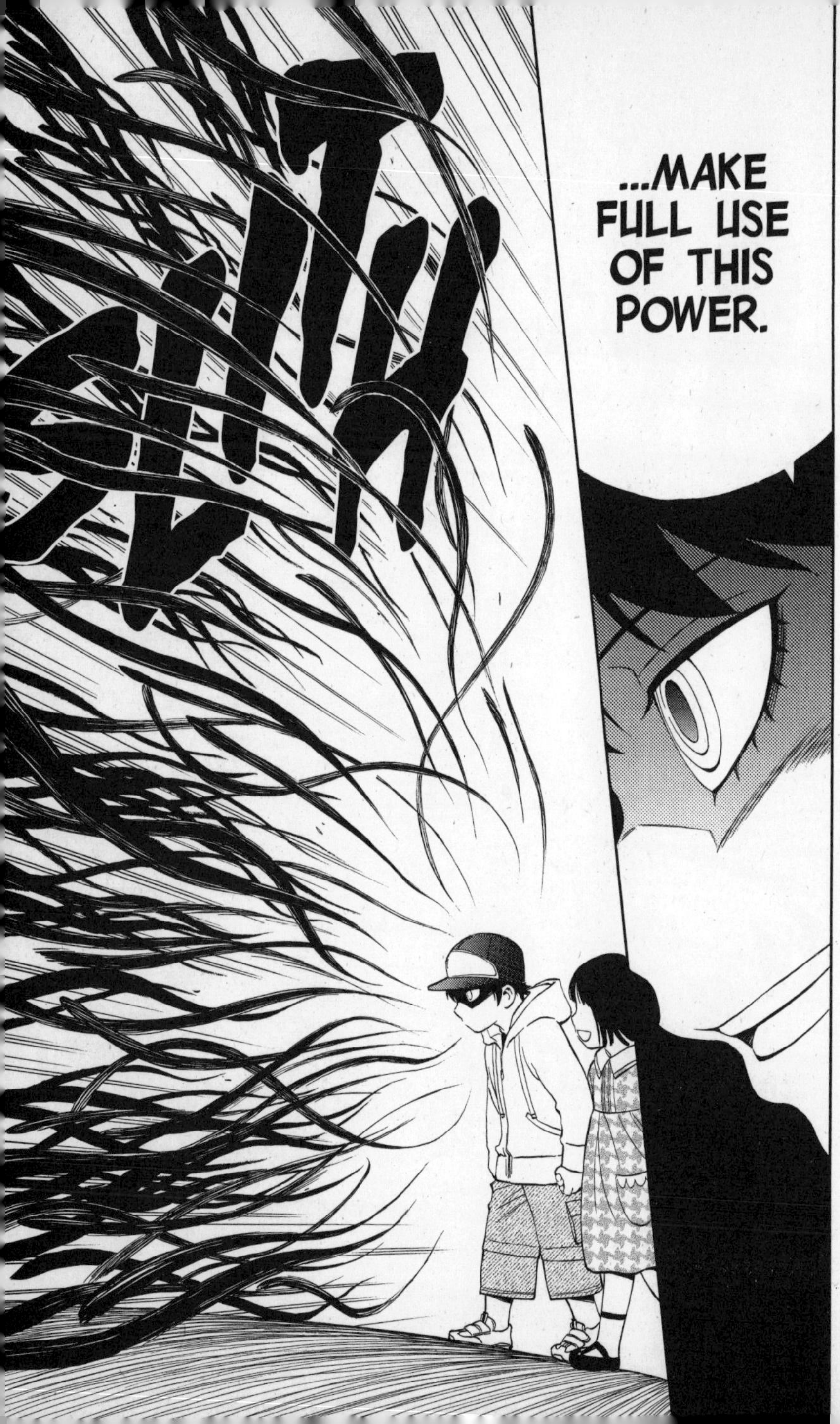
...MAKE FULL USE OF THIS POWER.

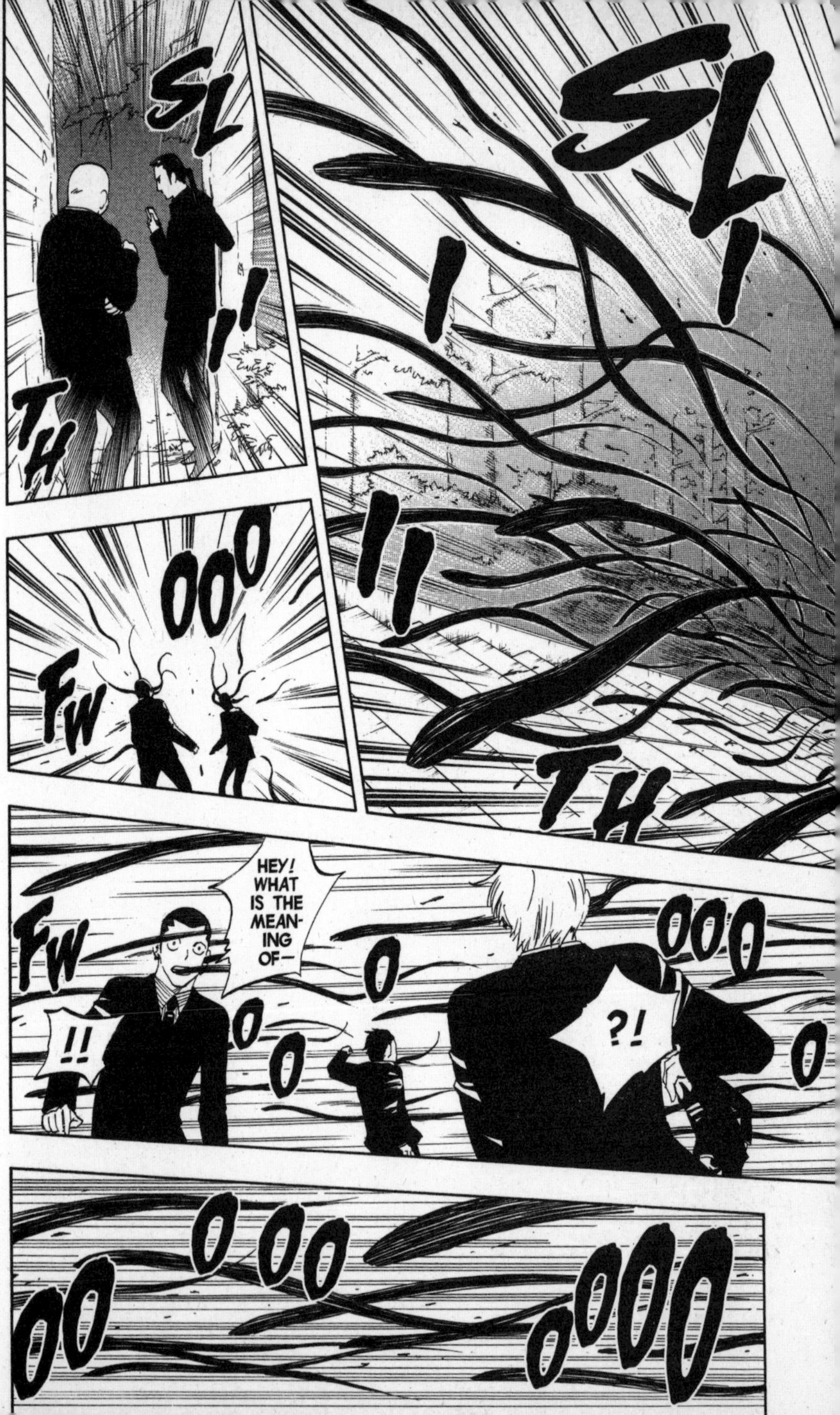

SLIIIITH
SLIIIITH
FWOOO
?!
OOOO
O
HEY! WHAT IS THE MEANING OF—
!!
FW
OOOO
OOO
OO

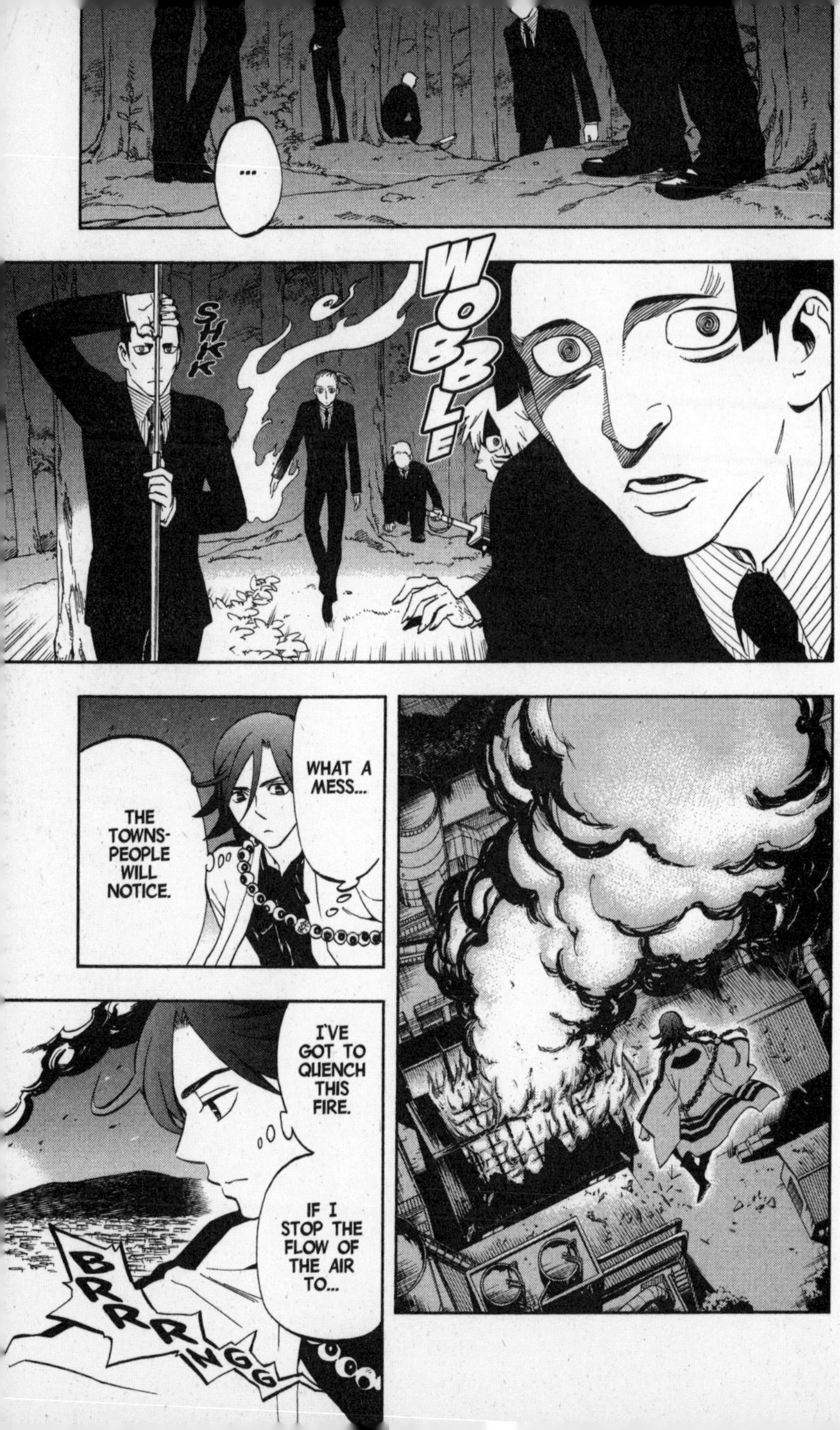

...
WOBBLE
SHKK
WHAT A MESS...
THE TOWNS-PEOPLE WILL NOTICE.
I'VE GOT TO QUENCH THIS FIRE.
IF I STOP THE FLOW OF THE AIR TO...
BRRRRINGG

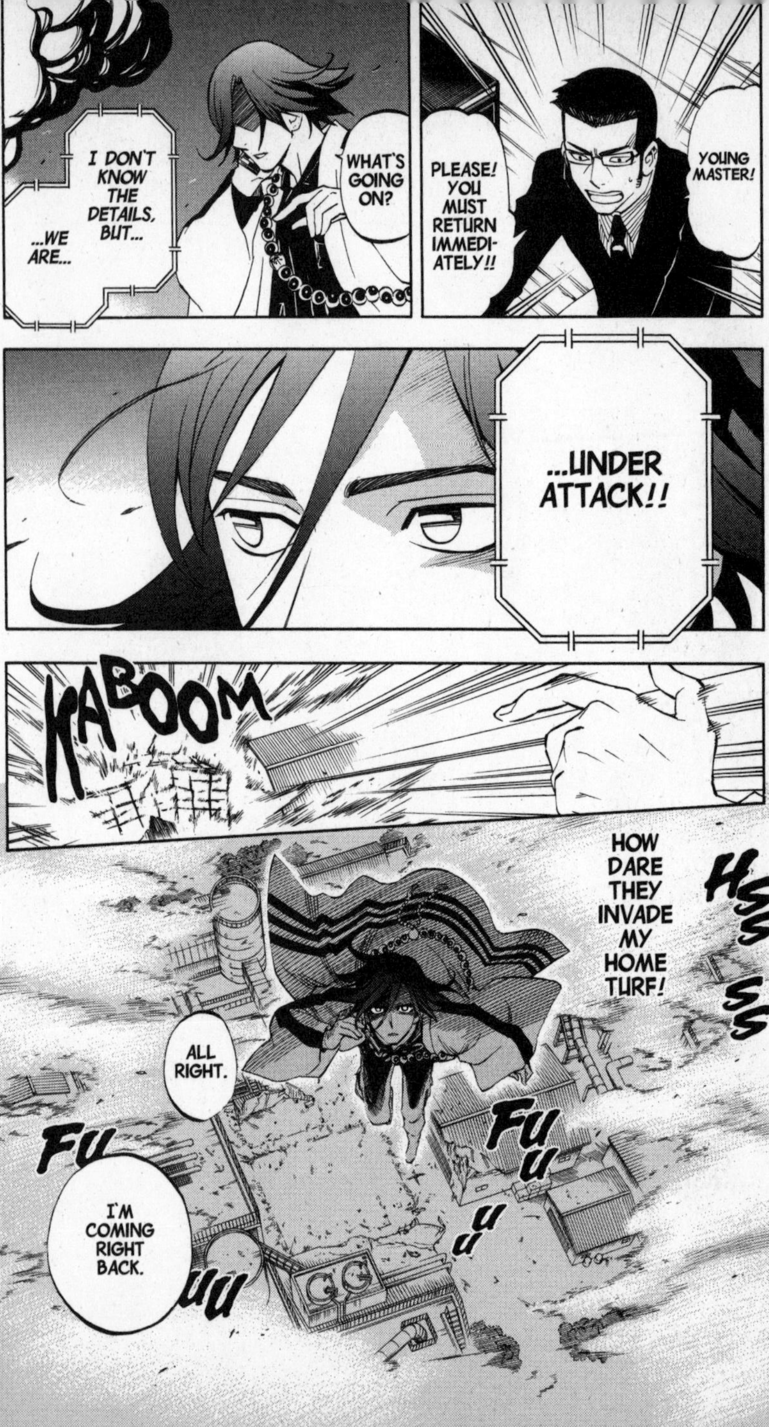
YOUNG MASTER!
PLEASE! YOU MUST RETURN IMMEDIATELY!!
WHAT'S GOING ON?
I DON'T KNOW THE DETAILS, BUT...
...WE ARE...
...UNDER ATTACK!!
KABOOM
HSSSS
HOW DARE THEY INVADE MY HOME TURF!
FUUUU
ALL RIGHT.
FUUU
I'M COMING RIGHT BACK.

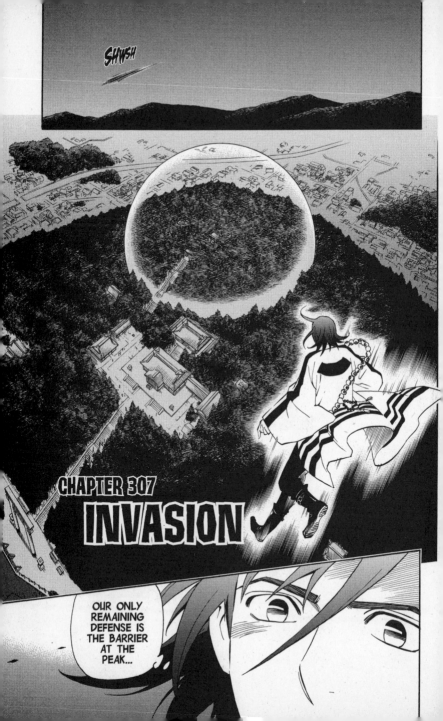

SHWSH

CHAPTER 307
INVASION

OUR ONLY
REMAINING
DEFENSE IS
THE BARRIER
AT THE
PEAK...

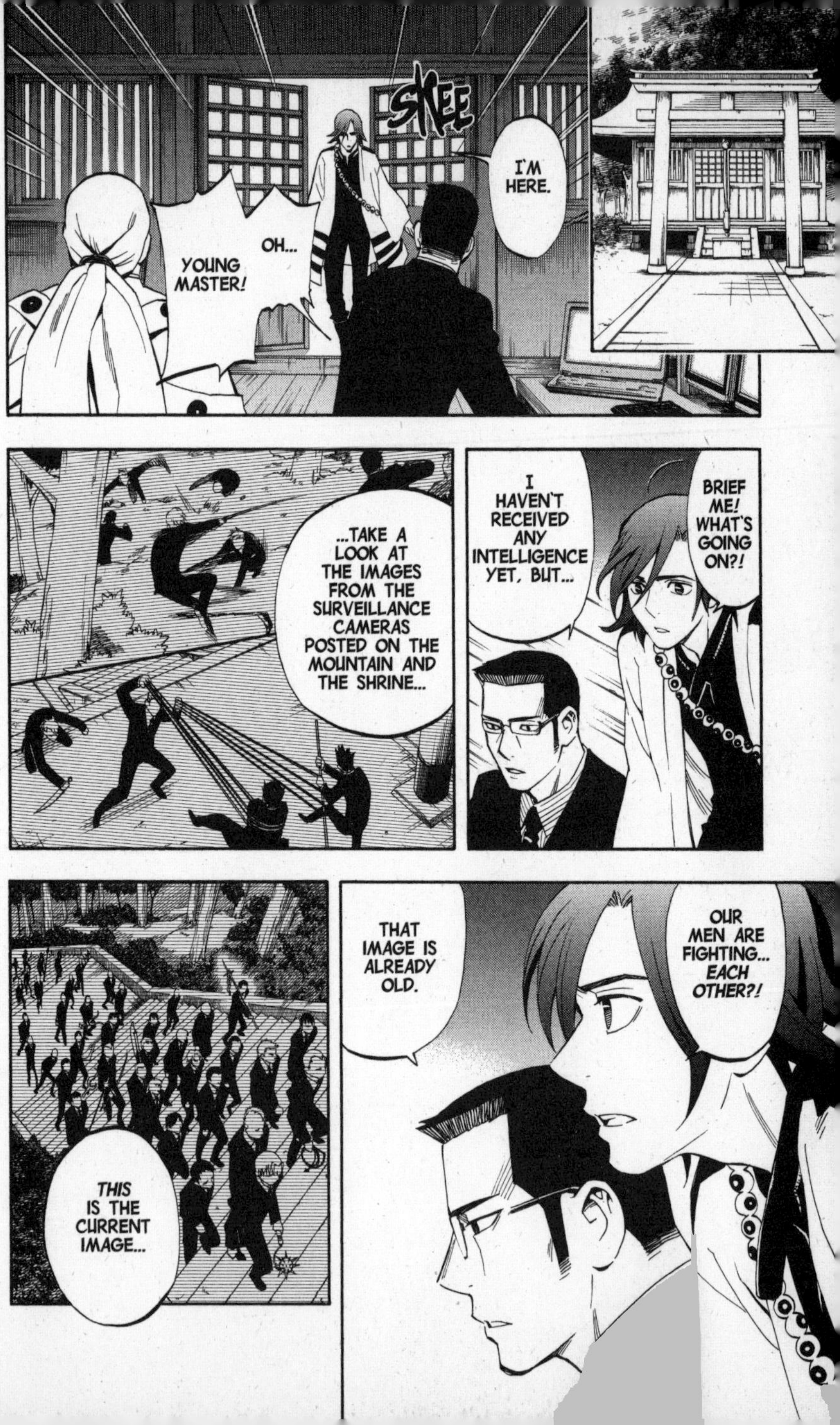
SKEE
I'M HERE.
OH... YOUNG MASTER!
BRIEF ME! WHAT'S GOING ON?!
I HAVEN'T RECEIVED ANY INTELLIGENCE YET, BUT...
...TAKE A LOOK AT THE IMAGES FROM THE SURVEILLANCE CAMERAS POSTED ON THE MOUNTAIN AND THE SHRINE...
OUR MEN ARE FIGHTING... EACH OTHER?!
THAT IMAGE IS ALREADY OLD.
THIS IS THE CURRENT IMAGE...

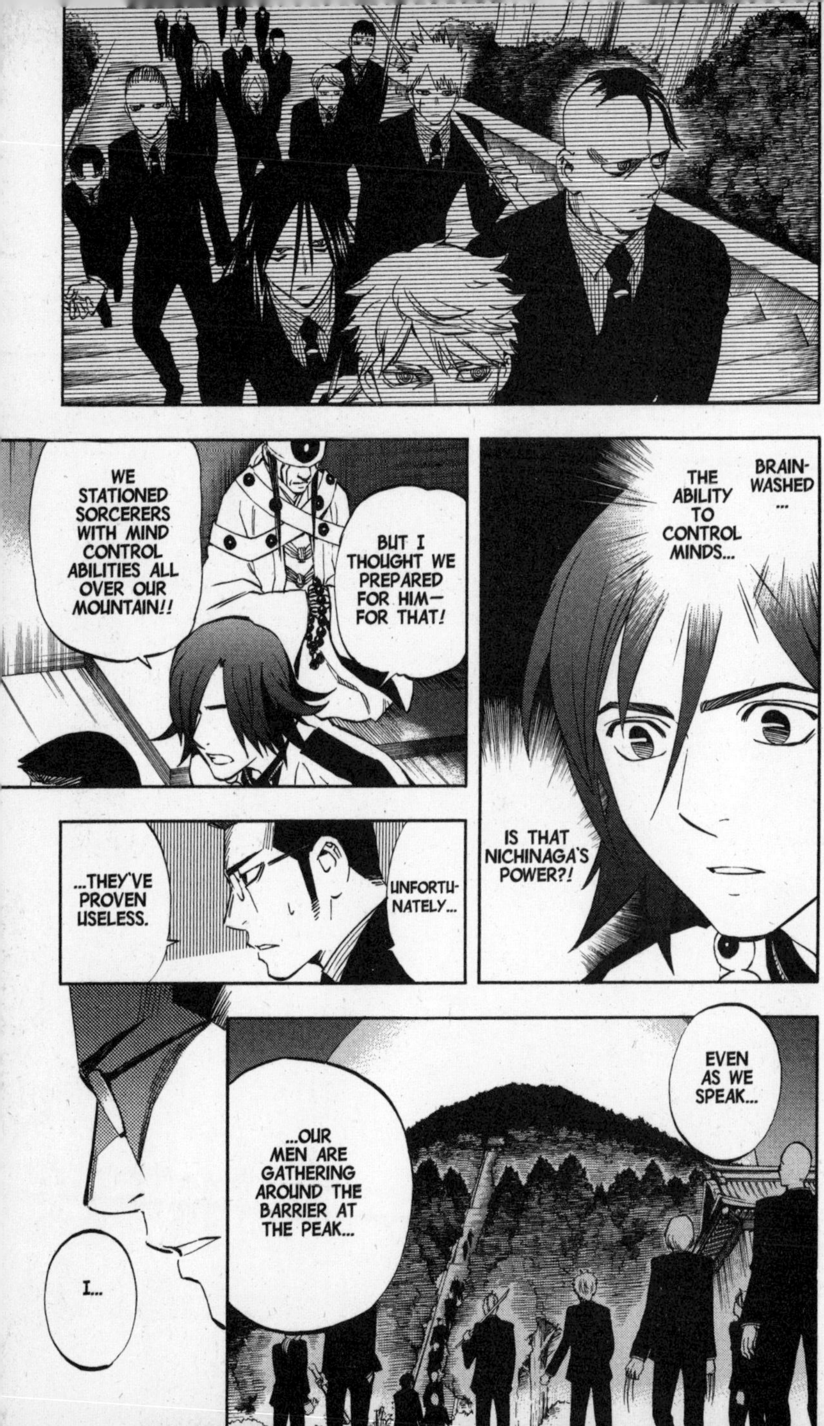
BRAIN-WASHED...
THE ABILITY TO CONTROL MINDS...
IS THAT NICHINAGA'S POWER?!
BUT I THOUGHT WE PREPARED FOR HIM—FOR THAT!
WE STATIONED SORCERERS WITH MIND CONTROL ABILITIES ALL OVER OUR MOUNTAIN!!
UNFORTUNATELY...
...THEY'VE PROVEN USELESS.
EVEN AS WE SPEAK...
...OUR MEN ARE GATHERING AROUND THE BARRIER AT THE PEAK...
I...

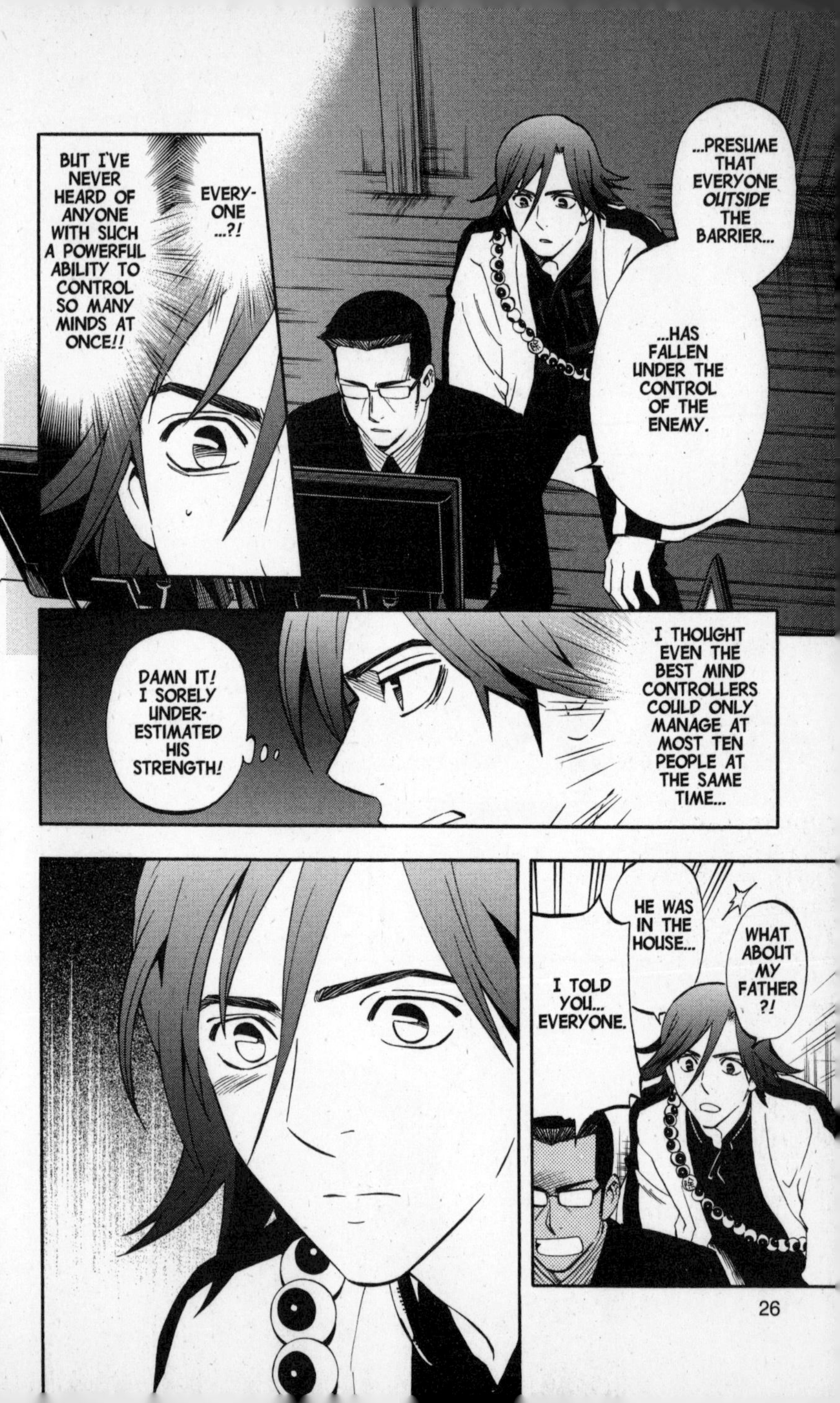
...PRESUME THAT EVERYONE *OUTSIDE* THE BARRIER...
...HAS FALLEN UNDER THE CONTROL OF THE ENEMY.
EVERY-ONE ...?!
BUT I'VE NEVER HEARD OF ANYONE WITH SUCH A POWERFUL ABILITY TO CONTROL SO MANY MINDS AT ONCE!!
I THOUGHT EVEN THE BEST MIND CONTROLLERS COULD ONLY MANAGE AT MOST TEN PEOPLE AT THE SAME TIME...
DAMN IT! I SORELY UNDER-ESTIMATED HIS STRENGTH!
WHAT ABOUT MY FATHER?!
HE WAS IN THE HOUSE...
I TOLD YOU... EVERYONE.

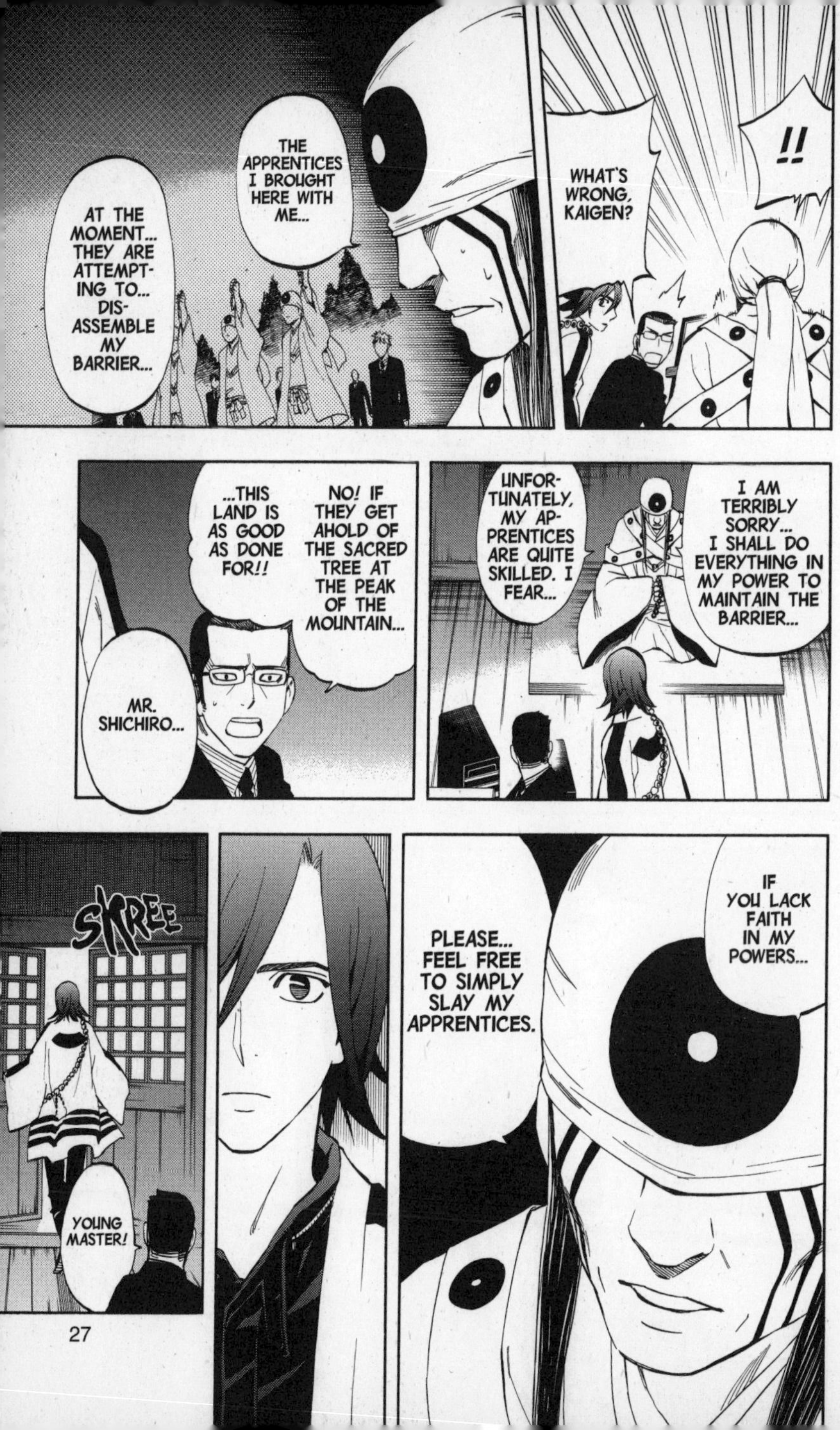
!!
WHAT'S WRONG, KAIGEN?
THE APPRENTICES I BROUGHT HERE WITH ME...
AT THE MOMENT... THEY ARE ATTEMPTING TO... DISASSEMBLE MY BARRIER...
I AM TERRIBLY SORRY... I SHALL DO EVERYTHING IN MY POWER TO MAINTAIN THE BARRIER...
UNFORTUNATELY, MY APPRENTICES ARE QUITE SKILLED. I FEAR...
NO! IF THEY GET AHOLD OF THE SACRED TREE AT THE PEAK OF THE MOUNTAIN...
...THIS LAND IS AS GOOD AS DONE FOR!!
MR. SHICHIRO...
IF YOU LACK FAITH IN MY POWERS...
PLEASE... FEEL FREE TO SIMPLY SLAY MY APPRENTICES.
SKREE
YOUNG MASTER!

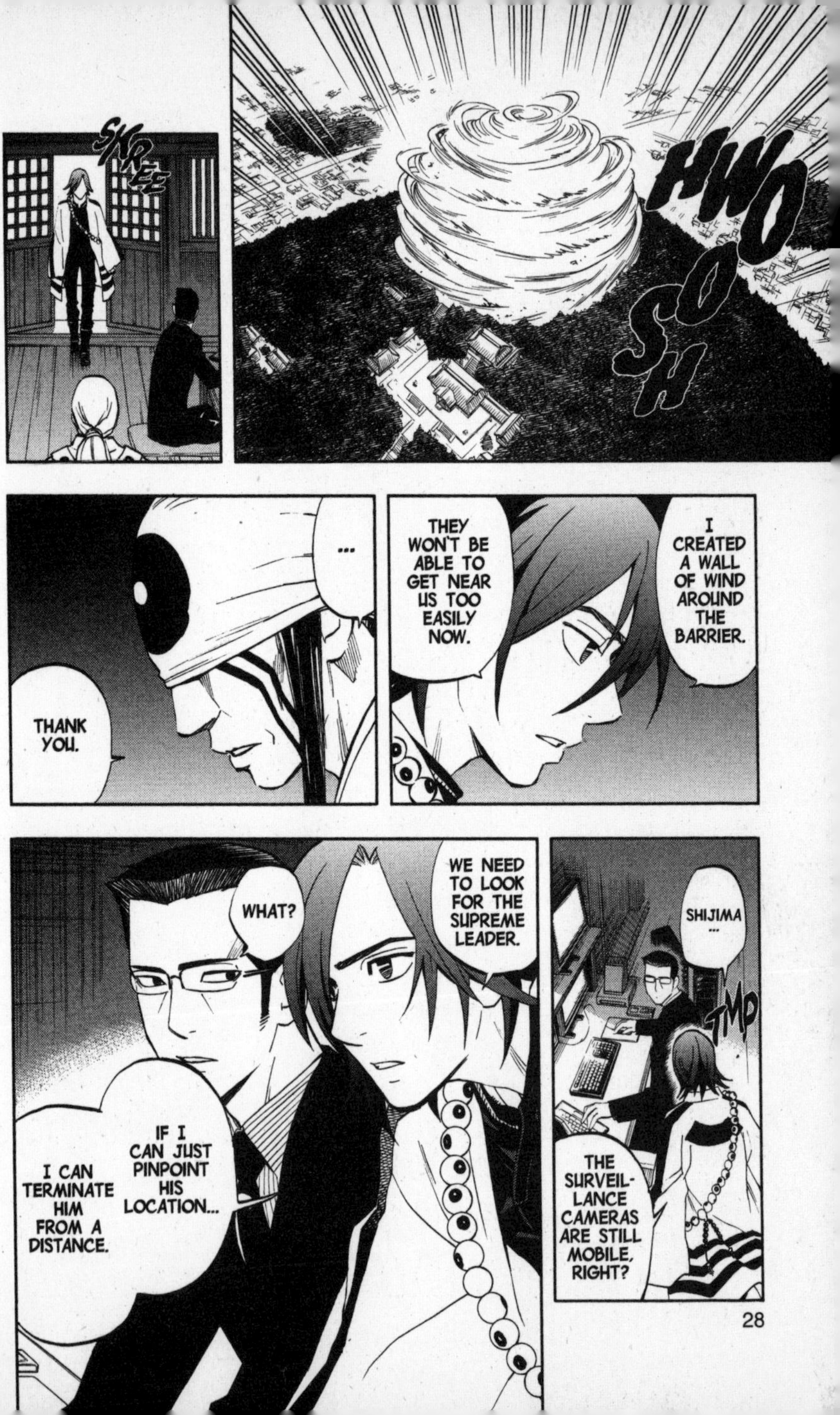
HWOOSH
SKREE
I CREATED A WALL OF WIND AROUND THE BARRIER.
THEY WON'T BE ABLE TO GET NEAR US TOO EASILY NOW.
...
THANK YOU.
SHIJIMA...
TMP
THE SURVEILLANCE CAMERAS ARE STILL MOBILE, RIGHT?
WE NEED TO LOOK FOR THE SUPREME LEADER.
WHAT?
IF I CAN JUST PINPOINT HIS LOCATION...
I CAN TERMINATE HIM FROM A DISTANCE.

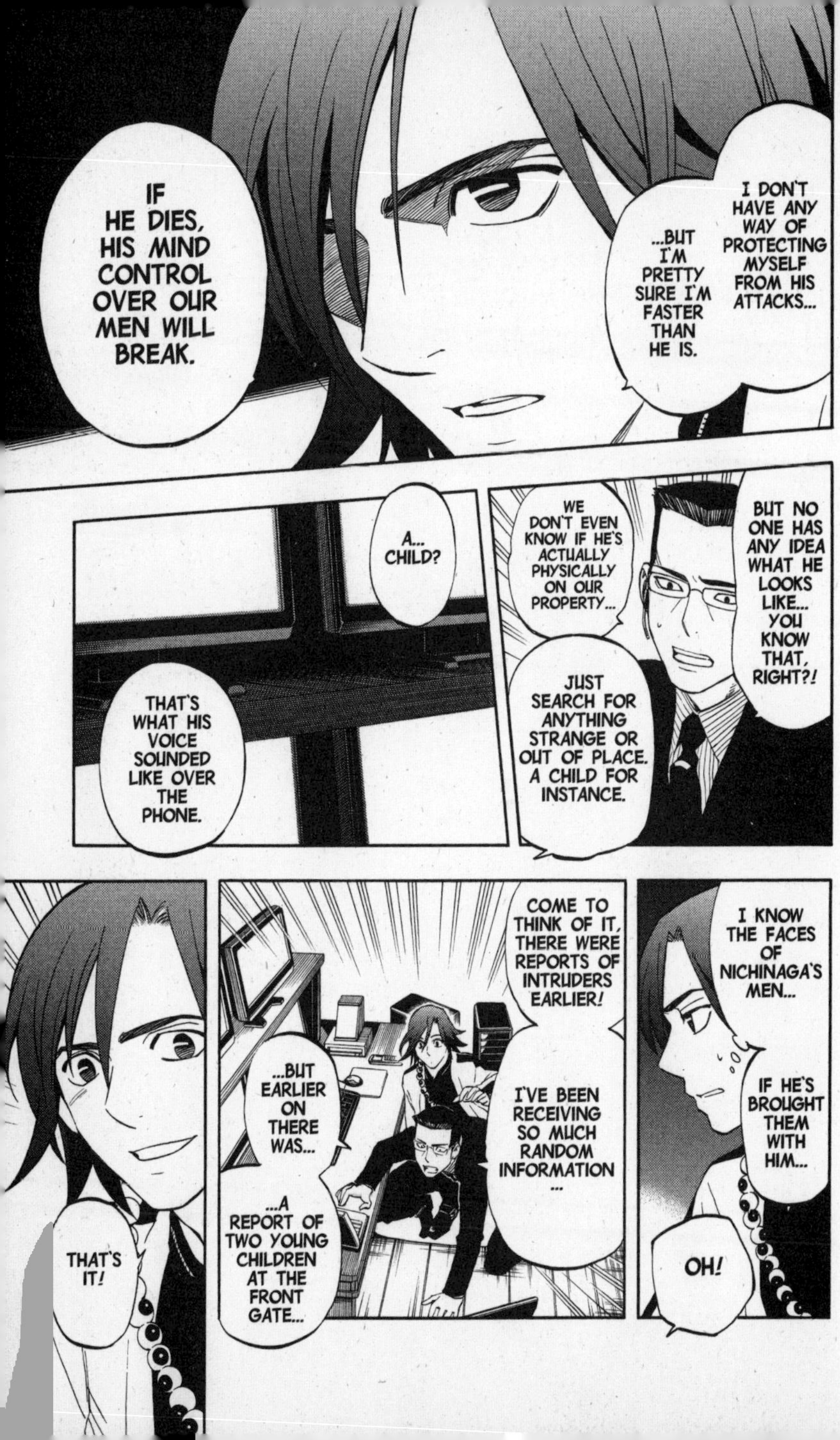
I DON'T HAVE ANY WAY OF PROTECTING MYSELF FROM HIS ATTACKS...
...BUT I'M PRETTY SURE I'M FASTER THAN HE IS.
IF HE DIES, HIS MIND CONTROL OVER OUR MEN WILL BREAK.
BUT NO ONE HAS ANY IDEA WHAT HE LOOKS LIKE... YOU KNOW THAT, RIGHT?!
WE DON'T EVEN KNOW IF HE'S ACTUALLY PHYSICALLY ON OUR PROPERTY...
JUST SEARCH FOR ANYTHING STRANGE OR OUT OF PLACE. A CHILD FOR INSTANCE.
A... CHILD?
THAT'S WHAT HIS VOICE SOUNDED LIKE OVER THE PHONE.
I KNOW THE FACES OF NICHINAGA'S MEN...
IF HE'S BROUGHT THEM WITH HIM...
OH!
COME TO THINK OF IT, THERE WERE REPORTS OF INTRUDERS EARLIER!
I'VE BEEN RECEIVING SO MUCH RANDOM INFORMATION...
...BUT EARLIER ON THERE WAS...
...A REPORT OF TWO YOUNG CHILDREN AT THE FRONT GATE...
THAT'S IT!

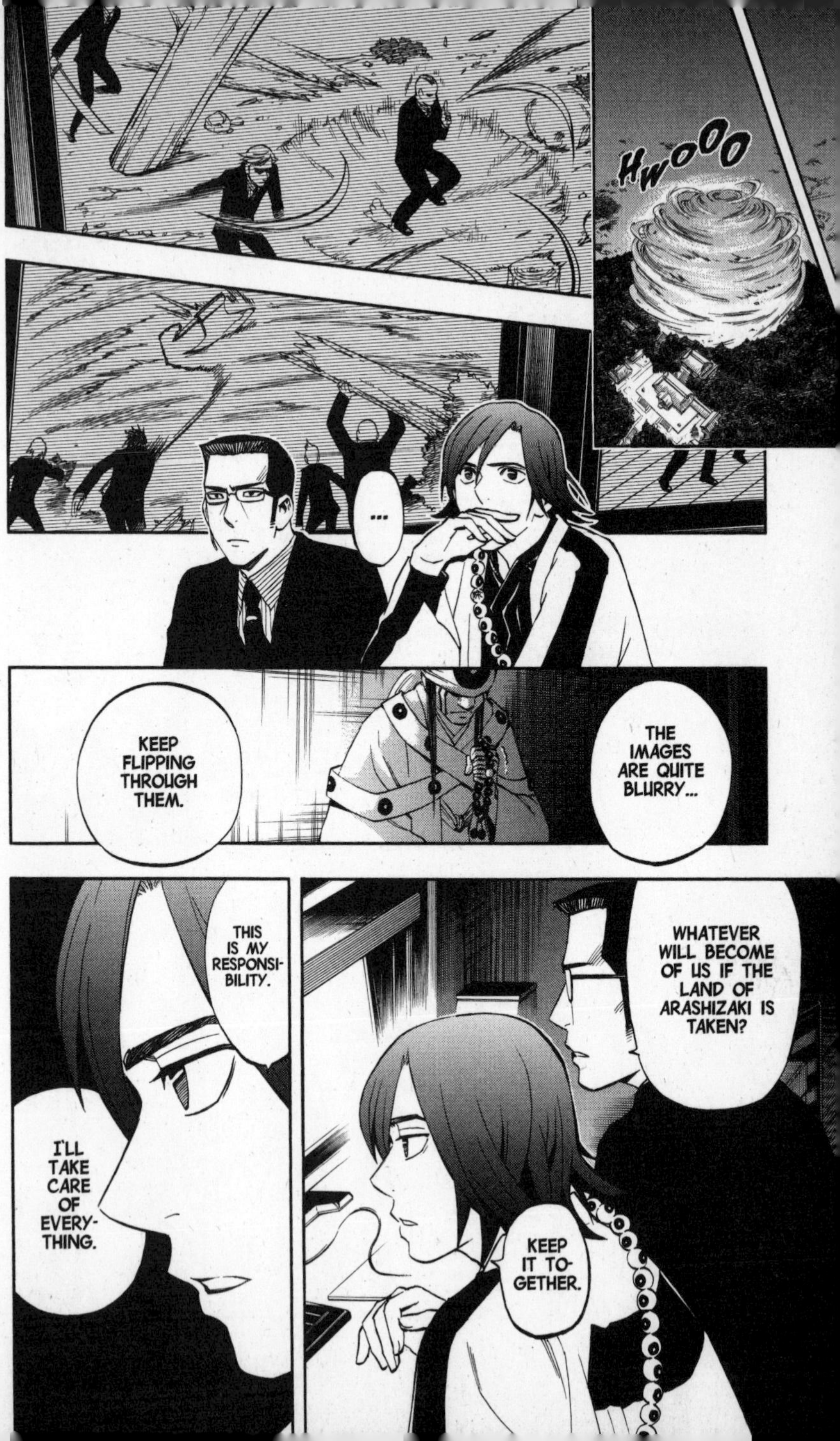
HWOOO
...
THE IMAGES ARE QUITE BLURRY...
KEEP FLIPPING THROUGH THEM.
WHATEVER WILL BECOME OF US IF THE LAND OF ARASHIZAKI IS TAKEN?
KEEP IT TOGETHER.
THIS IS MY RESPONSIBILITY.
I'LL TAKE CARE OF EVERYTHING.

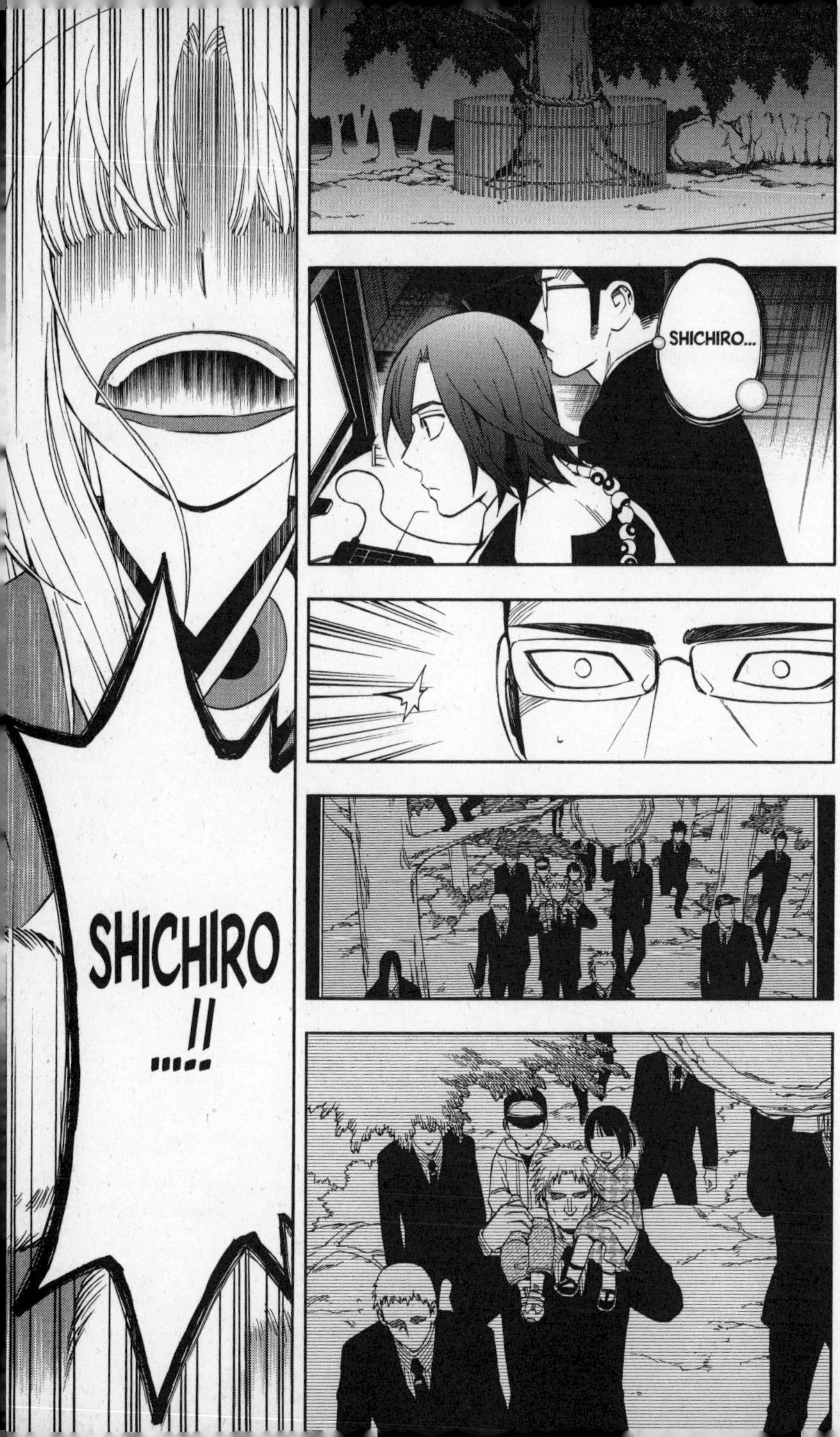
SHICHIRO...
SHICHIRO ...!!

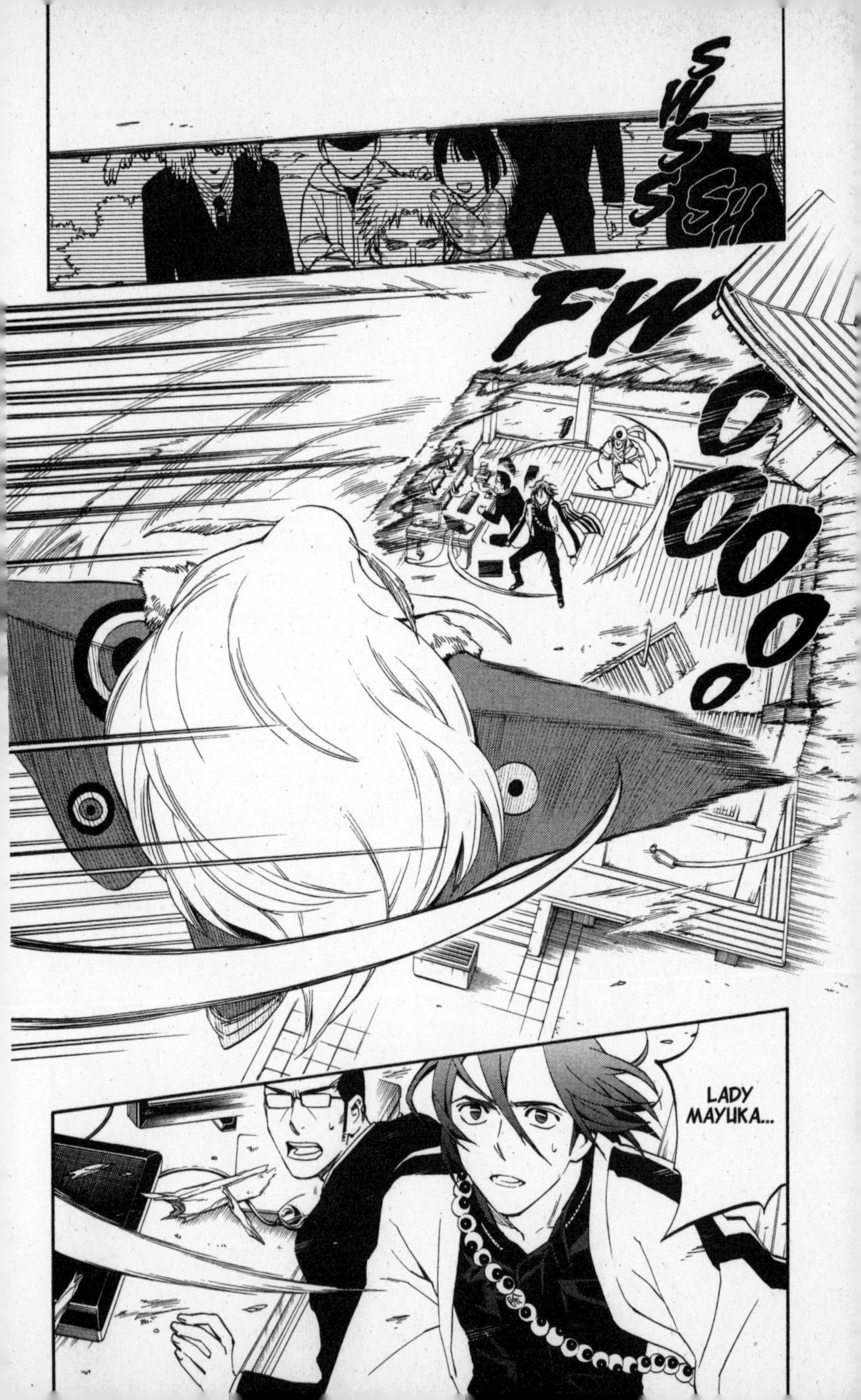
SWSSSH
FWOOOOO
LADY MAYUKA...

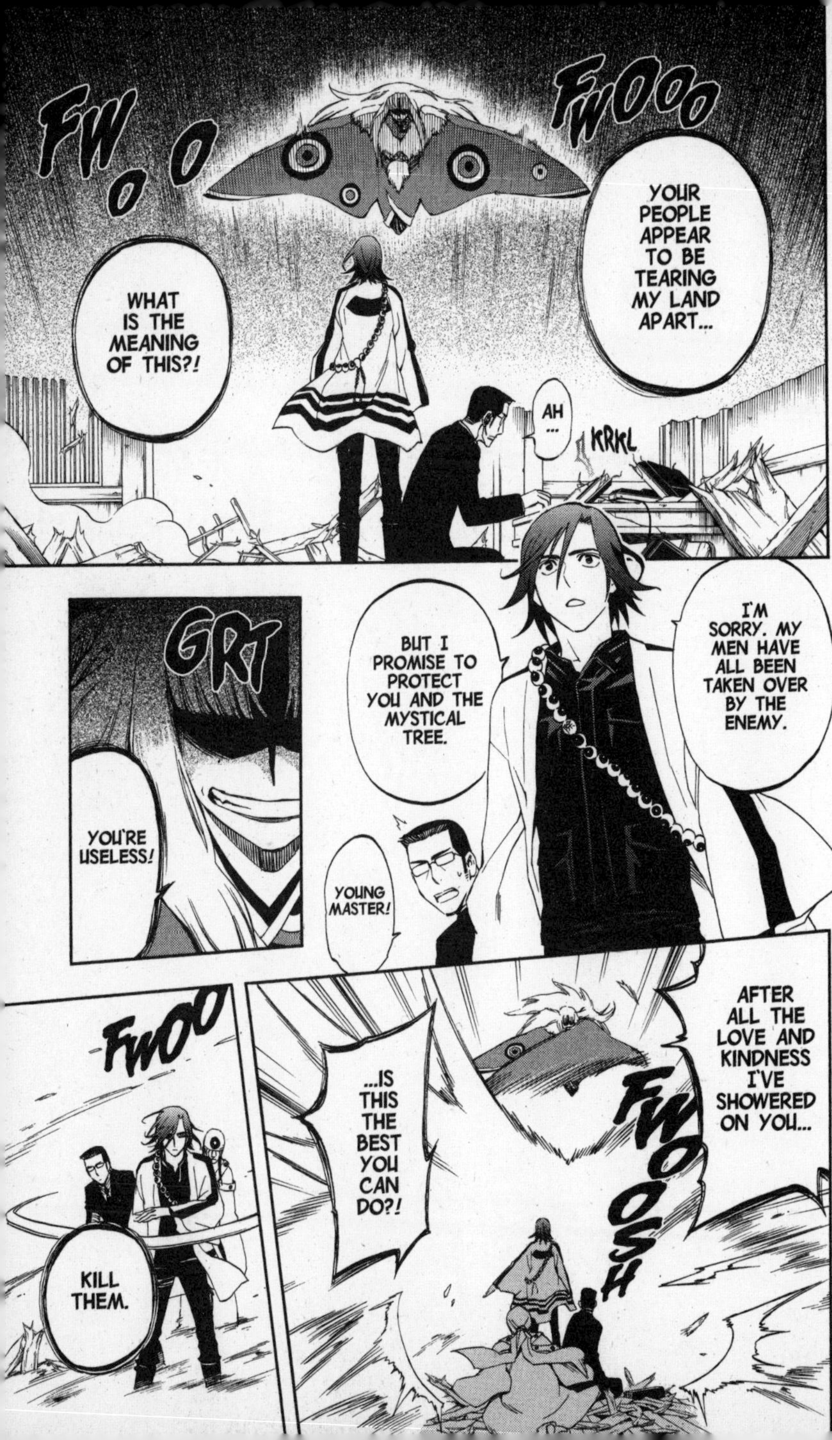
FWOOO
YOUR PEOPLE APPEAR TO BE TEARING MY LAND APART...
FWOOO
WHAT IS THE MEANING OF THIS?!
AH ...
KRKL
I'M SORRY. MY MEN HAVE ALL BEEN TAKEN OVER BY THE ENEMY.
BUT I PROMISE TO PROTECT YOU AND THE MYSTICAL TREE.
YOUNG MASTER!
GRT
YOU'RE USELESS!
AFTER ALL THE LOVE AND KINDNESS I'VE SHOWERED ON YOU...
FWOOOSH
...IS THIS THE BEST YOU CAN DO?!
FWOO
KILL THEM.

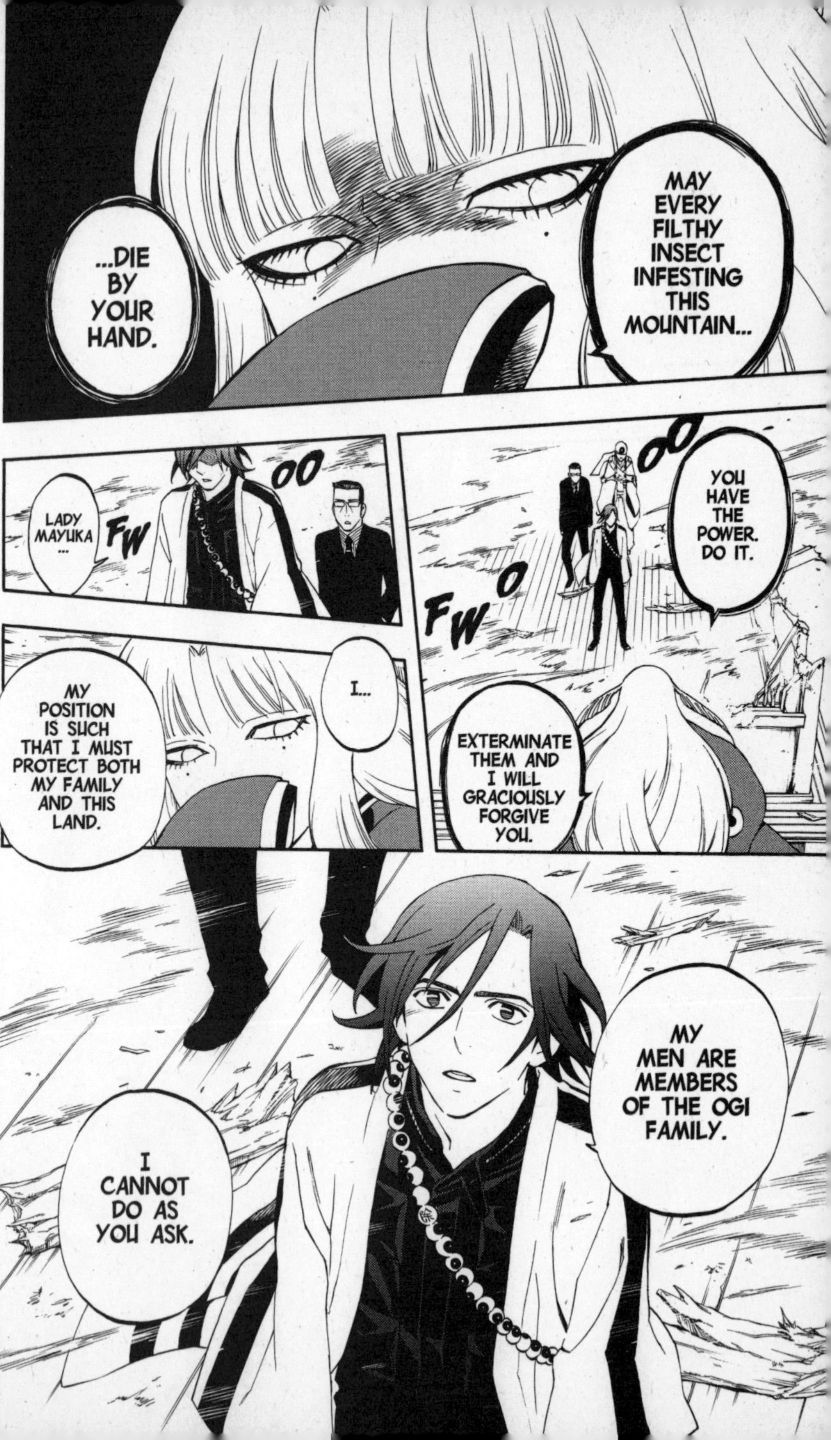
MAY EVERY FILTHY INSECT INFESTING THIS MOUNTAIN...
...DIE BY YOUR HAND.
OO
YOU HAVE THE POWER. DO IT.
FWO
EXTERMINATE THEM AND I WILL GRACIOUSLY FORGIVE YOU.
OO
FW
LADY MAYUKA ...
I...
MY POSITION IS SUCH THAT I MUST PROTECT BOTH MY FAMILY AND THIS LAND.
MY MEN ARE MEMBERS OF THE OGI FAMILY.
I CANNOT DO AS YOU ASK.

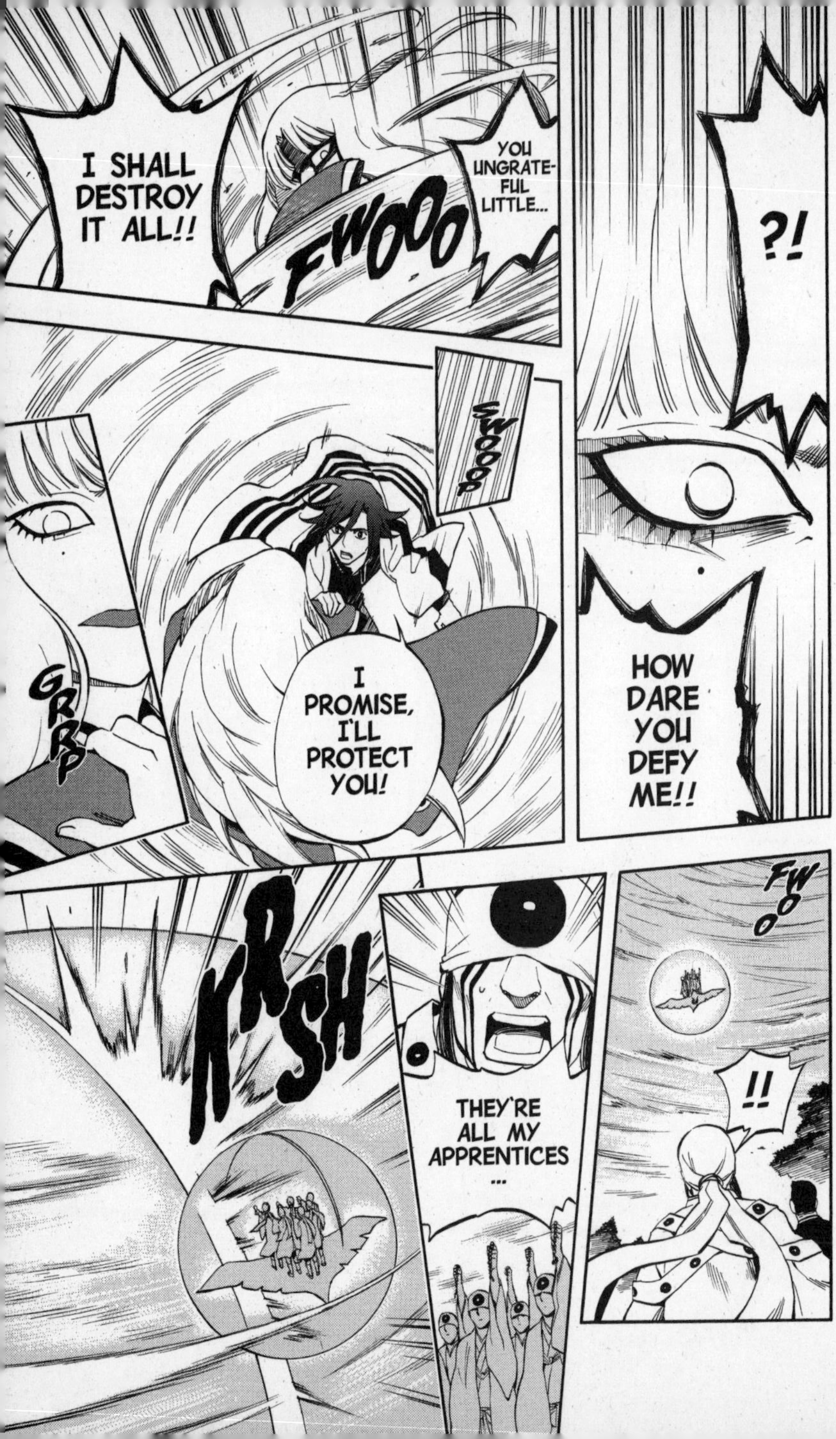
?!
HOW DARE YOU DEFY ME!!
YOU UNGRATEFUL LITTLE...
FWOOO
I SHALL DESTROY IT ALL!!
SWOOOP
I PROMISE, I'LL PROTECT YOU!
GRRP
FWOOO
!!
THEY'RE ALL MY APPRENTICES ...
KRSH

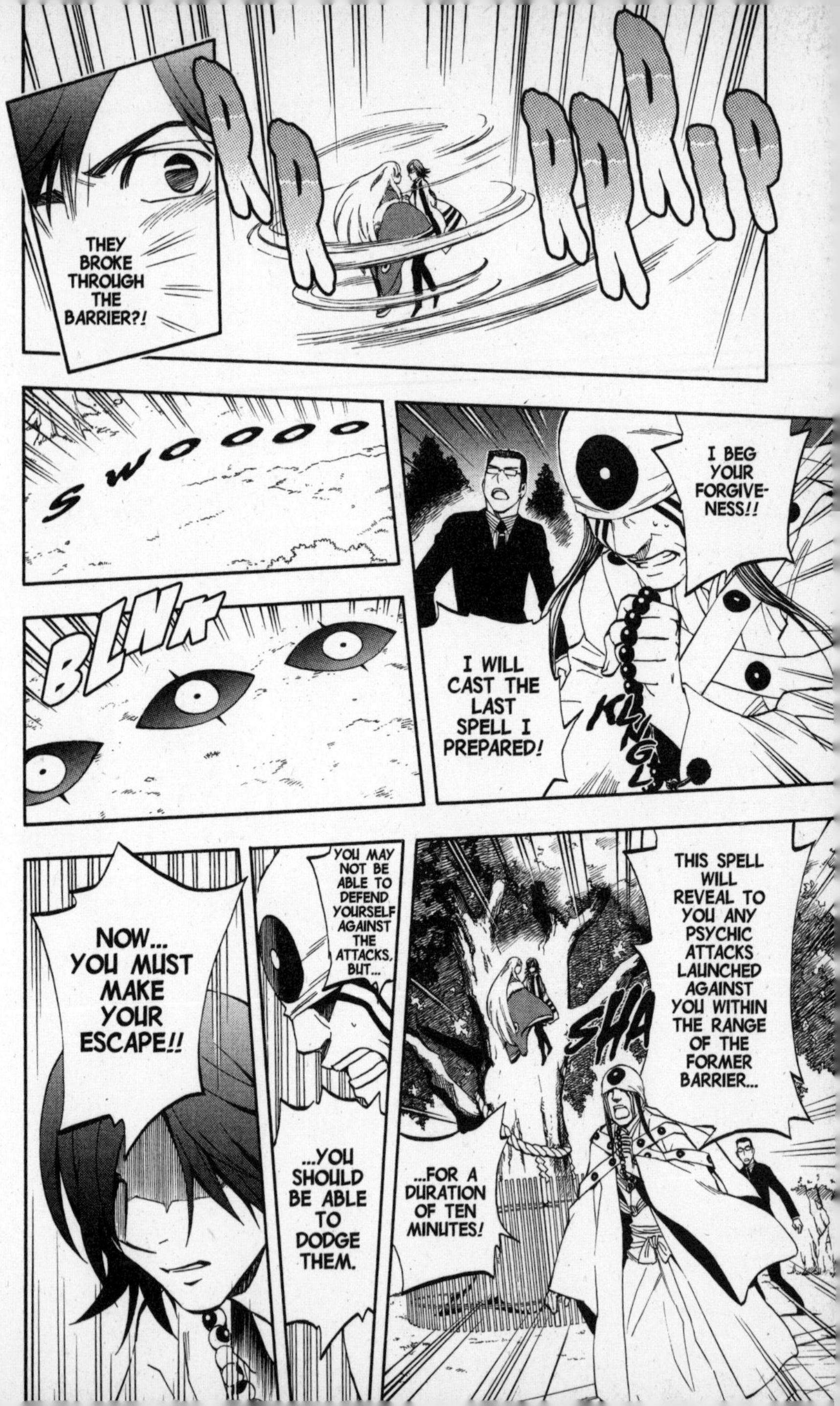
RRRRIP
RR
THEY BROKE THROUGH THE BARRIER?!
I BEG YOUR FORGIVE-NESS!!
I WILL CAST THE LAST SPELL I PREPARED!
KLNGL
SWOOOO
BLNK
THIS SPELL WILL REVEAL TO YOU ANY PSYCHIC ATTACKS LAUNCHED AGAINST YOU WITHIN THE RANGE OF THE FORMER BARRIER...
SHA
...FOR A DURATION OF TEN MINUTES!
YOU MAY NOT BE ABLE TO DEFEND YOURSELF AGAINST THE ATTACKS, BUT...
...YOU SHOULD BE ABLE TO DODGE THEM.
NOW... YOU MUST MAKE YOUR ESCAPE!!

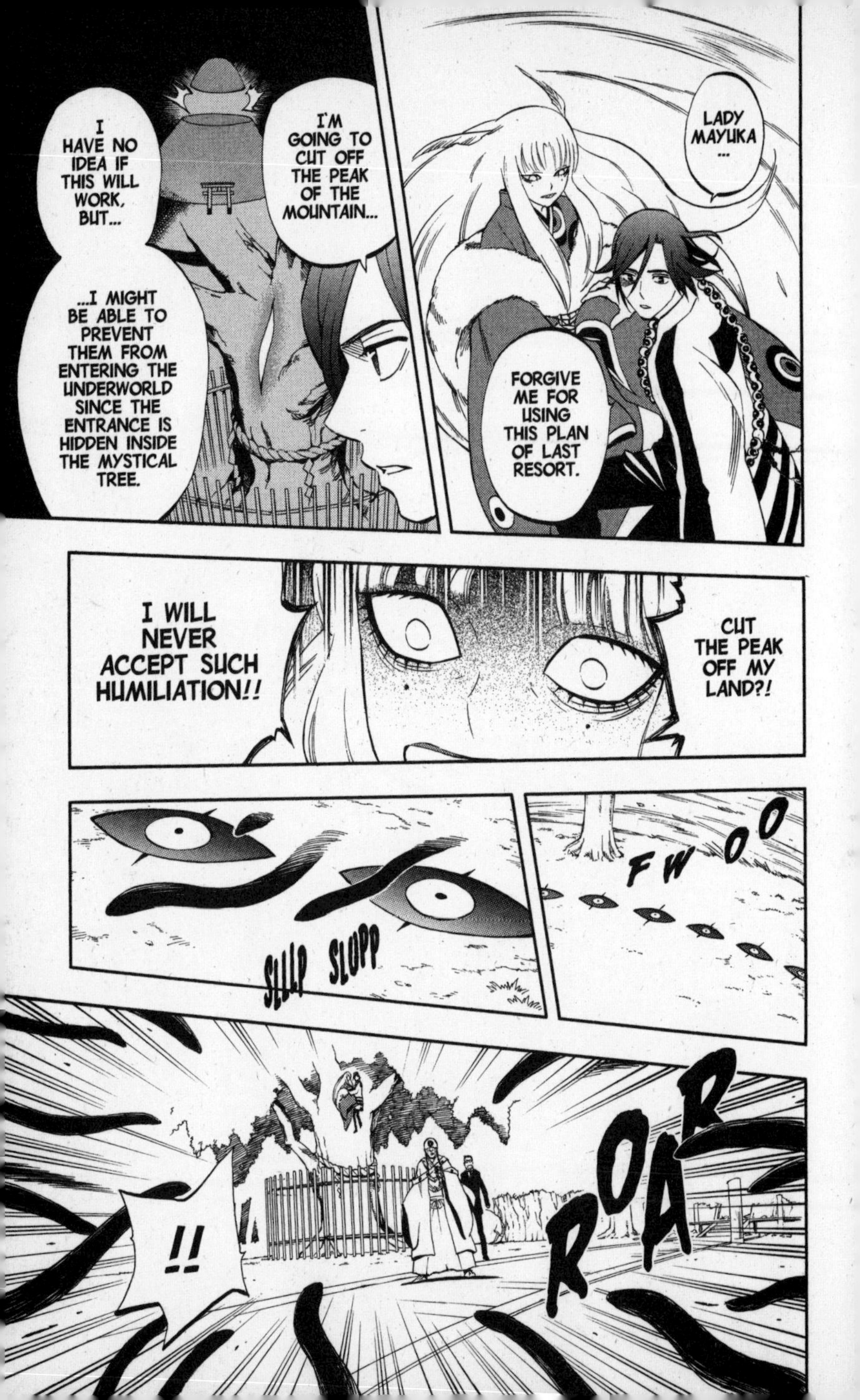
LADY MAYUKA ...
FORGIVE ME FOR USING THIS PLAN OF LAST RESORT.
I'M GOING TO CUT OFF THE PEAK OF THE MOUNTAIN...
I HAVE NO IDEA IF THIS WILL WORK, BUT...
...I MIGHT BE ABLE TO PREVENT THEM FROM ENTERING THE UNDERWORLD SINCE THE ENTRANCE IS HIDDEN INSIDE THE MYSTICAL TREE.
CUT THE PEAK OFF MY LAND?!
I WILL NEVER ACCEPT SUCH HUMILIATION!!
FWOOO
SLLLP SLUPP
ROAR
!!

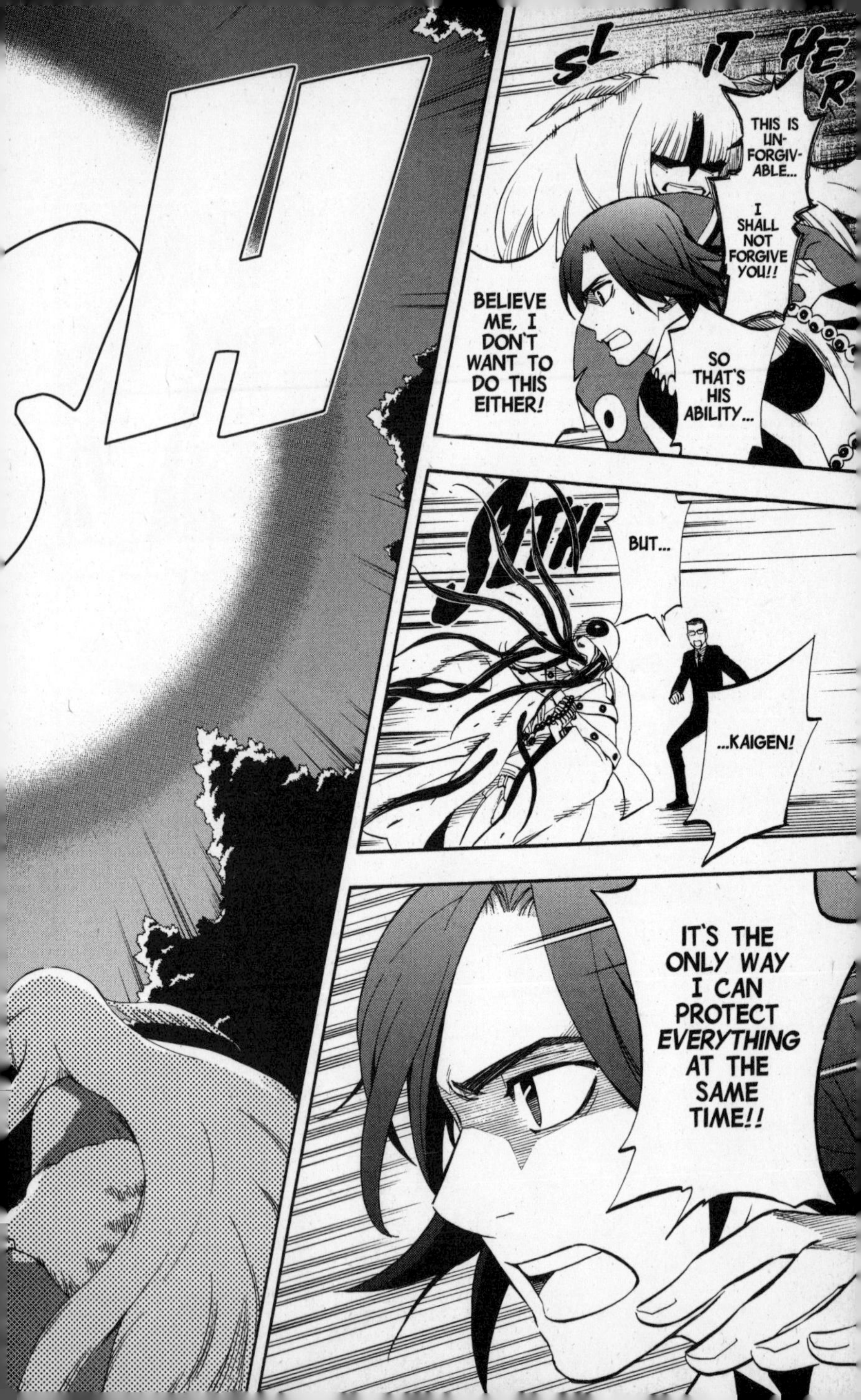
SL IT HER
THIS IS UN-FORGIV-ABLE...
I SHALL NOT FORGIVE YOU!!
SO THAT'S HIS ABILITY...
BELIEVE ME, I DON'T WANT TO DO THIS EITHER!
BUT...
...KAIGEN!
IT'S THE ONLY WAY I CAN PROTECT *EVERYTHING* AT THE SAME TIME!!

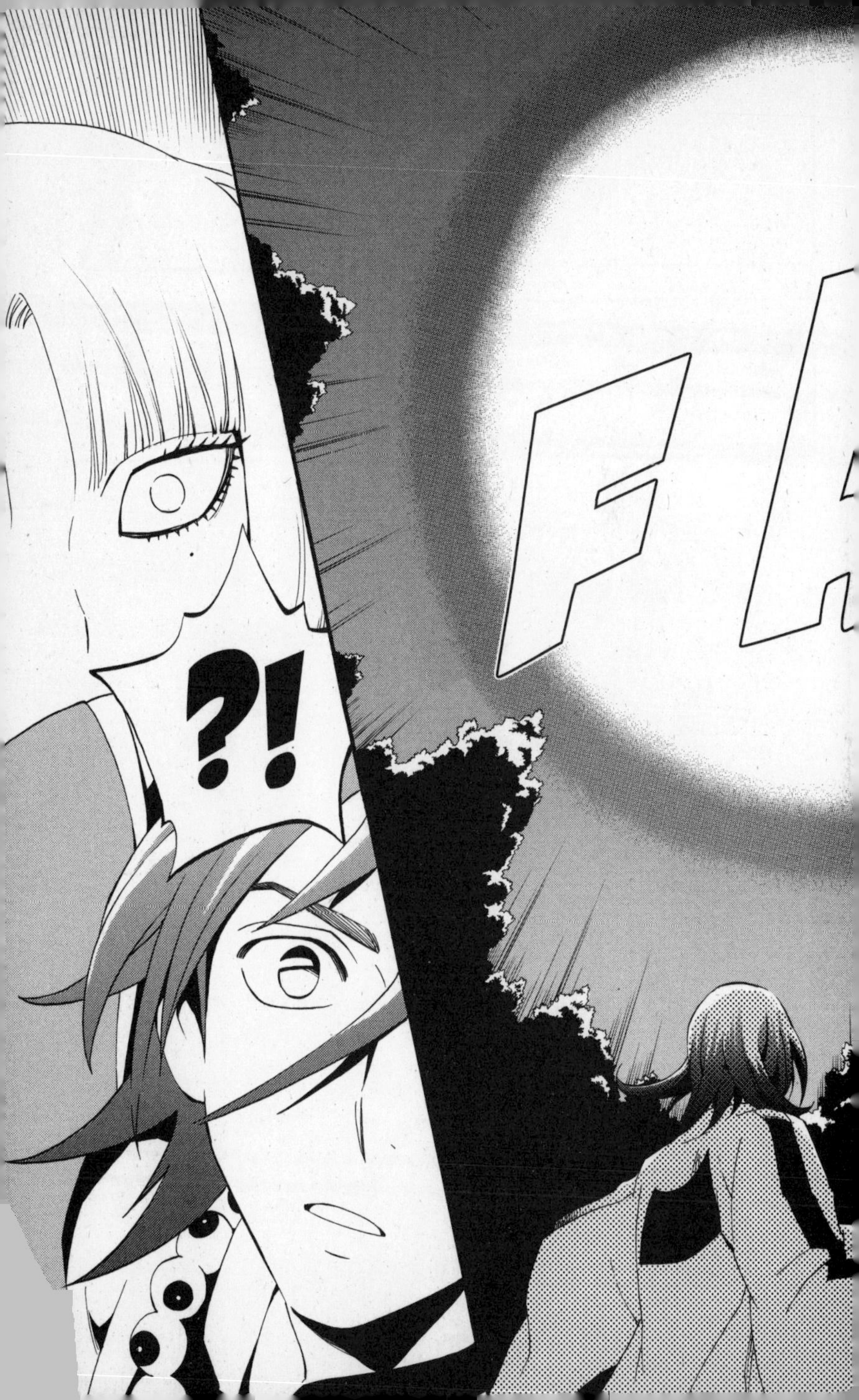
FA
?!

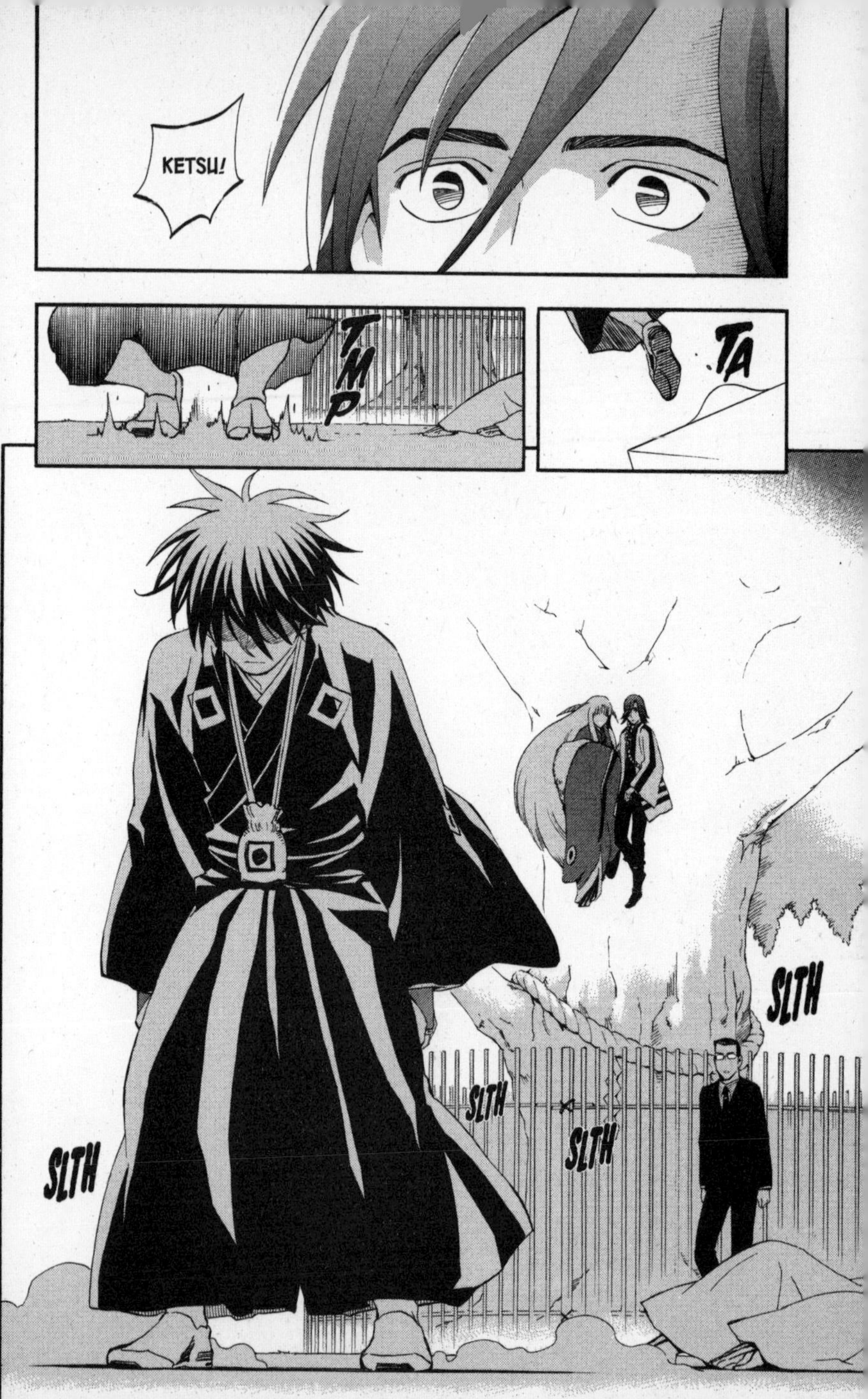
KETSU!
TA
TMP
SLTH
SLTH
SLTH
SLTH

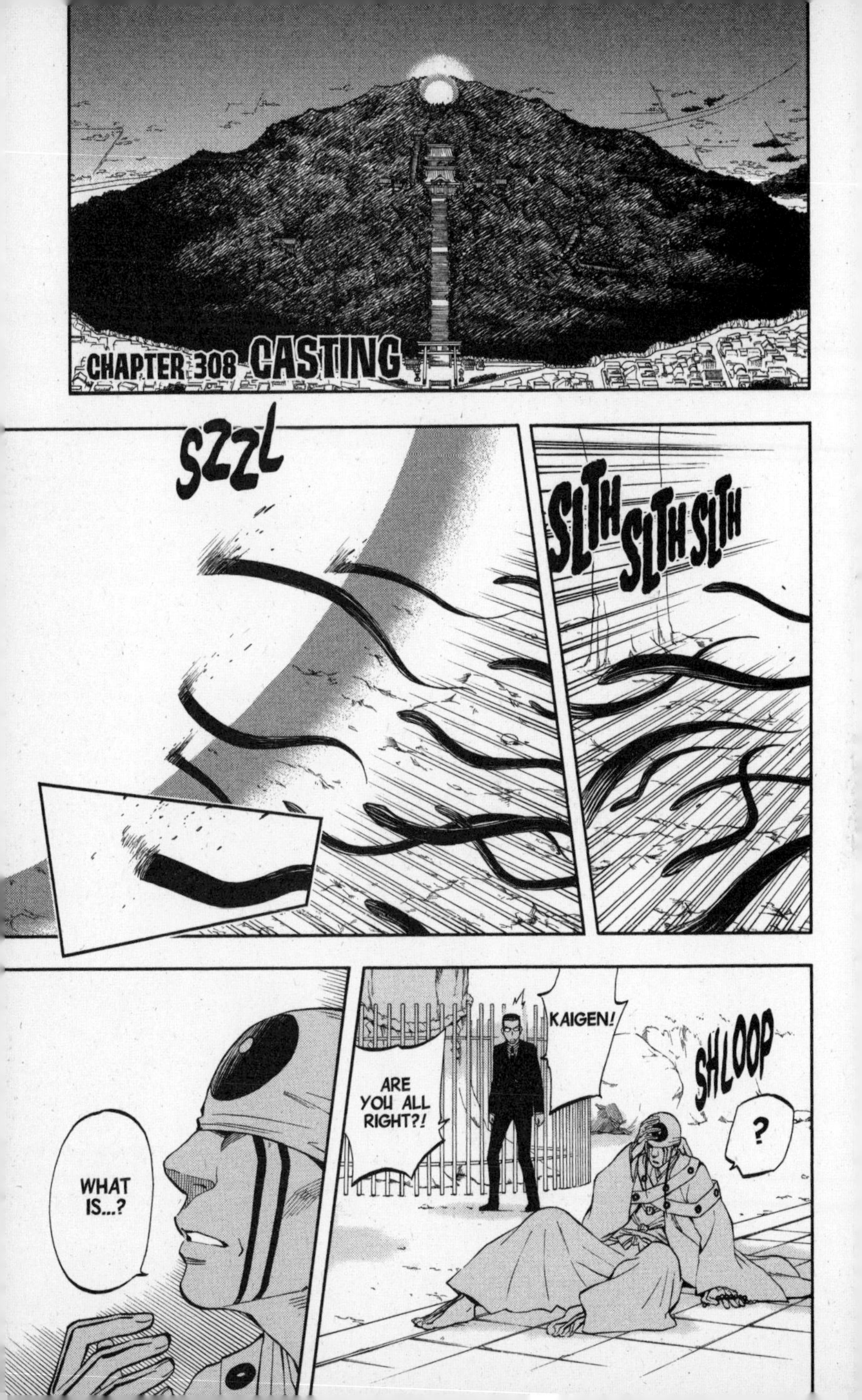
CHAPTER 308 CASTING
SLTH SLTH SLTH
SZZL
SHLOOP
KAIGEN!
?
ARE YOU ALL RIGHT?!
WHAT IS...?

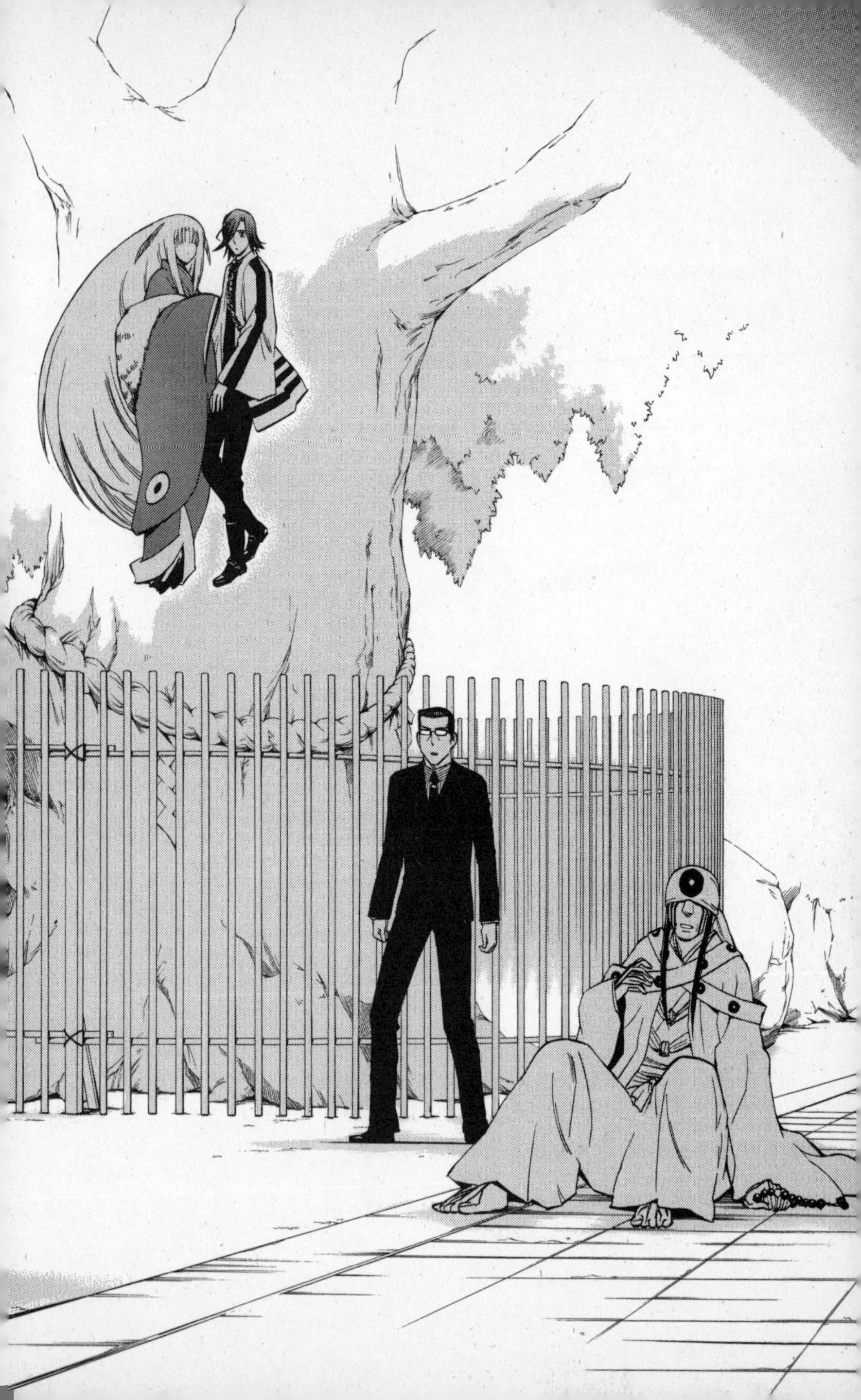

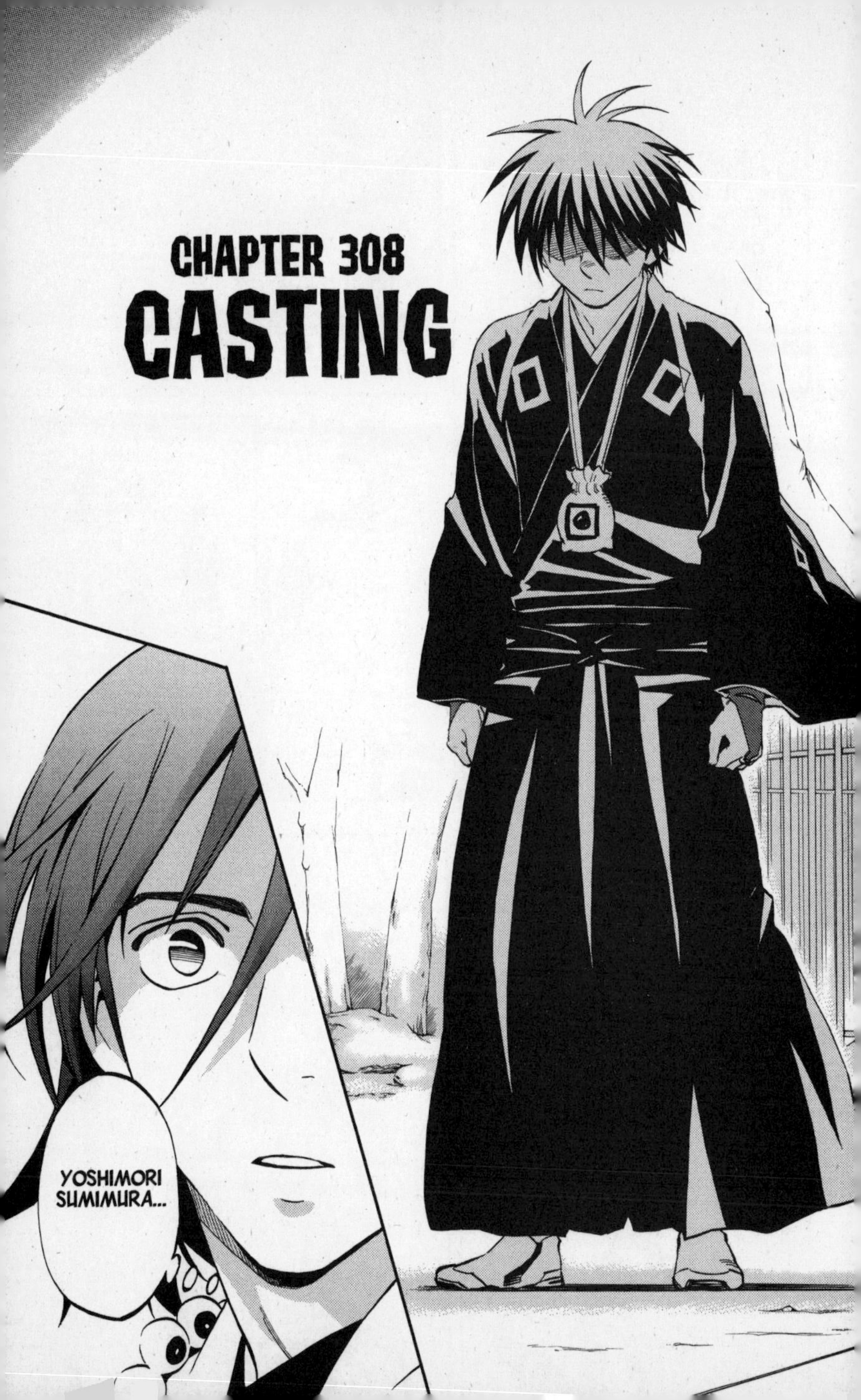
CHAPTER 308
CASTING
YOSHIMORI SUMIMURA...

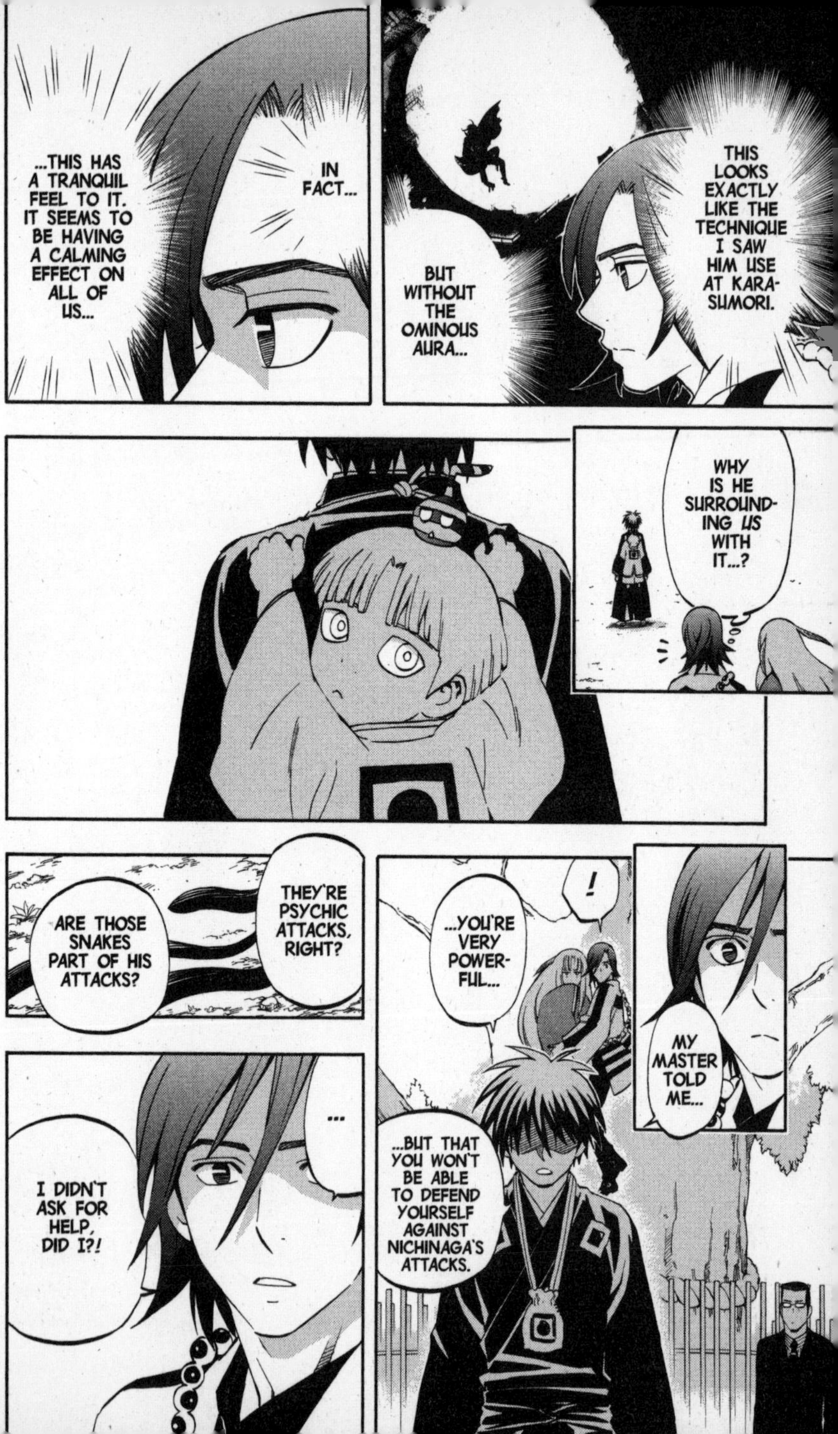
THIS LOOKS EXACTLY LIKE THE TECHNIQUE I SAW HIM USE AT KARA-SUMORI.
BUT WITHOUT THE OMINOUS AURA...
IN FACT...
...THIS HAS A TRANQUIL FEEL TO IT. IT SEEMS TO BE HAVING A CALMING EFFECT ON ALL OF US...
WHY IS HE SURROUND-ING *US* WITH IT...?
MY MASTER TOLD ME...
!
...YOU'RE VERY POWER-FUL...
...BUT THAT YOU WON'T BE ABLE TO DEFEND YOURSELF AGAINST NICHINAGA'S ATTACKS.
THEY'RE PSYCHIC ATTACKS, RIGHT?
ARE THOSE SNAKES PART OF HIS ATTACKS?
...
I DIDN'T ASK FOR HELP, DID I?!

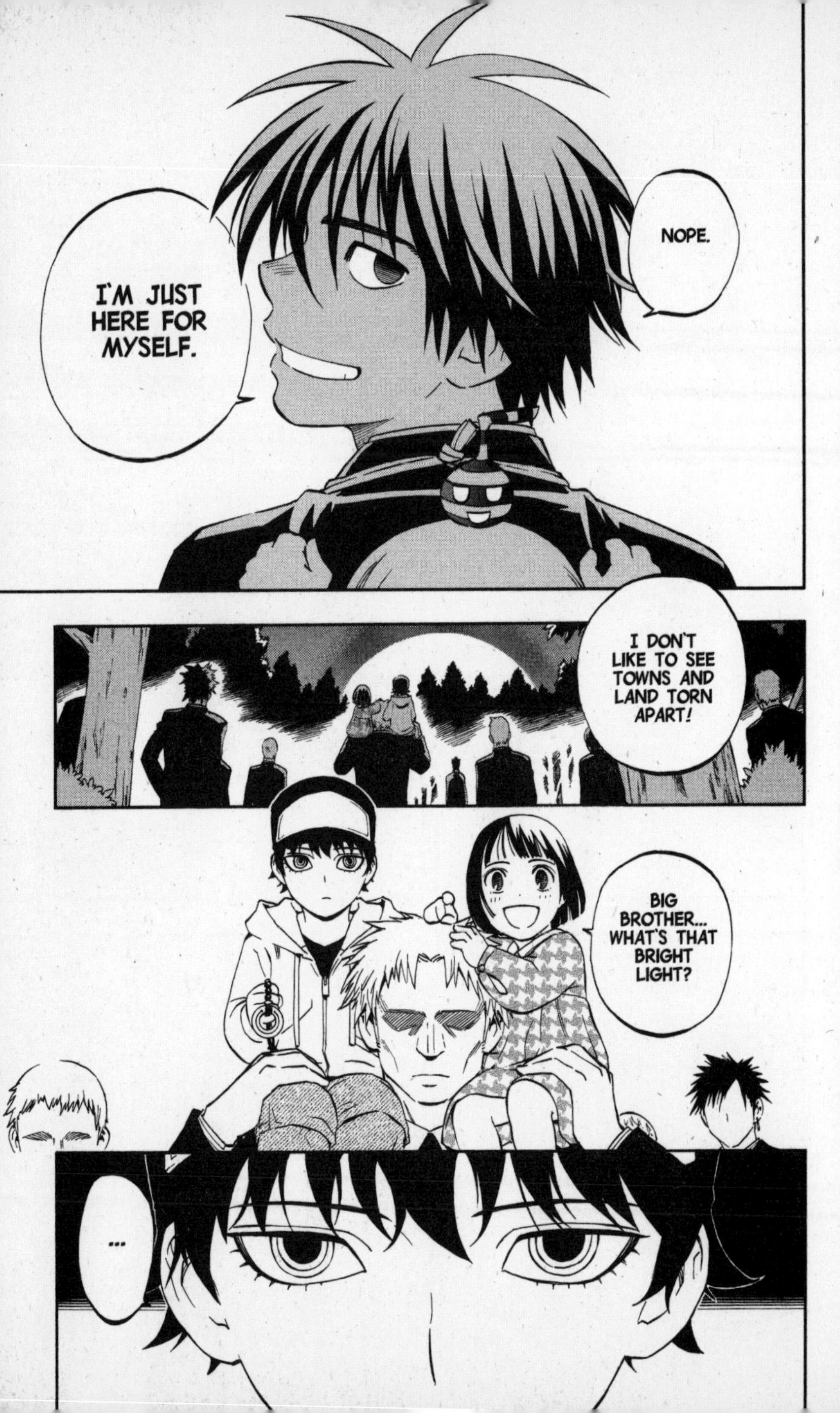
NOPE.
I'M JUST HERE FOR MYSELF.
I DON'T LIKE TO SEE TOWNS AND LAND TORN APART!
BIG BROTHER... WHAT'S THAT BRIGHT LIGHT?
...

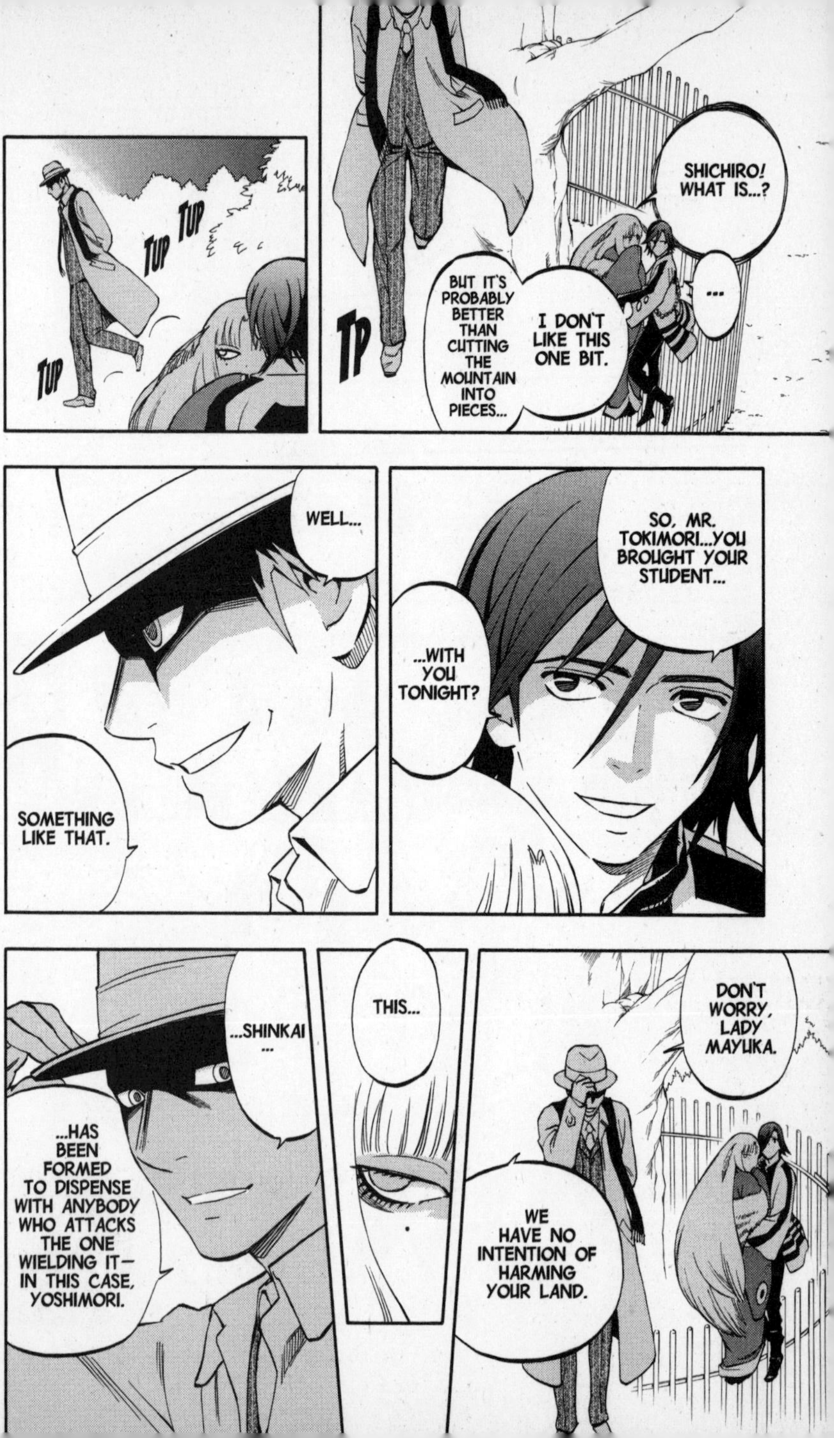
SHICHIRO! WHAT IS...?
...
I DON'T LIKE THIS ONE BIT.
BUT IT'S PROBABLY BETTER THAN CUTTING THE MOUNTAIN INTO PIECES...
TP
TUP TUP
TUP
SO, MR. TOKIMORI...YOU BROUGHT YOUR STUDENT...
...WITH YOU TONIGHT?
WELL...
SOMETHING LIKE THAT.
DON'T WORRY, LADY MAYUKA.
WE HAVE NO INTENTION OF HARMING YOUR LAND.
THIS...
...SHINKAI...
...HAS BEEN FORMED TO DISPENSE WITH ANYBODY WHO ATTACKS THE ONE WIELDING IT— IN THIS CASE, YOSHIMORI.

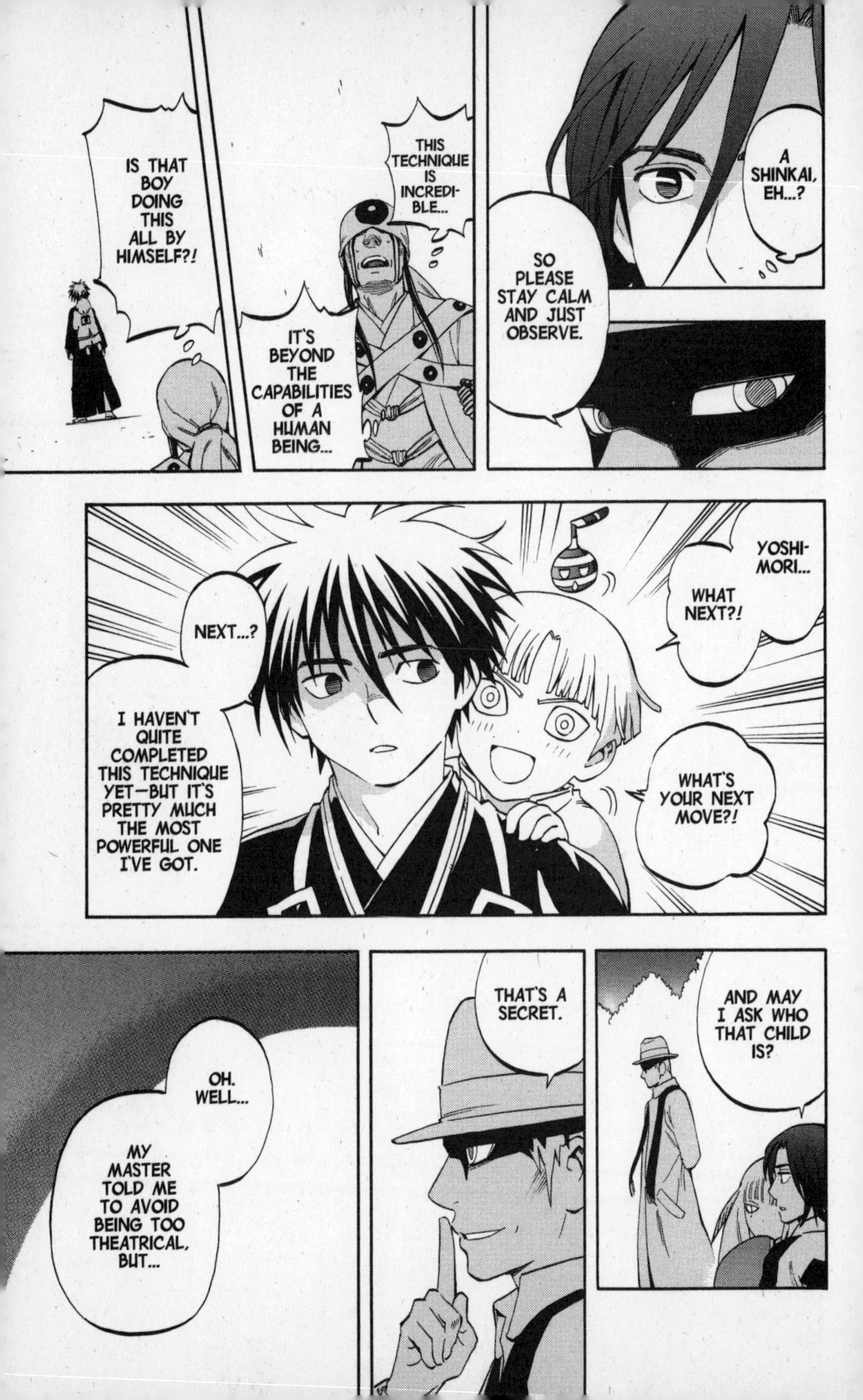

A SHINKAI, EH...?
SO PLEASE STAY CALM AND JUST OBSERVE.
THIS TECHNIQUE IS INCREDIBLE...
IT'S BEYOND THE CAPABILITIES OF A HUMAN BEING...
IS THAT BOY DOING THIS ALL BY HIMSELF?!
YOSHIMORI...
WHAT NEXT?!
NEXT...?
WHAT'S YOUR NEXT MOVE?!
I HAVEN'T QUITE COMPLETED THIS TECHNIQUE YET—BUT IT'S PRETTY MUCH THE MOST POWERFUL ONE I'VE GOT.
AND MAY I ASK WHO THAT CHILD IS?
THAT'S A SECRET.
OH. WELL...
MY MASTER TOLD ME TO AVOID BEING TOO THEATRICAL, BUT...

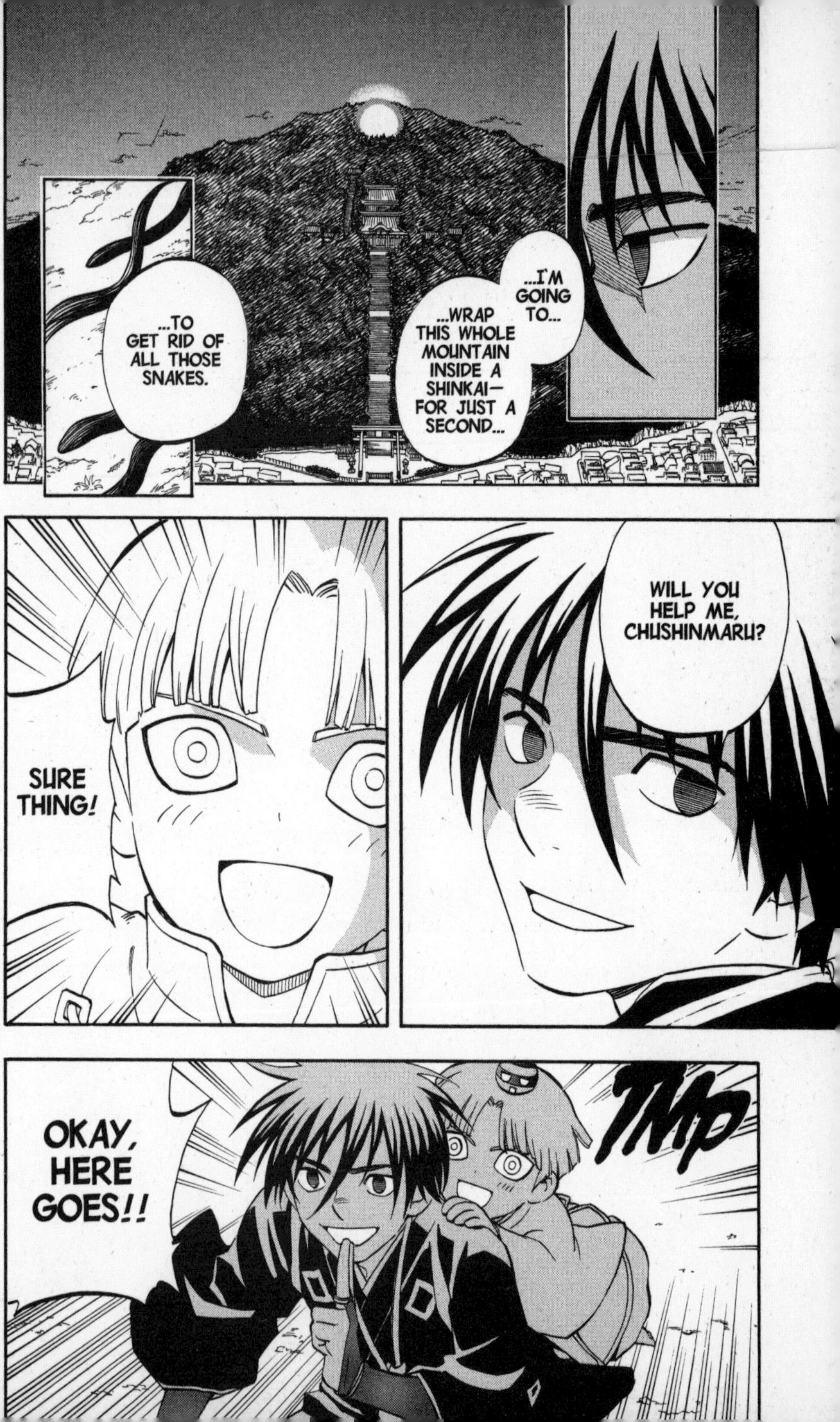
...I'M GOING TO...
...WRAP THIS WHOLE MOUNTAIN INSIDE A SHINKAI— FOR JUST A SECOND...
...TO GET RID OF ALL THOSE SNAKES.
WILL YOU HELP ME, CHUSHINMARU?
SURE THING!
TMP
OKAY, HERE GOES!!

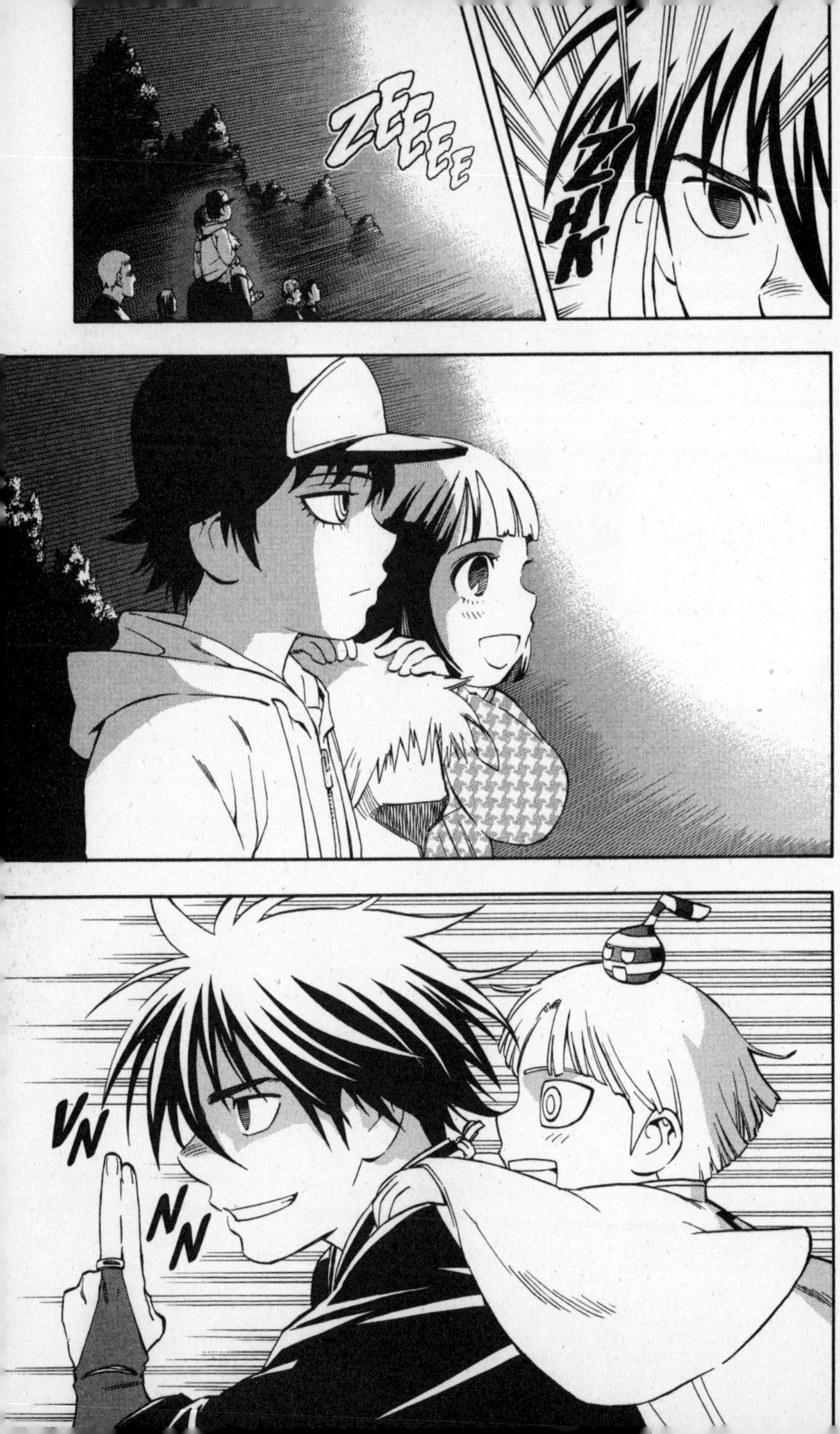
ZHK
ZEEEEE
VN
NN

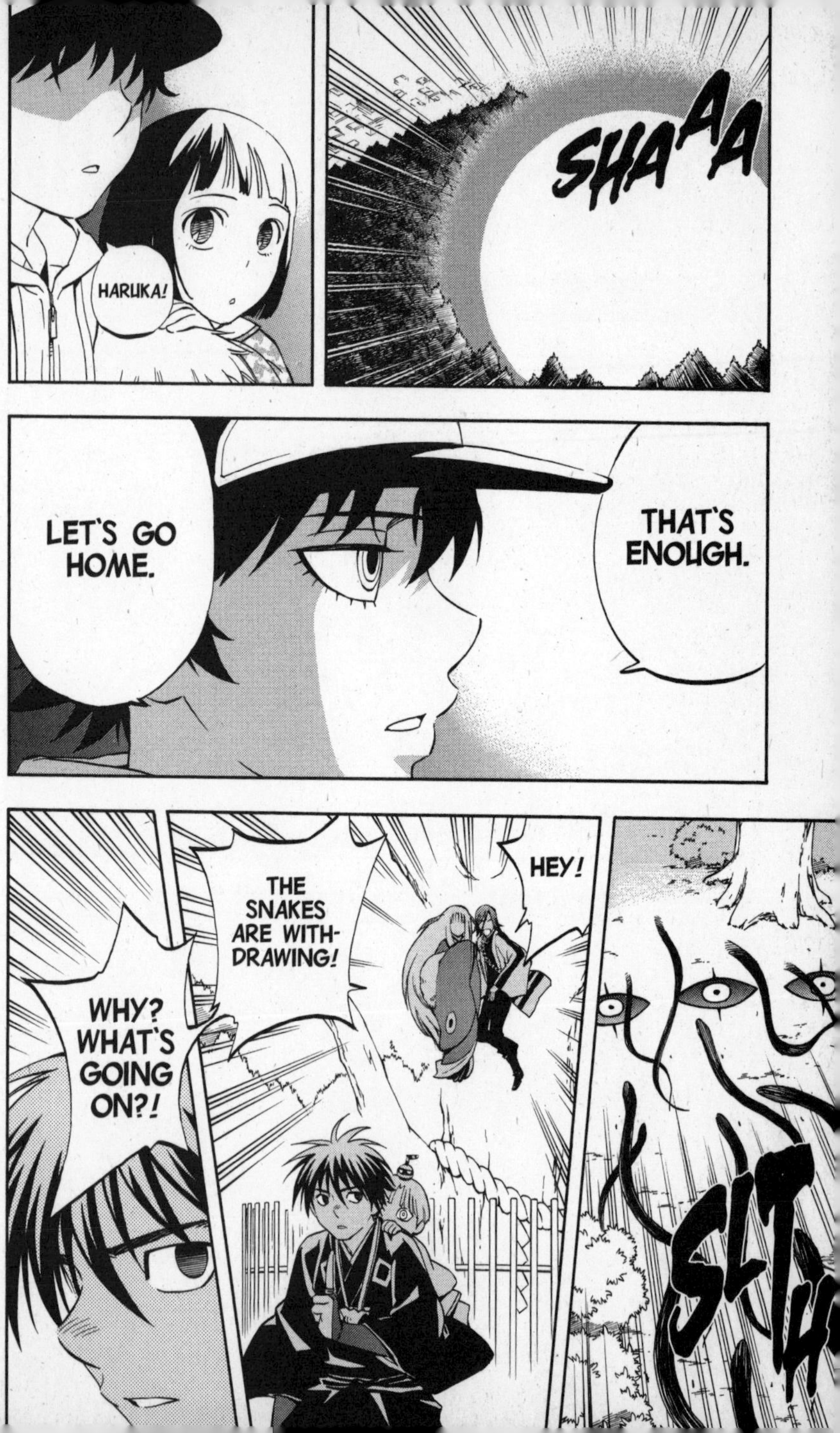
SHAAA
HARUKA!
THAT'S ENOUGH.
LET'S GO HOME.
HEY!
THE SNAKES ARE WITH-DRAWING!
WHY? WHAT'S GOING ON?!

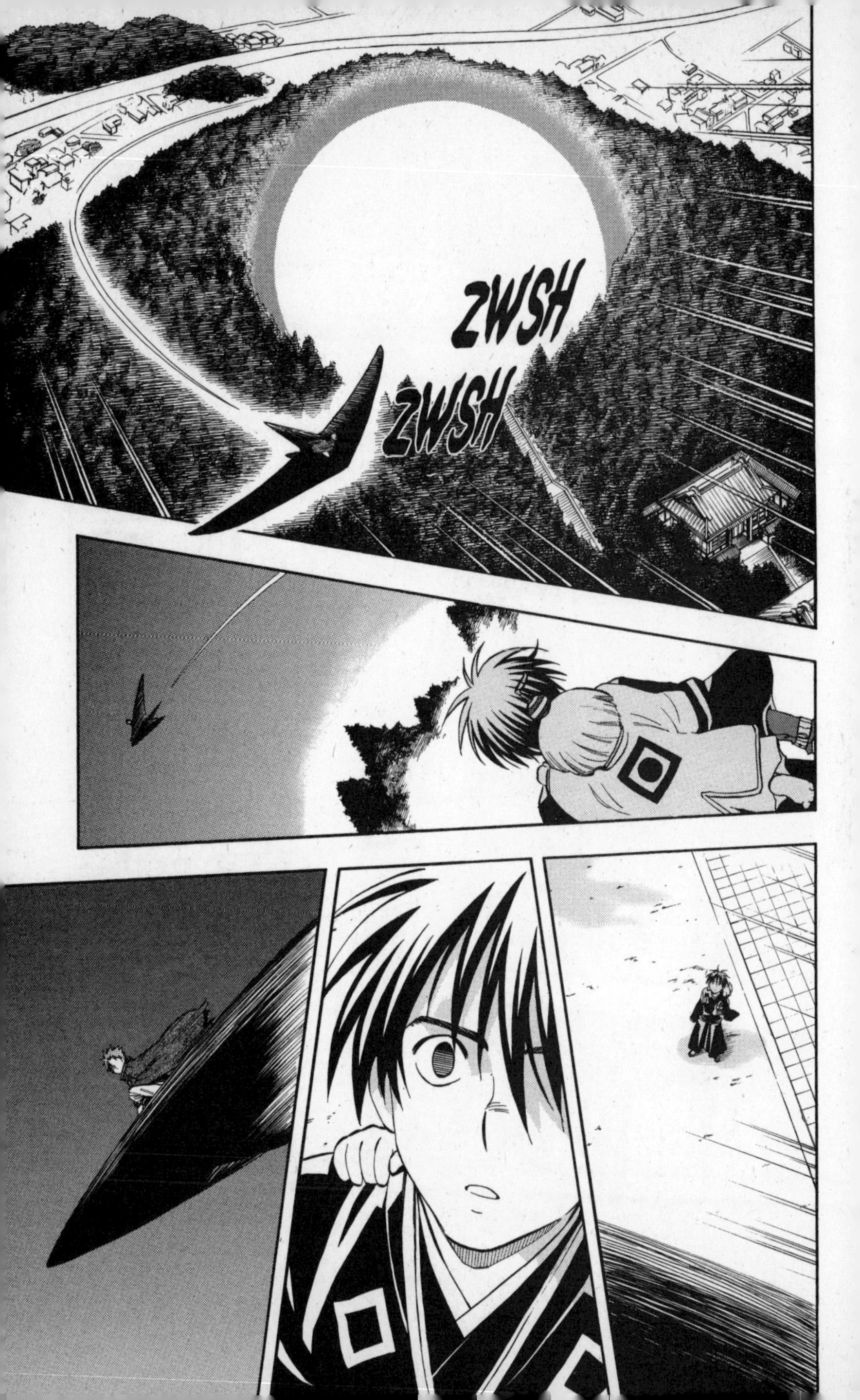
ZWSH
ZWSH

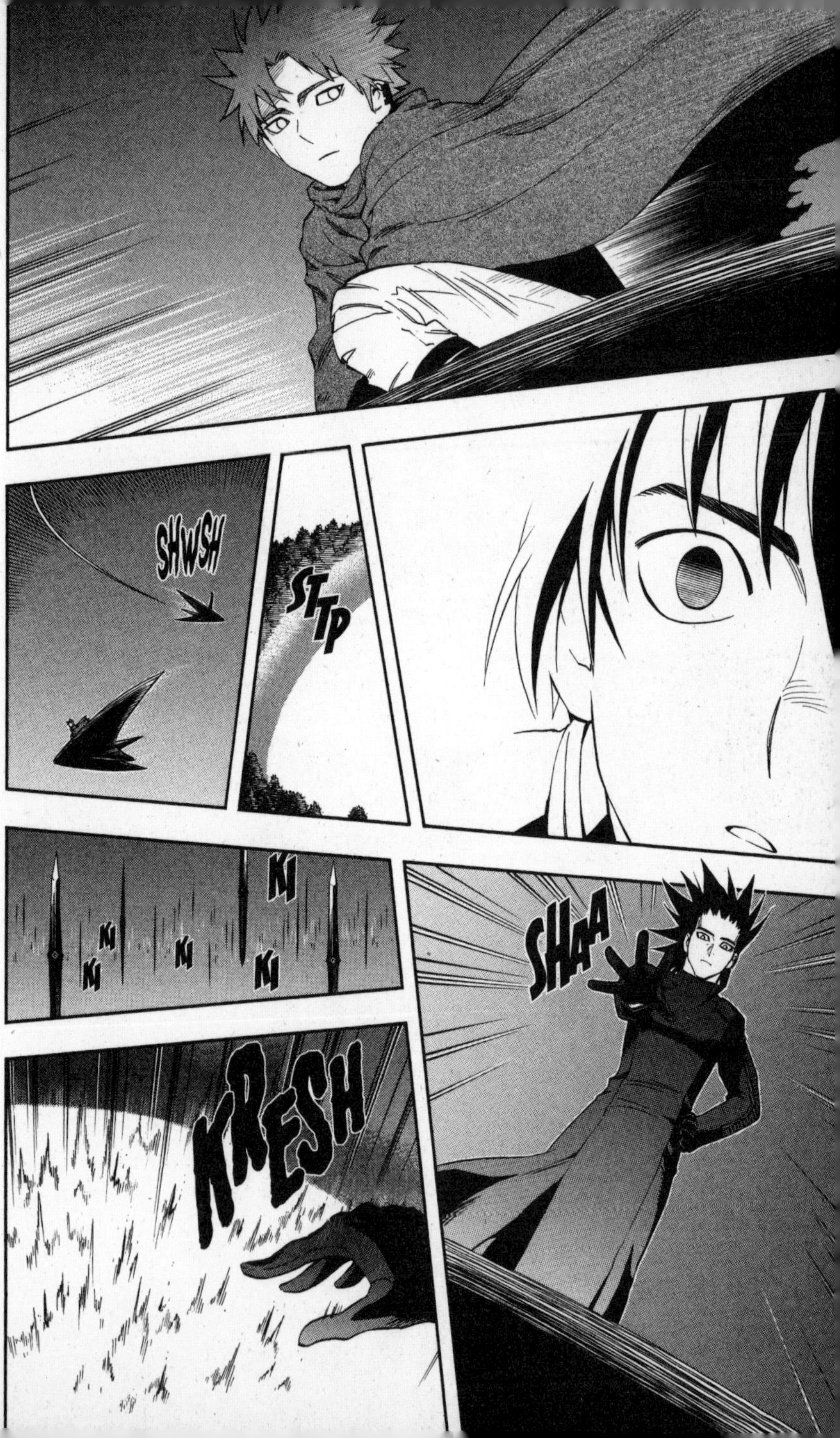
STTP
SHWSH
SHAA
KI
KI
KI
KI
KI
KRESH

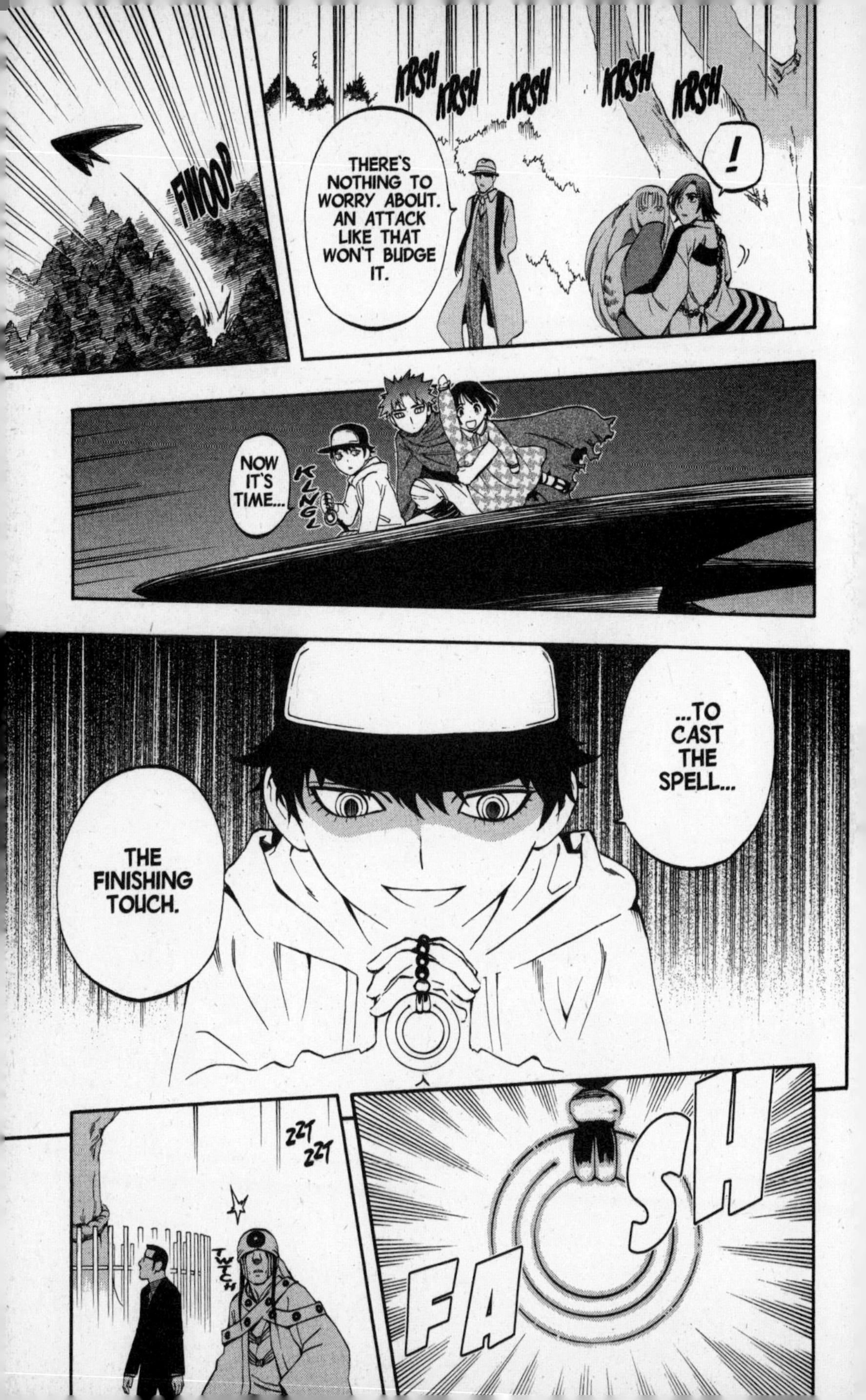
KRSH
KRSH
KRSH
KRSH
KRSH
!
THERE'S NOTHING TO WORRY ABOUT. AN ATTACK LIKE THAT WON'T BUDGE IT.
FWOOP
KLNGL
NOW IT'S TIME...
...TO CAST THE SPELL...
THE FINISHING TOUCH.
FASH
ZZT ZZT
TWITCH

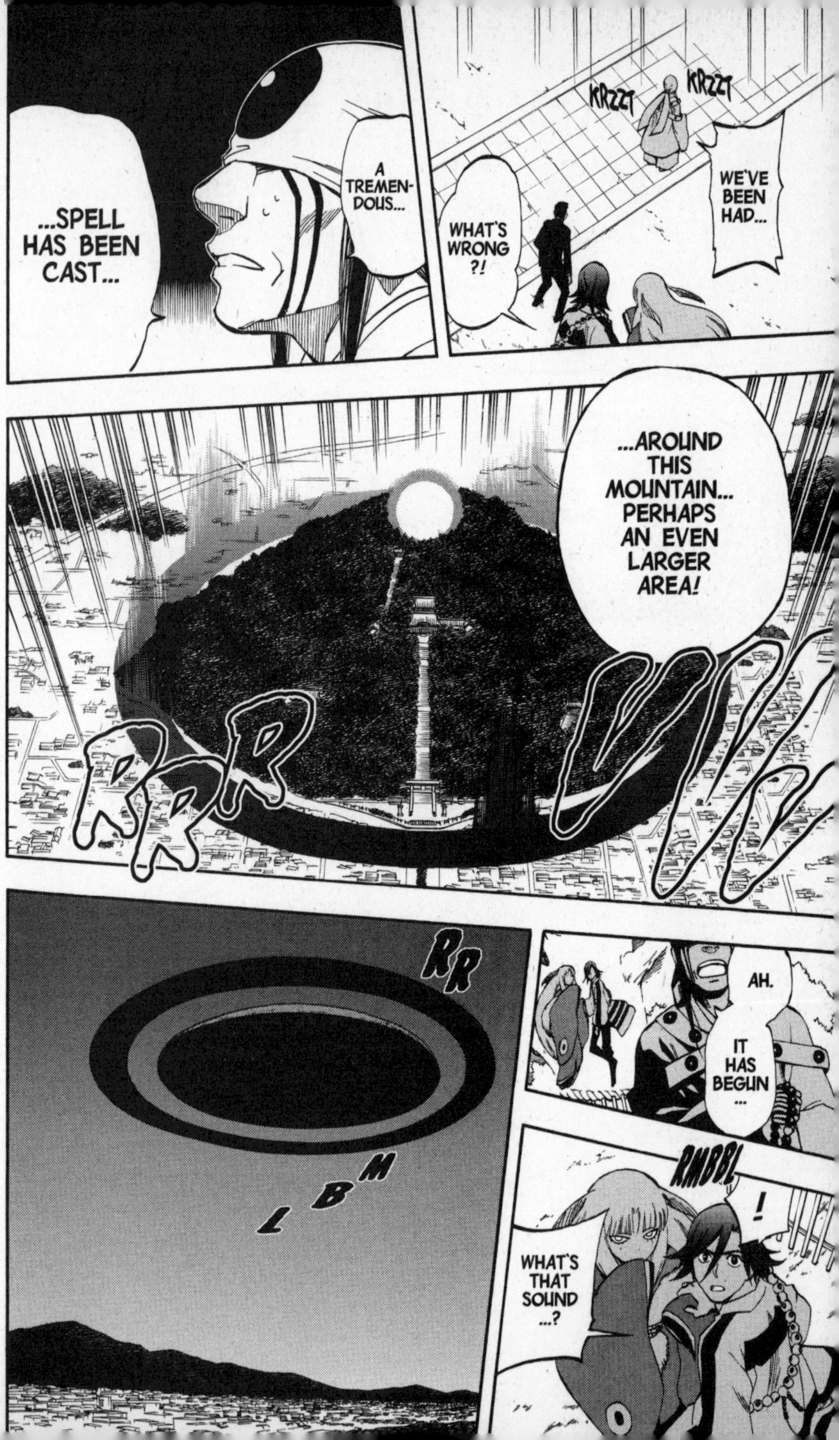
KRZZT KRZZT
WE'VE BEEN HAD...
WHAT'S WRONG?!
A TREMEN-DOUS...
...SPELL HAS BEEN CAST...
...AROUND THIS MOUNTAIN... PERHAPS AN EVEN LARGER AREA!
RRRUUUU
AH.
IT HAS BEGUN...
RMBBL
!
WHAT'S THAT SOUND...?
RR
LBM

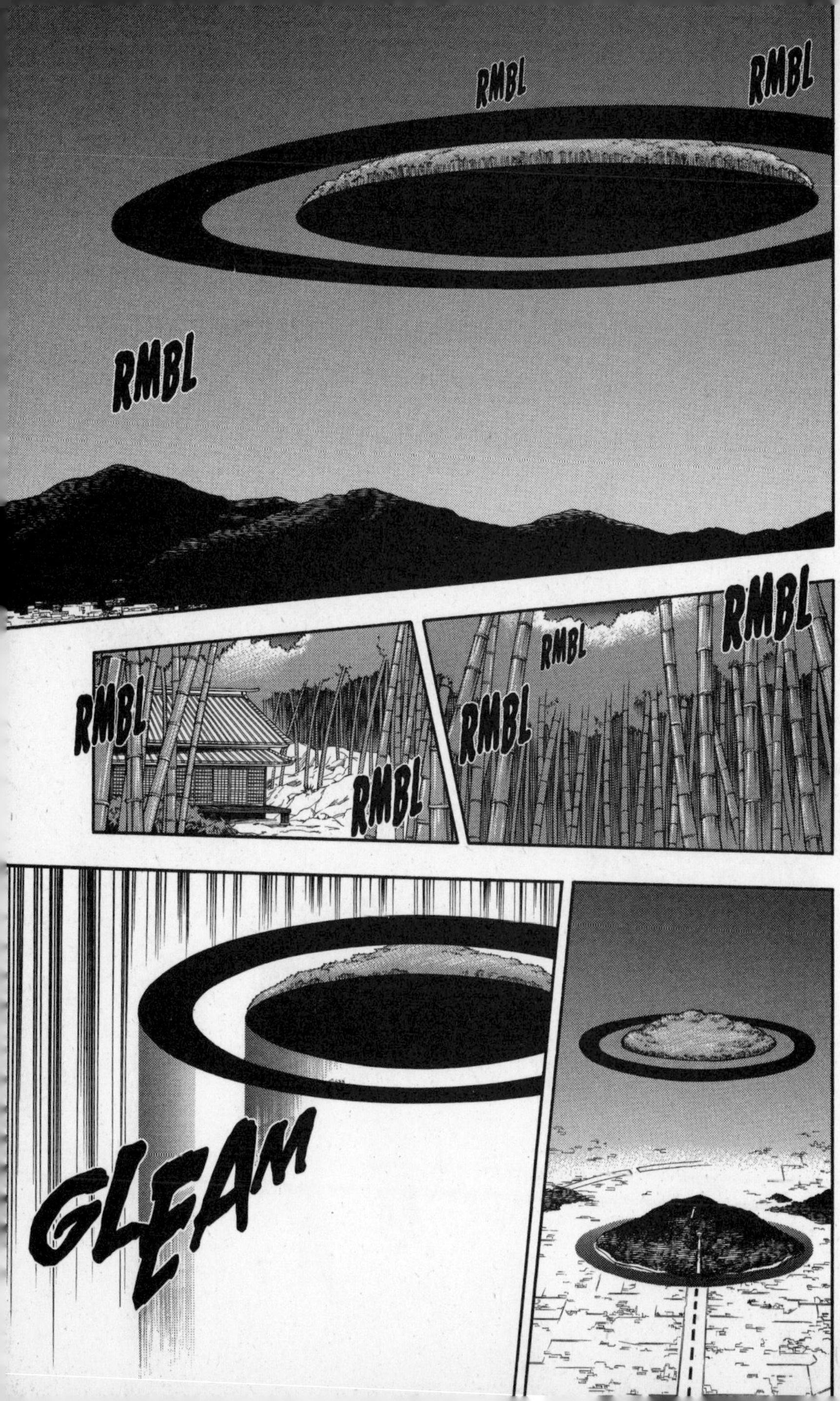
RMBL
RMBL
RMBL
RMBL
RMBL
RMBL
RMBL
RMBL
GLEAM

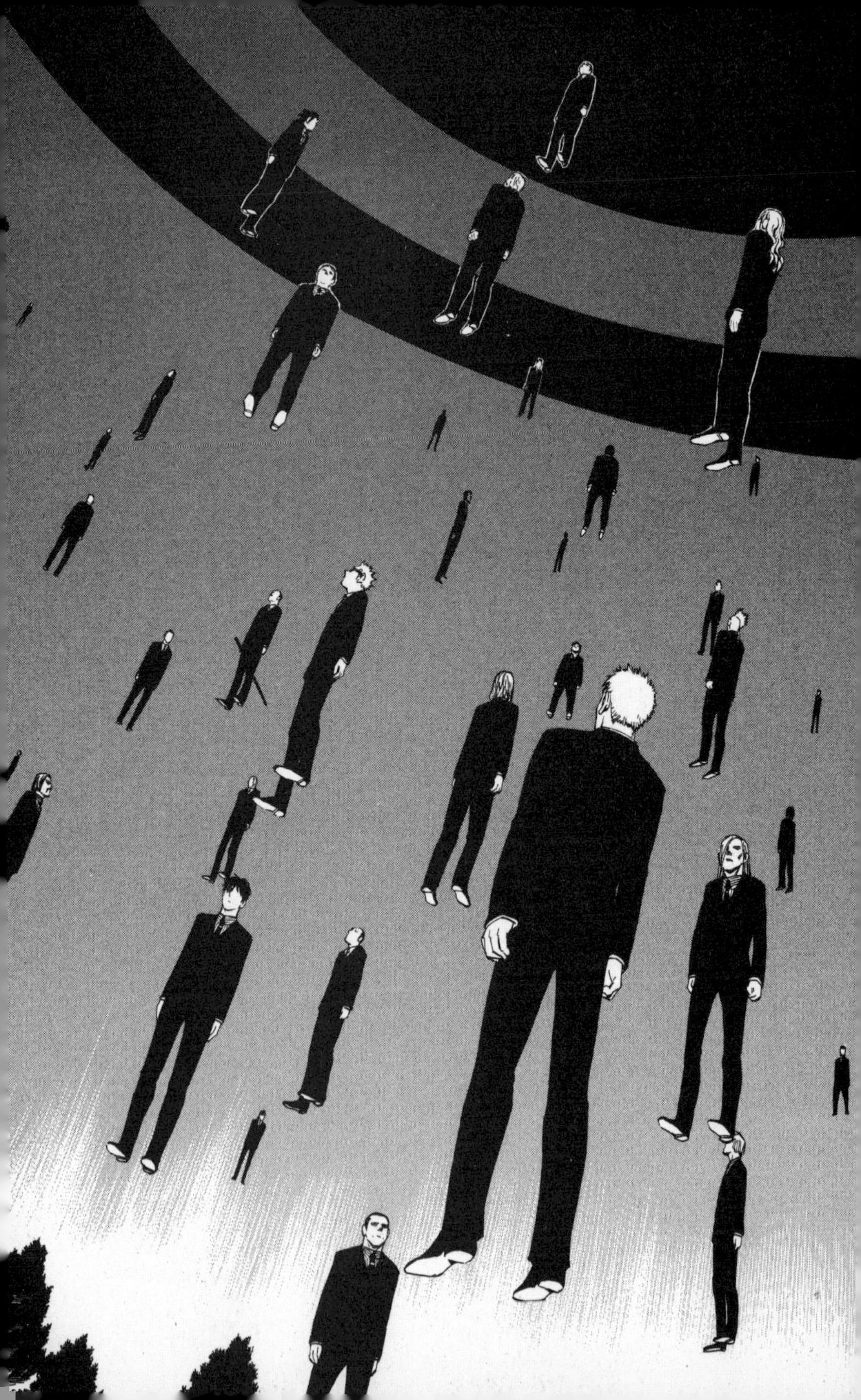

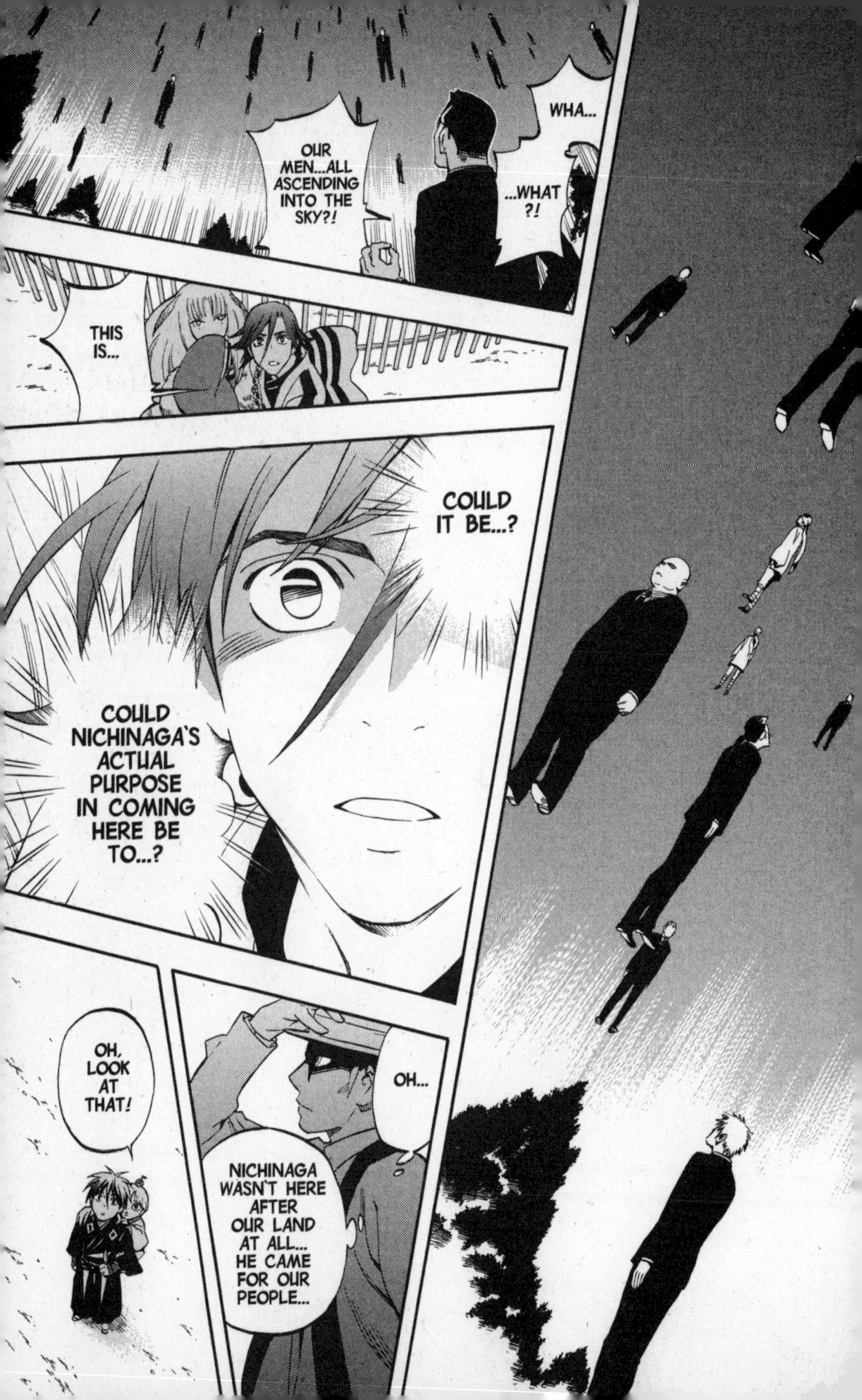
WHA...
...WHAT?!
OUR MEN...ALL ASCENDING INTO THE SKY?!
THIS IS...
COULD IT BE...?
COULD NICHINAGA'S ACTUAL PURPOSE IN COMING HERE BE TO...?
OH...
NICHINAGA WASN'T HERE AFTER OUR LAND AT ALL... HE CAME FOR OUR PEOPLE...
OH, LOOK AT THAT!

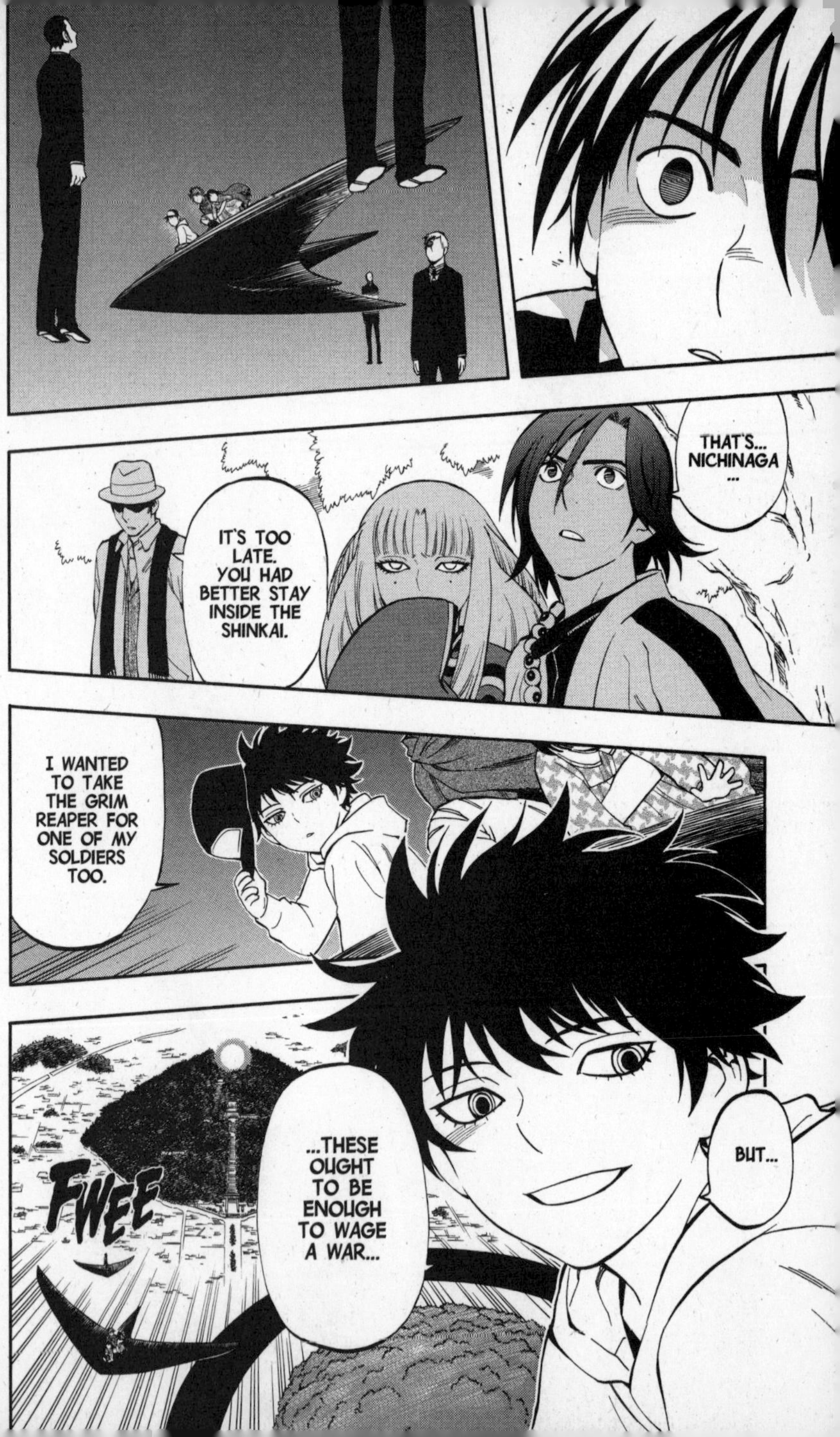
THAT'S... NICHINAGA ...
IT'S TOO LATE. YOU HAD BETTER STAY INSIDE THE SHINKAI.
I WANTED TO TAKE THE GRIM REAPER FOR ONE OF MY SOLDIERS TOO.
BUT...
...THESE OUGHT TO BE ENOUGH TO WAGE A WAR...
FWEE

CHAPTER 309 DEFEAT

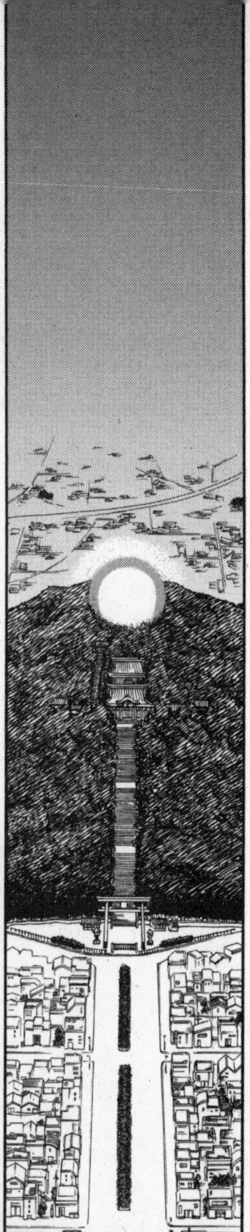

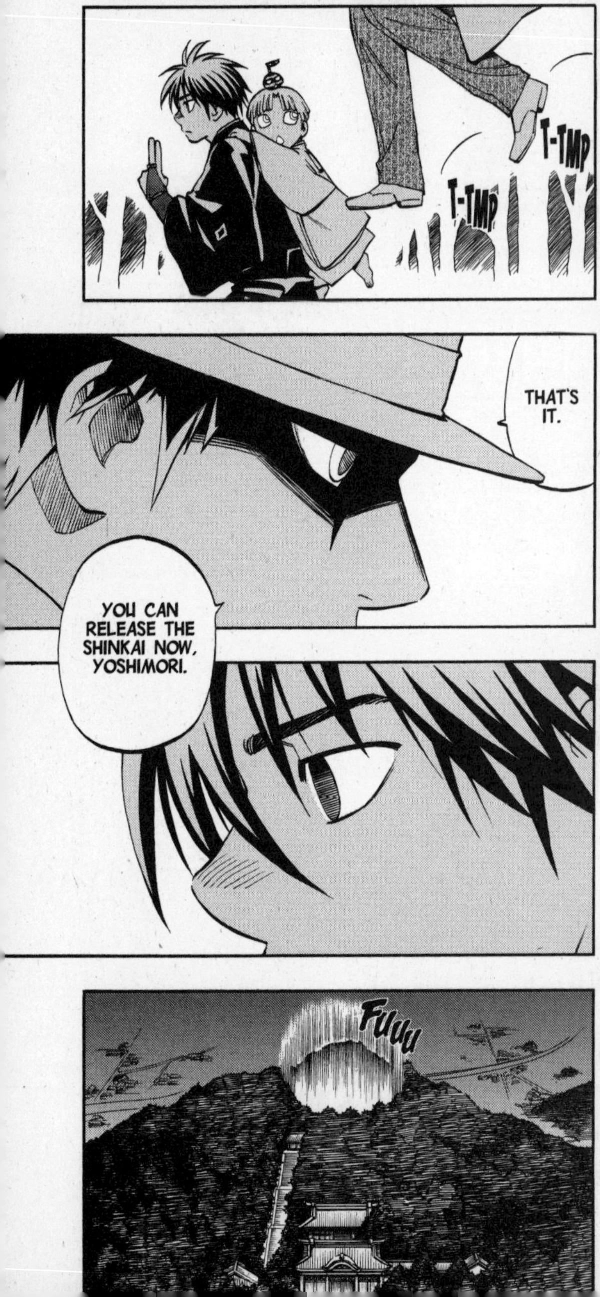
T-TMP
T-TMP
THAT'S IT.
YOU CAN RELEASE THE SHINKAI NOW, YOSHIMORI.
FUUU

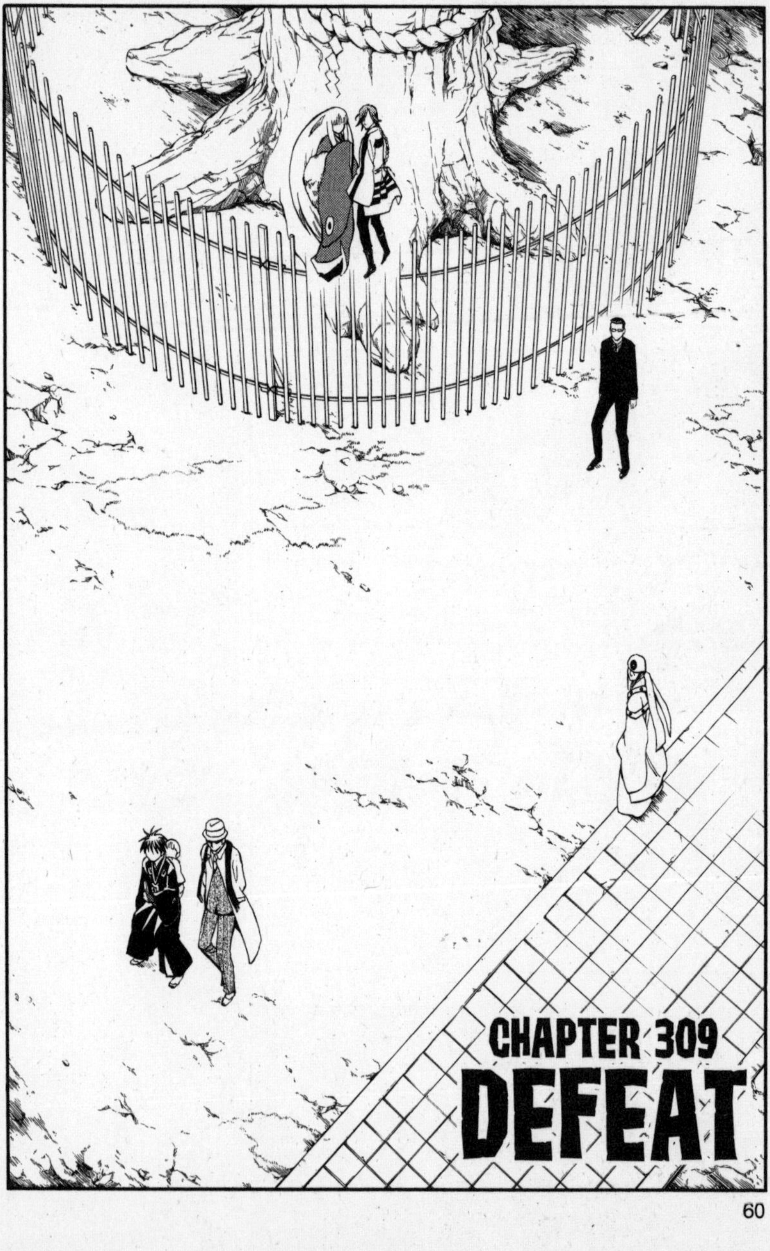
CHAPTER 309
DEFEAT

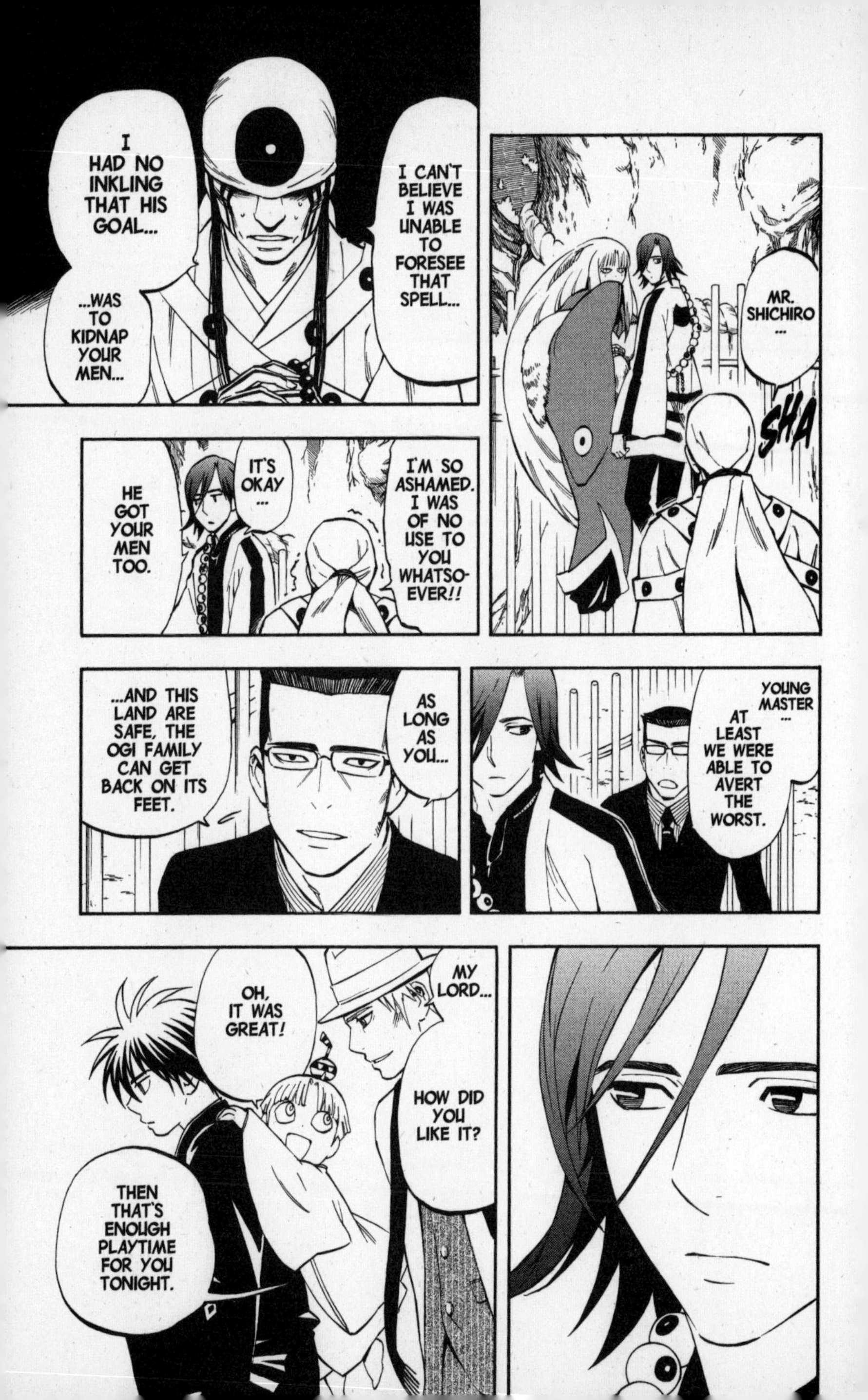

I CAN'T BELIEVE I WAS UNABLE TO FORESEE THAT SPELL...
I HAD NO INKLING THAT HIS GOAL...
...WAS TO KIDNAP YOUR MEN...
MR. SHICHIRO...
SHA
I'M SO ASHAMED. I WAS OF NO USE TO YOU WHATSOEVER!!
IT'S OKAY...
HE GOT YOUR MEN TOO.
YOUNG MASTER... AT LEAST WE WERE ABLE TO AVERT THE WORST.
AS LONG AS YOU...
...AND THIS LAND ARE SAFE, THE OGI FAMILY CAN GET BACK ON ITS FEET.
MY LORD...
HOW DID YOU LIKE IT?
OH, IT WAS GREAT!
THEN THAT'S ENOUGH PLAYTIME FOR YOU TONIGHT.

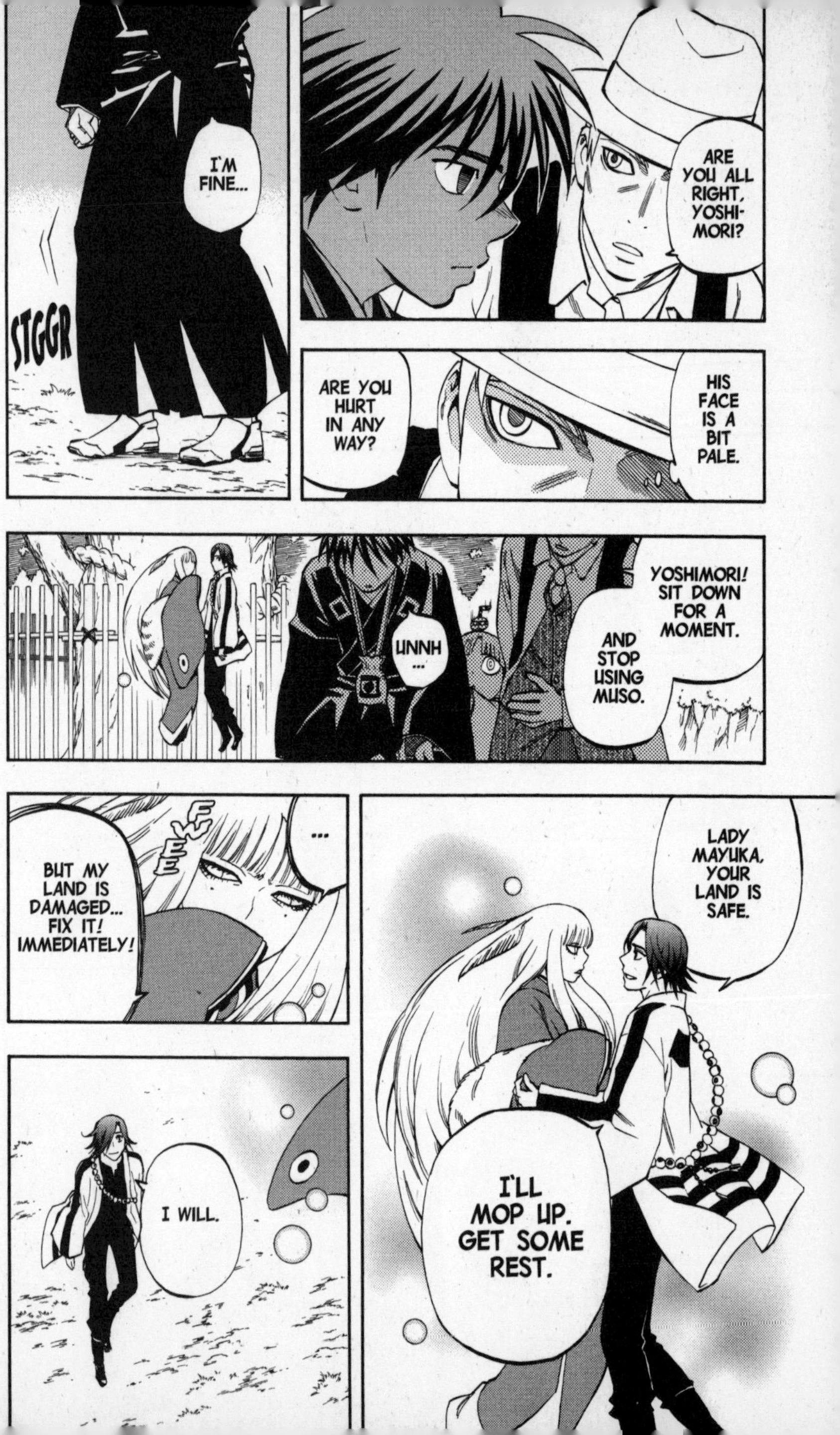
ARE YOU ALL RIGHT, YOSHIMORI?
HIS FACE IS A BIT PALE.
ARE YOU HURT IN ANY WAY?
I'M FINE...
STGGR
YOSHIMORI! SIT DOWN FOR A MOMENT.
AND STOP USING MUSO.
UNNH...
LADY MAYUKA, YOUR LAND IS SAFE.
I'LL MOP UP. GET SOME REST.
...
FWEE
BUT MY LAND IS DAMAGED... FIX IT! IMMEDIATELY!
I WILL.

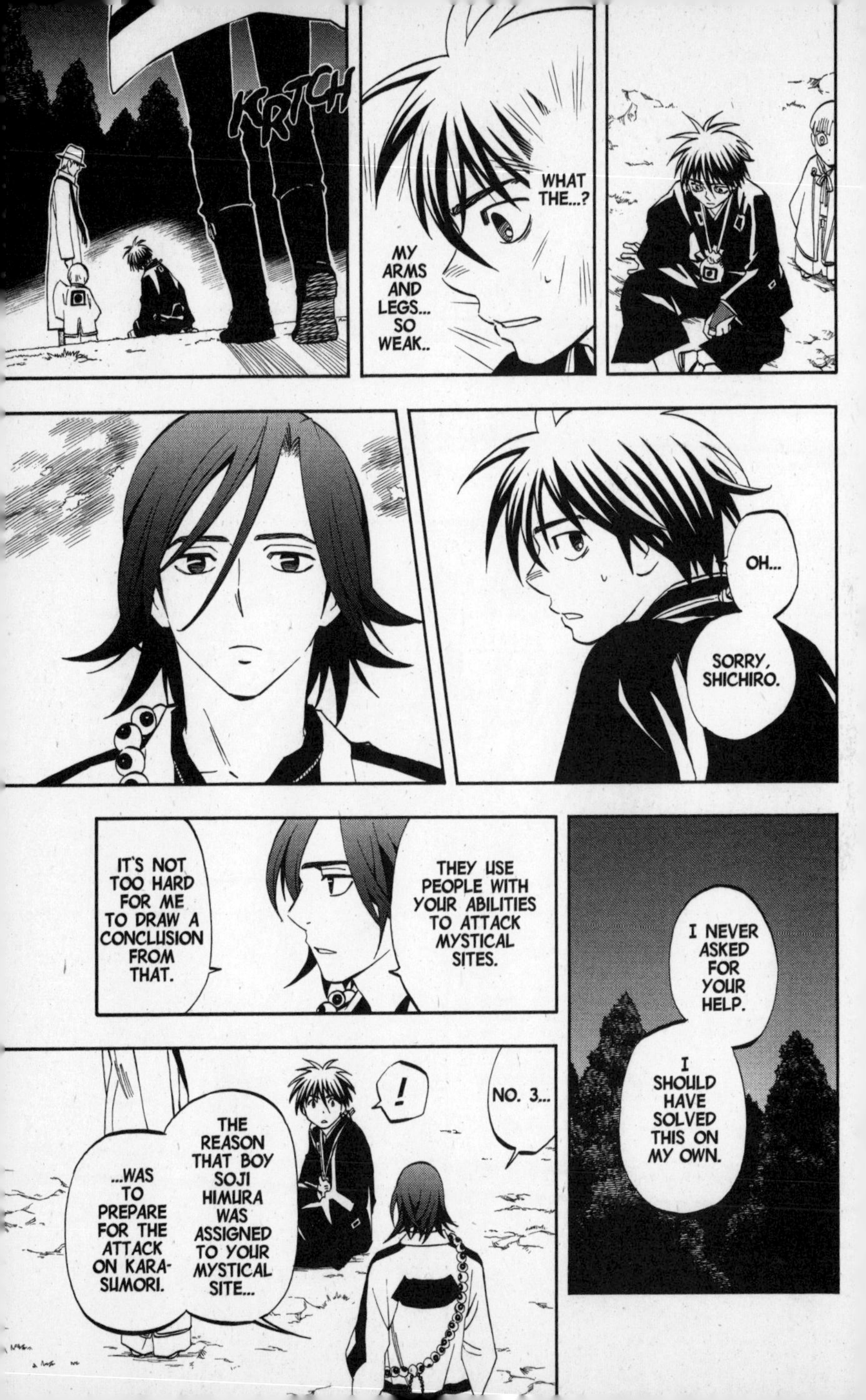
WHAT THE...?
MY ARMS AND LEGS... SO WEAK..
KRTCH
OH...
SORRY, SHICHIRO.
I NEVER ASKED FOR YOUR HELP.
I SHOULD HAVE SOLVED THIS ON MY OWN.
THEY USE PEOPLE WITH YOUR ABILITIES TO ATTACK MYSTICAL SITES.
IT'S NOT TOO HARD FOR ME TO DRAW A CONCLUSION FROM THAT.
NO. 3...
!
THE REASON THAT BOY SOJI HIMURA WAS ASSIGNED TO YOUR MYSTICAL SITE...
...WAS TO PREPARE FOR THE ATTACK ON KARA-SUMORI.

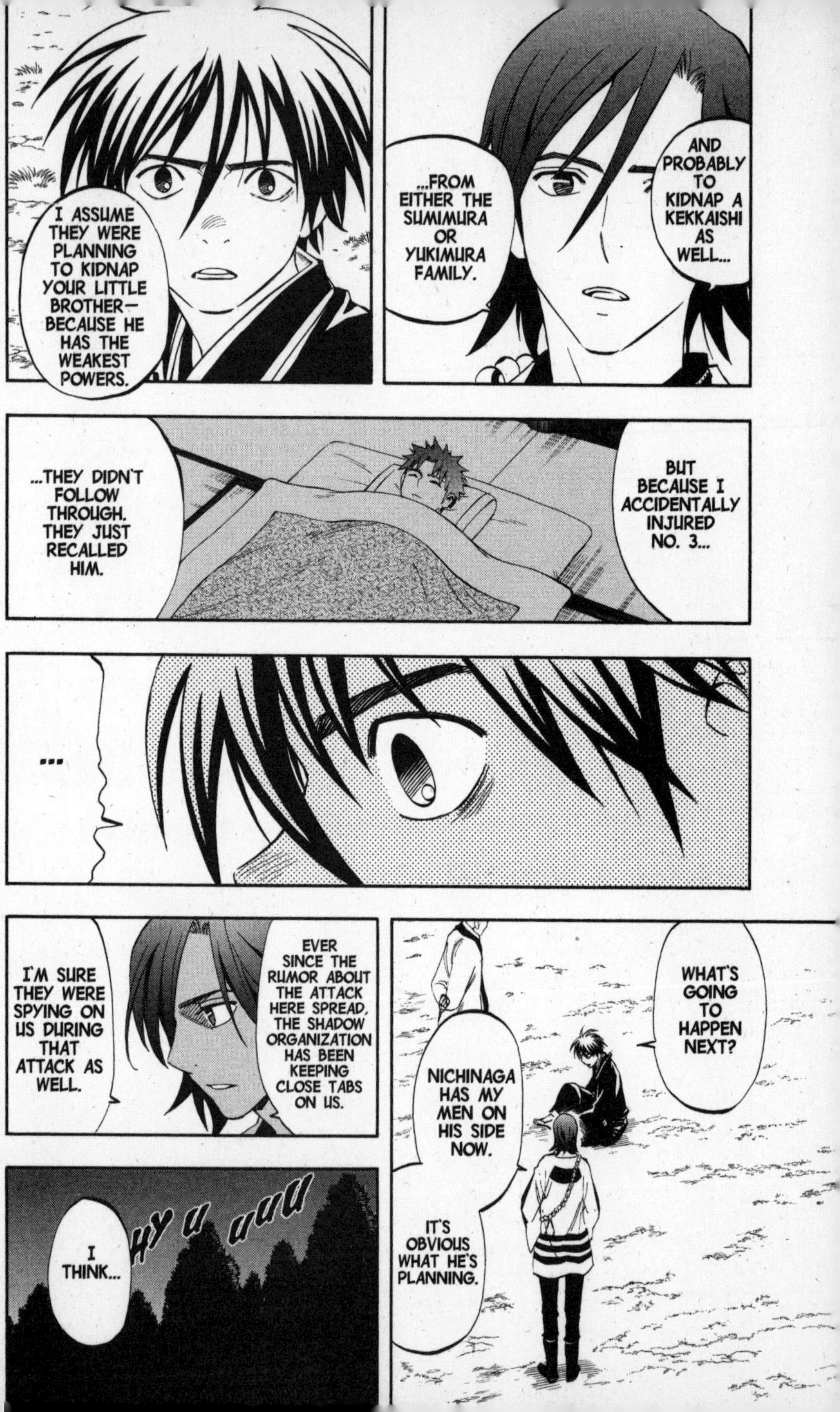
AND PROBABLY TO KIDNAP A KEKKAISHI AS WELL...
...FROM EITHER THE SUMIMURA OR YUKIMURA FAMILY.
I ASSUME THEY WERE PLANNING TO KIDNAP YOUR LITTLE BROTHER— BECAUSE HE HAS THE WEAKEST POWERS.
BUT BECAUSE I ACCIDENTALLY INJURED NO. 3...
...THEY DIDN'T FOLLOW THROUGH. THEY JUST RECALLED HIM.
...
WHAT'S GOING TO HAPPEN NEXT?
NICHINAGA HAS MY MEN ON HIS SIDE NOW.
IT'S OBVIOUS WHAT HE'S PLANNING.
EVER SINCE THE RUMOR ABOUT THE ATTACK HERE SPREAD, THE SHADOW ORGANIZATION HAS BEEN KEEPING CLOSE TABS ON US.
I'M SURE THEY WERE SPYING ON US DURING THAT ATTACK AS WELL.
HYU U UUU
I THINK...

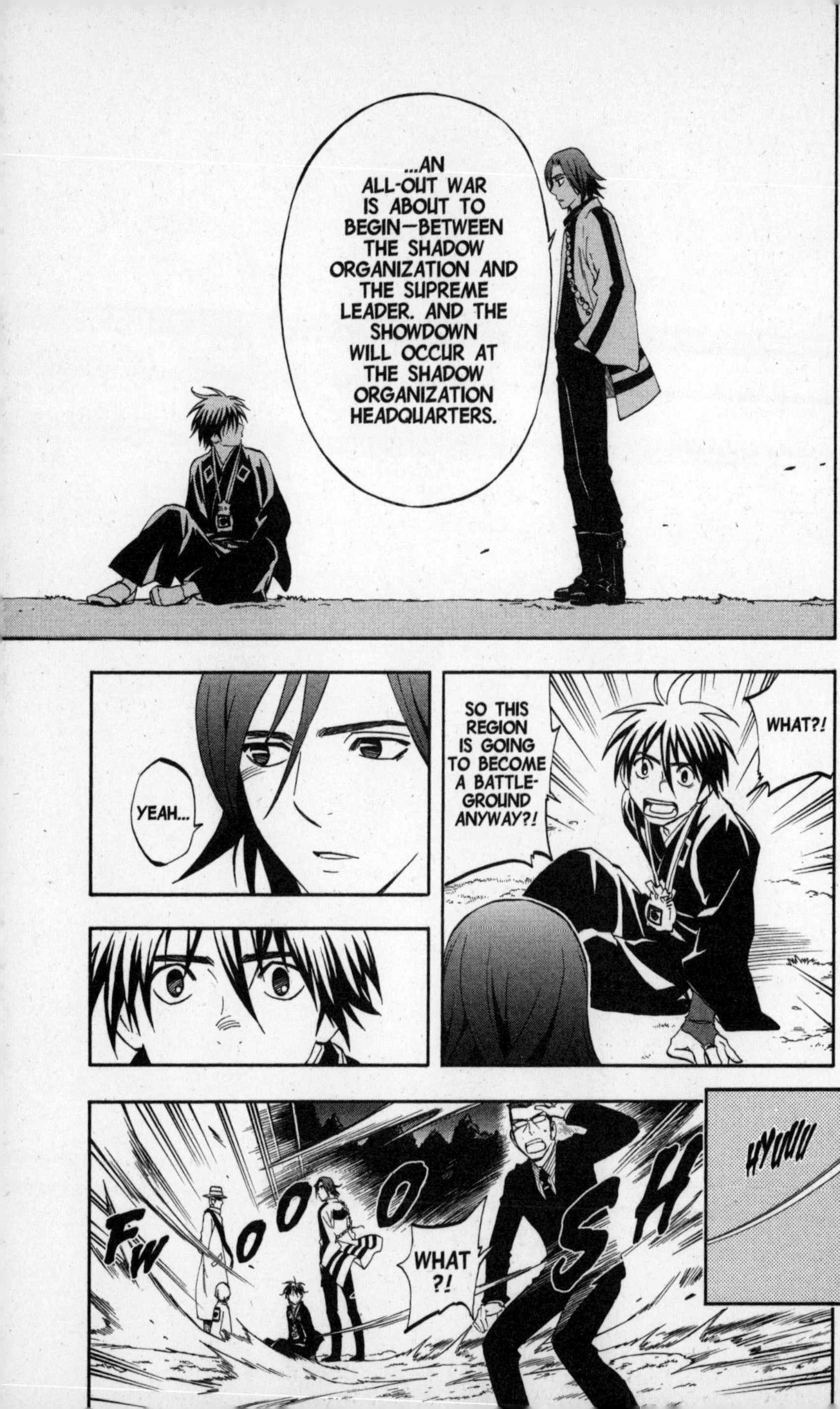
...AN ALL-OUT WAR IS ABOUT TO BEGIN—BETWEEN THE SHADOW ORGANIZATION AND THE SUPREME LEADER. AND THE SHOWDOWN WILL OCCUR AT THE SHADOW ORGANIZATION HEADQUARTERS.
WHAT?!
SO THIS REGION IS GOING TO BECOME A BATTLE-GROUND ANYWAY?!
YEAH...
HYUUU
WHAT ?!
FWOOOOSH

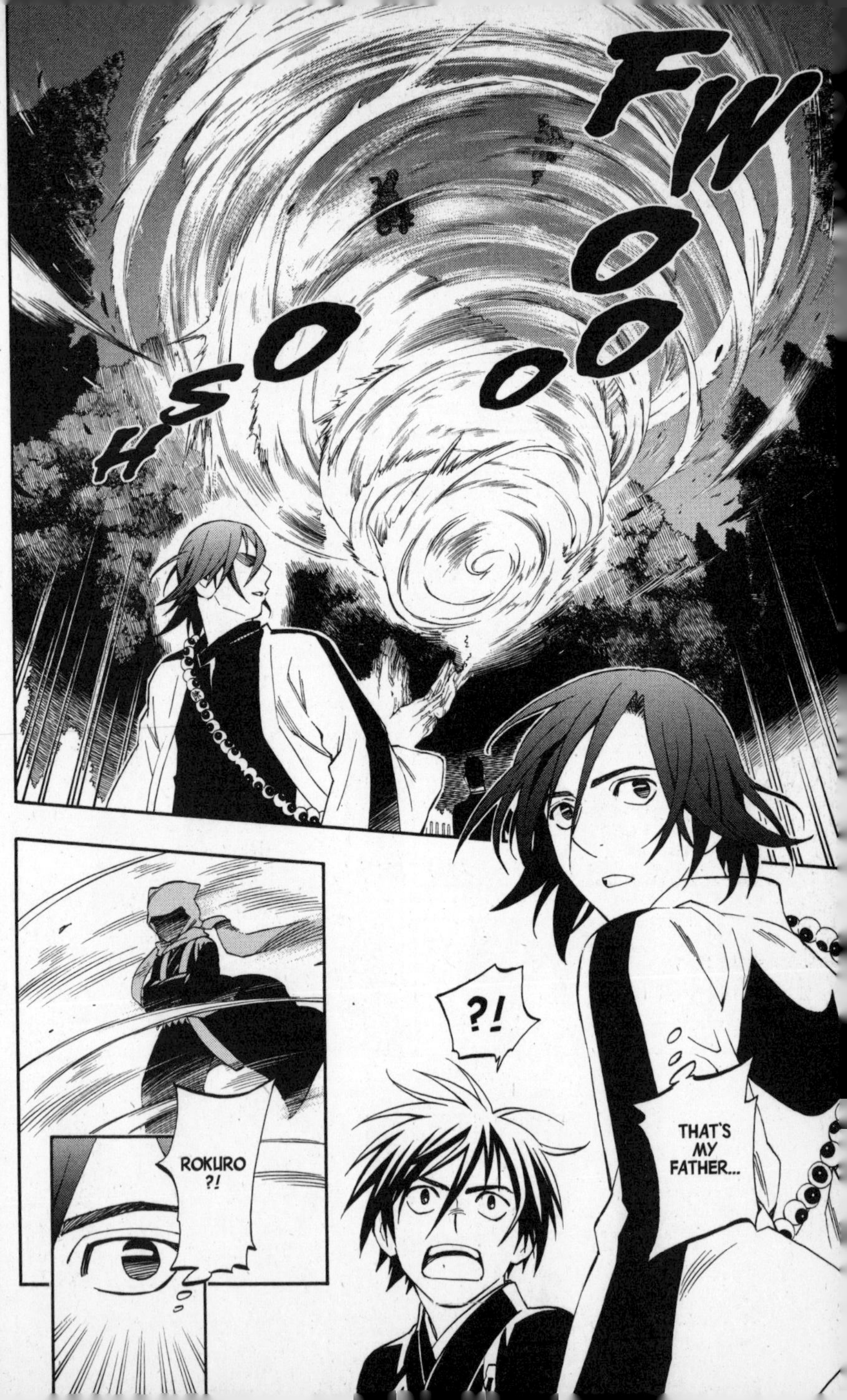
FWOOOO
HSOOO
?!
THAT'S MY FATHER...
ROKURO ?!

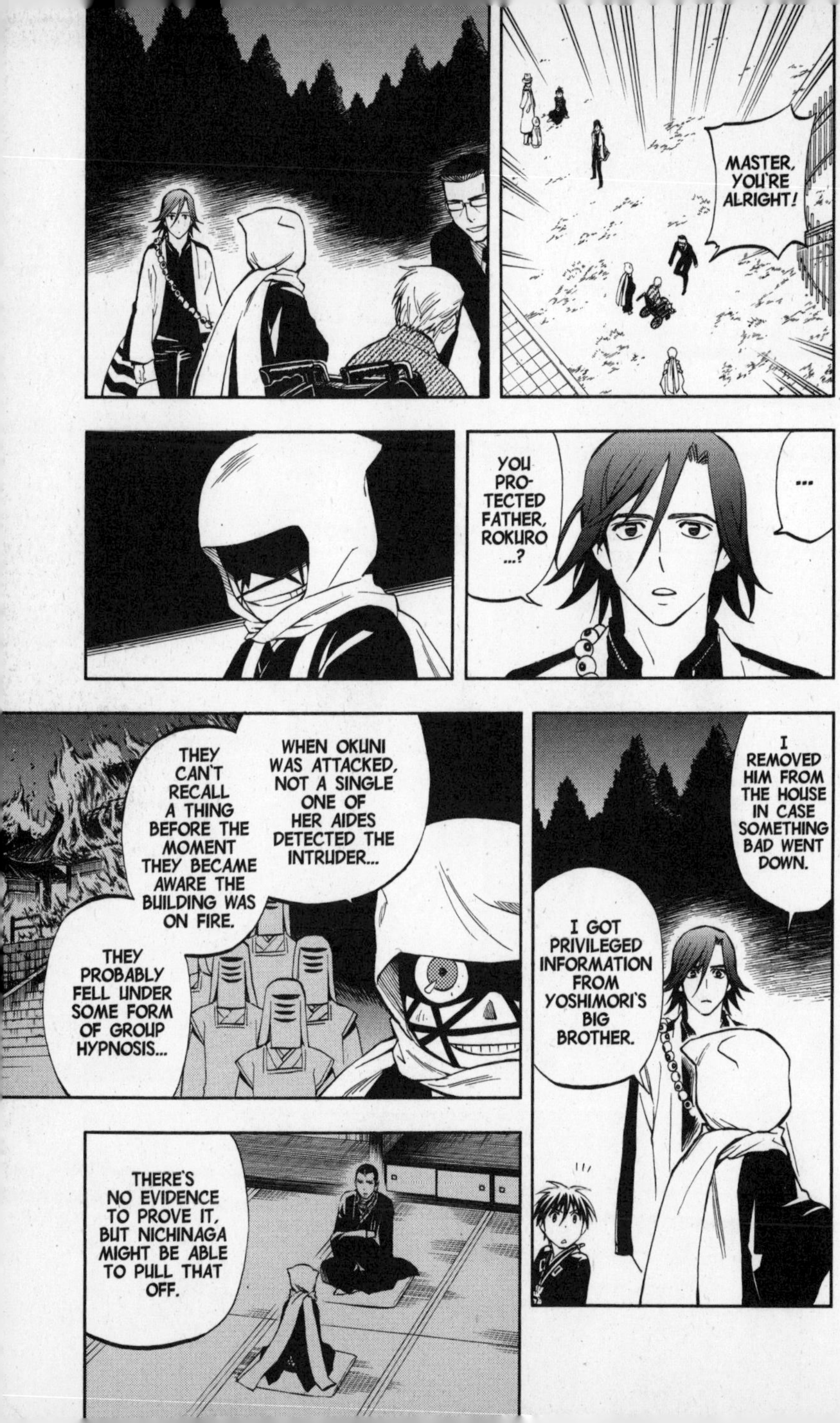

MASTER, YOU'RE ALRIGHT!
...
YOU PROTECTED FATHER, ROKURO ...?
I REMOVED HIM FROM THE HOUSE IN CASE SOMETHING BAD WENT DOWN.
I GOT PRIVILEGED INFORMATION FROM YOSHIMORI'S BIG BROTHER.
WHEN OKUNI WAS ATTACKED, NOT A SINGLE ONE OF HER AIDES DETECTED THE INTRUDER...
THEY CAN'T RECALL A THING BEFORE THE MOMENT THEY BECAME AWARE THE BUILDING WAS ON FIRE.
THEY PROBABLY FELL UNDER SOME FORM OF GROUP HYPNOSIS...
THERE'S NO EVIDENCE TO PROVE IT, BUT NICHINAGA MIGHT BE ABLE TO PULL THAT OFF.

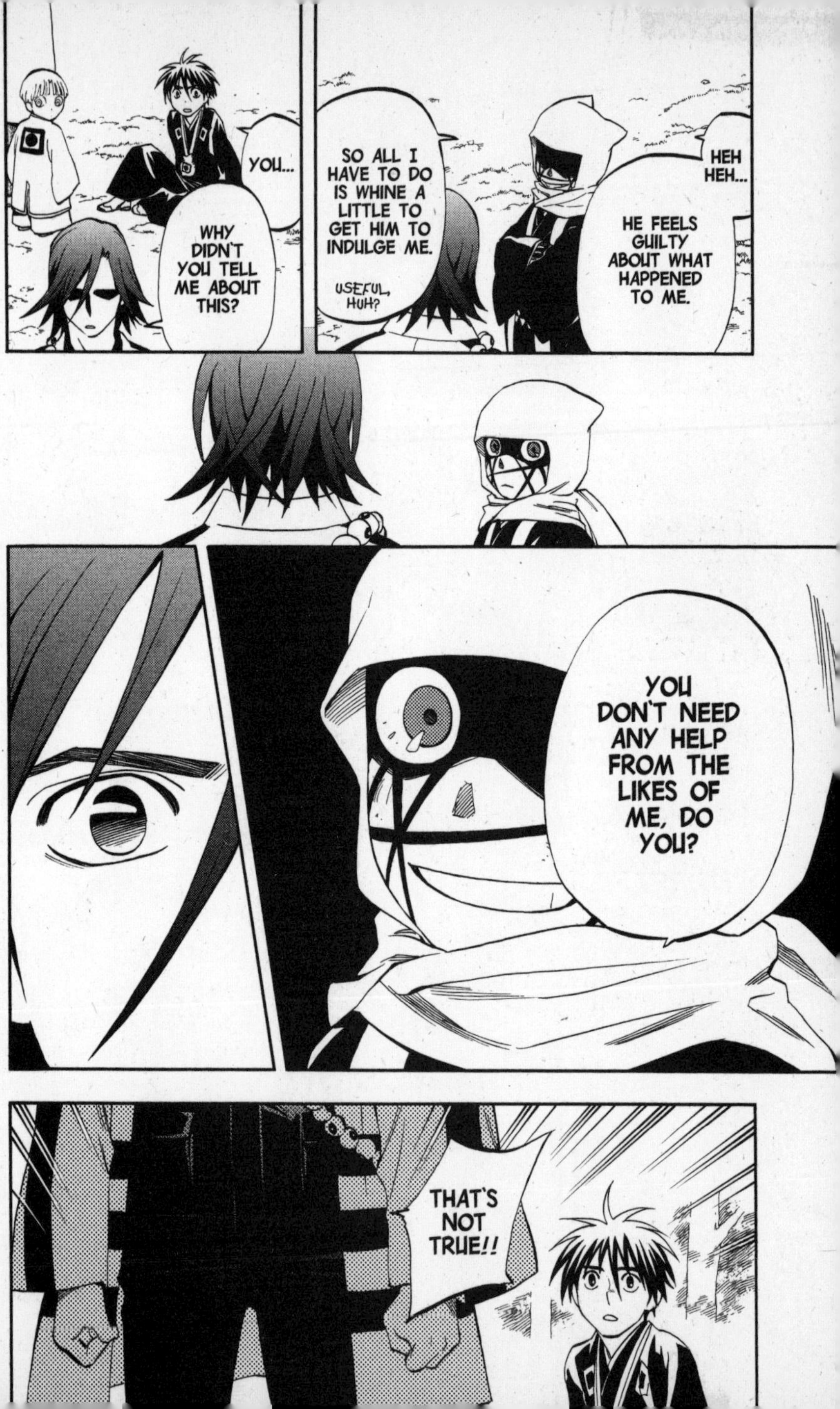
HEH HEH...
HE FEELS GUILTY ABOUT WHAT HAPPENED TO ME.
SO ALL I HAVE TO DO IS WHINE A LITTLE TO GET HIM TO INDULGE ME.
USEFUL, HUH?
YOU...
WHY DIDN'T YOU TELL ME ABOUT THIS?
YOU DON'T NEED ANY HELP FROM THE LIKES OF ME, DO YOU?
THAT'S NOT TRUE!!

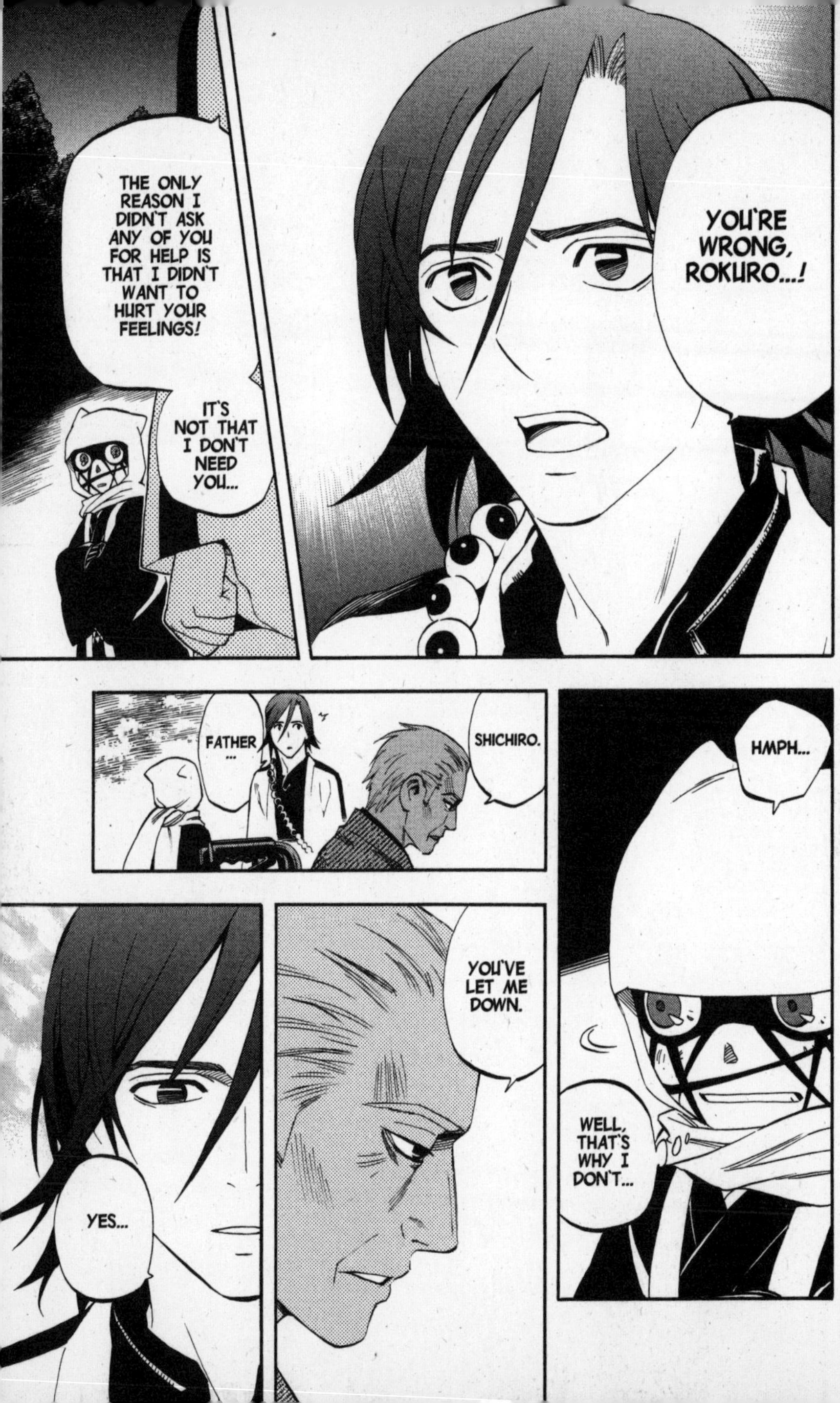
YOU'RE WRONG, ROKURO...!
THE ONLY REASON I DIDN'T ASK ANY OF YOU FOR HELP IS THAT I DIDN'T WANT TO HURT YOUR FEELINGS!
IT'S NOT THAT I DON'T NEED YOU...
HMPH...
WELL, THAT'S WHY I DON'T...
SHICHIRO.
FATHER ...
YOU'VE LET ME DOWN.
YES...

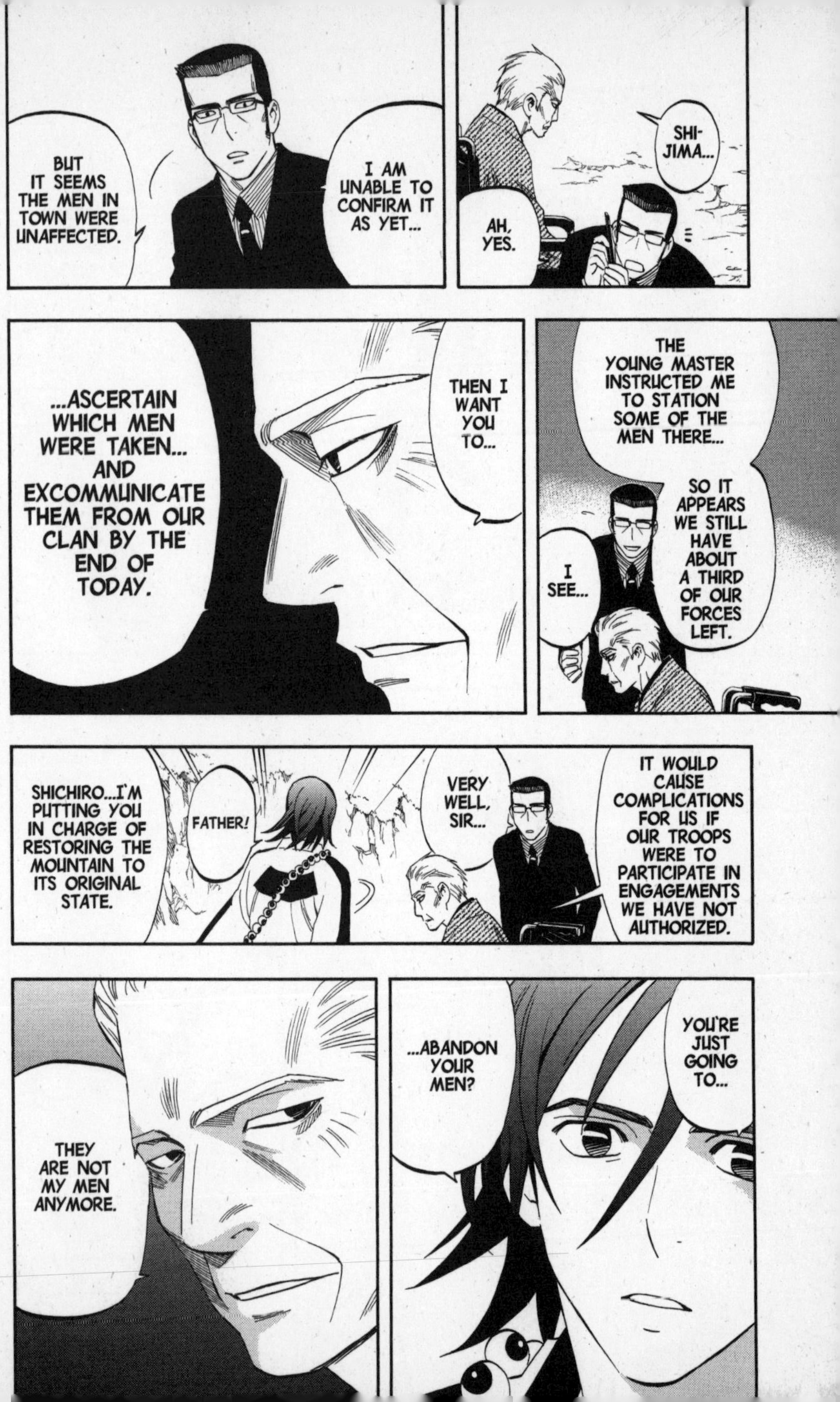
SHI-JIMA...
AH, YES.
I AM UNABLE TO CONFIRM IT AS YET...
BUT IT SEEMS THE MEN IN TOWN WERE UNAFFECTED.
THE YOUNG MASTER INSTRUCTED ME TO STATION SOME OF THE MEN THERE...
SO IT APPEARS WE STILL HAVE ABOUT A THIRD OF OUR FORCES LEFT.
I SEE...
THEN I WANT YOU TO...
...ASCERTAIN WHICH MEN WERE TAKEN... AND EXCOMMUNICATE THEM FROM OUR CLAN BY THE END OF TODAY.
IT WOULD CAUSE COMPLICATIONS FOR US IF OUR TROOPS WERE TO PARTICIPATE IN ENGAGEMENTS WE HAVE NOT AUTHORIZED.
VERY WELL, SIR...
FATHER!
SHICHIRO...I'M PUTTING YOU IN CHARGE OF RESTORING THE MOUNTAIN TO ITS ORIGINAL STATE.
YOU'RE JUST GOING TO...
...ABANDON YOUR MEN?
THEY ARE NOT MY MEN ANYMORE.

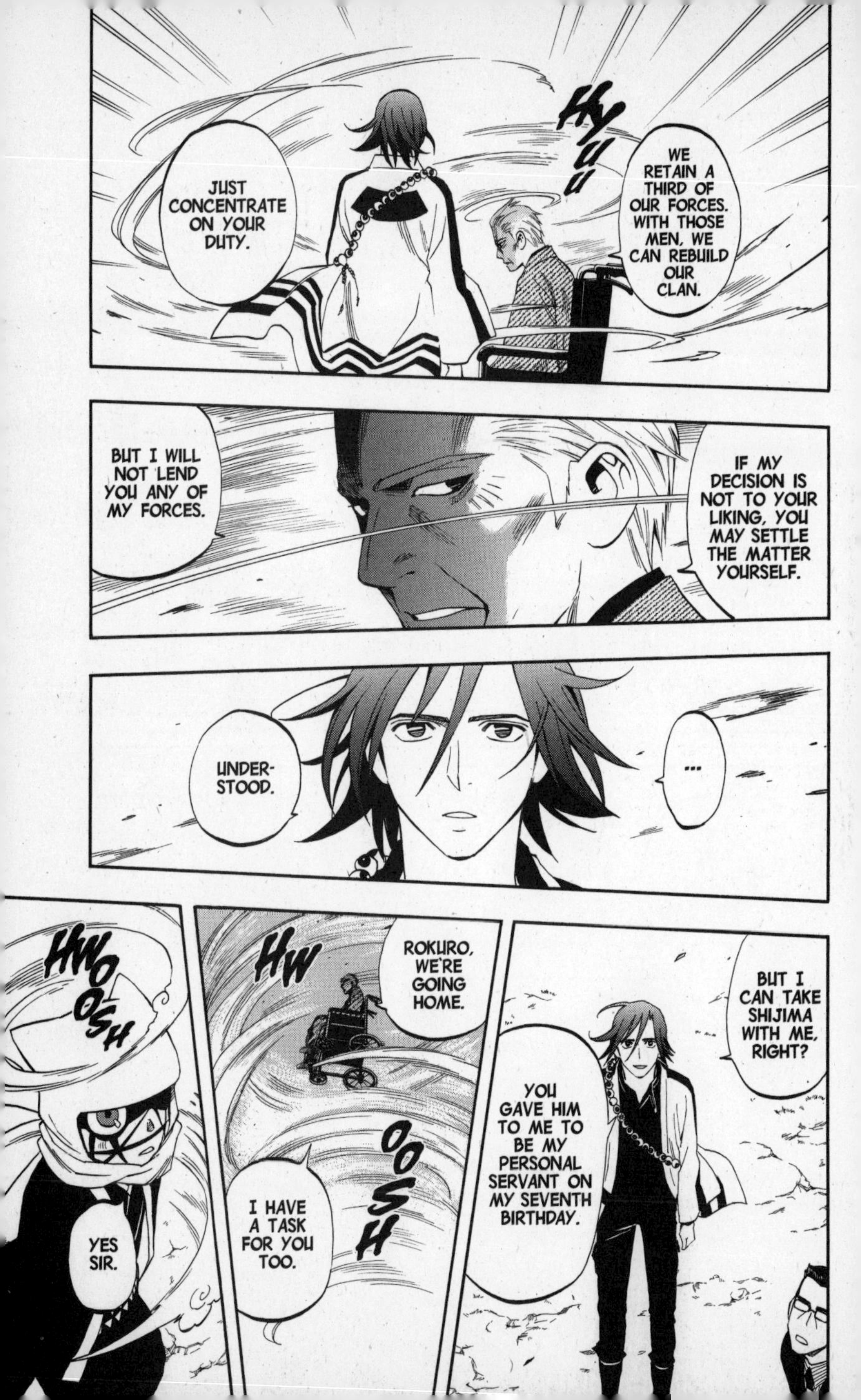
WE RETAIN A THIRD OF OUR FORCES. WITH THOSE MEN, WE CAN REBUILD OUR CLAN.
HYUUU
JUST CONCENTRATE ON YOUR DUTY.
IF MY DECISION IS NOT TO YOUR LIKING, YOU MAY SETTLE THE MATTER YOURSELF.
BUT I WILL NOT LEND YOU ANY OF MY FORCES.
...
UNDER-STOOD.
BUT I CAN TAKE SHIJIMA WITH ME, RIGHT?
YOU GAVE HIM TO ME TO BE MY PERSONAL SERVANT ON MY SEVENTH BIRTHDAY.
ROKURO, WE'RE GOING HOME.
HW
OOSH
I HAVE A TASK FOR YOU TOO.
HWOOSH
YES SIR.

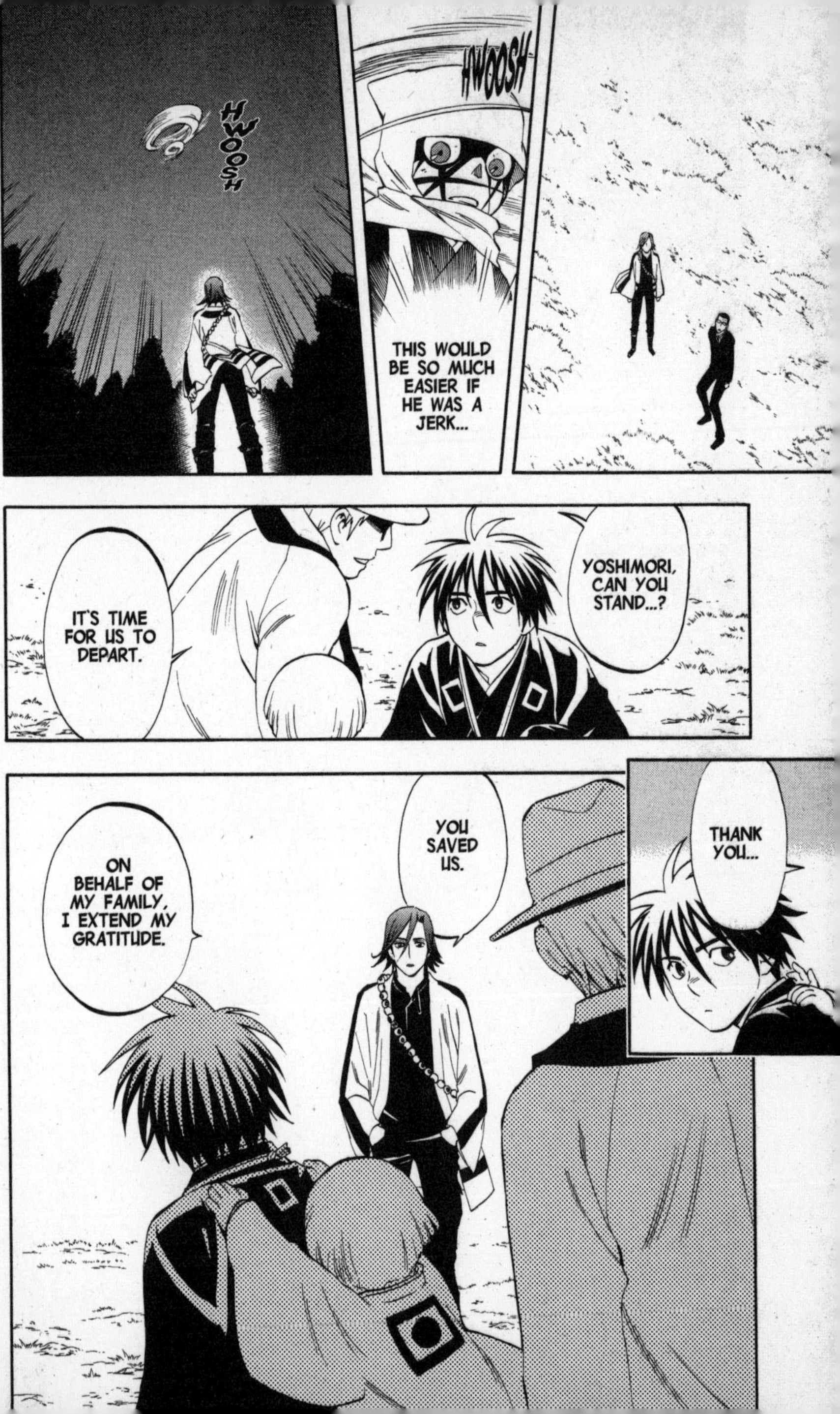
HWOOSH
THIS WOULD BE SO MUCH EASIER IF HE WAS A JERK...
HWOOSH
YOSHIMORI, CAN YOU STAND...?
IT'S TIME FOR US TO DEPART.
THANK YOU...
YOU SAVED US.
ON BEHALF OF MY FAMILY, I EXTEND MY GRATITUDE.

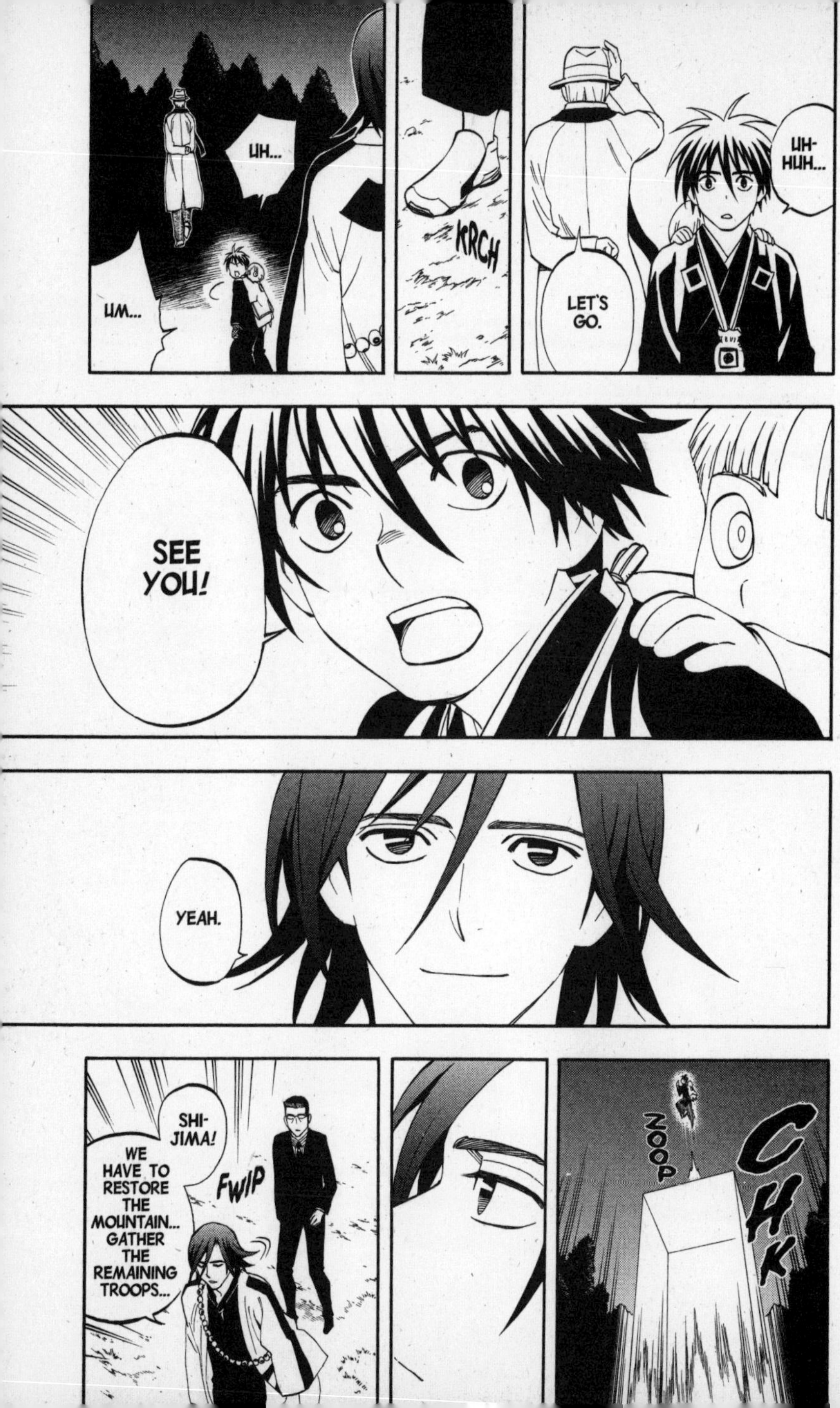
UH-HUH...
LET'S GO.
KRCH
UH...
UM...
SEE YOU!
YEAH.
ZOOP
CHK
SHI-JIMA!
WE HAVE TO RESTORE THE MOUNTAIN... GATHER THE REMAINING TROOPS...
FWIP

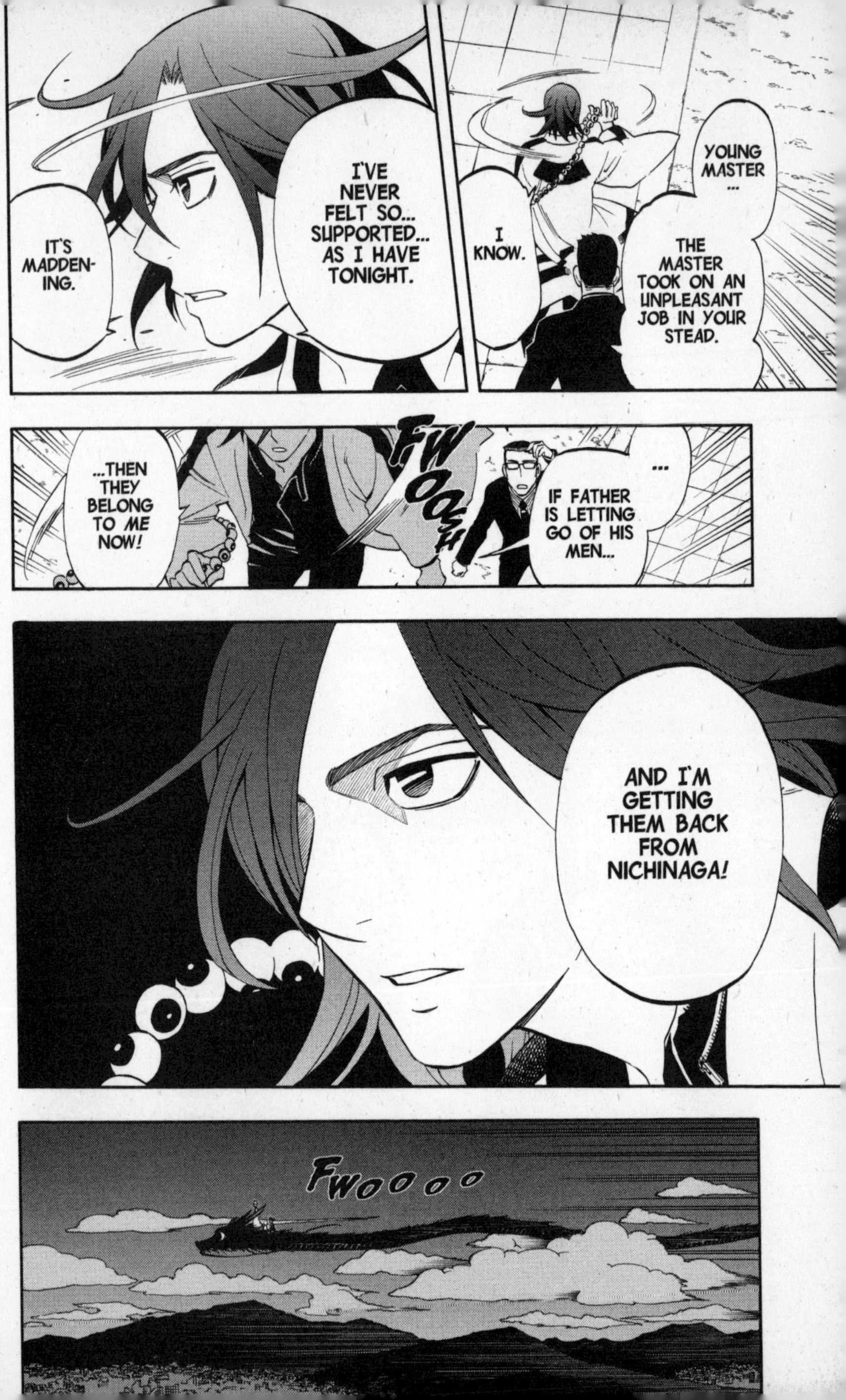
YOUNG MASTER ...
THE MASTER TOOK ON AN UNPLEASANT JOB IN YOUR STEAD.
I KNOW.
I'VE NEVER FELT SO... SUPPORTED... AS I HAVE TONIGHT.
IT'S MADDEN-ING.
...
IF FATHER IS LETTING GO OF HIS MEN...
FWOOOSH
...THEN THEY BELONG TO *ME* NOW!
AND I'M GETTING THEM BACK FROM NICHINAGA!
FWOOOOO

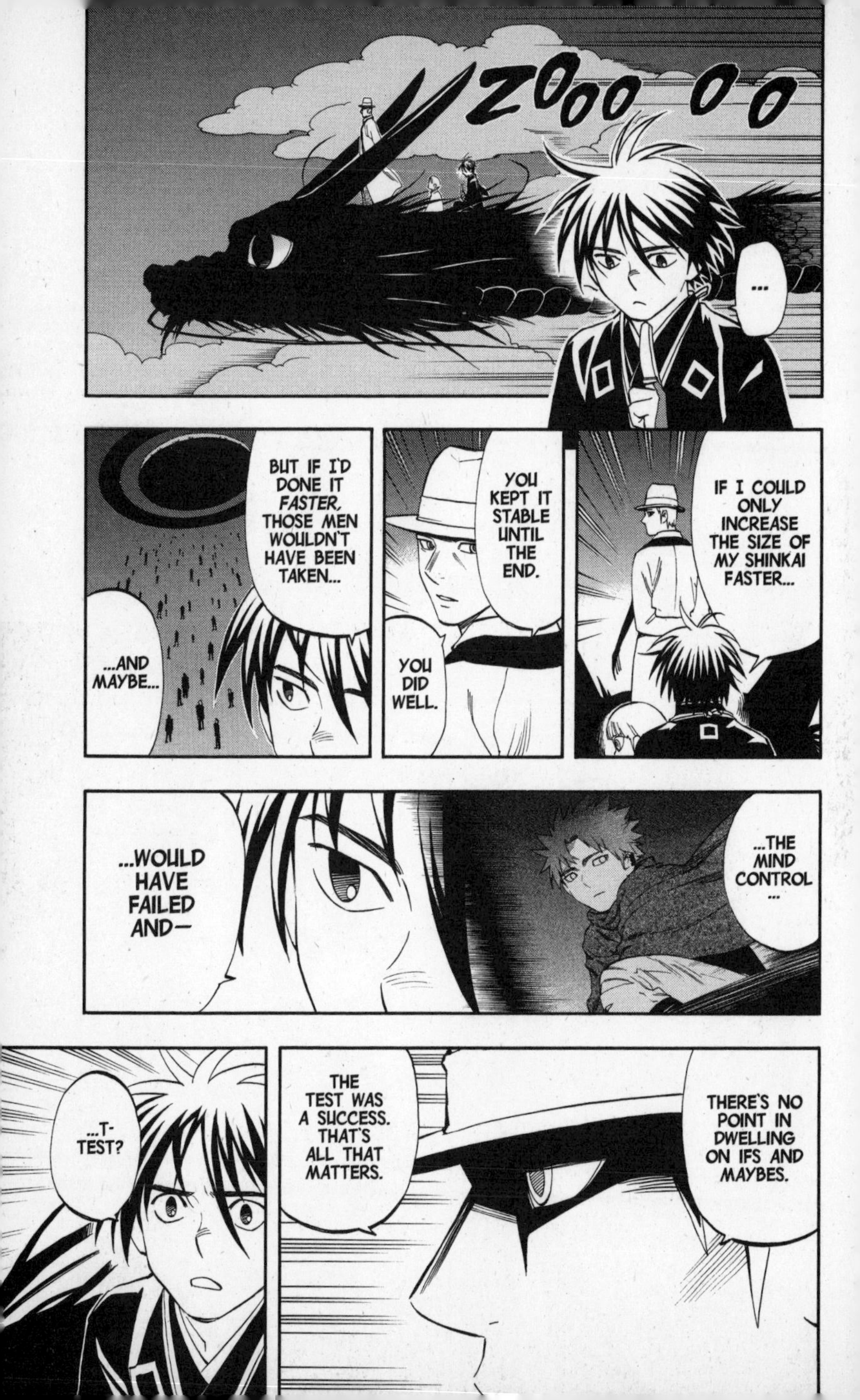
ZOOOO O O
...
IF I COULD ONLY INCREASE THE SIZE OF MY SHINKAI FASTER...
YOU KEPT IT STABLE UNTIL THE END.
YOU DID WELL.
BUT IF I'D DONE IT *FASTER,* THOSE MEN WOULDN'T HAVE BEEN TAKEN...
...AND MAYBE...
...THE MIND CONTROL ...
...WOULD HAVE FAILED AND—
THERE'S NO POINT IN DWELLING ON IFS AND MAYBES.
THE TEST WAS A SUCCESS. THAT'S ALL THAT MATTERS.
...T-TEST?

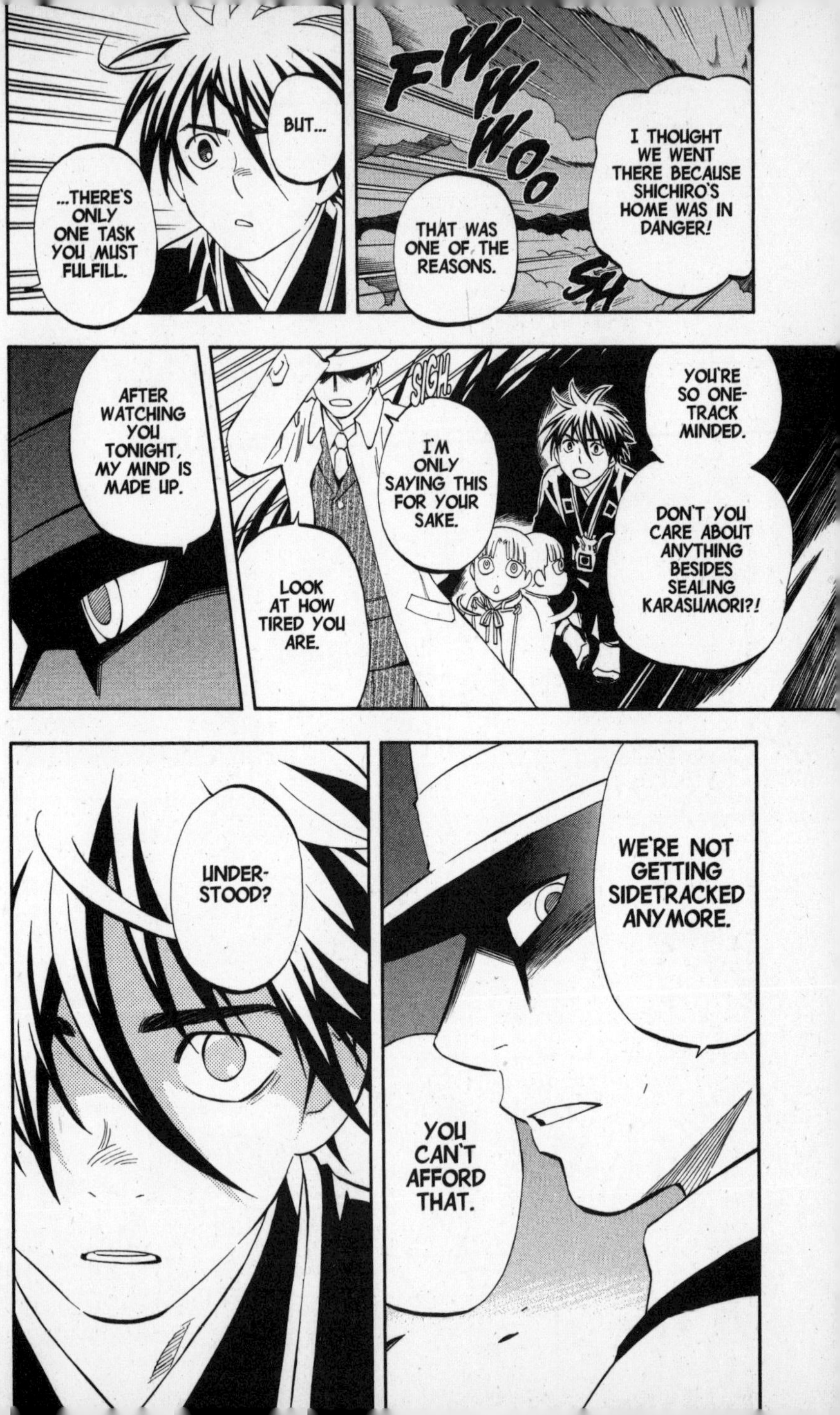
I THOUGHT WE WENT THERE BECAUSE SHICHIRO'S HOME WAS IN DANGER!
FWWWOO
SH
THAT WAS ONE OF THE REASONS.
BUT...
...THERE'S ONLY ONE TASK YOU MUST FULFILL.
YOU'RE SO ONE-TRACK MINDED.
DON'T YOU CARE ABOUT ANYTHING BESIDES SEALING KARASUMORI?!
SIGH
I'M ONLY SAYING THIS FOR YOUR SAKE.
LOOK AT HOW TIRED YOU ARE.
AFTER WATCHING YOU TONIGHT, MY MIND IS MADE UP.
WE'RE NOT GETTING SIDETRACKED ANYMORE.
YOU CAN'T AFFORD THAT.
UNDER-STOOD?

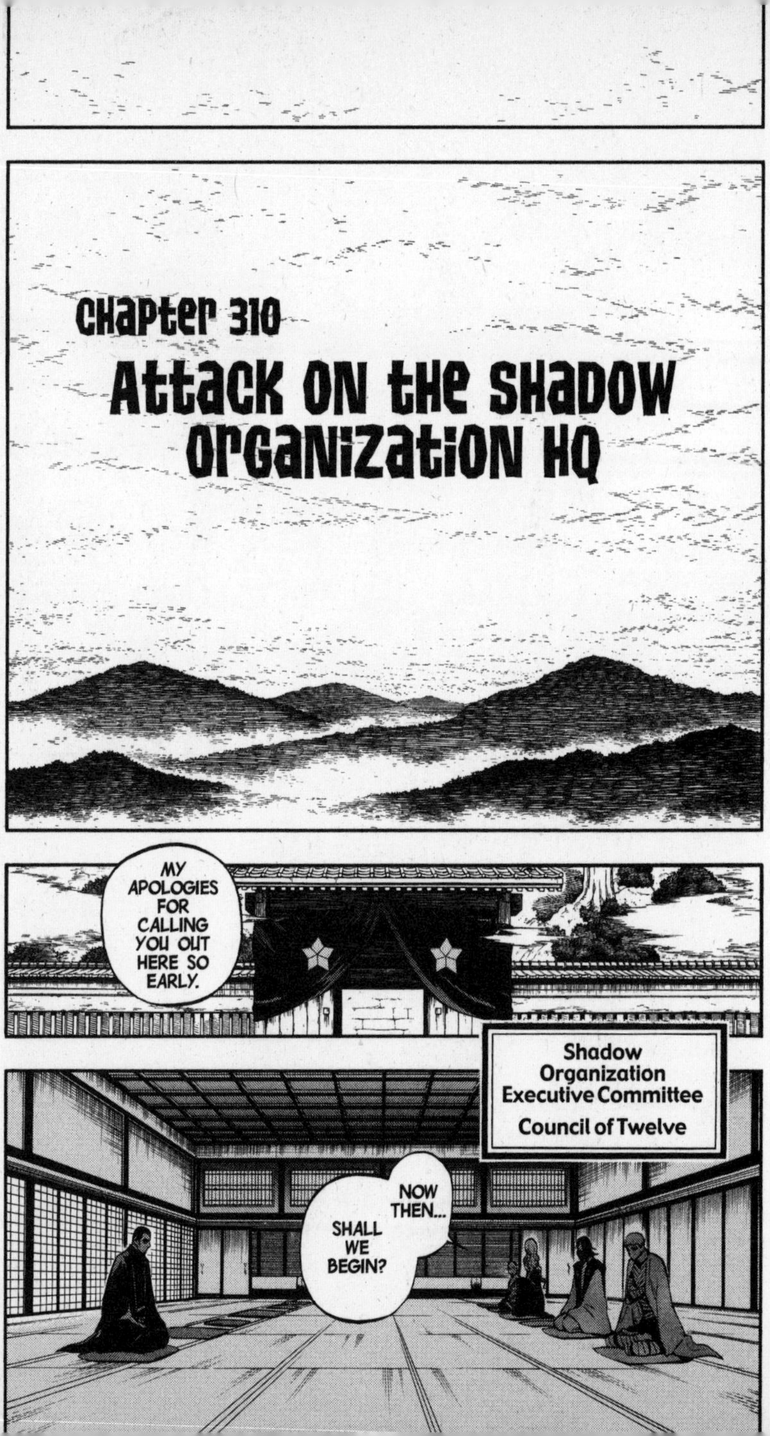
Chapter 310
Attack on the Shadow Organization HQ
MY APOLOGIES FOR CALLING YOU OUT HERE SO EARLY.
Shadow Organization Executive Committee
Council of Twelve
NOW THEN... SHALL WE BEGIN?

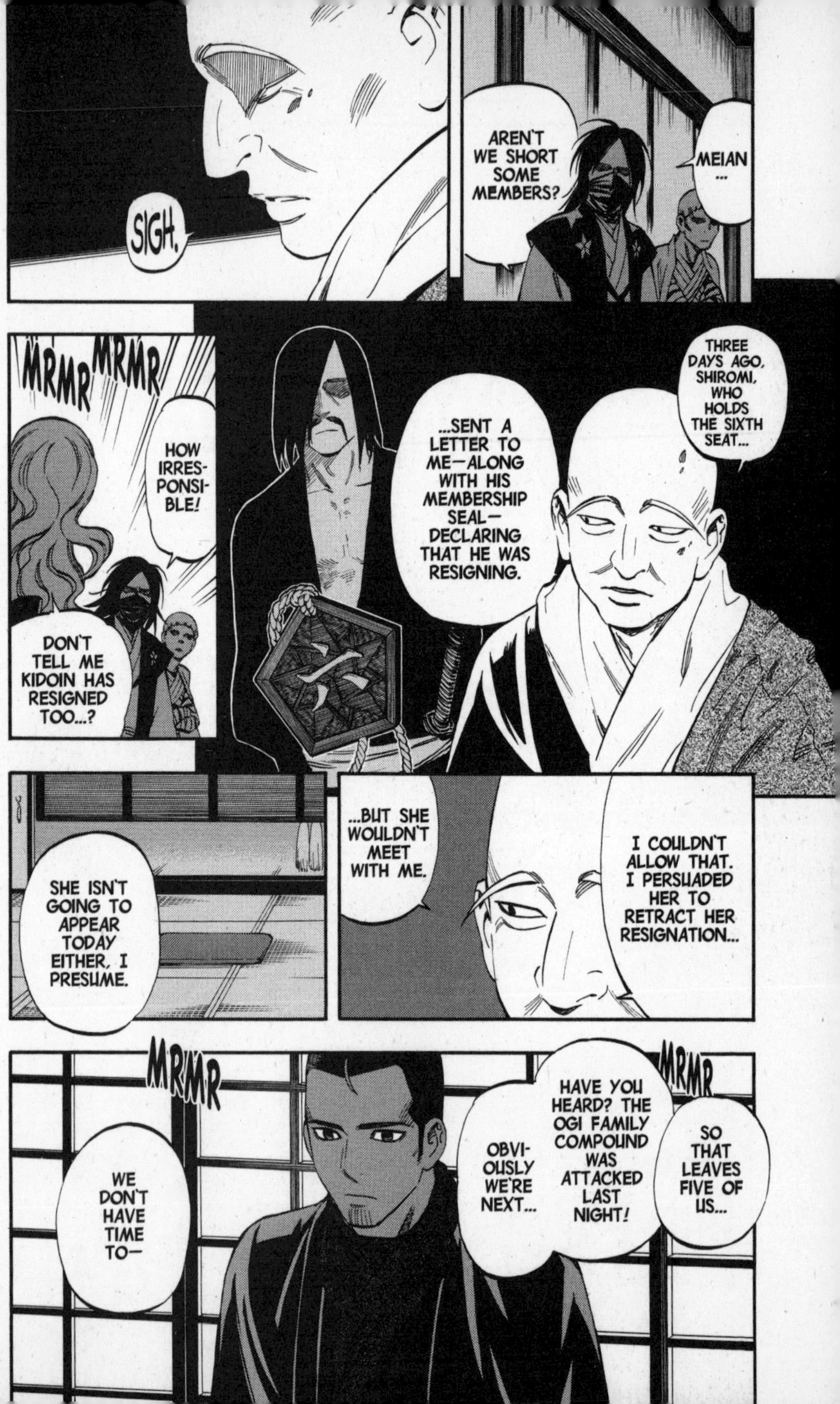
MEIAN...
AREN'T WE SHORT SOME MEMBERS?
SIGH.
THREE DAYS AGO, SHIROMI, WHO HOLDS THE SIXTH SEAT...
...SENT A LETTER TO ME—ALONG WITH HIS MEMBERSHIP SEAL—DECLARING THAT HE WAS RESIGNING.
MRMR MRMR
HOW IRRES-PONSI-BLE!
DON'T TELL ME KIDOIN HAS RESIGNED TOO...?
I COULDN'T ALLOW THAT. I PERSUADED HER TO RETRACT HER RESIGNATION...
...BUT SHE WOULDN'T MEET WITH ME.
SHE ISN'T GOING TO APPEAR TODAY EITHER, I PRESUME.
MRMR
SO THAT LEAVES FIVE OF US...
HAVE YOU HEARD? THE OGI FAMILY COMPOUND WAS ATTACKED LAST NIGHT!
OBVI-OUSLY WE'RE NEXT...
MRMR
WE DON'T HAVE TIME TO—

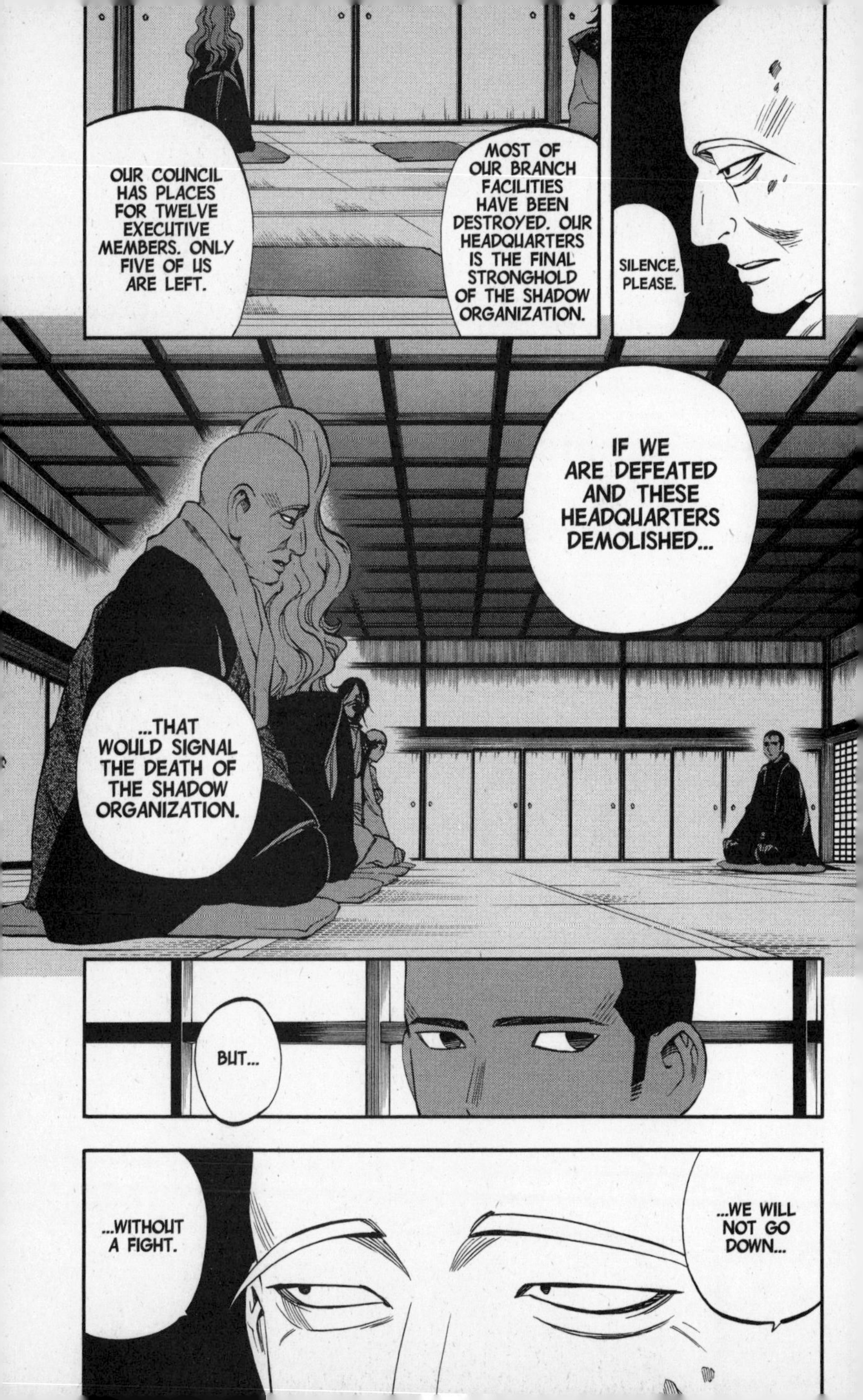
SILENCE, PLEASE.
MOST OF OUR BRANCH FACILITIES HAVE BEEN DESTROYED. OUR HEADQUARTERS IS THE FINAL STRONGHOLD OF THE SHADOW ORGANIZATION.
OUR COUNCIL HAS PLACES FOR TWELVE EXECUTIVE MEMBERS. ONLY FIVE OF US ARE LEFT.
IF WE ARE DEFEATED AND THESE HEADQUARTERS DEMOLISHED...
...THAT WOULD SIGNAL THE DEATH OF THE SHADOW ORGANIZATION.
BUT...
...WE WILL NOT GO DOWN...
...WITHOUT A FIGHT.

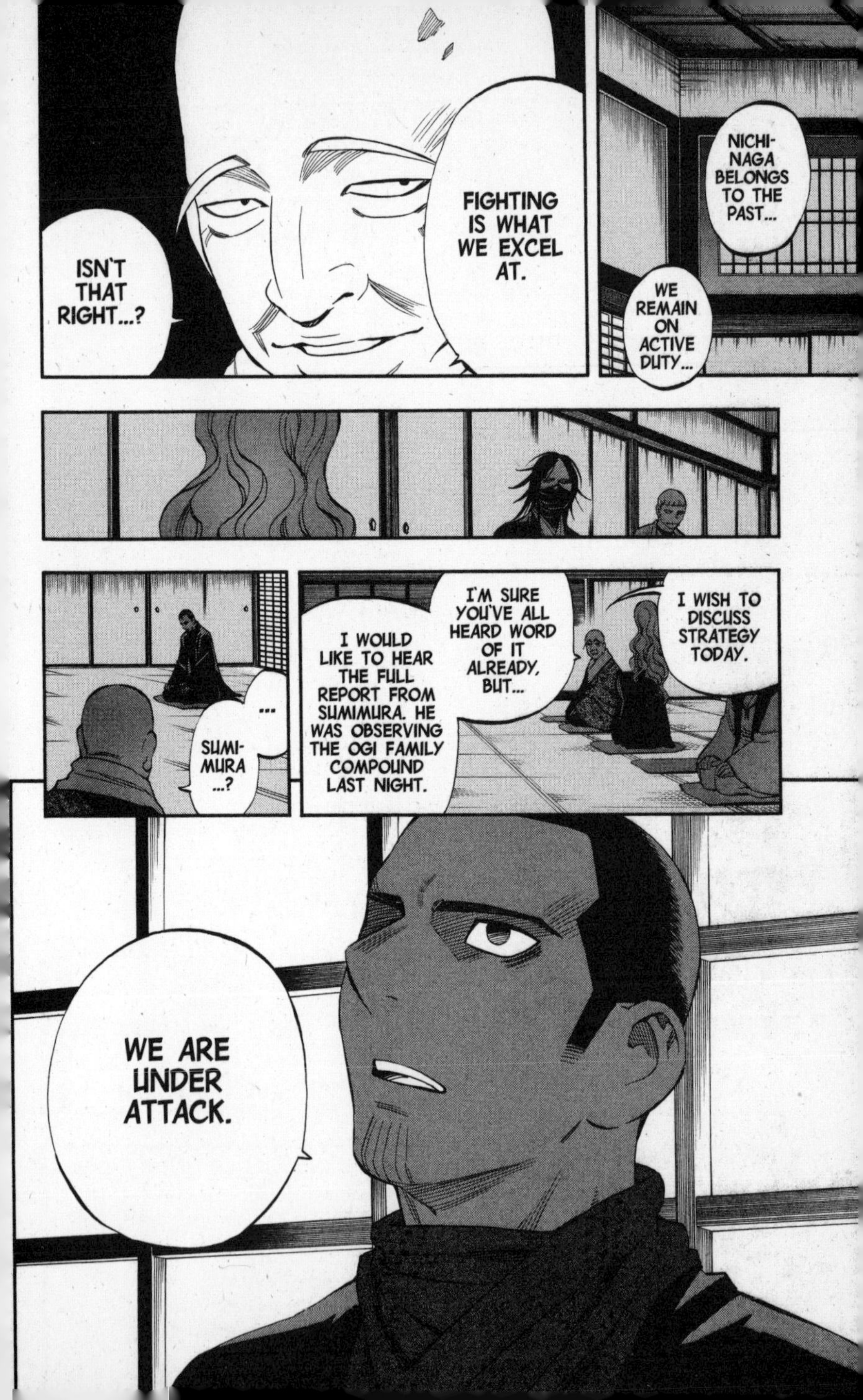
NICHI-NAGA BELONGS TO THE PAST...
WE REMAIN ON ACTIVE DUTY...
FIGHTING IS WHAT WE EXCEL AT.
ISN'T THAT RIGHT...?
I WISH TO DISCUSS STRATEGY TODAY.
I'M SURE YOU'VE ALL HEARD WORD OF IT ALREADY, BUT...
I WOULD LIKE TO HEAR THE FULL REPORT FROM SUMIMURA. HE WAS OBSERVING THE OGI FAMILY COMPOUND LAST NIGHT.
...
SUMI-MURA ...?
WE ARE UNDER ATTACK.

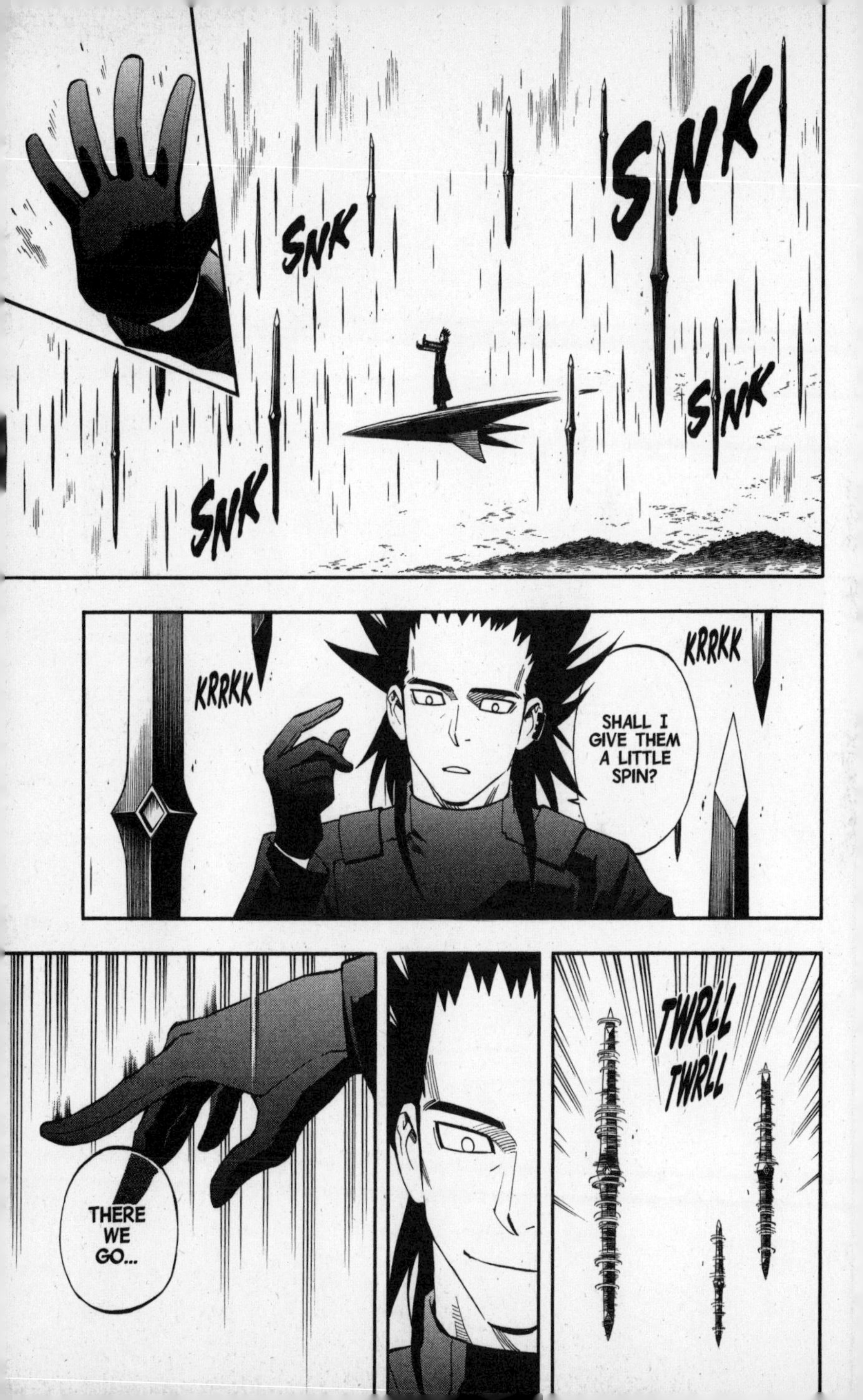
SNK
SNK
SNK
SNK
KRRKK
SHALL I GIVE THEM A LITTLE SPIN?
KRRKK
TWRLL TWRLL
THERE WE GO...

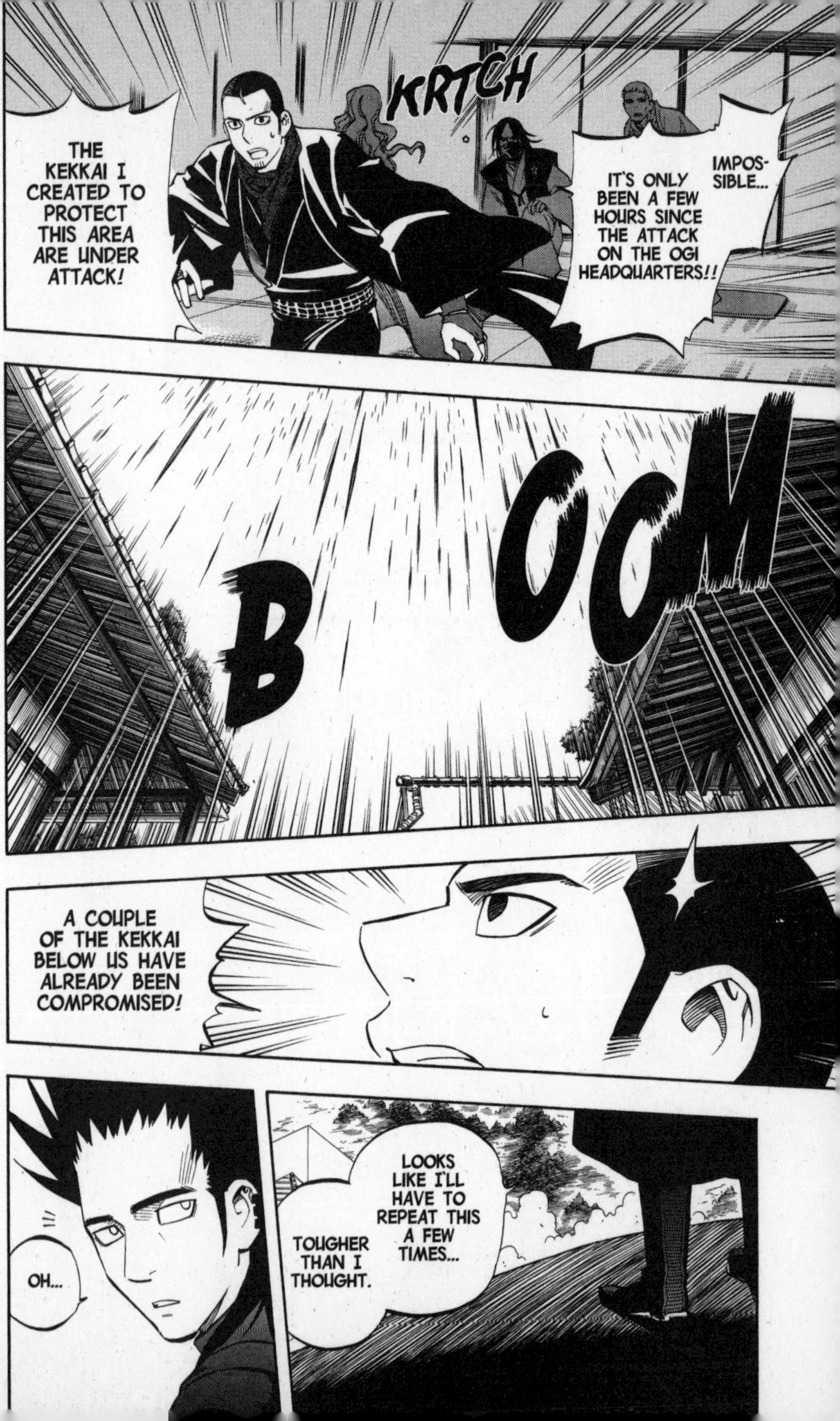
KRTCH
IMPOSSIBLE... IT'S ONLY BEEN A FEW HOURS SINCE THE ATTACK ON THE OGI HEADQUARTERS!!
THE KEKKAI I CREATED TO PROTECT THIS AREA ARE UNDER ATTACK!
BOOM
A COUPLE OF THE KEKKAI BELOW US HAVE ALREADY BEEN COMPROMISED!
LOOKS LIKE I'LL HAVE TO REPEAT THIS A FEW TIMES...
TOUGHER THAN I THOUGHT.
OH...

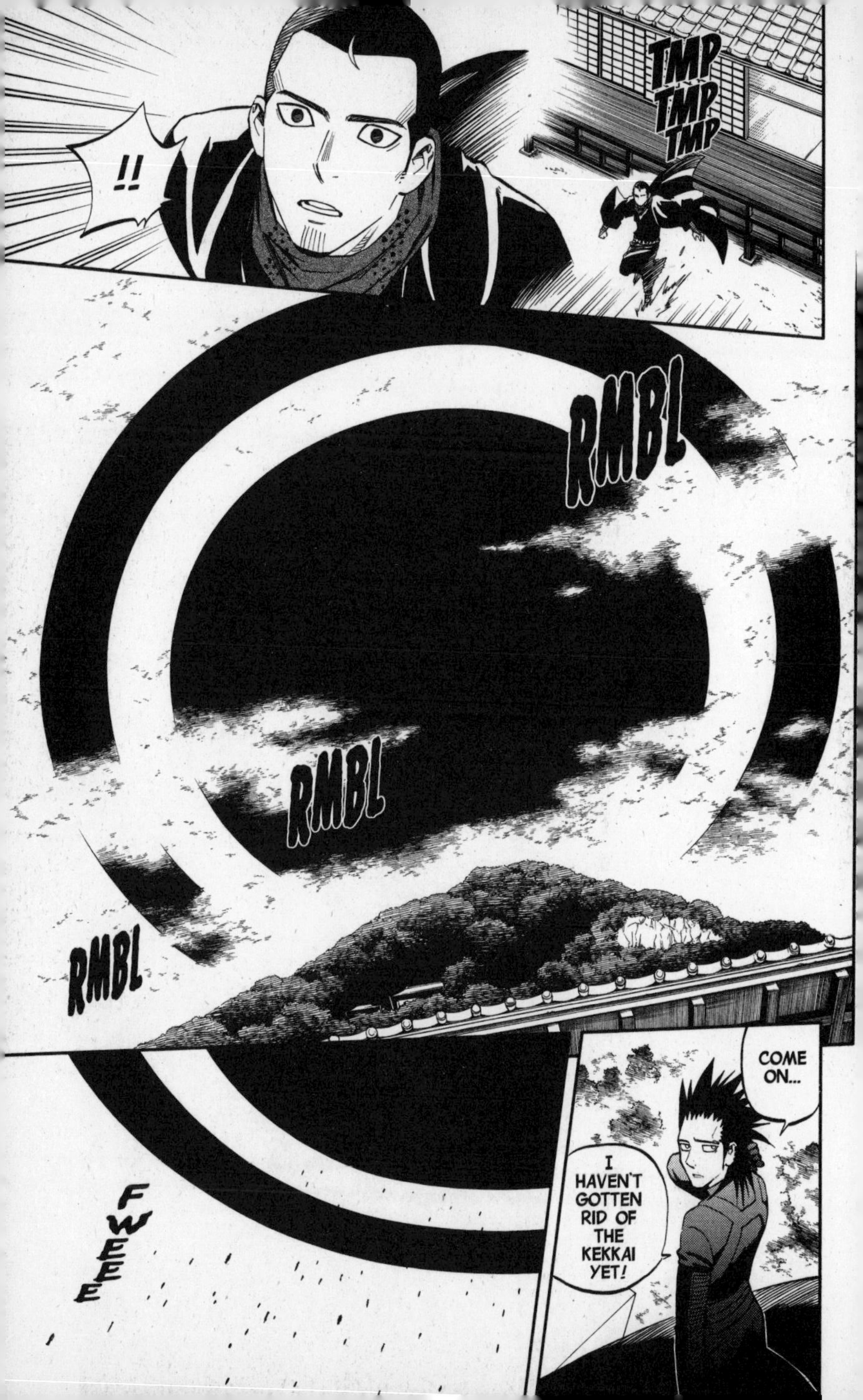
TMP TMP TMP
!!
RMBL
RMBL
RMBL
COME ON...
I HAVEN'T GOTTEN RID OF THE KEKKAI YET!
FWEEE

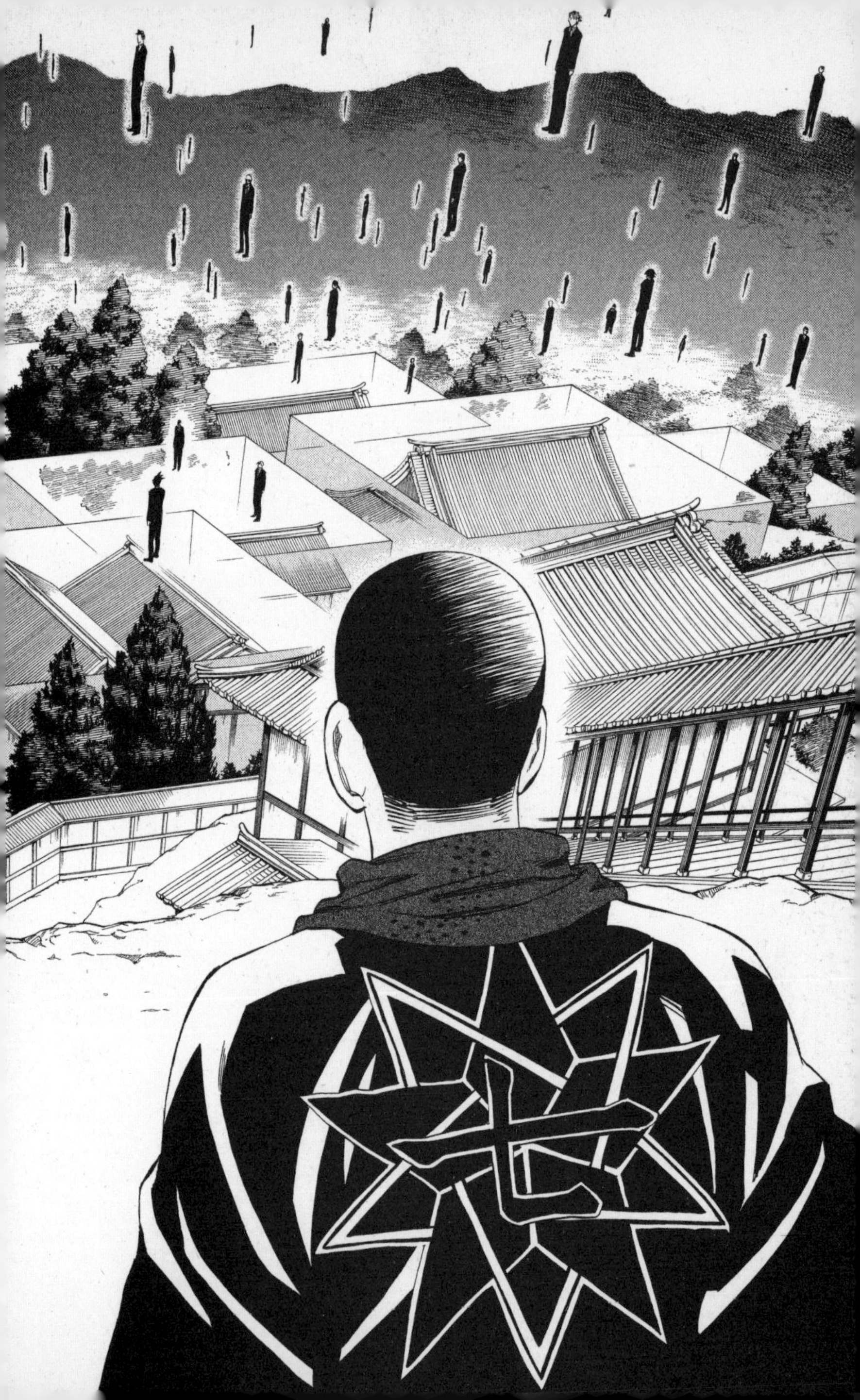

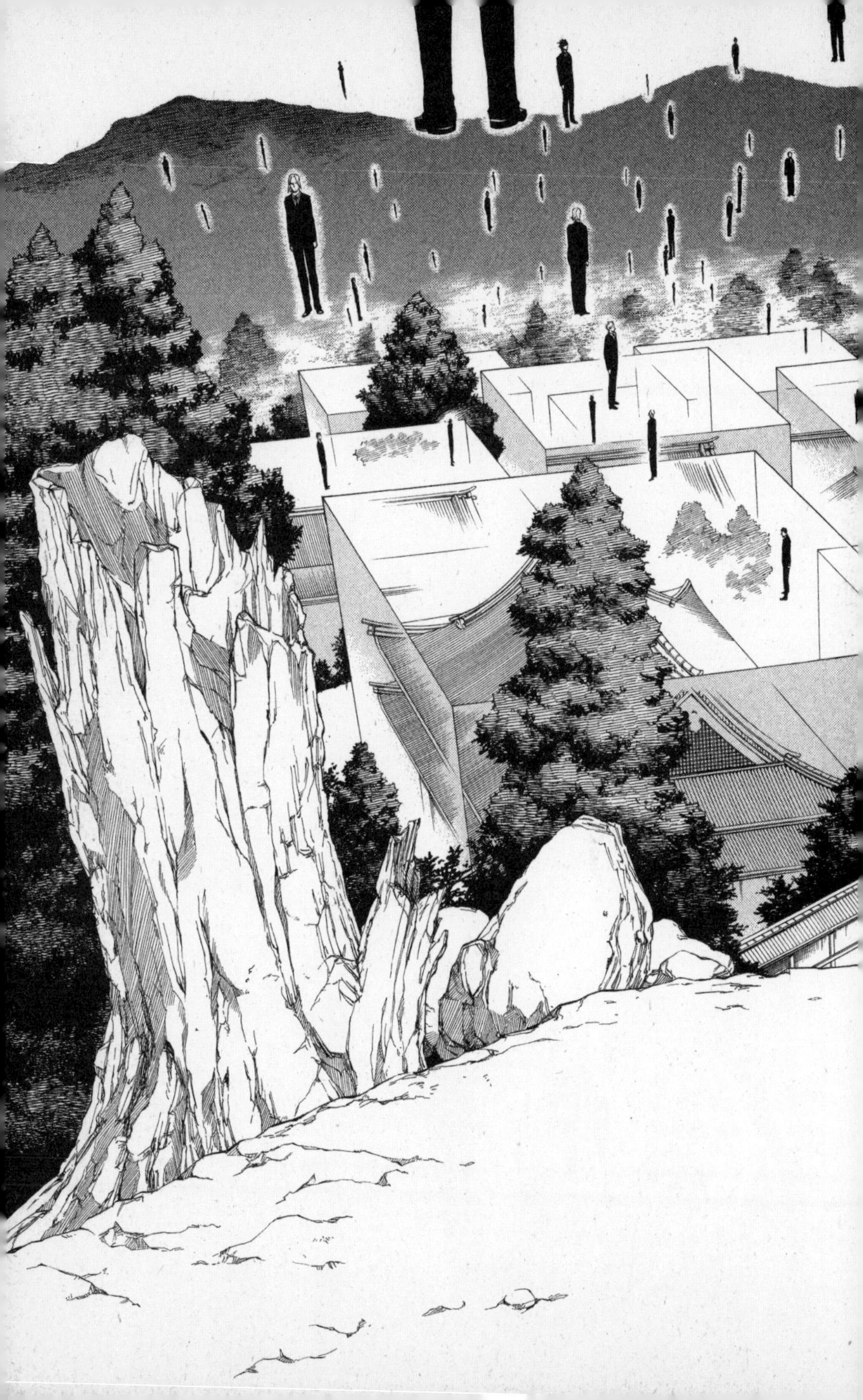

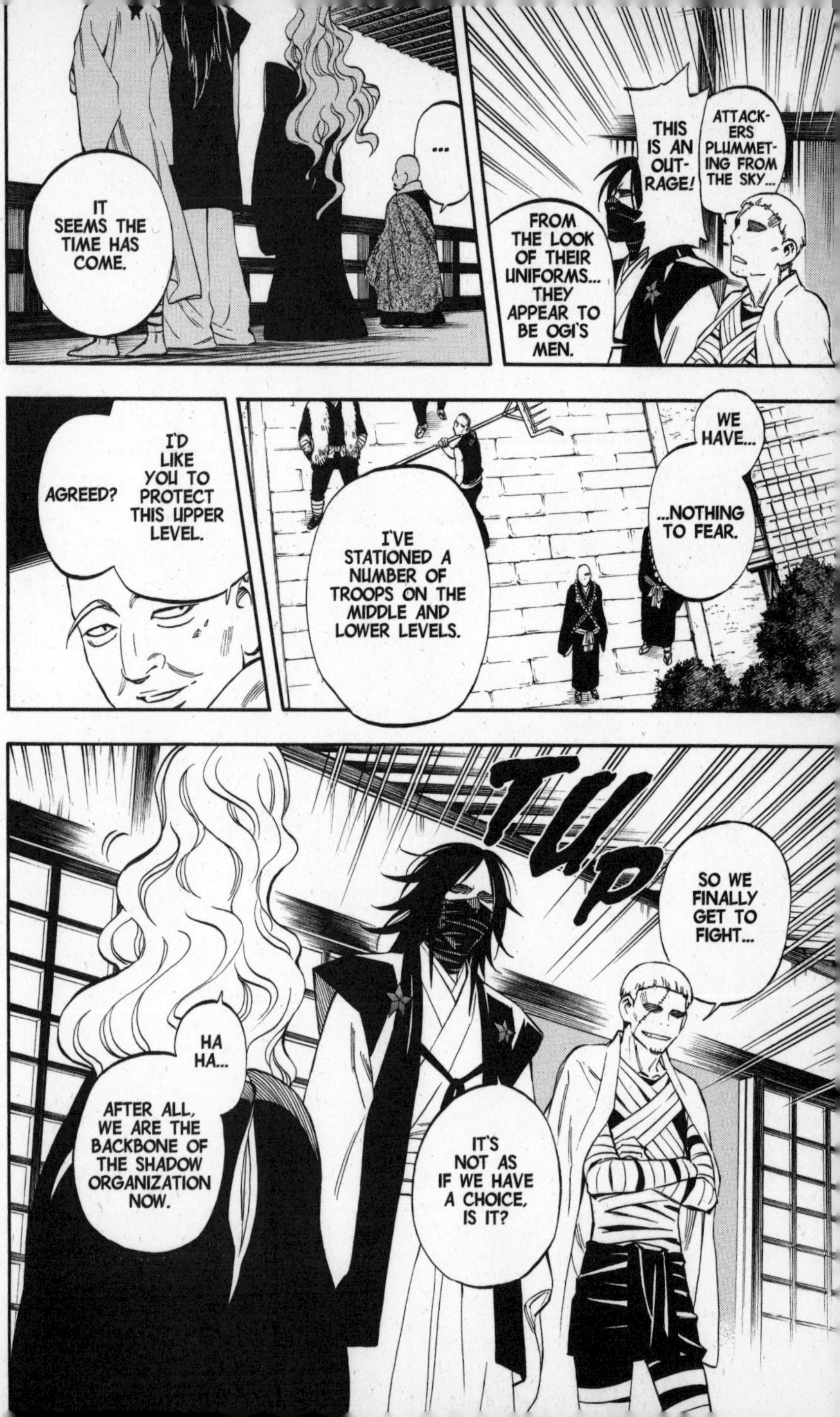
ATTACKERS PLUMMETING FROM THE SKY...
THIS IS AN OUTRAGE!
FROM THE LOOK OF THEIR UNIFORMS... THEY APPEAR TO BE OGI'S MEN.
...
IT SEEMS THE TIME HAS COME.
WE HAVE...
...NOTHING TO FEAR.
I'VE STATIONED A NUMBER OF TROOPS ON THE MIDDLE AND LOWER LEVELS.
I'D LIKE YOU TO PROTECT THIS UPPER LEVEL.
AGREED?
TUP
SO WE FINALLY GET TO FIGHT...
IT'S NOT AS IF WE HAVE A CHOICE, IS IT?
HA HA...
AFTER ALL, WE ARE THE BACKBONE OF THE SHADOW ORGANIZATION NOW.

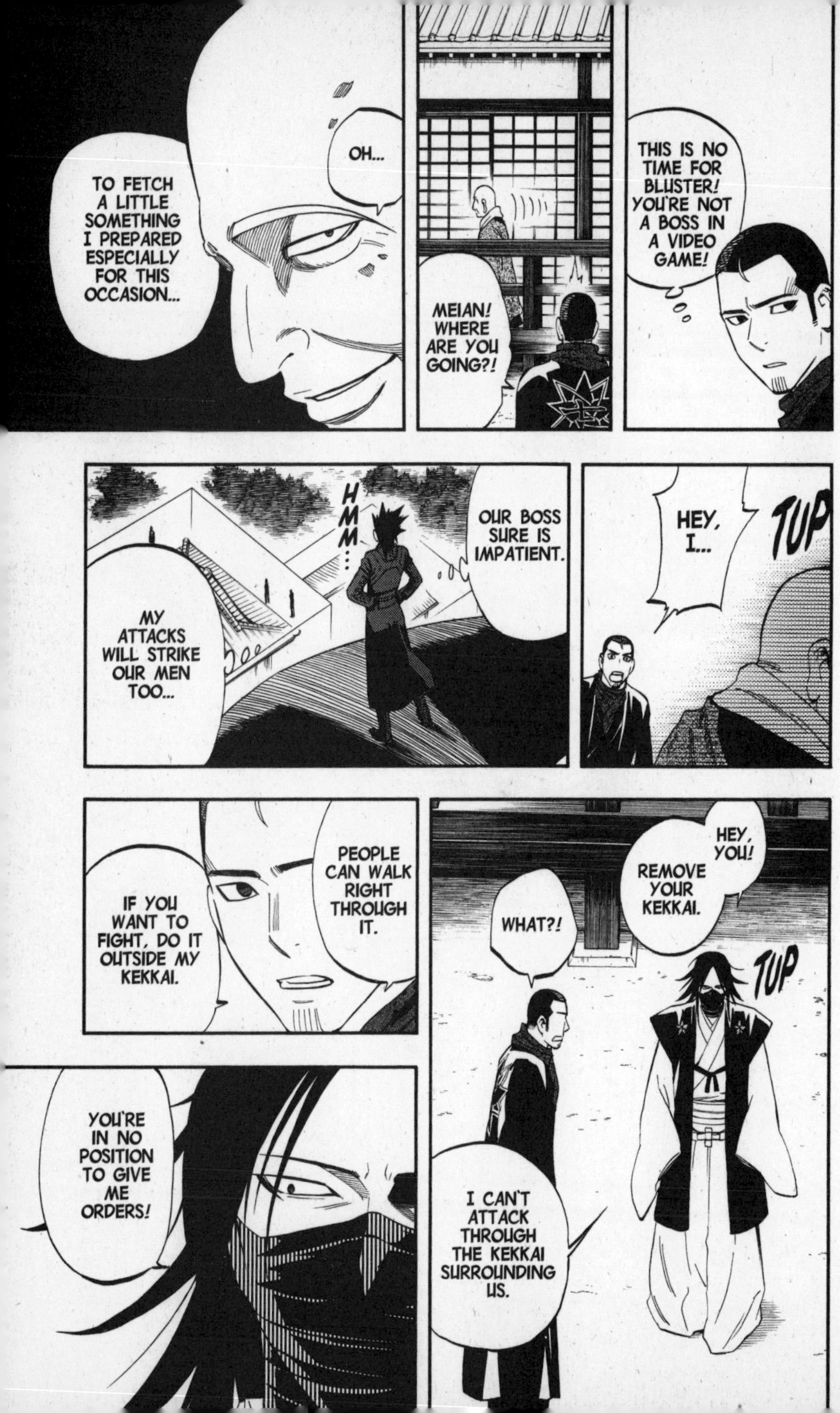
THIS IS NO TIME FOR BLUSTER! YOU'RE NOT A BOSS IN A VIDEO GAME!
MEIAN! WHERE ARE YOU GOING?!
OH...
TO FETCH A LITTLE SOMETHING I PREPARED ESPECIALLY FOR THIS OCCASION...
HEY, I...
TUP
OUR BOSS SURE IS IMPATIENT.
HMM...
MY ATTACKS WILL STRIKE OUR MEN TOO...
HEY, YOU!
REMOVE YOUR KEKKAI.
TUP
WHAT?!
I CAN'T ATTACK THROUGH THE KEKKAI SURROUNDING US.
PEOPLE CAN WALK RIGHT THROUGH IT.
IF YOU WANT TO FIGHT, DO IT OUTSIDE MY KEKKAI.
YOU'RE IN NO POSITION TO GIVE ME ORDERS!

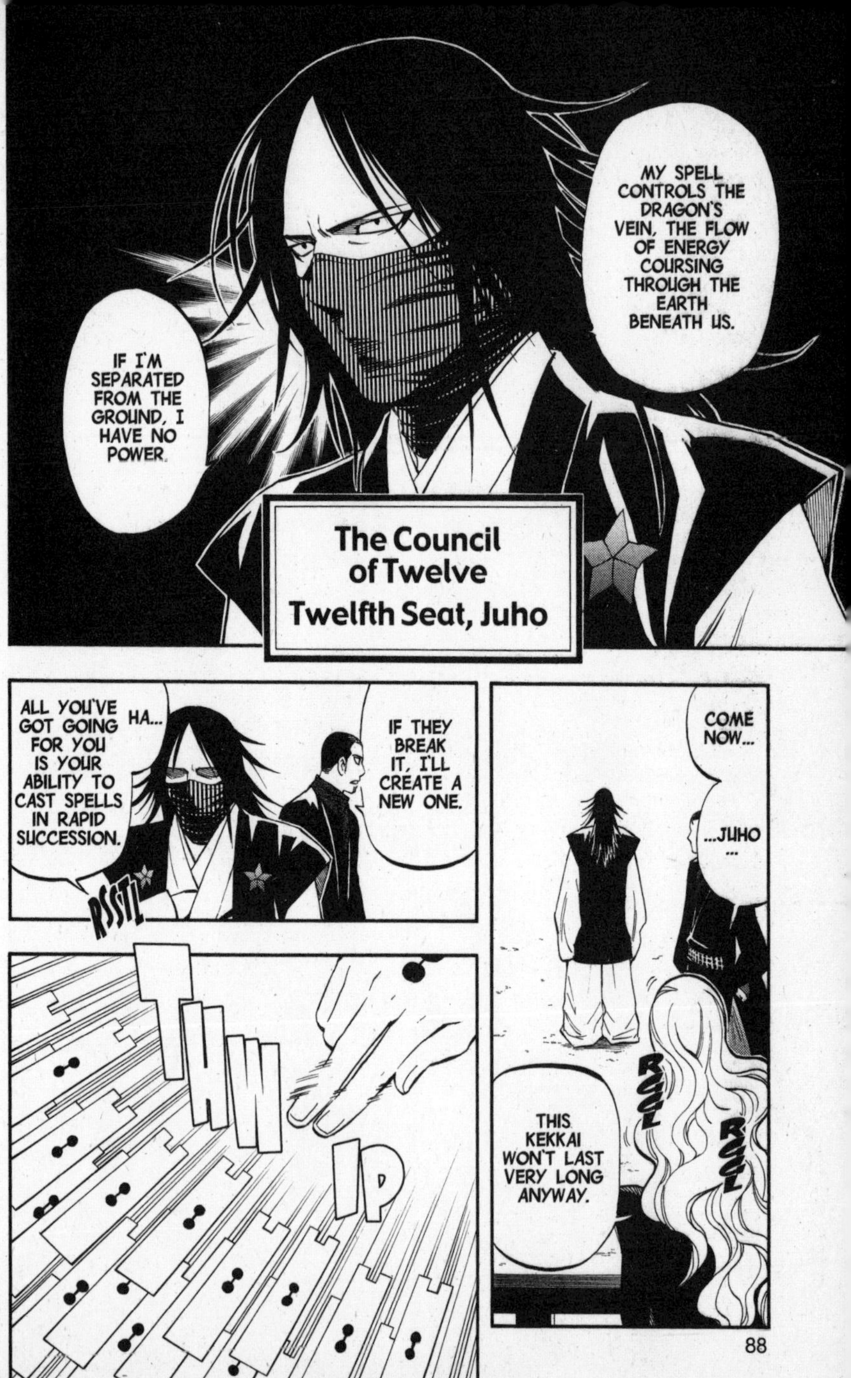
MY SPELL CONTROLS THE DRAGON'S VEIN, THE FLOW OF ENERGY COURSING THROUGH THE EARTH BENEATH US.
IF I'M SEPARATED FROM THE GROUND, I HAVE NO POWER.
The Council of Twelve
Twelfth Seat, Juho
COME NOW...
...JUHO...
RCCL RCCL
THIS KEKKAI WON'T LAST VERY LONG ANYWAY.
IF THEY BREAK IT, I'LL CREATE A NEW ONE.
HA...
ALL YOU'VE GOT GOING FOR YOU IS YOUR ABILITY TO CAST SPELLS IN RAPID SUCCESSION.
RSSTL
THWIP

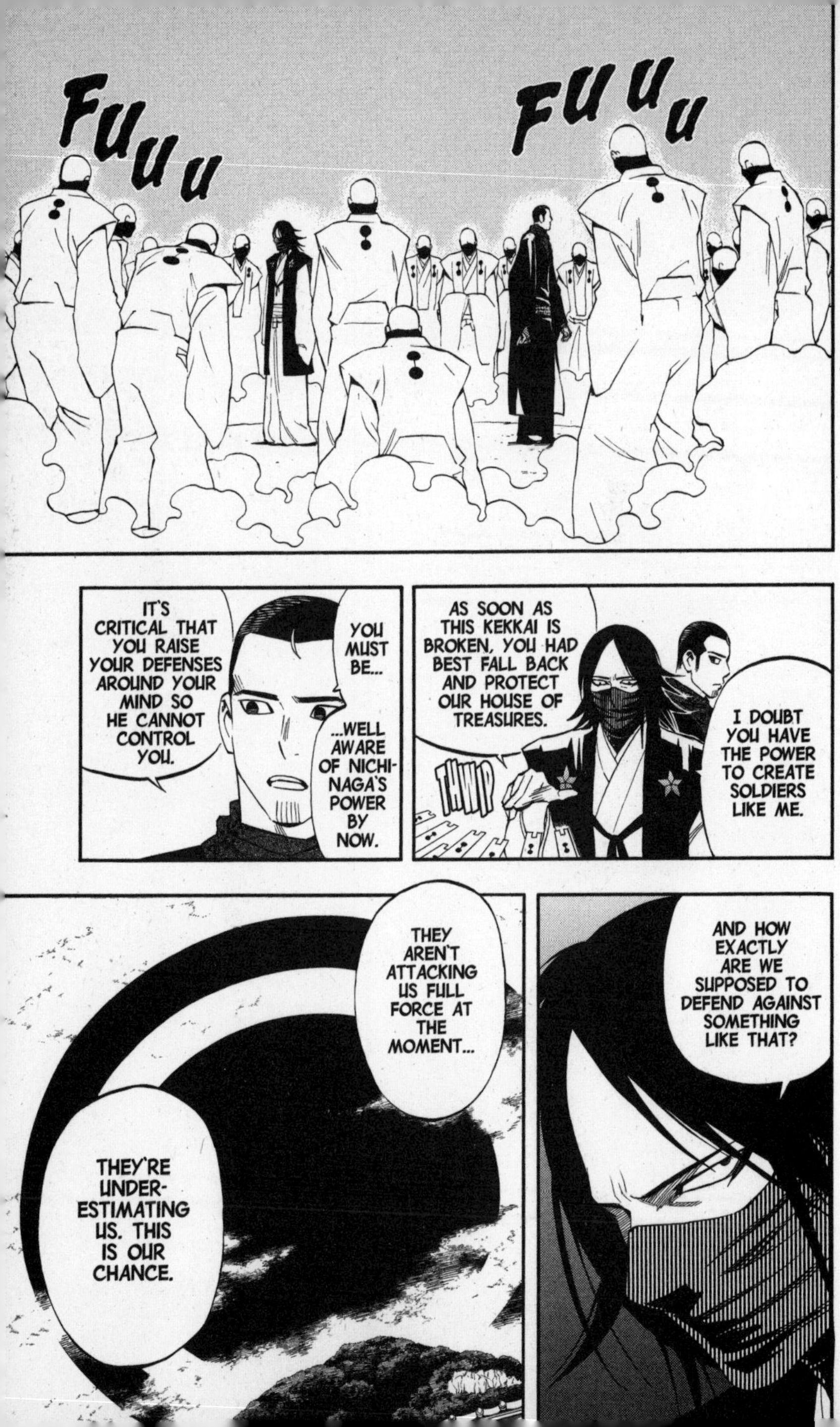
FUUUU
FUUUU
AS SOON AS THIS KEKKAI IS BROKEN, YOU HAD BEST FALL BACK AND PROTECT OUR HOUSE OF TREASURES.
I DOUBT YOU HAVE THE POWER TO CREATE SOLDIERS LIKE ME.
THWIP
YOU MUST BE...
...WELL AWARE OF NICHI-NAGA'S POWER BY NOW.
IT'S CRITICAL THAT YOU RAISE YOUR DEFENSES AROUND YOUR MIND SO HE CANNOT CONTROL YOU.
AND HOW EXACTLY ARE WE SUPPOSED TO DEFEND AGAINST SOMETHING LIKE THAT?
THEY AREN'T ATTACKING US FULL FORCE AT THE MOMENT...
THEY'RE UNDER-ESTIMATING US. THIS IS OUR CHANCE.

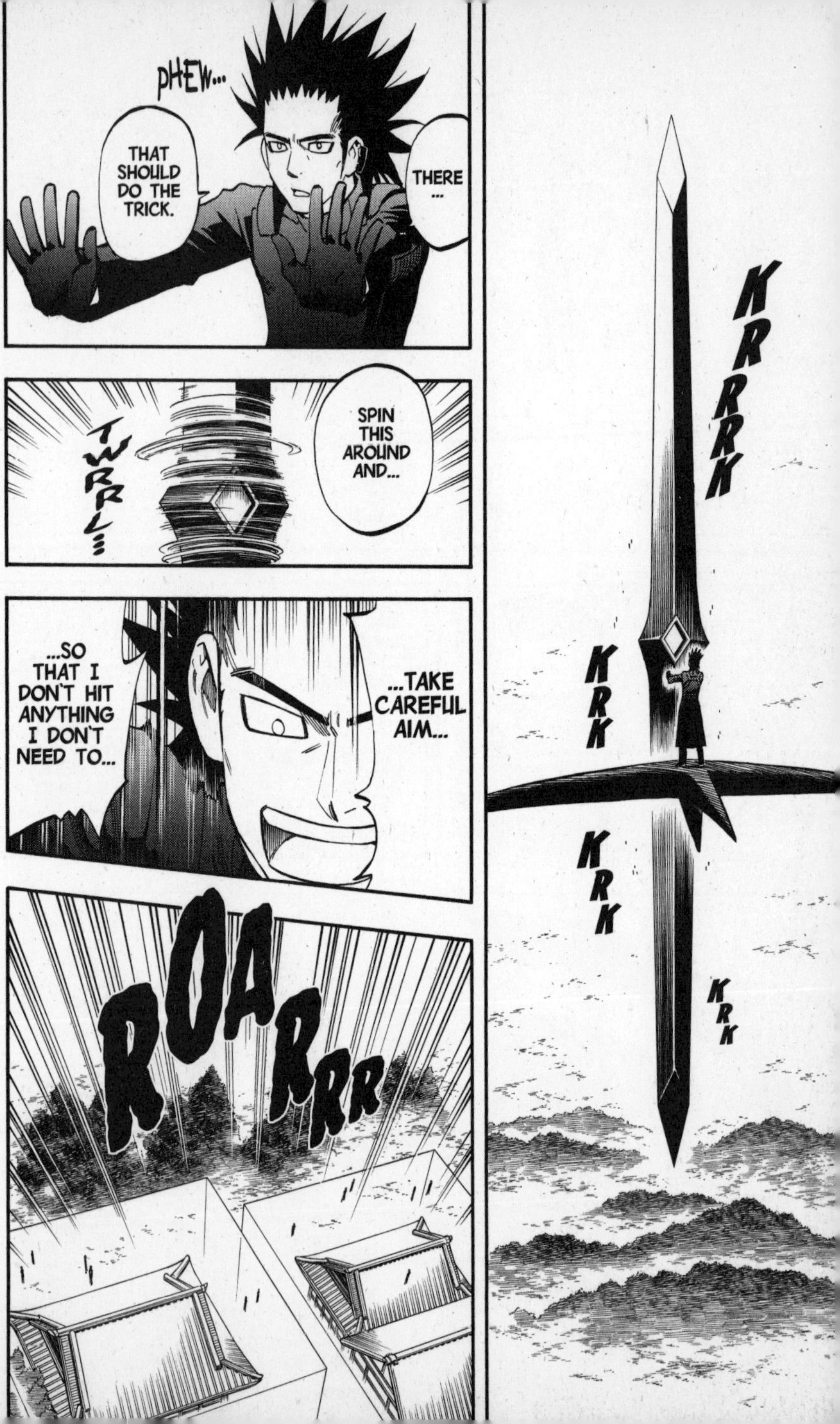
KRRRRN
KRK
KRK
KRK
THERE...
PHEW...
THAT SHOULD DO THE TRICK.
SPIN THIS AROUND AND...
TWRRL!!
...TAKE CAREFUL AIM...
...SO THAT I DON'T HIT ANYTHING I DON'T NEED TO...
ROARRR

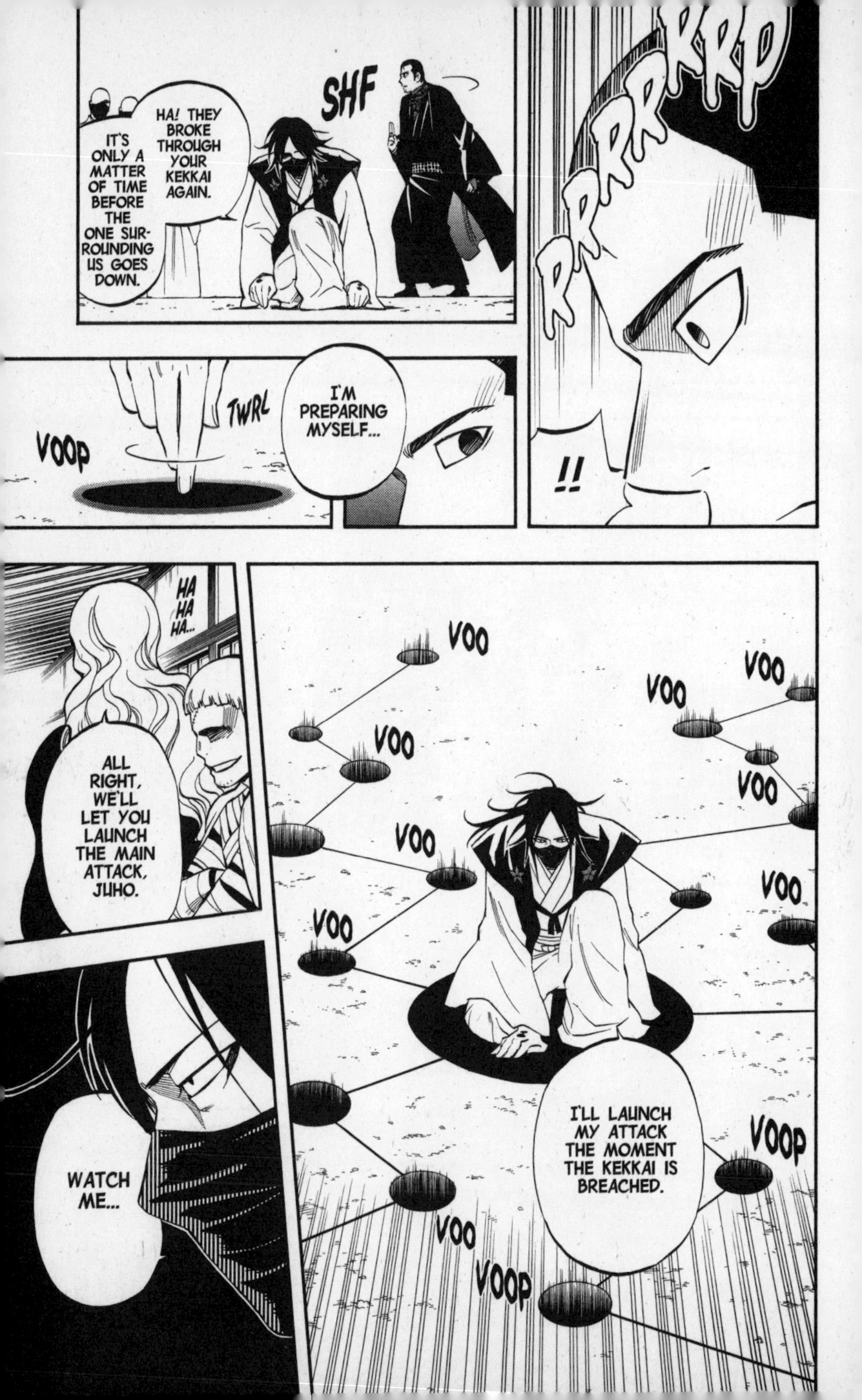
RRRRRRD
!!
SHF
HA! THEY BROKE THROUGH YOUR KEKKAI AGAIN.
IT'S ONLY A MATTER OF TIME BEFORE THE ONE SURROUNDING US GOES DOWN.
I'M PREPARING MYSELF...
TWRL
VOOP
VOO
VOO
VOO
VOO
VOO
VOO
VOO
VOO
I'LL LAUNCH MY ATTACK THE MOMENT THE KEKKAI IS BREACHED.
VOOP
VOO
VOOP
HA HA HA...
ALL RIGHT, WE'LL LET YOU LAUNCH THE MAIN ATTACK, JUHO.
WATCH ME...

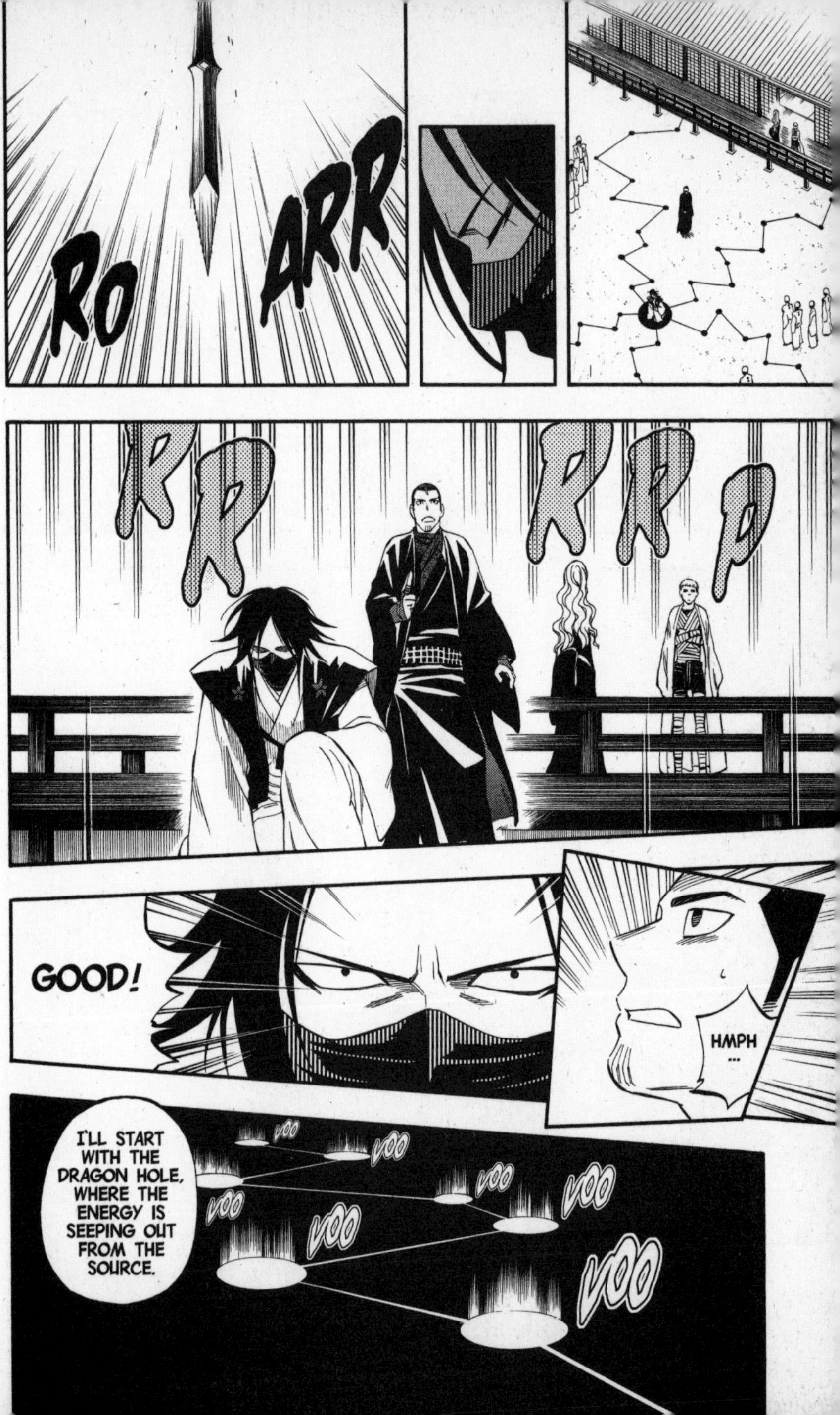
RO ARR
RR RRRP
HMPH...
GOOD!
I'LL START WITH THE DRAGON HOLE, WHERE THE ENERGY IS SEEPING OUT FROM THE SOURCE.
VOO VOO VOO VOO VOO VOO VOO

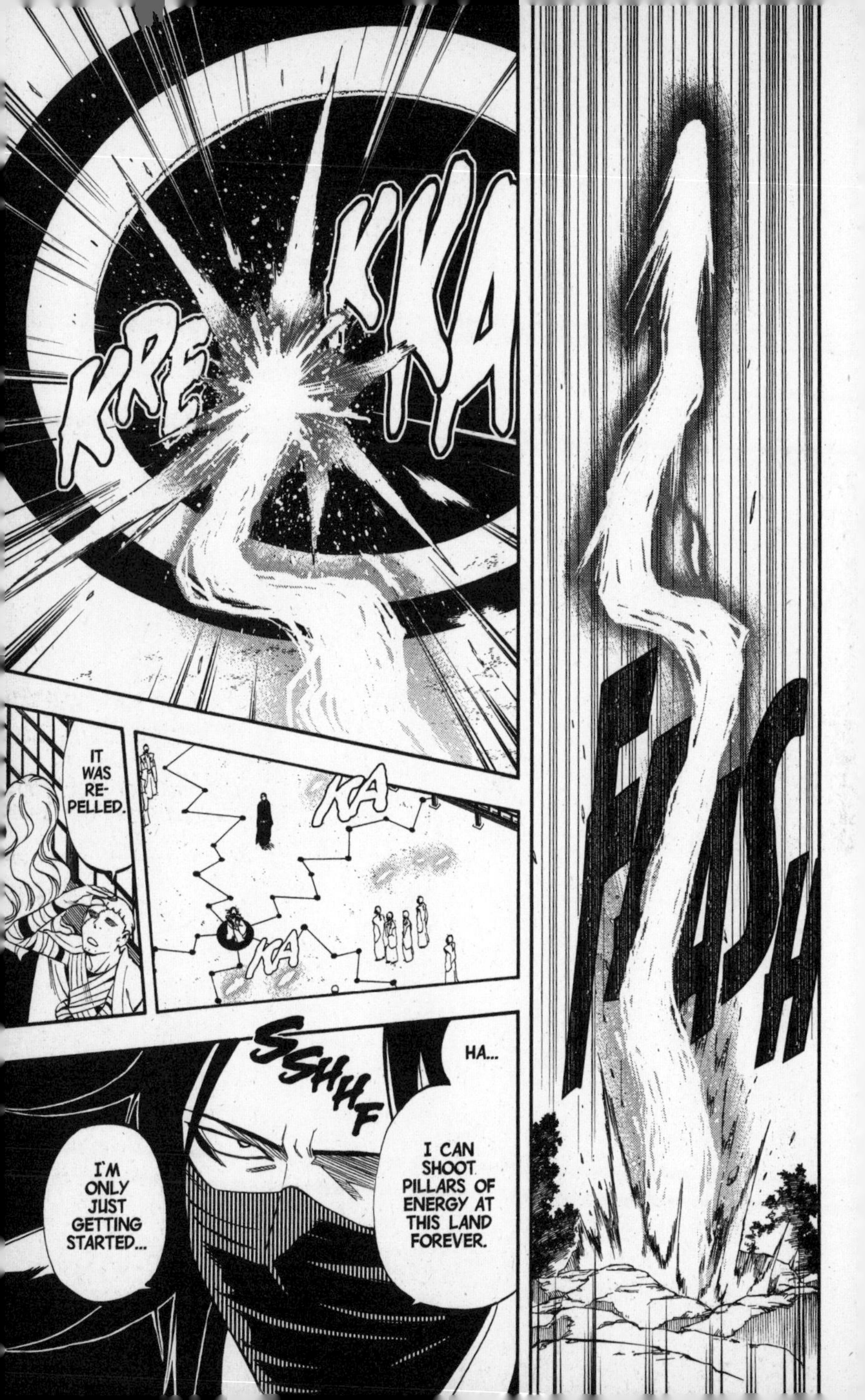
FLASH
KRE
KKA
KA
KA
IT WAS REPELLED.
SSHHF
HA...
I CAN SHOOT PILLARS OF ENERGY AT THIS LAND FOREVER.
I'M ONLY JUST GETTING STARTED...

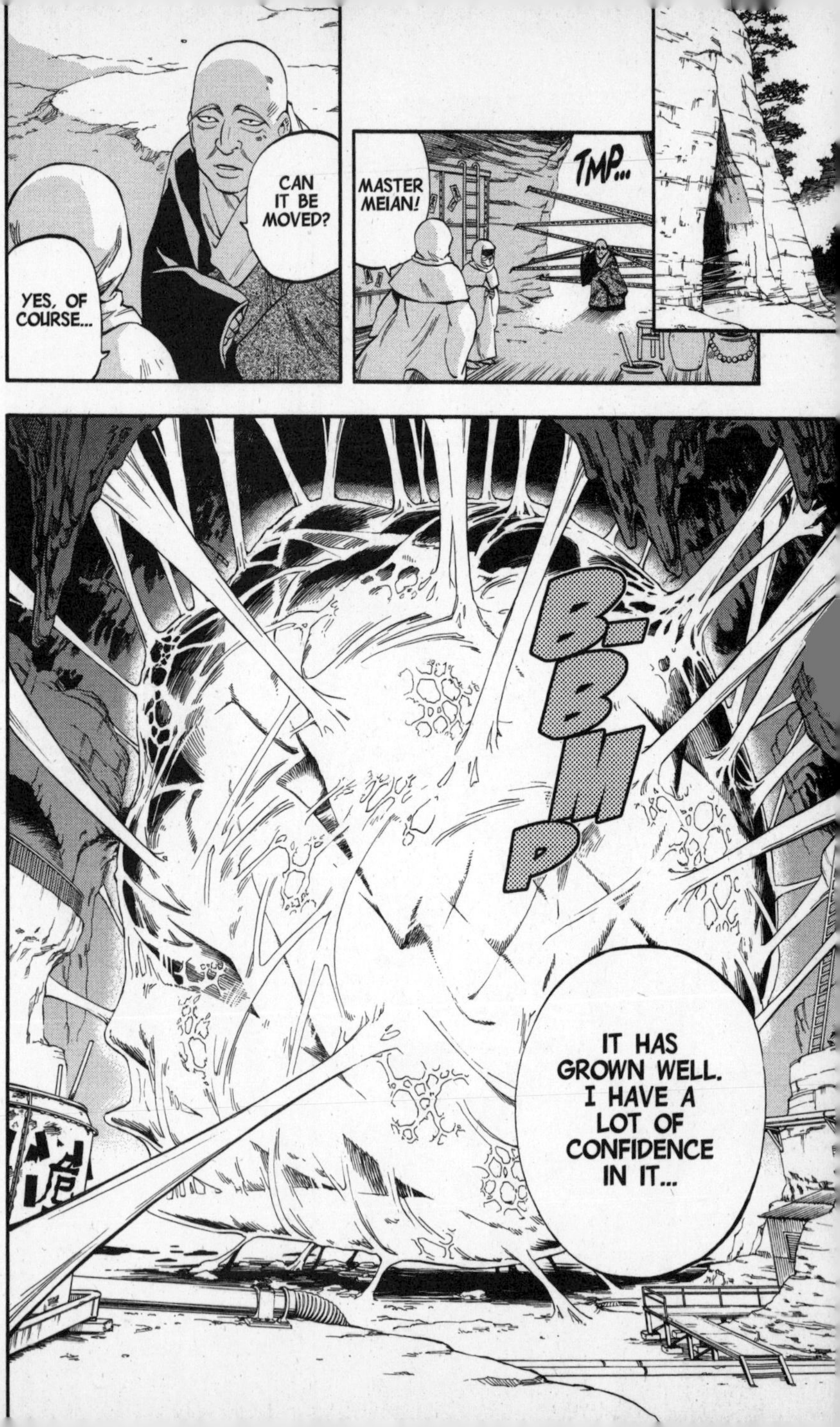
TMP...
MASTER MEIAN!
CAN IT BE MOVED?
YES, OF COURSE...
B-BMP
IT HAS GROWN WELL. I HAVE A LOT OF CONFIDENCE IN IT...

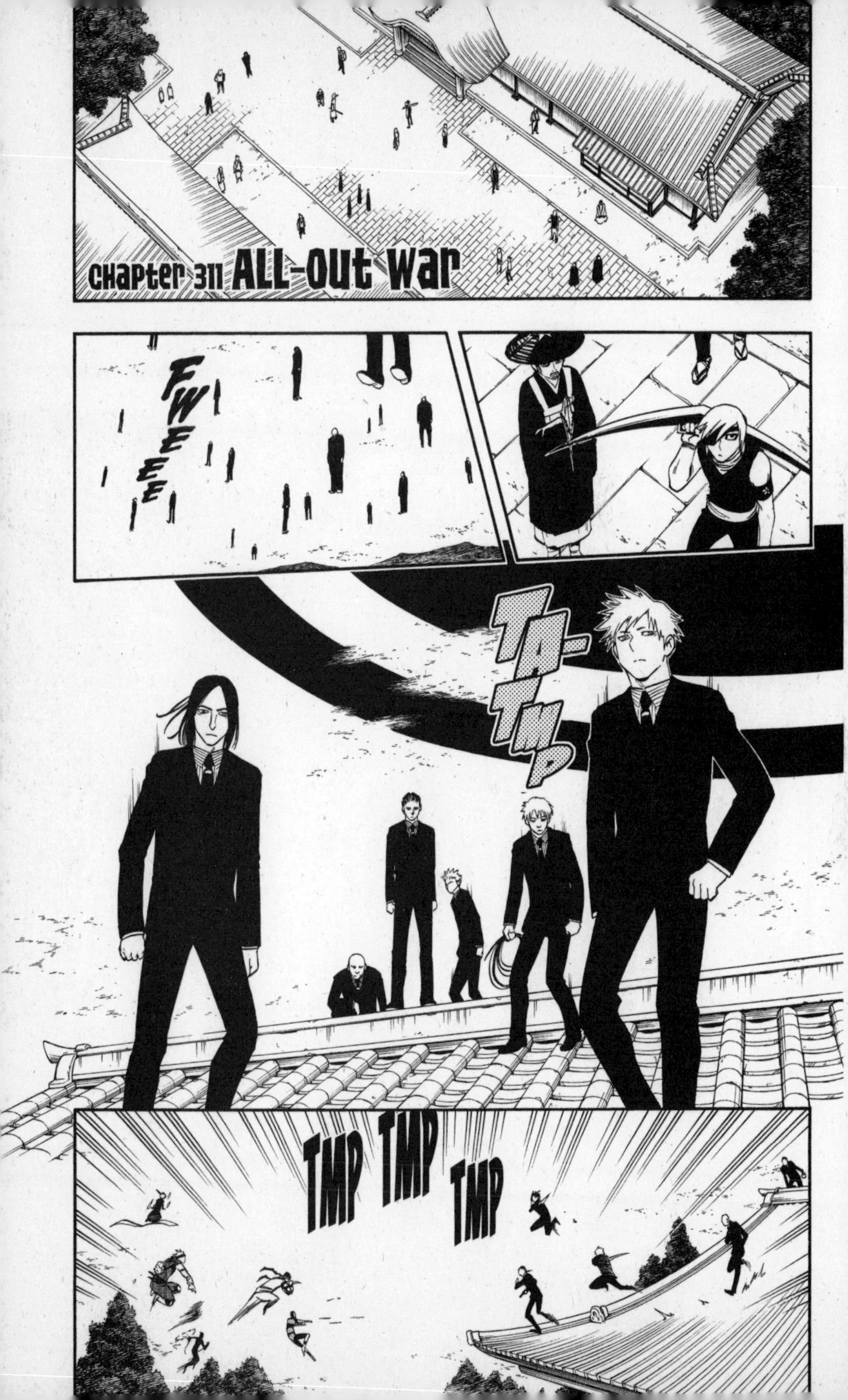
Chapter 311 ALL-out war
FWEEEE
TA-TMP
TMP TMP TMP

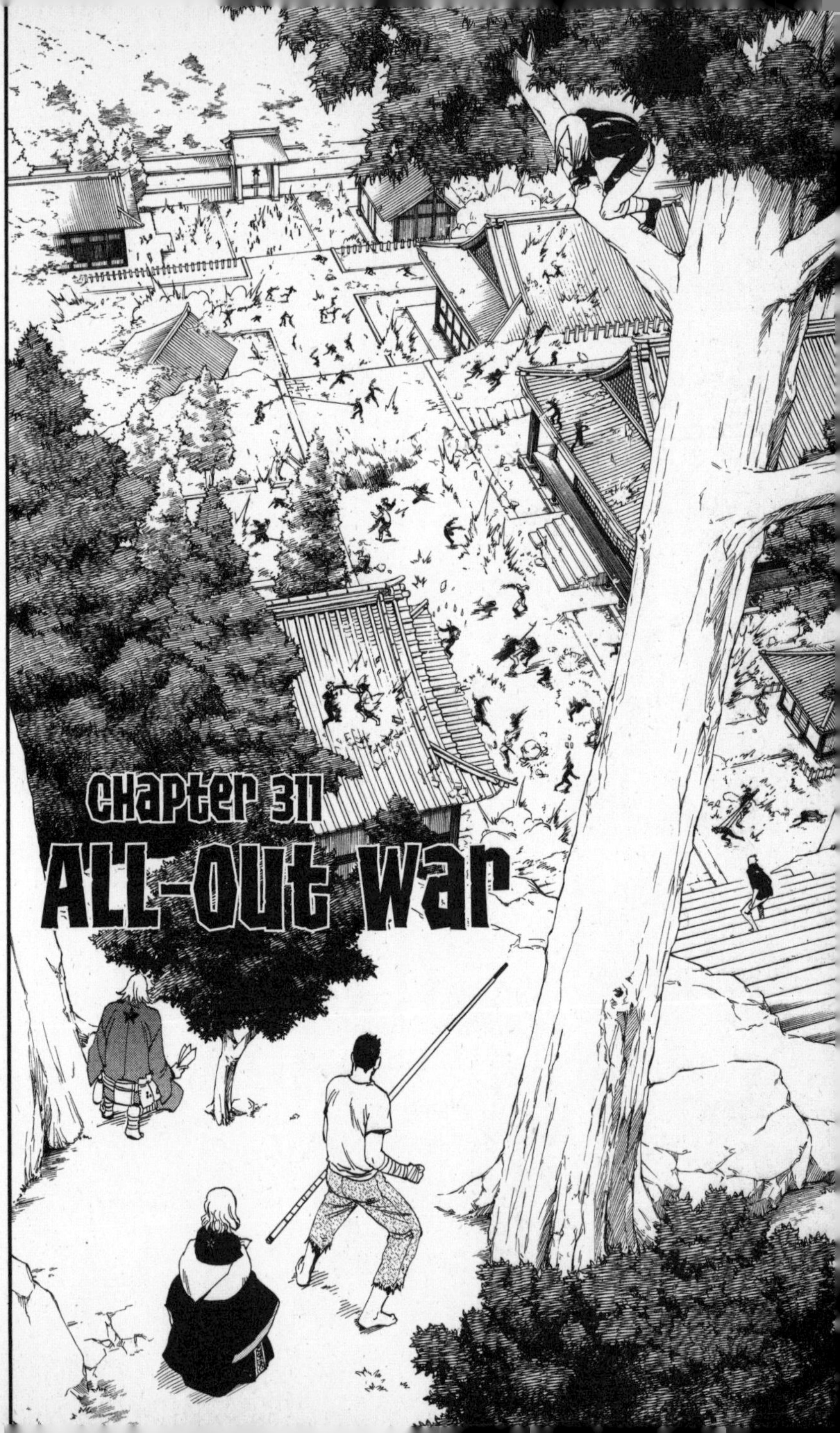
CHAPTER 311
ALL-OUT WAR

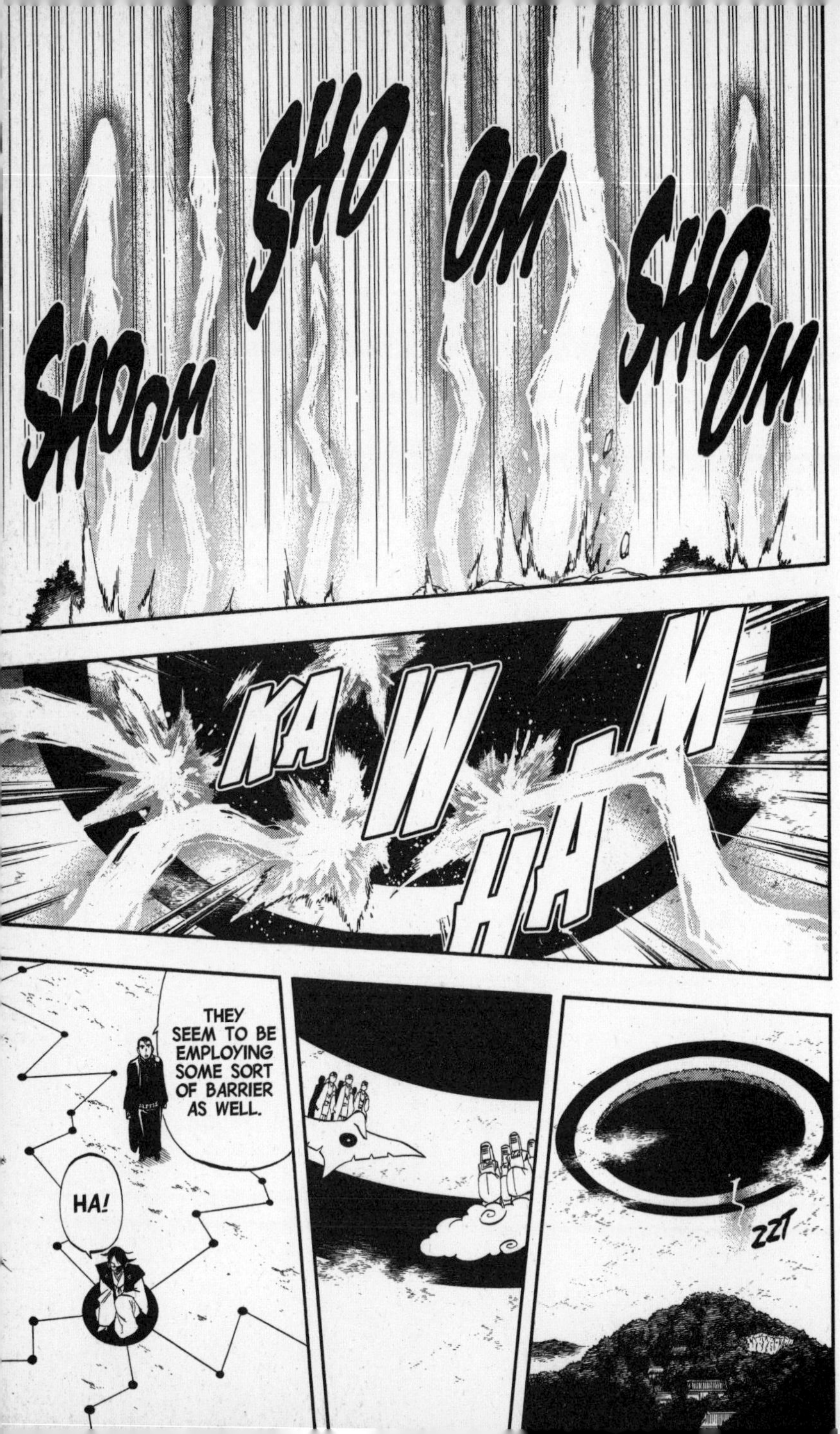
SHOOM
SHOOM
SHOOM
KAWHAM
ZZT
THEY SEEM TO BE EMPLOYING SOME SORT OF BARRIER AS WELL.
HA!

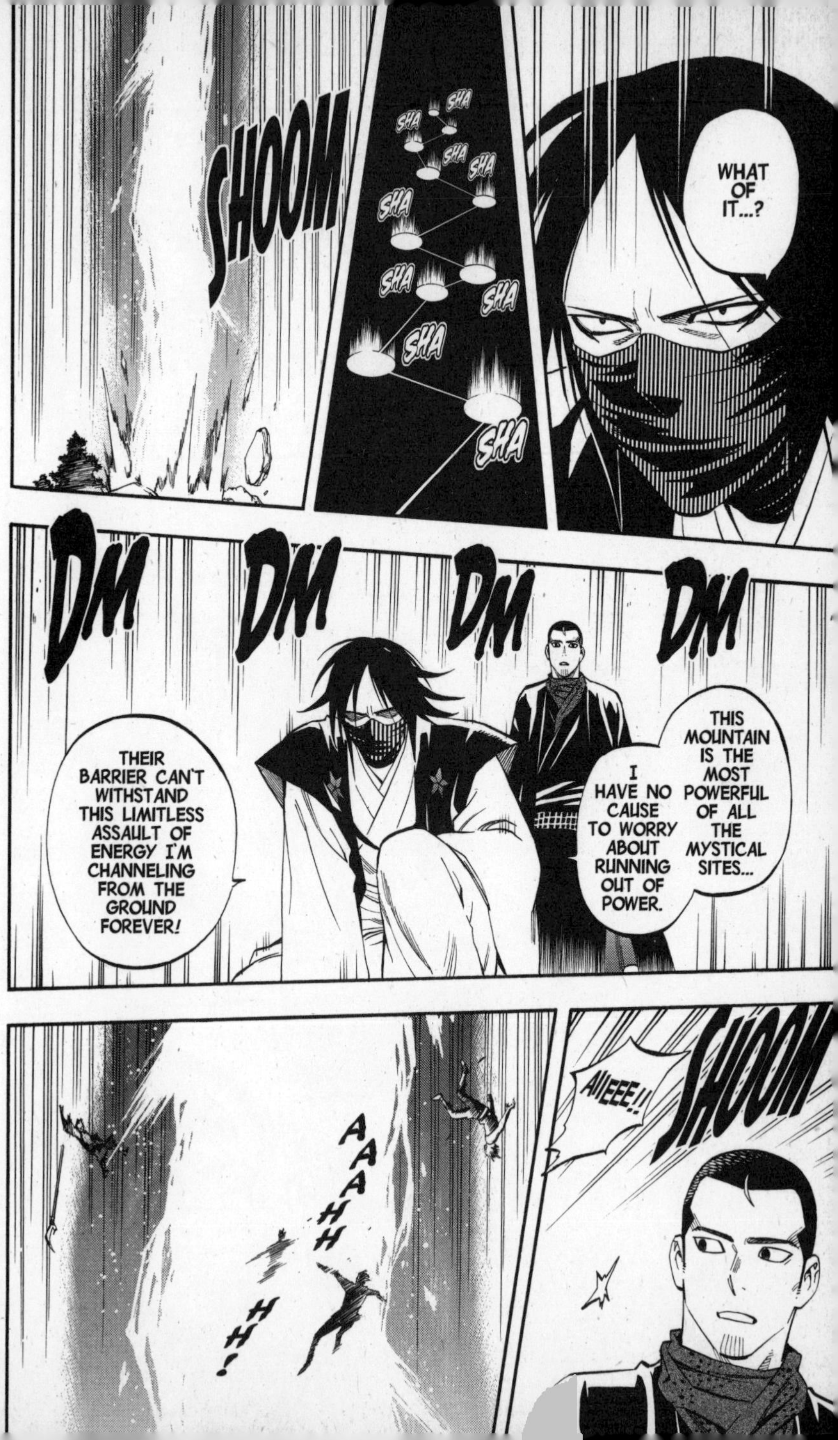
WHAT OF IT...?
SHA SHA SHA SHA SHA SHA SHA SHA SHA
SHOOM
DM DM DM DM
THIS MOUNTAIN IS THE MOST POWERFUL OF ALL THE MYSTICAL SITES...
I HAVE NO CAUSE TO WORRY ABOUT RUNNING OUT OF POWER.
THEIR BARRIER CAN'T WITHSTAND THIS LIMITLESS ASSAULT OF ENERGY I'M CHANNELING FROM THE GROUND FOREVER!
SHOOM
AIIEEE!!
AAAAHHHH!

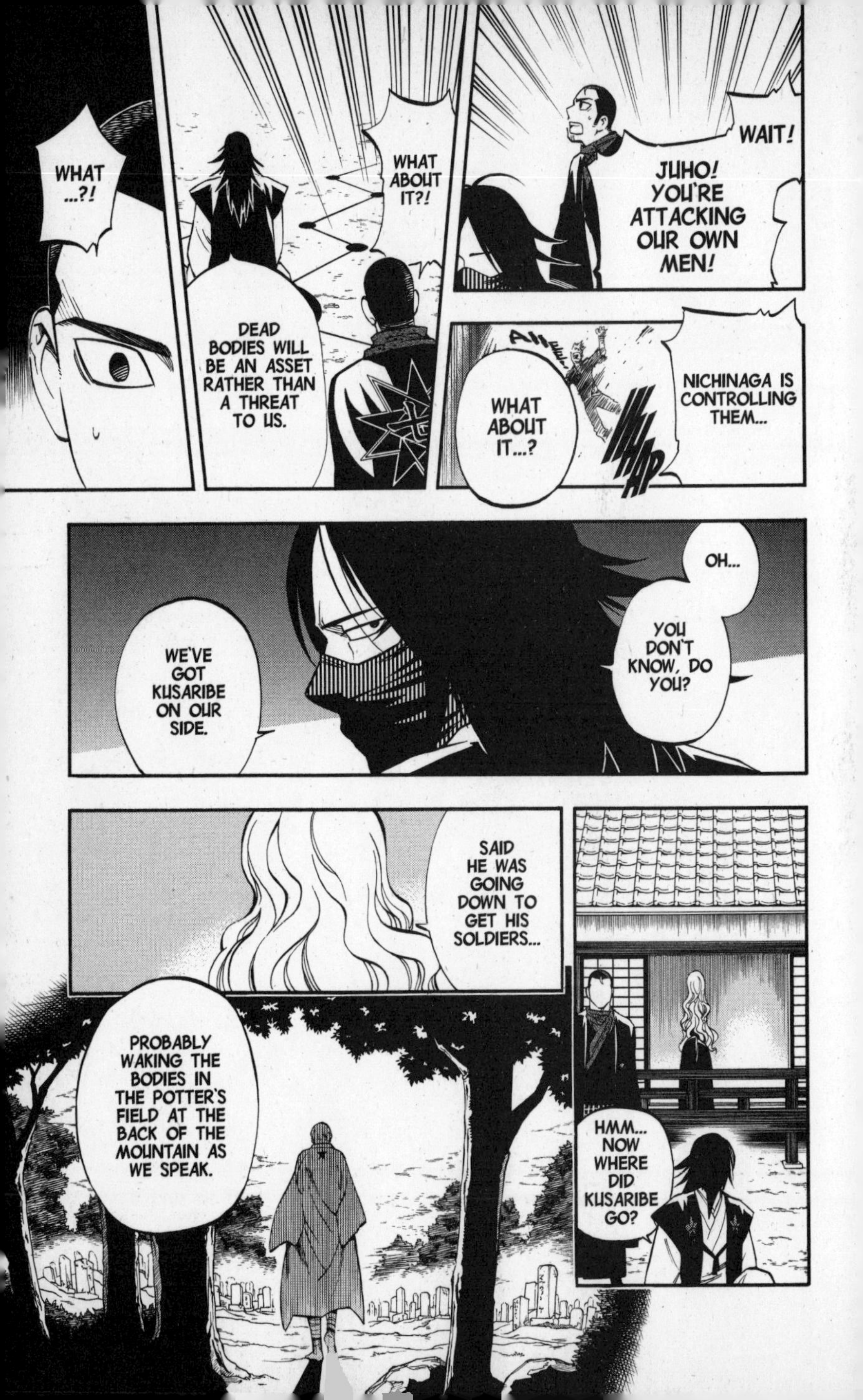
WAIT!
JUHO! YOU'RE ATTACKING OUR OWN MEN!
NICHINAGA IS CONTROLLING THEM...
WHAT ABOUT IT...?
WHAP
WHAT ABOUT IT?!
DEAD BODIES WILL BE AN ASSET RATHER THAN A THREAT TO US.
WHAT ...?!
OH...
YOU DON'T KNOW, DO YOU?
WE'VE GOT KUSARIBE ON OUR SIDE.
HMM... NOW WHERE DID KUSARIBE GO?
SAID HE WAS GOING DOWN TO GET HIS SOLDIERS...
PROBABLY WAKING THE BODIES IN THE POTTER'S FIELD AT THE BACK OF THE MOUNTAIN AS WE SPEAK.

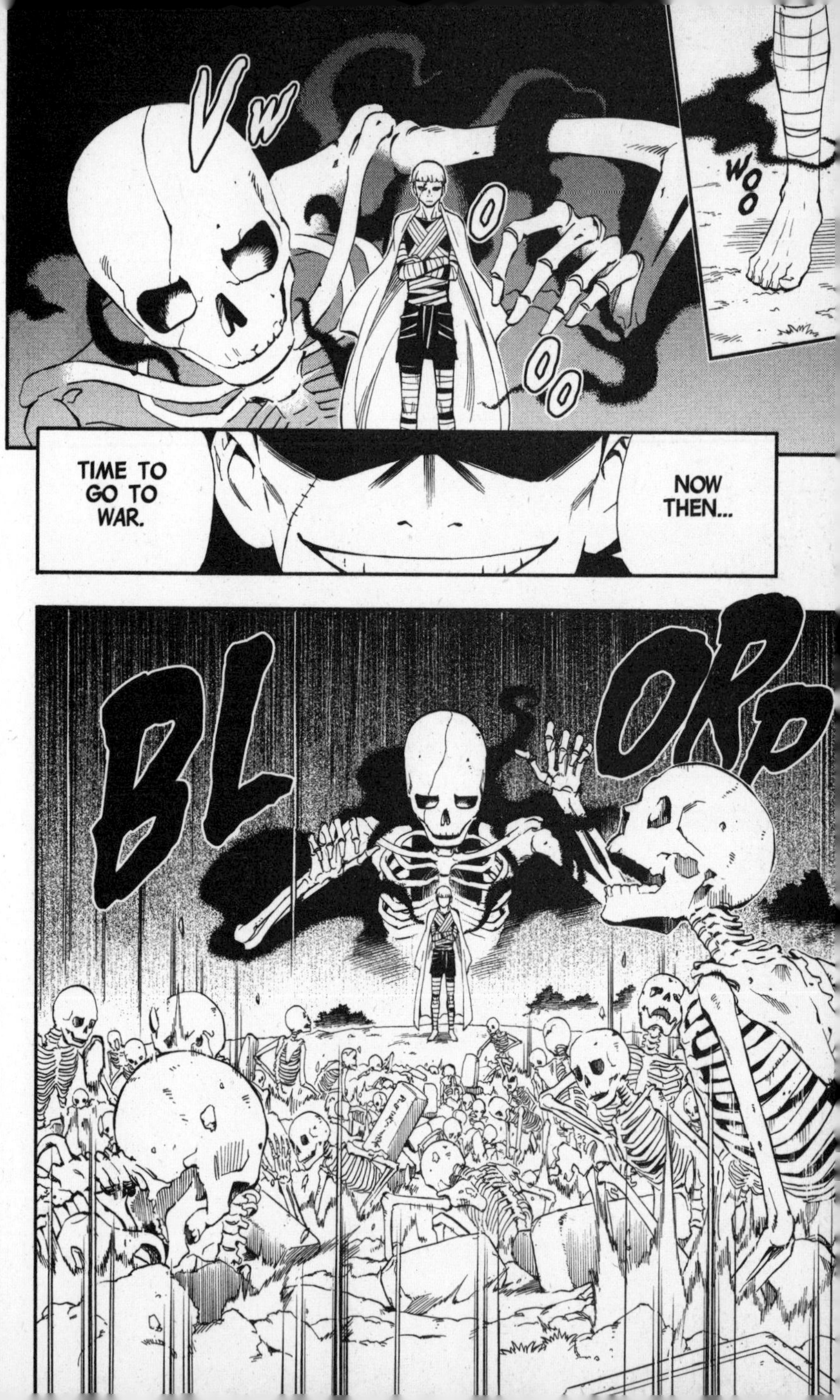
WOOO
VW
OOOO
NOW THEN...
TIME TO GO TO WAR.
BLORP

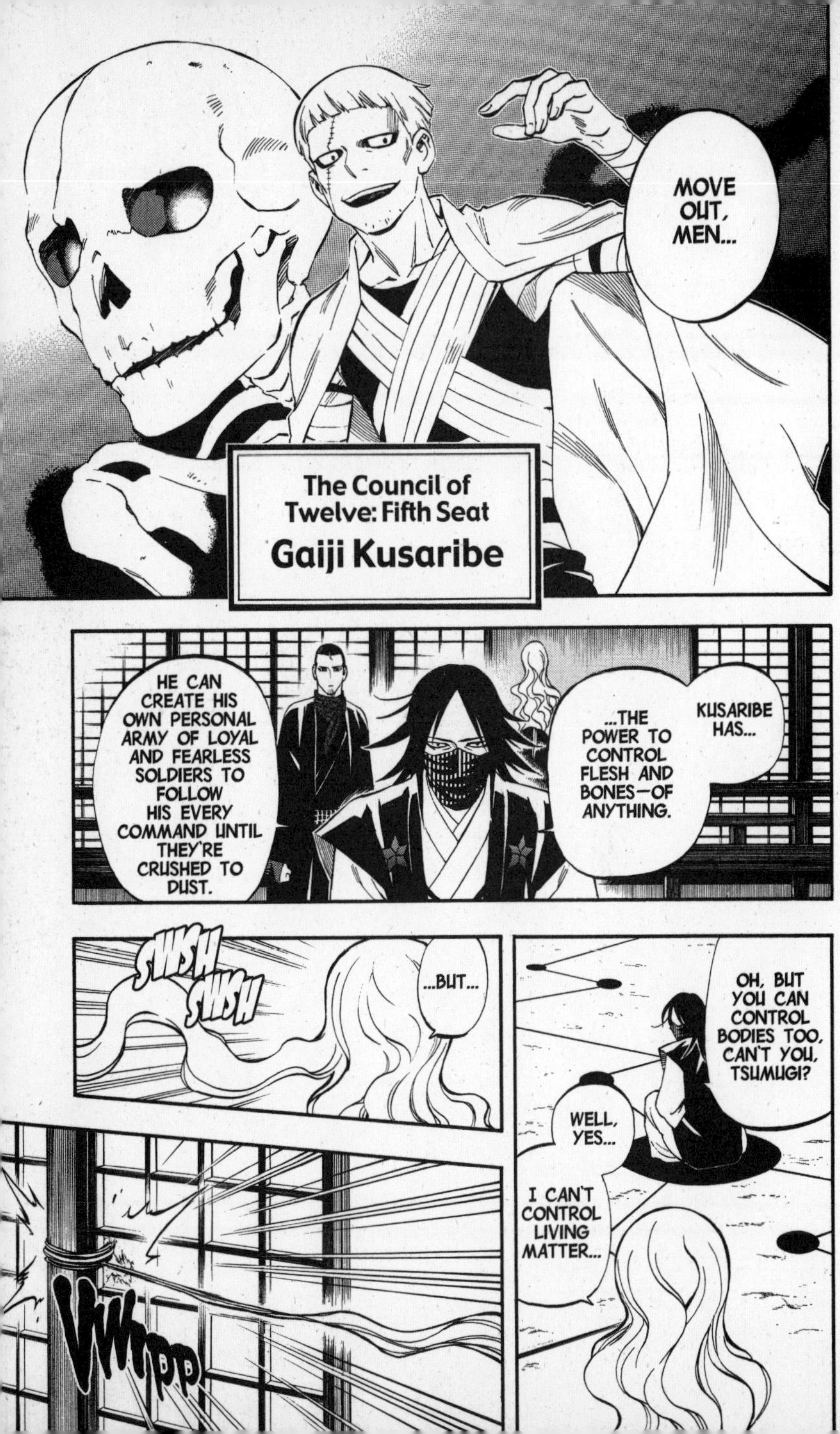
MOVE OUT, MEN...
The Council of Twelve: Fifth Seat
Gaiji Kusaribe
KUSARIBE HAS...
...THE POWER TO CONTROL FLESH AND BONES—OF ANYTHING.
HE CAN CREATE HIS OWN PERSONAL ARMY OF LOYAL AND FEARLESS SOLDIERS TO FOLLOW HIS EVERY COMMAND UNTIL THEY'RE CRUSHED TO DUST.
OH, BUT YOU CAN CONTROL BODIES TOO, CAN'T YOU, TSUMUGI?
WELL, YES...
I CAN'T CONTROL LIVING MATTER...
SWISH SWISH
...BUT...
VWHPP

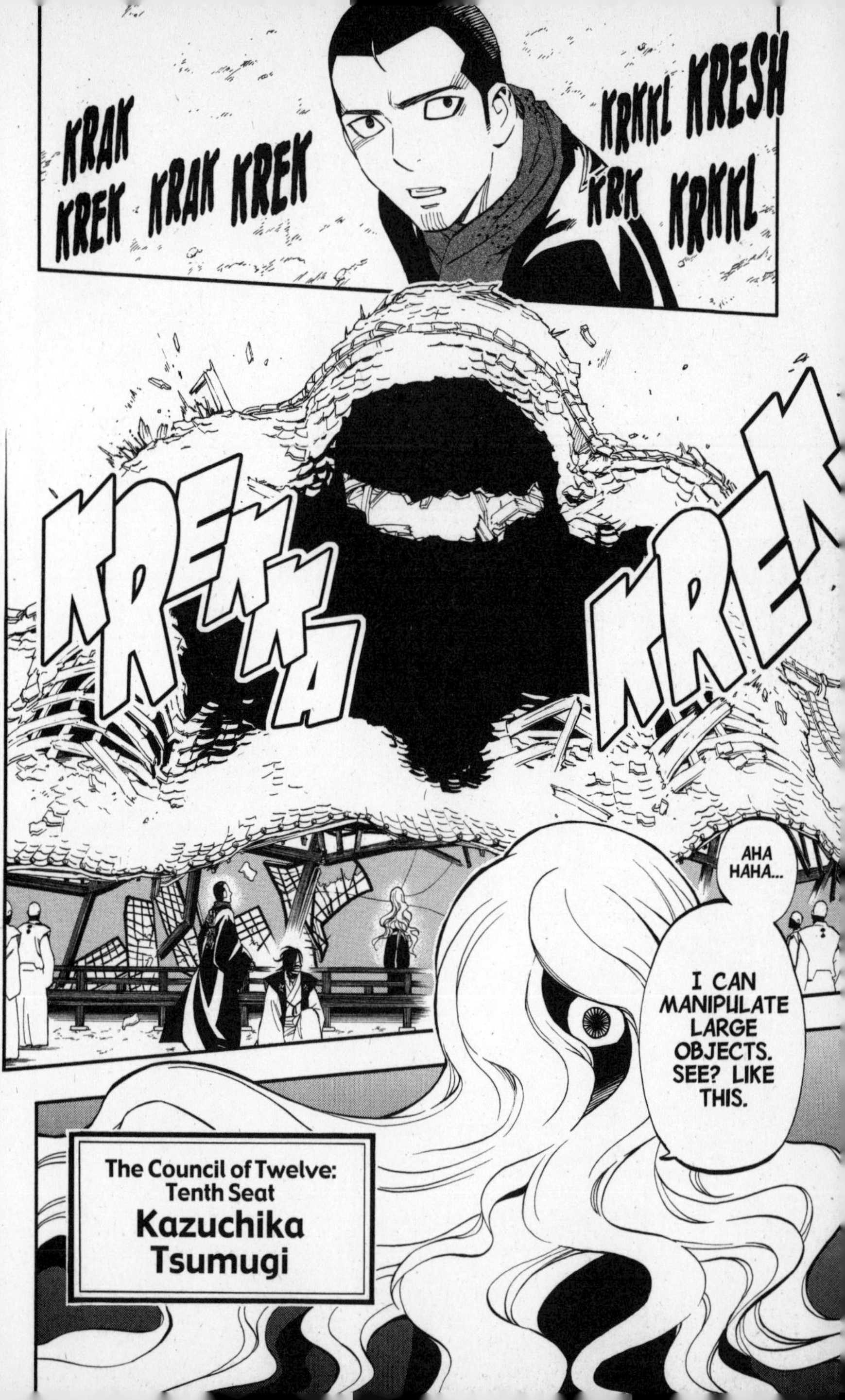
KRKKL KRESH
KRK KRKKL
KRAK KREK
KRAK KREK
AHA HAHA...
I CAN MANIPULATE LARGE OBJECTS. SEE? LIKE THIS.
The Council of Twelve: Tenth Seat
Kazuchika Tsumugi

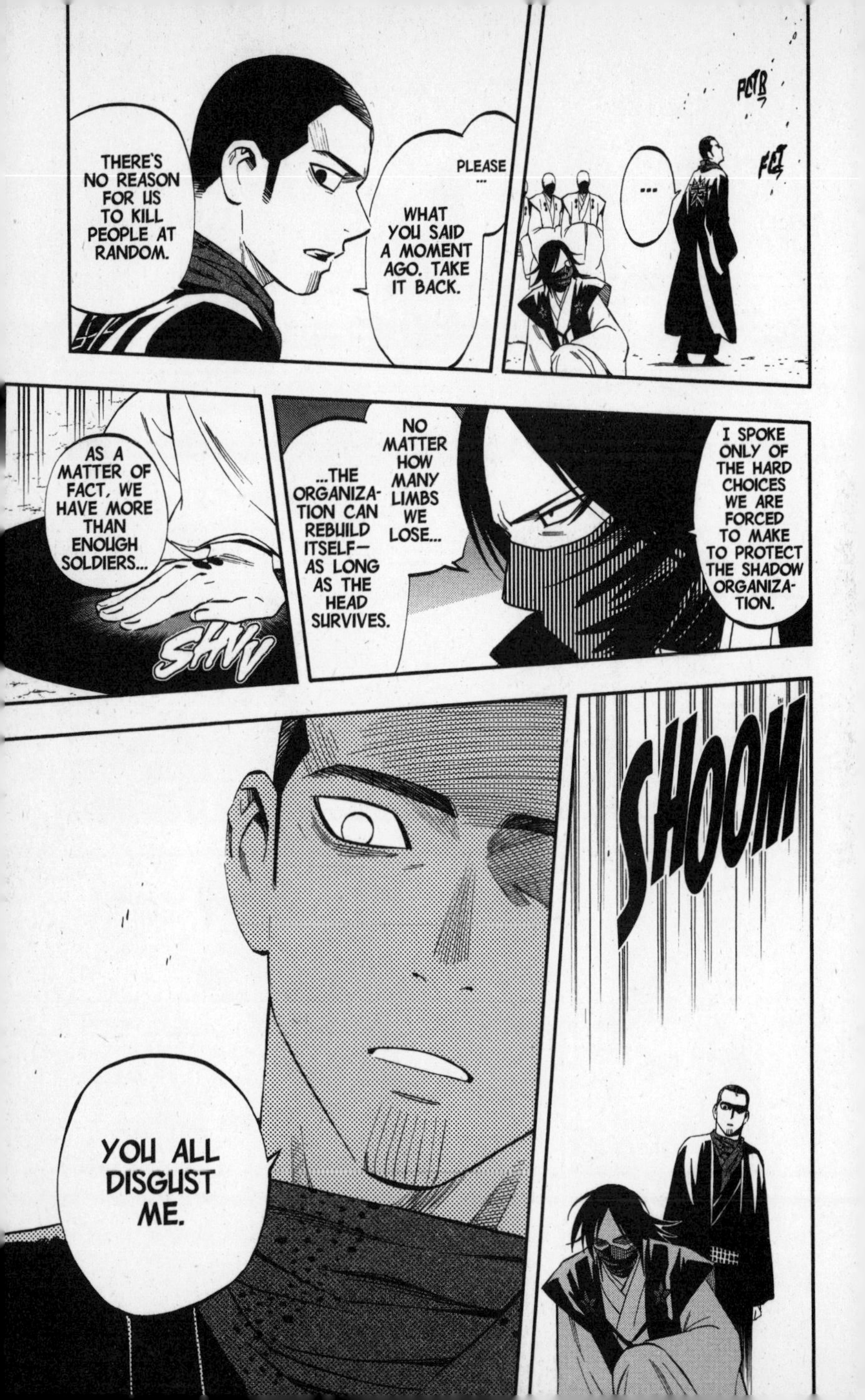

FLTR
FLT
...
PLEASE ...
WHAT YOU SAID A MOMENT AGO. TAKE IT BACK.
THERE'S NO REASON FOR US TO KILL PEOPLE AT RANDOM.
I SPOKE ONLY OF THE HARD CHOICES WE ARE FORCED TO MAKE TO PROTECT THE SHADOW ORGANIZATION.
NO MATTER HOW MANY LIMBS WE LOSE...
...THE ORGANIZATION CAN REBUILD ITSELF— AS LONG AS THE HEAD SURVIVES.
AS A MATTER OF FACT, WE HAVE MORE THAN ENOUGH SOLDIERS...
SHVV
SHOOM
YOU ALL DISGUST ME.

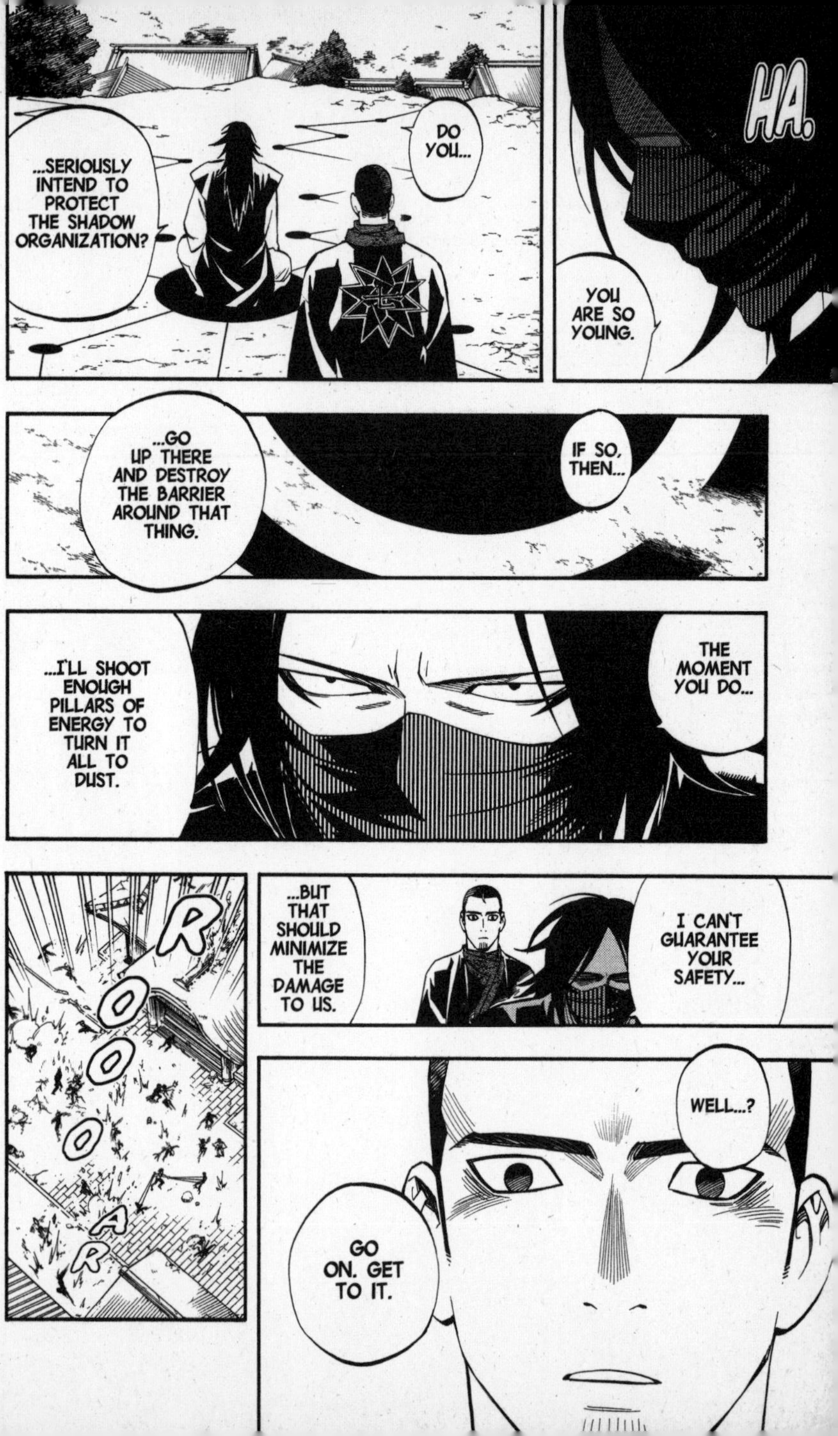
HA.
YOU ARE SO YOUNG.
DO YOU...
...SERIOUSLY INTEND TO PROTECT THE SHADOW ORGANIZATION?
IF SO, THEN...
...GO UP THERE AND DESTROY THE BARRIER AROUND THAT THING.
THE MOMENT YOU DO...
...I'LL SHOOT ENOUGH PILLARS OF ENERGY TO TURN IT ALL TO DUST.
I CAN'T GUARANTEE YOUR SAFETY...
...BUT THAT SHOULD MINIMIZE THE DAMAGE TO US.
WELL...?
GO ON. GET TO IT.
ROOOOAR

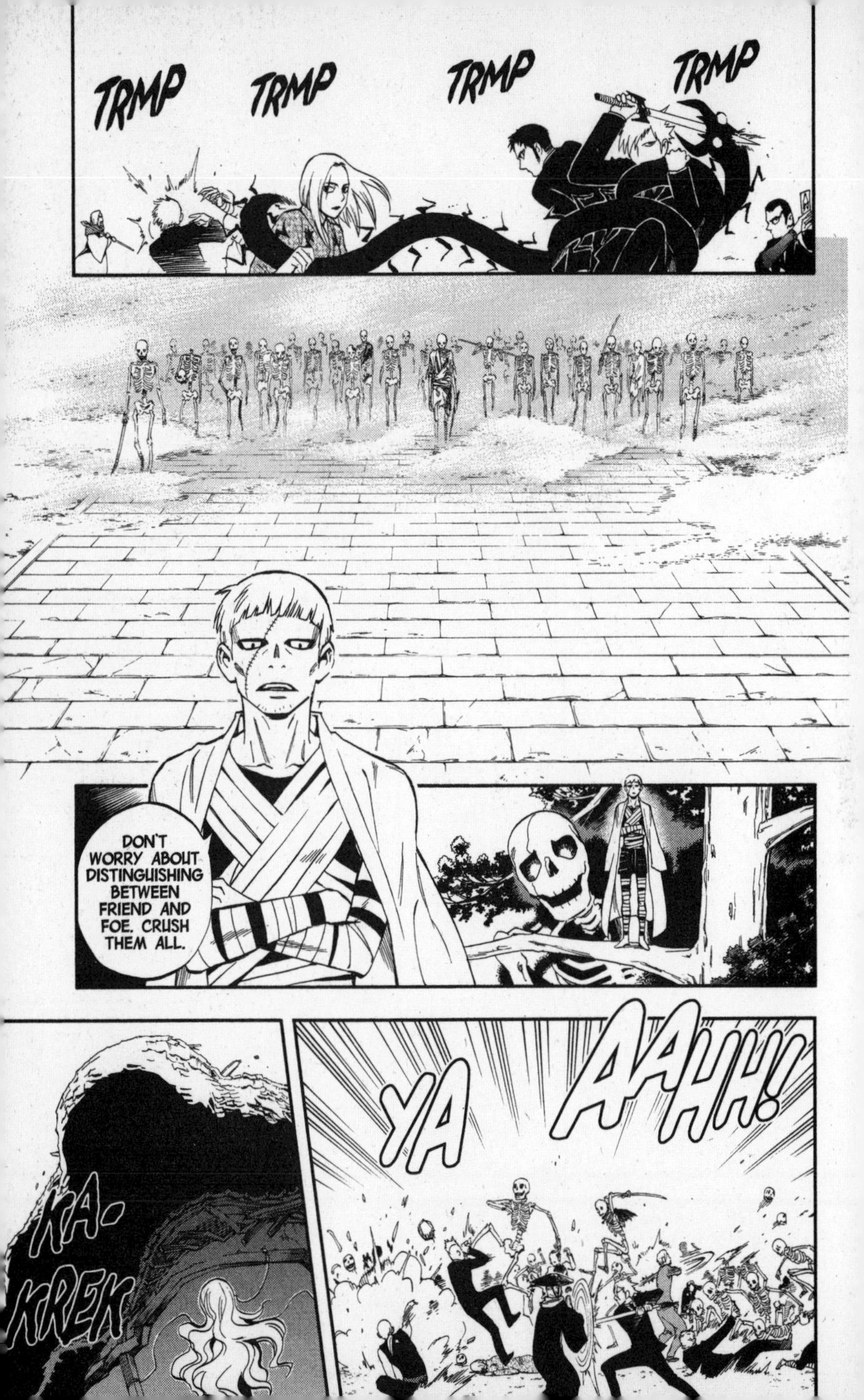
TRMP
TRMP
TRMP
TRMP
DON'T WORRY ABOUT DISTINGUISHING BETWEEN FRIEND AND FOE. CRUSH THEM ALL.
YA AAHH!
KA-KREK

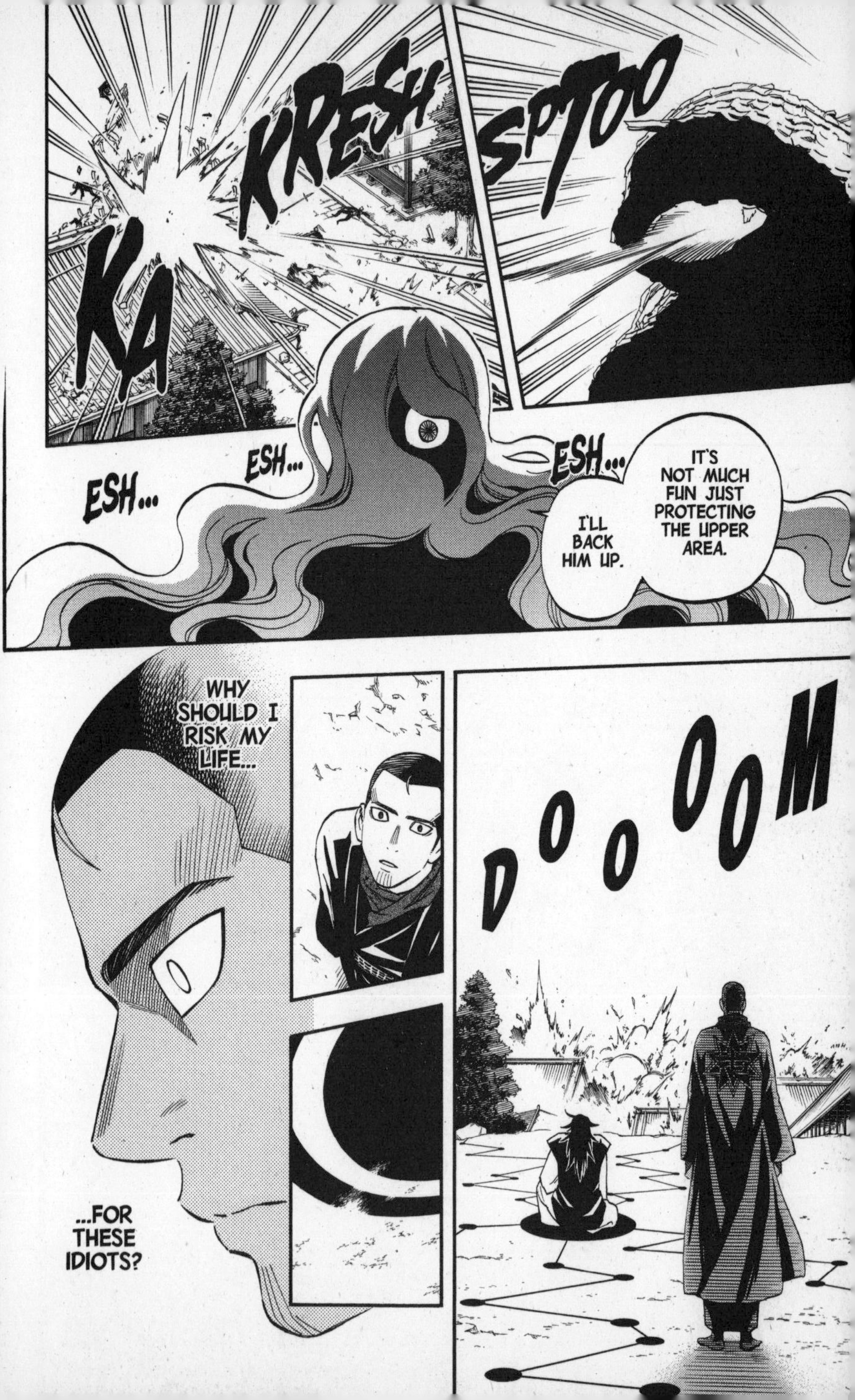
SPTOO
KA
KRESH
IT'S NOT MUCH FUN JUST PROTECTING THE UPPER AREA.
I'LL BACK HIM UP.
ESH...
ESH...
ESH...
DOOOOM
WHY SHOULD I RISK MY LIFE...
...FOR THESE IDIOTS?

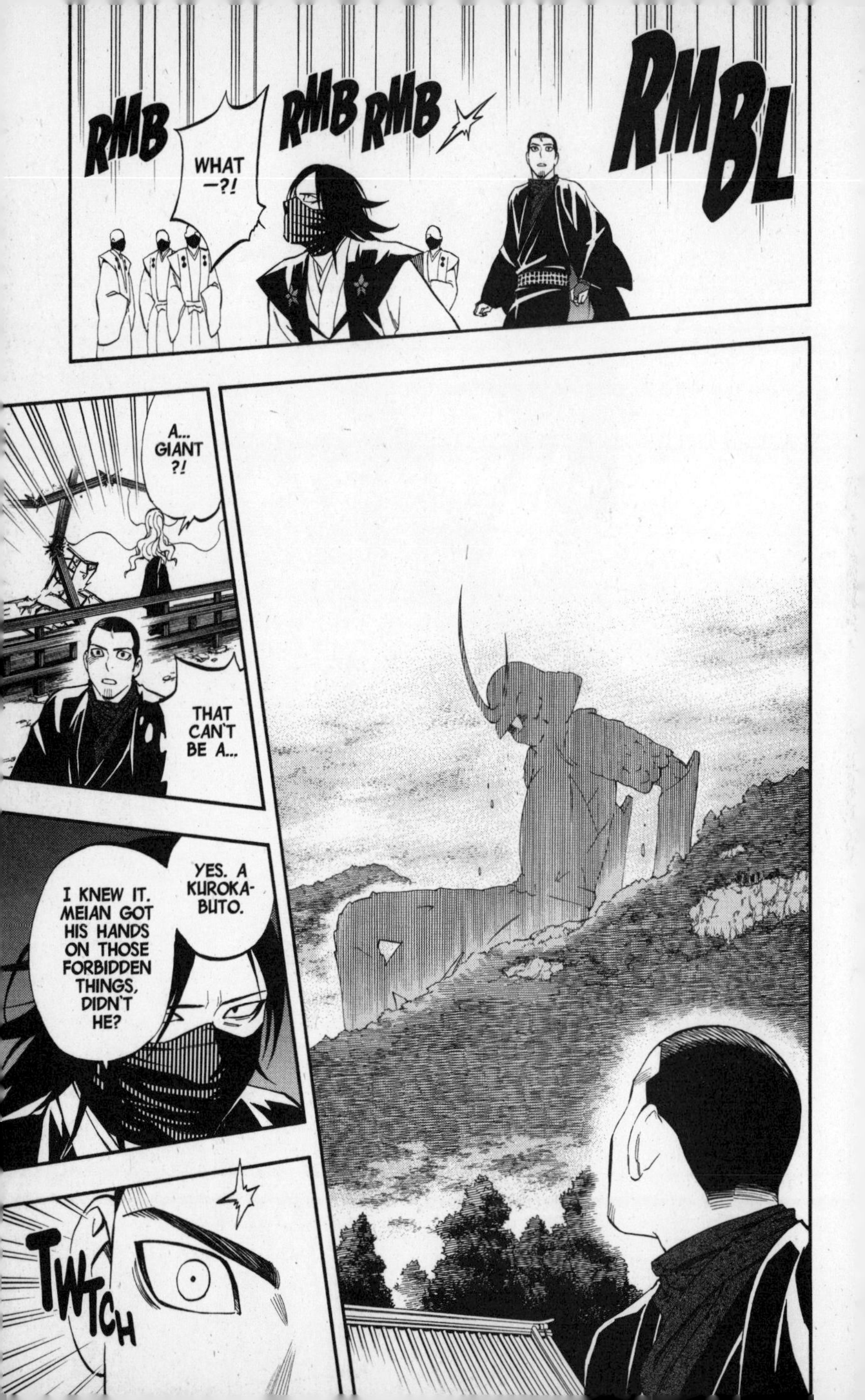
RMBL
RMB RMB
WHAT—?!
RMB
A... GIANT?!
THAT CAN'T BE A...
YES. A KUROKA-BUTO.
I KNEW IT. MEIAN GOT HIS HANDS ON THOSE FORBIDDEN THINGS, DIDN'T HE?
TWITCH

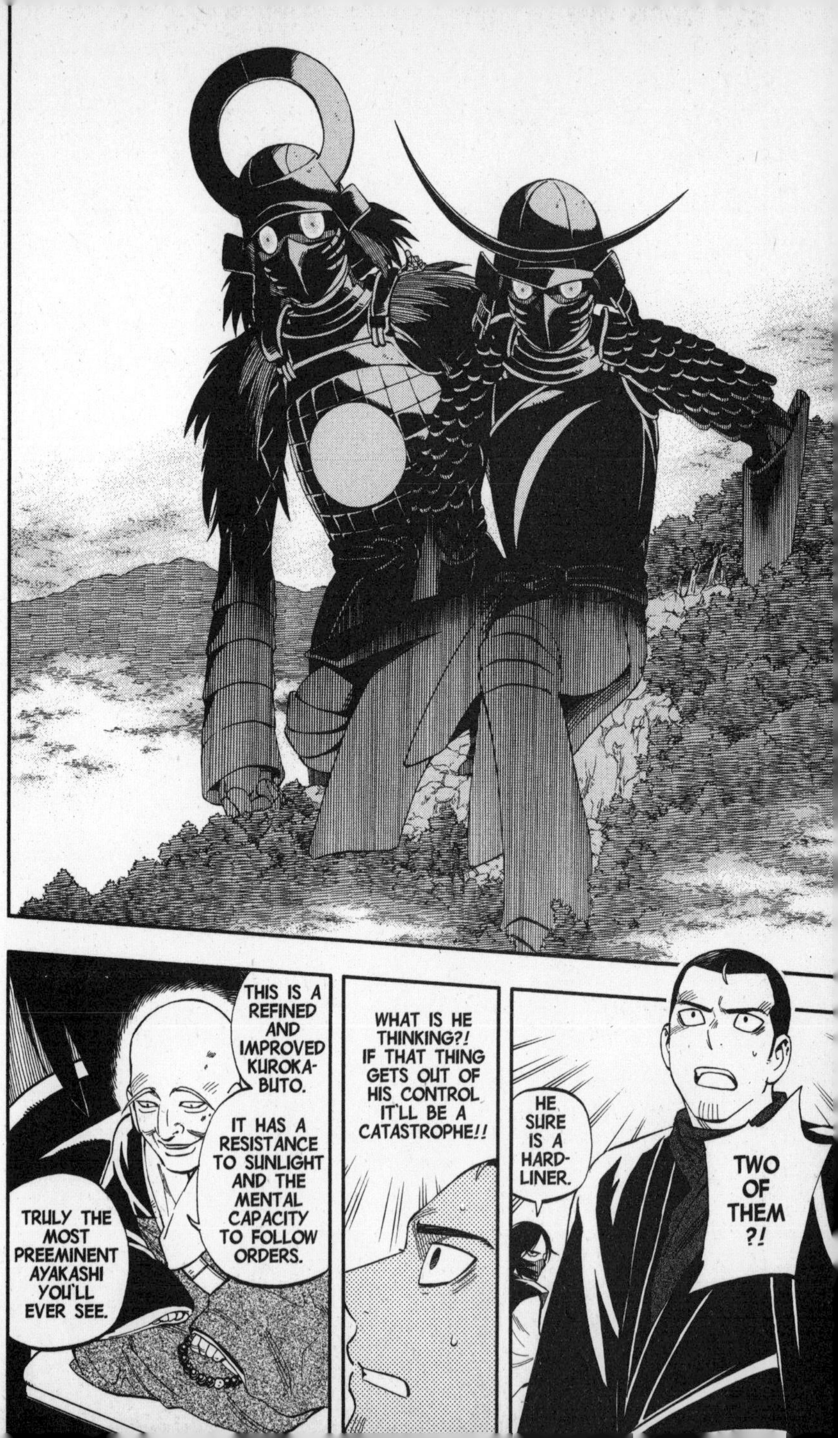
TWO OF THEM?!
HE SURE IS A HARD-LINER.
WHAT IS HE THINKING?! IF THAT THING GETS OUT OF HIS CONTROL IT'LL BE A CATASTROPHE!!
THIS IS A REFINED AND IMPROVED KUROKA-BUTO.
IT HAS A RESISTANCE TO SUNLIGHT AND THE MENTAL CAPACITY TO FOLLOW ORDERS.
TRULY THE MOST PREEMINENT AYAKASHI YOU'LL EVER SEE.

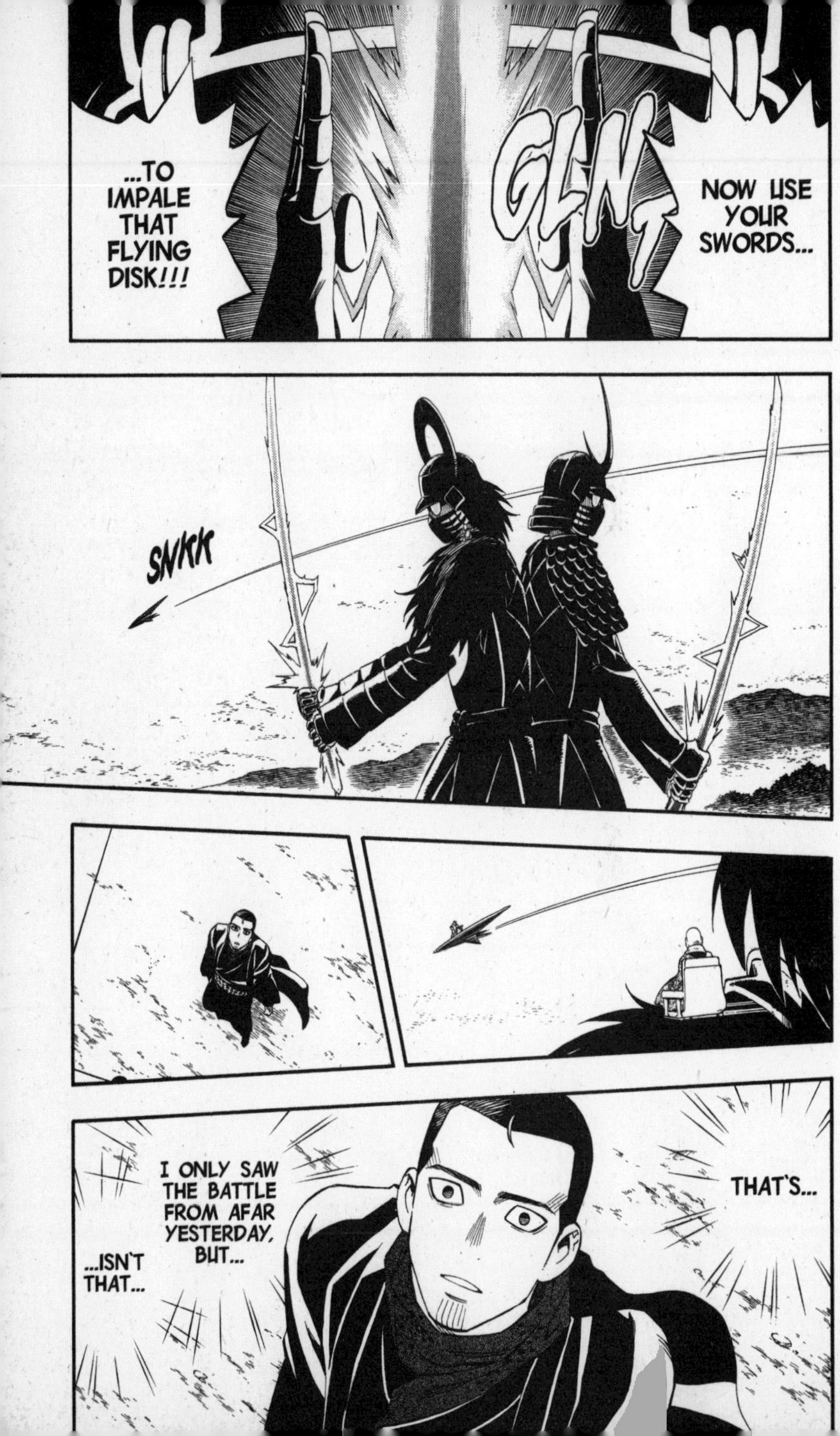
NOW USE YOUR SWORDS...
GLINT
...TO IMPALE THAT FLYING DISK!!!
SNKK
THAT'S...
I ONLY SAW THE BATTLE FROM AFAR YESTERDAY, BUT...
...ISN'T THAT...

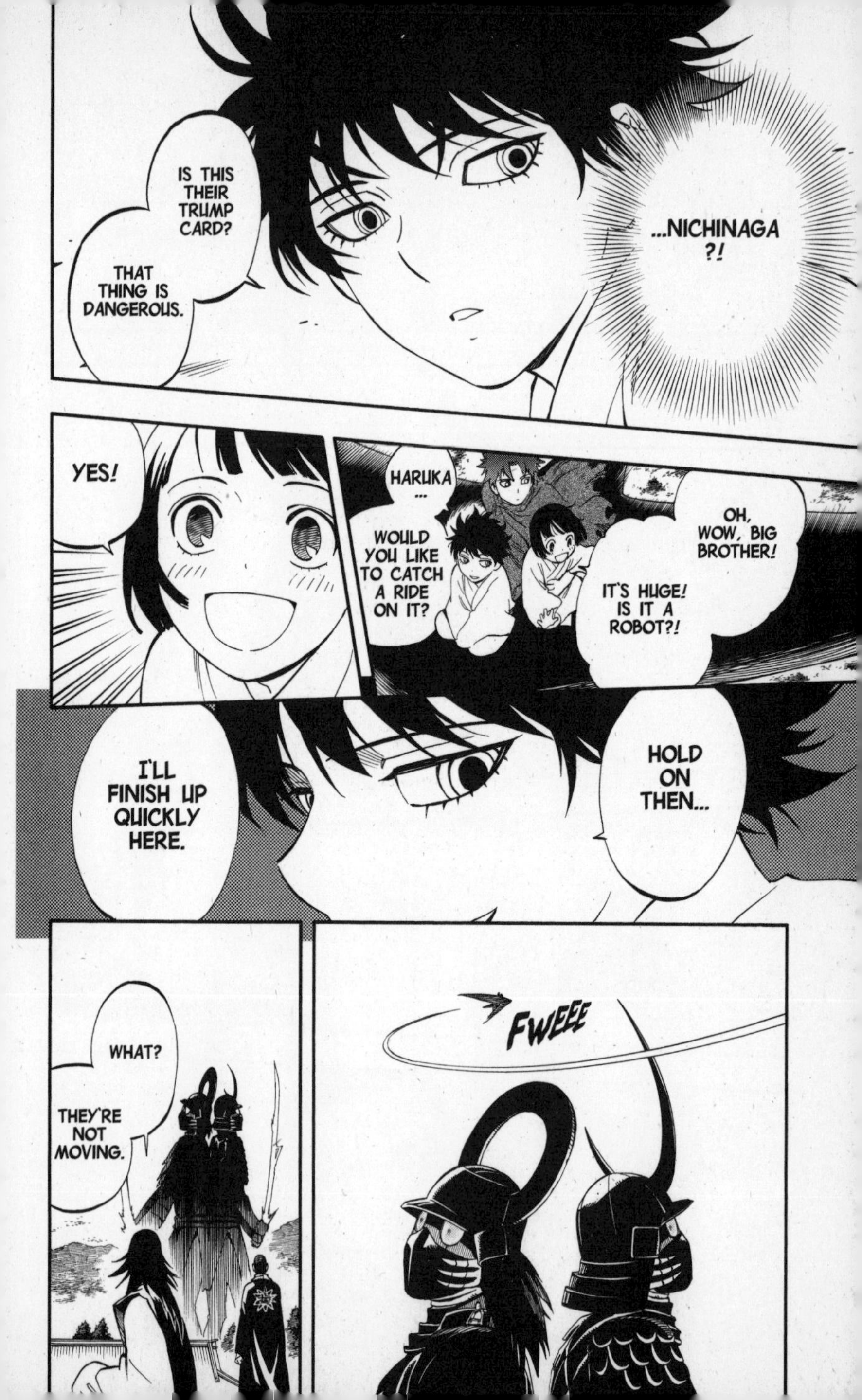
...NICHINAGA ?!
IS THIS THEIR TRUMP CARD?
THAT THING IS DANGEROUS.
OH, WOW, BIG BROTHER!
IT'S HUGE! IS IT A ROBOT?!
HARUKA... WOULD YOU LIKE TO CATCH A RIDE ON IT?
YES!
HOLD ON THEN...
I'LL FINISH UP QUICKLY HERE.
FWEEE
WHAT?
THEY'RE NOT MOVING.

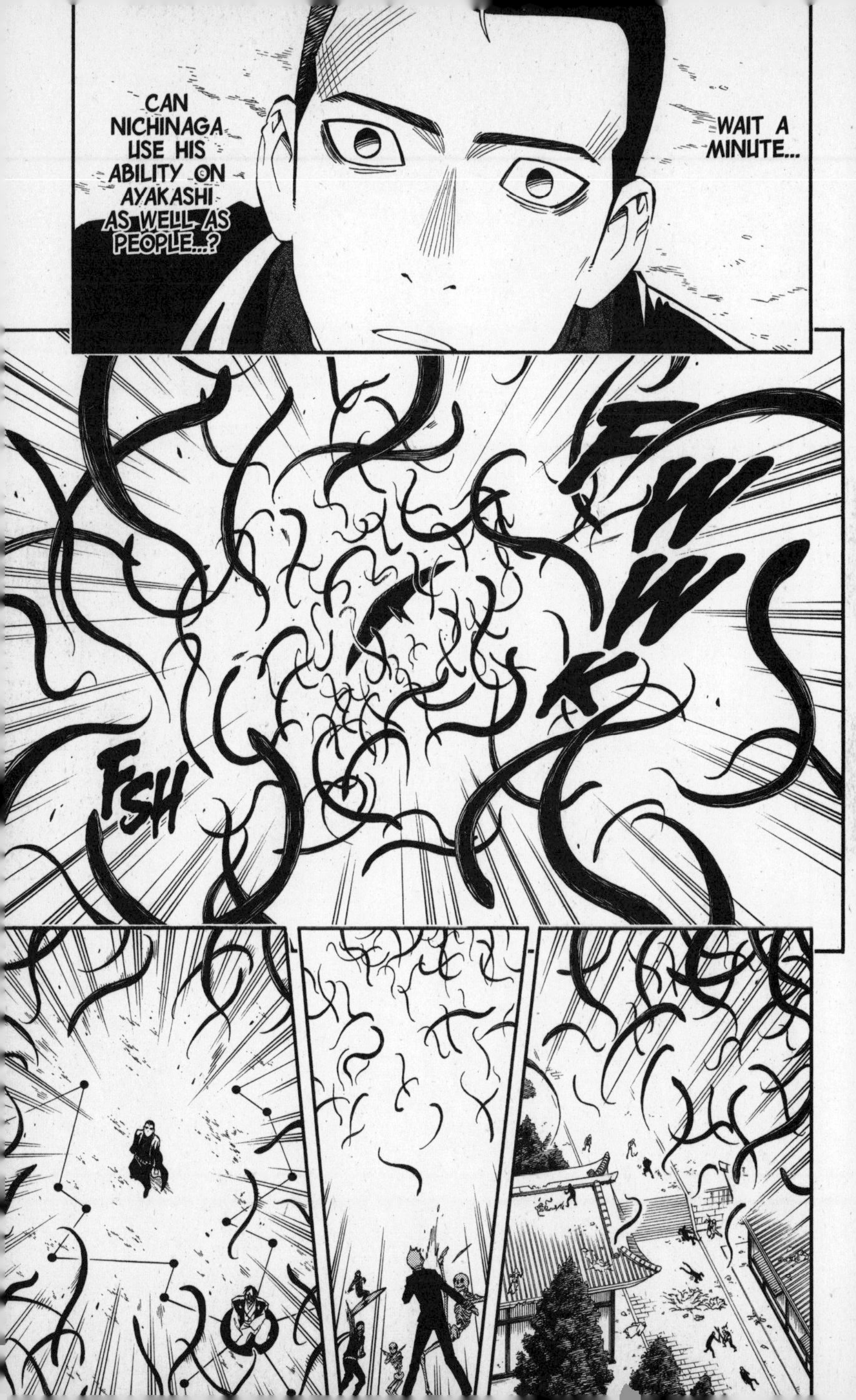
WAIT A MINUTE...
CAN NICHINAGA USE HIS ABILITY ON AYAKASHI AS WELL AS PEOPLE...?
FWWK
FSH

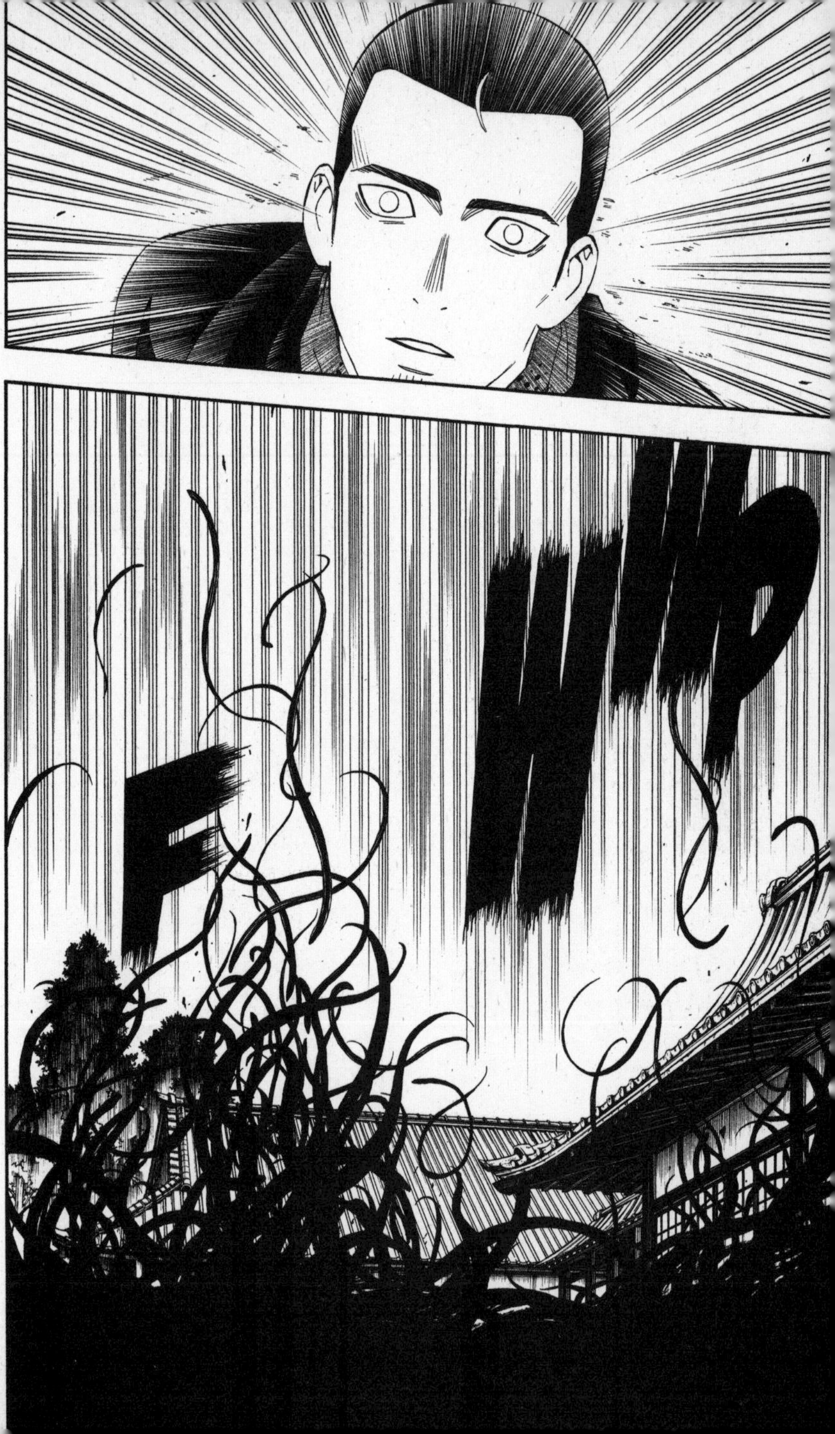
FWIP

CHAPTER 312
UNDERDOG

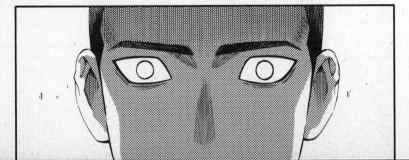

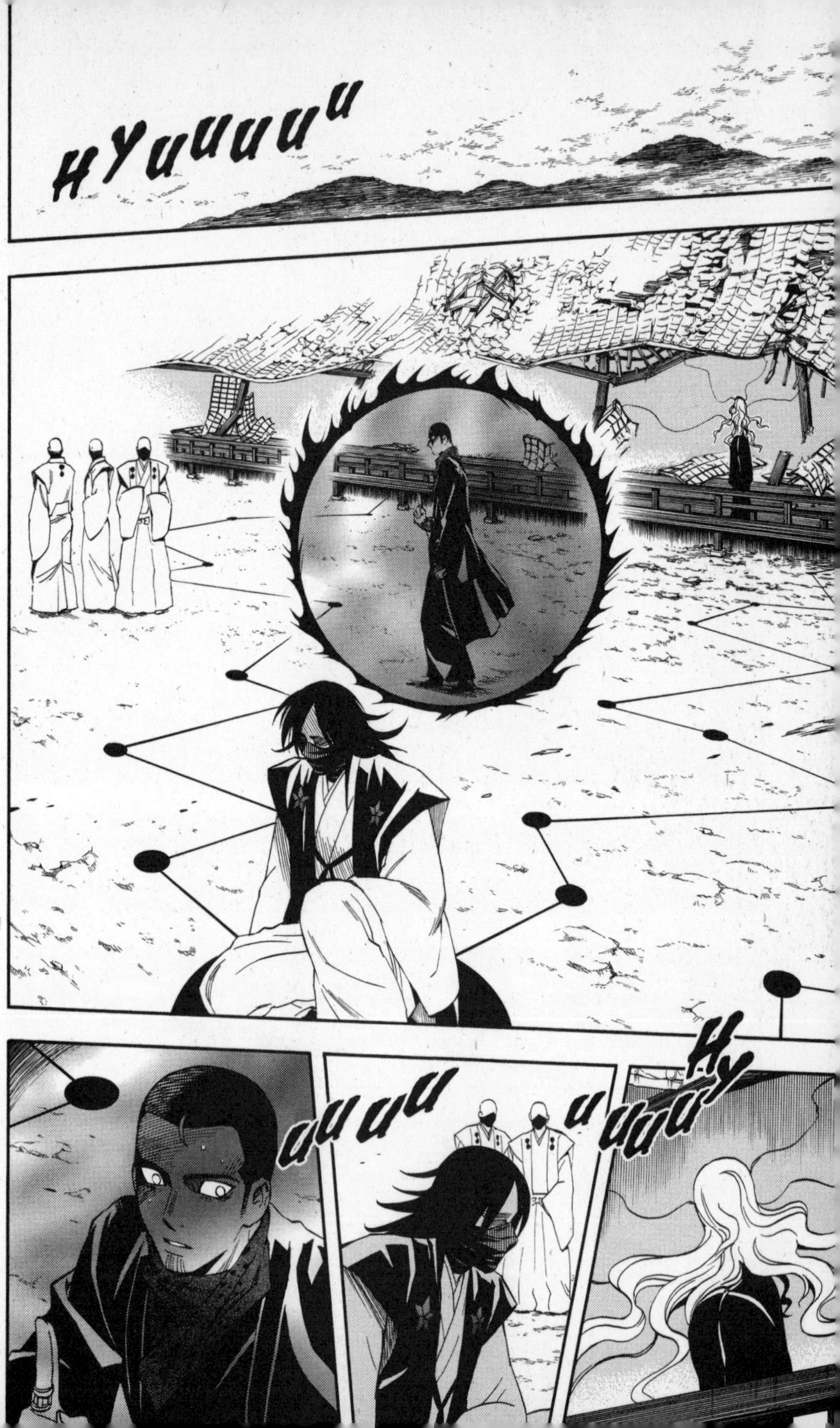
HYUUUUUU
HYUUUUU
UUUUU

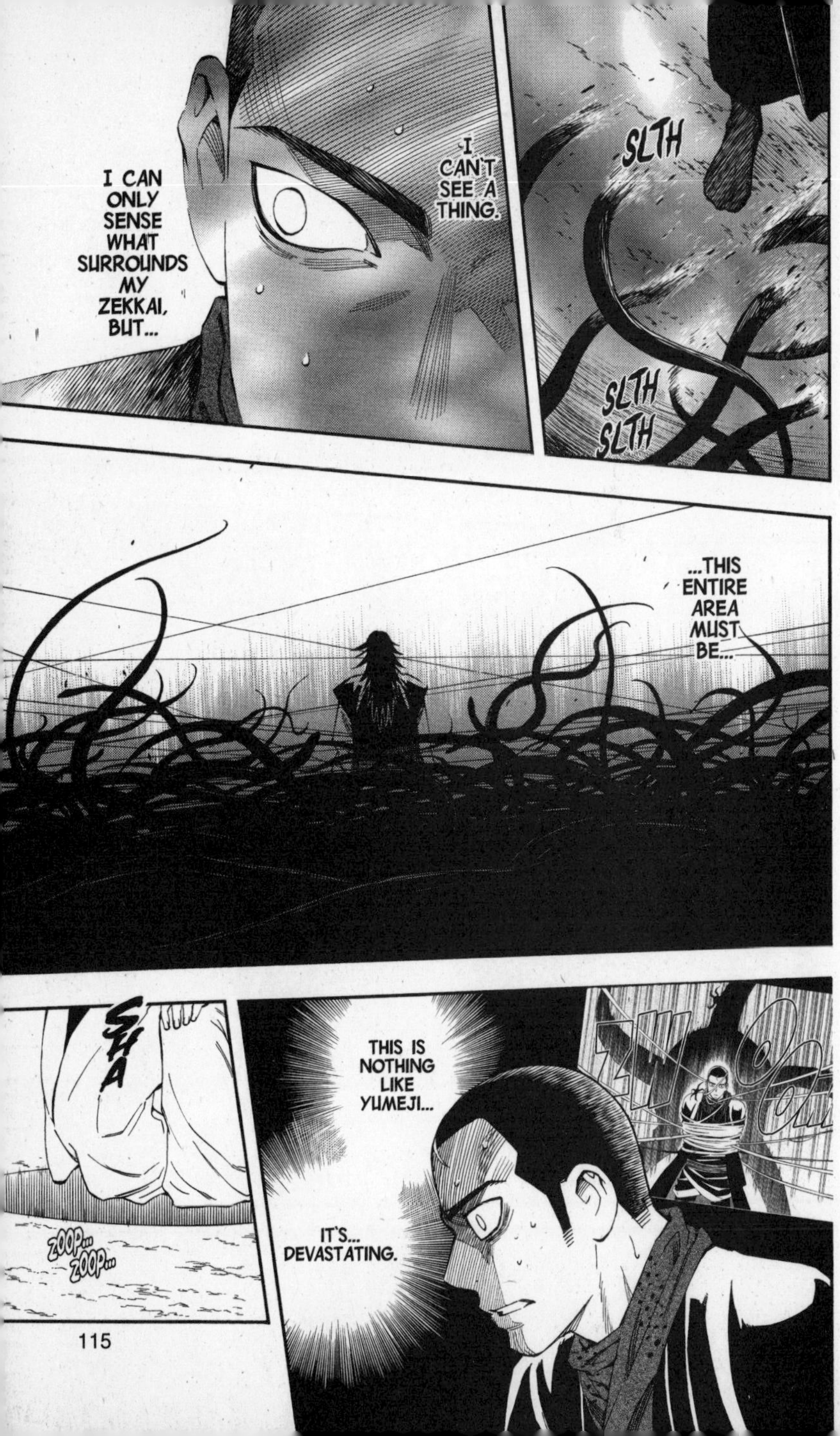
SLTH
SLTH SLTH
I CAN'T SEE A THING.
I CAN ONLY SENSE WHAT SURROUNDS MY ZEKKAI, BUT...
...THIS ENTIRE AREA MUST BE...
THIS IS NOTHING LIKE YUMEJI...
IT'S... DEVASTATING.
SHA
ZOOP... ZOOP...

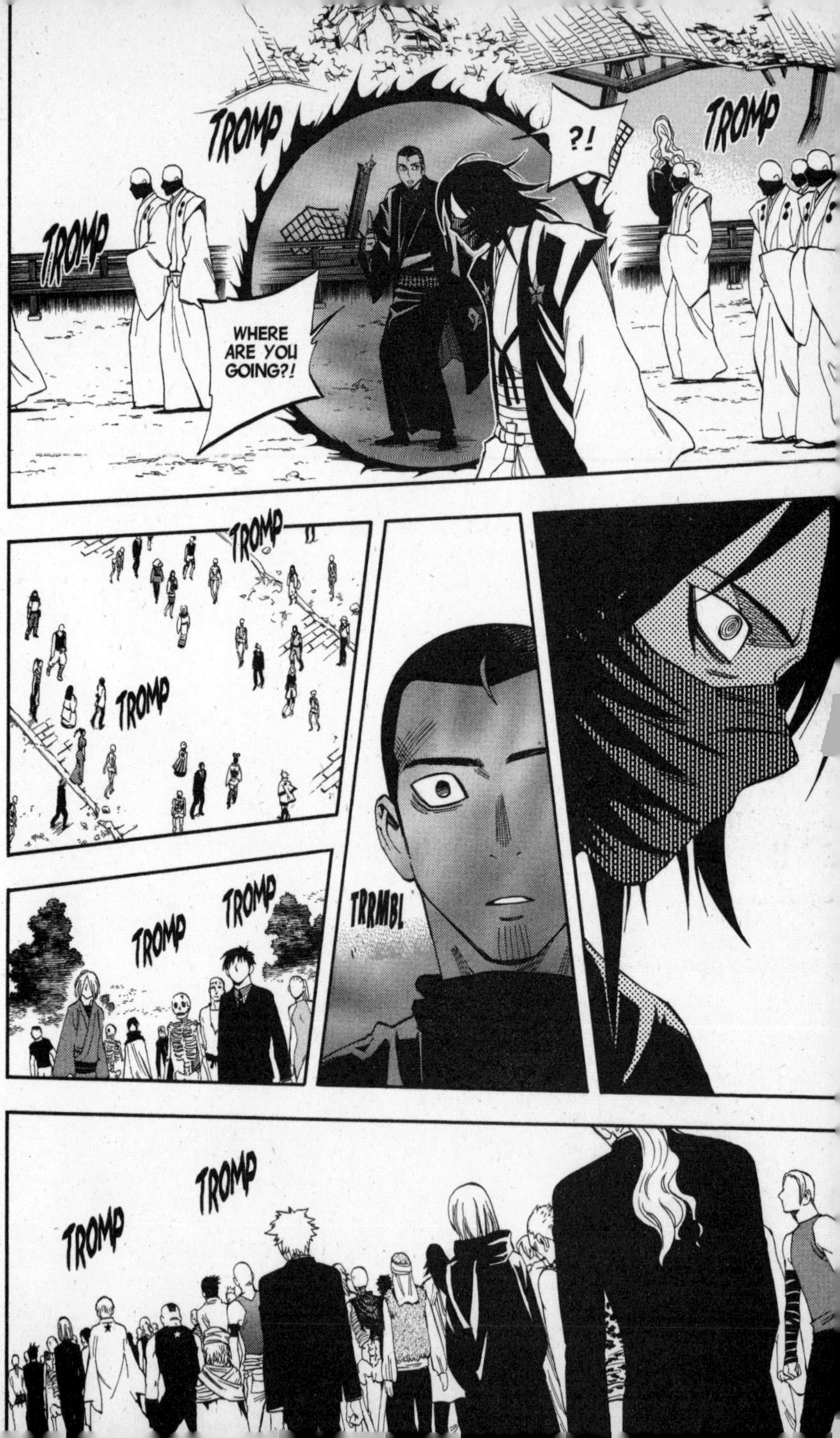
TROMP
?!
TROMP
TROMP
WHERE ARE YOU GOING?!
TRRMBL
TROMP
TROMP
TROMP
TROMP
TROMP
TROMP

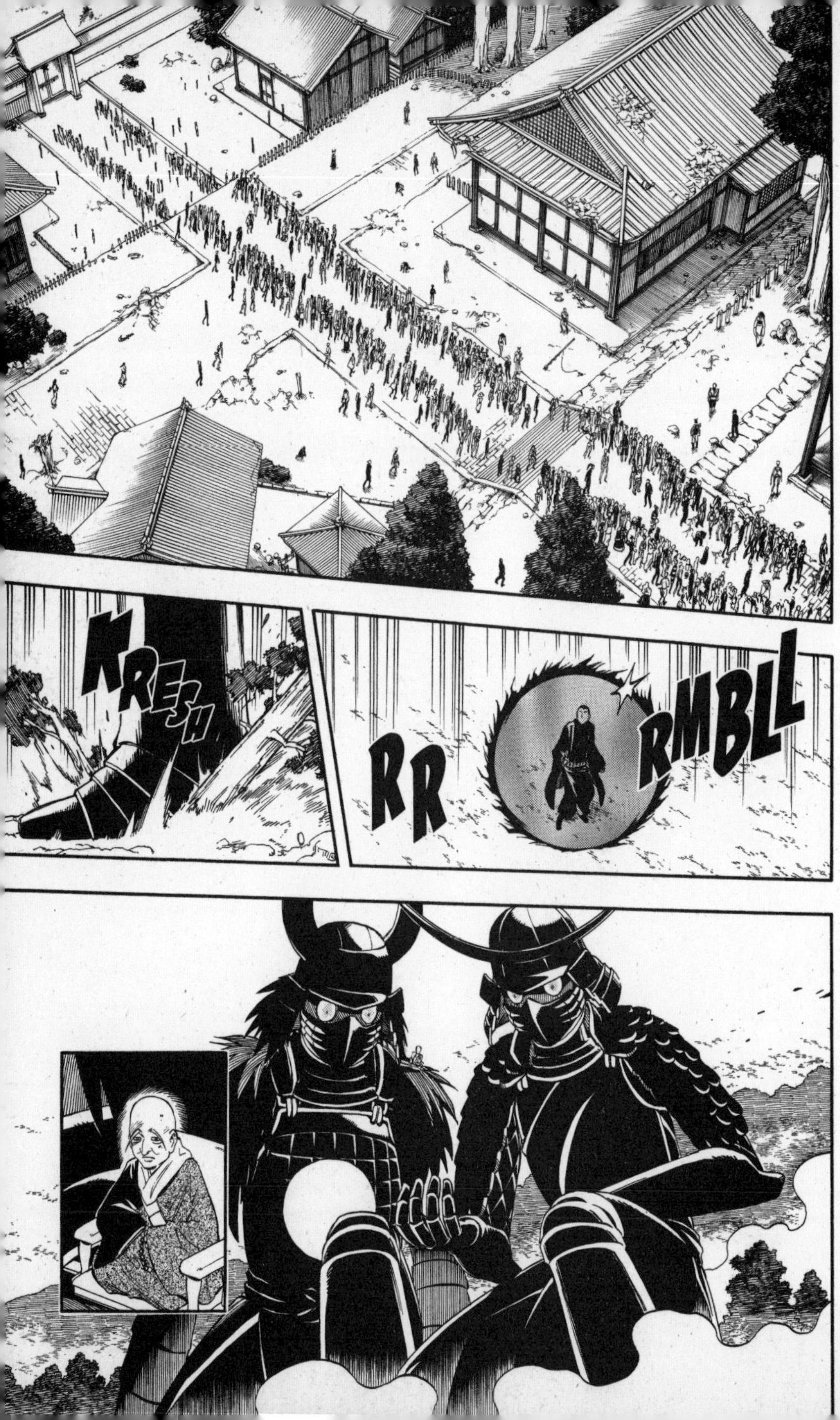
RR
RMBLL
KRESH

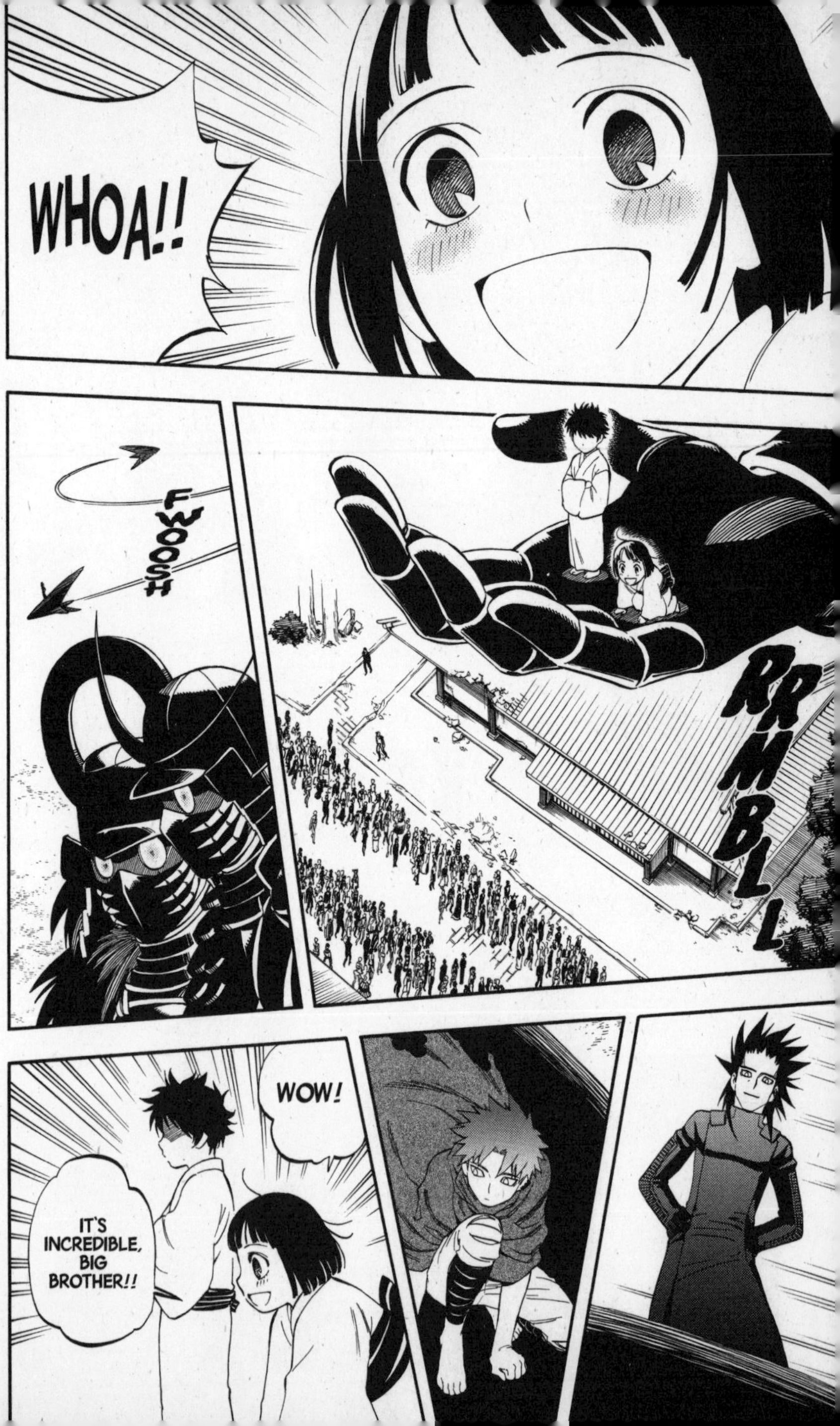
WHOA!!
RRMBLL
FWOOSH
WOW!
IT'S INCREDIBLE, BIG BROTHER!!

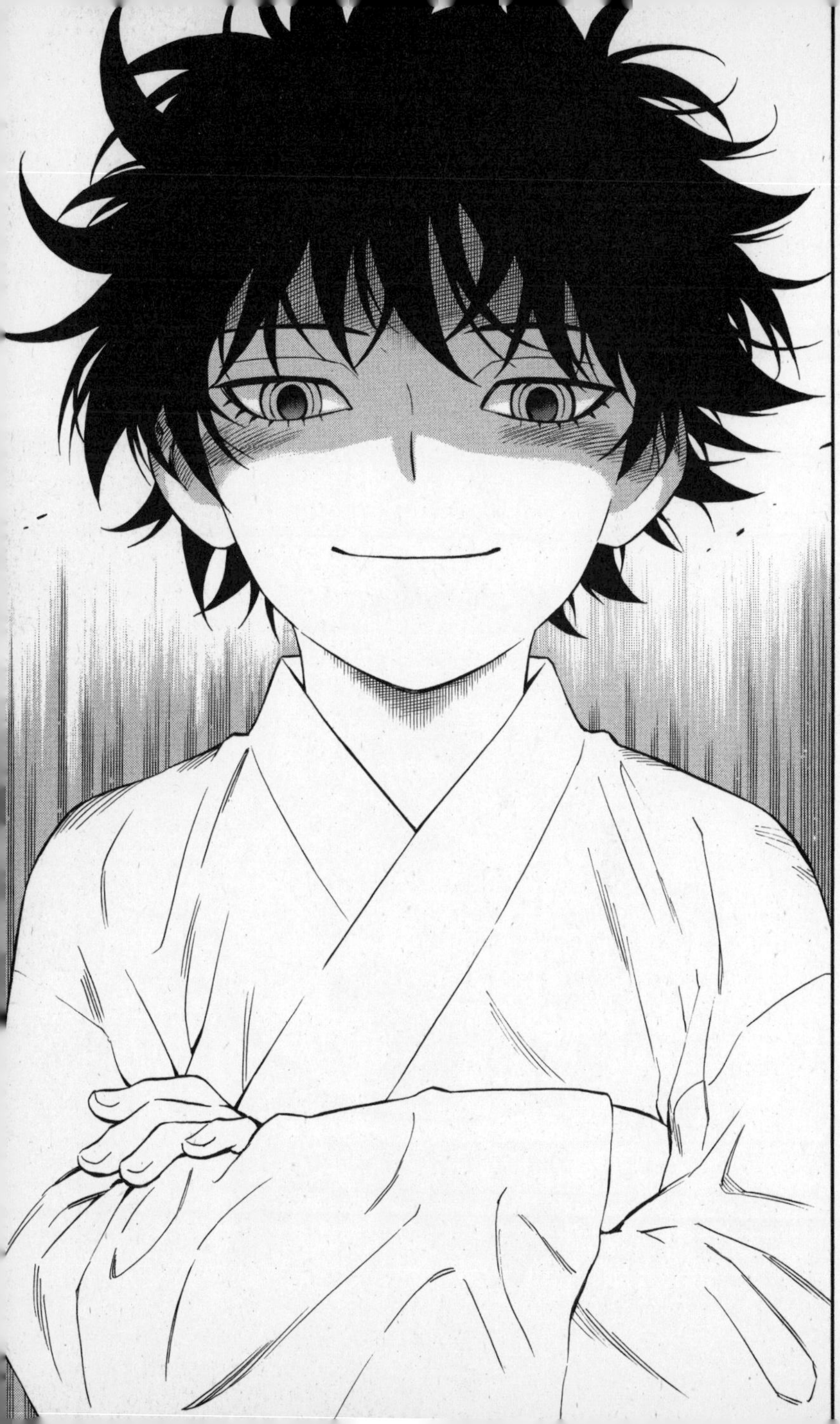

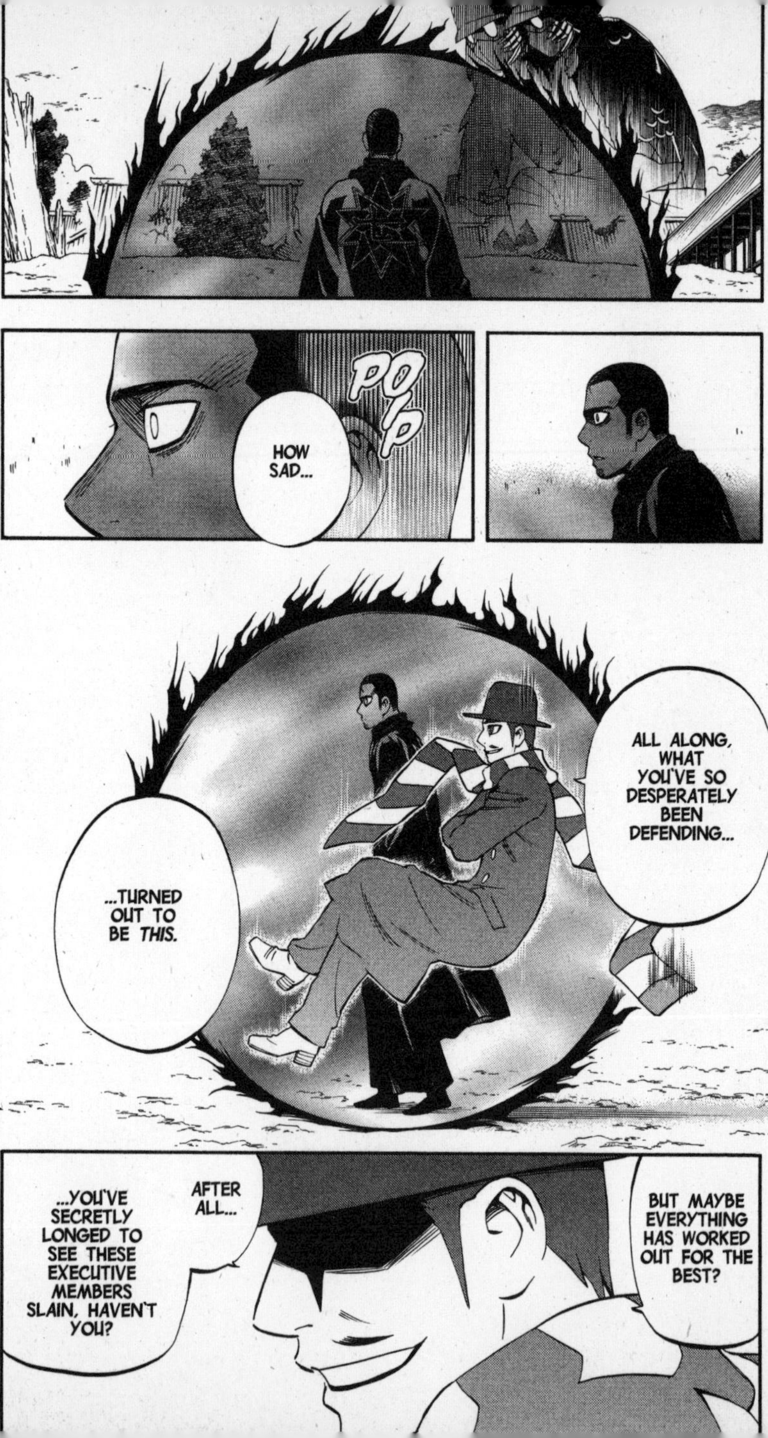
POP
HOW SAD...
ALL ALONG, WHAT YOU'VE SO DESPERATELY BEEN DEFENDING...
...TURNED OUT TO BE *THIS.*
BUT MAYBE EVERYTHING HAS WORKED OUT FOR THE BEST?
AFTER ALL...
...YOU'VE SECRETLY LONGED TO SEE THESE EXECUTIVE MEMBERS SLAIN, HAVEN'T YOU?

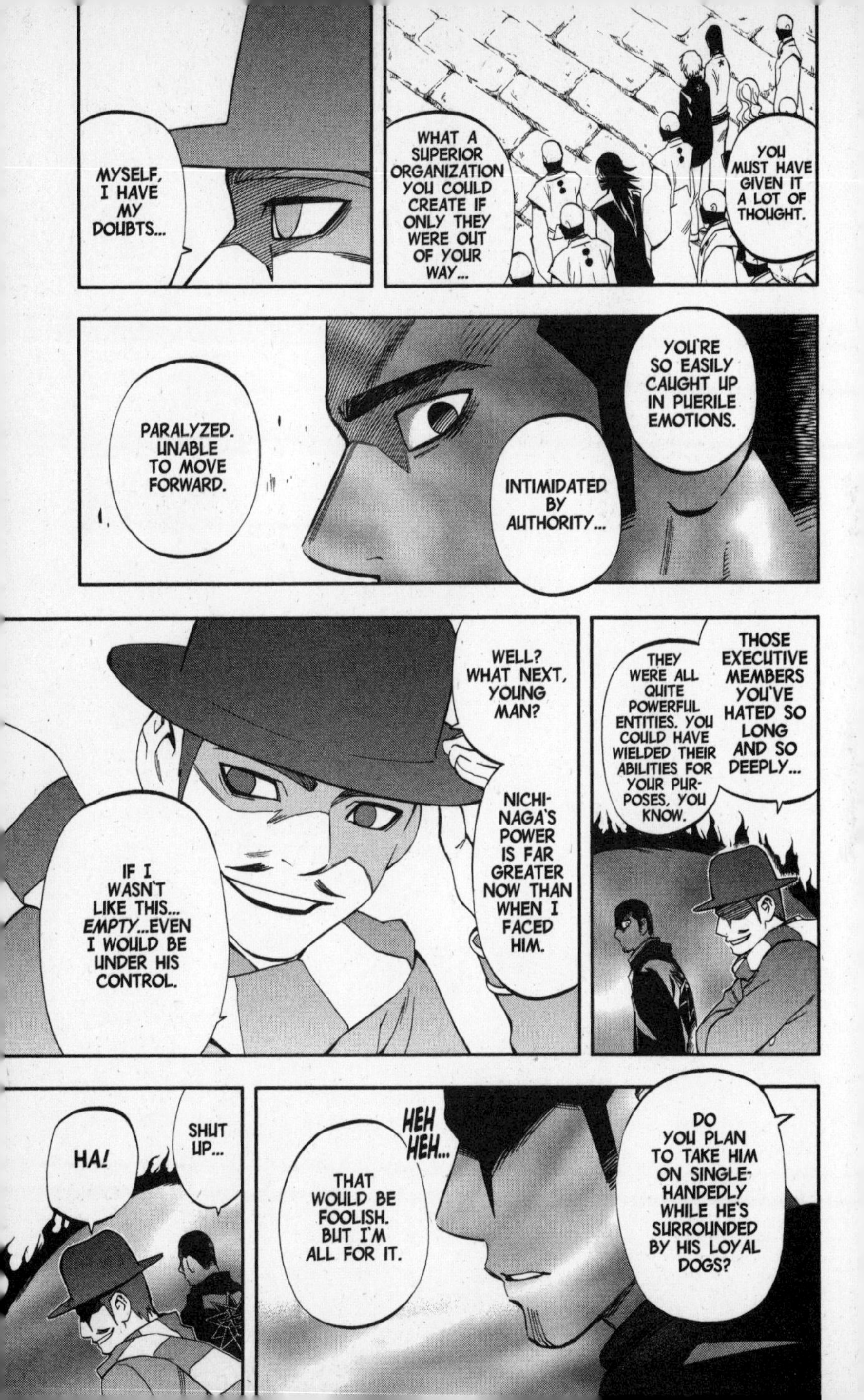
YOU MUST HAVE GIVEN IT A LOT OF THOUGHT.
WHAT A SUPERIOR ORGANIZATION YOU COULD CREATE IF ONLY THEY WERE OUT OF YOUR WAY...
MYSELF, I HAVE MY DOUBTS...
YOU'RE SO EASILY CAUGHT UP IN PUERILE EMOTIONS.
INTIMIDATED BY AUTHORITY...
PARALYZED. UNABLE TO MOVE FORWARD.
THOSE EXECUTIVE MEMBERS YOU'VE HATED SO LONG AND SO DEEPLY...
THEY WERE ALL QUITE POWERFUL ENTITIES. YOU COULD HAVE WIELDED THEIR ABILITIES FOR YOUR PURPOSES, YOU KNOW.
WELL? WHAT NEXT, YOUNG MAN?
NICHINAGA'S POWER IS FAR GREATER NOW THAN WHEN I FACED HIM.
IF I WASN'T LIKE THIS... *EMPTY*...EVEN I WOULD BE UNDER HIS CONTROL.
DO YOU PLAN TO TAKE HIM ON SINGLE-HANDEDLY WHILE HE'S SURROUNDED BY HIS LOYAL DOGS?
HEH HEH...
THAT WOULD BE FOOLISH. BUT I'M ALL FOR IT.
SHUT UP...
HA!

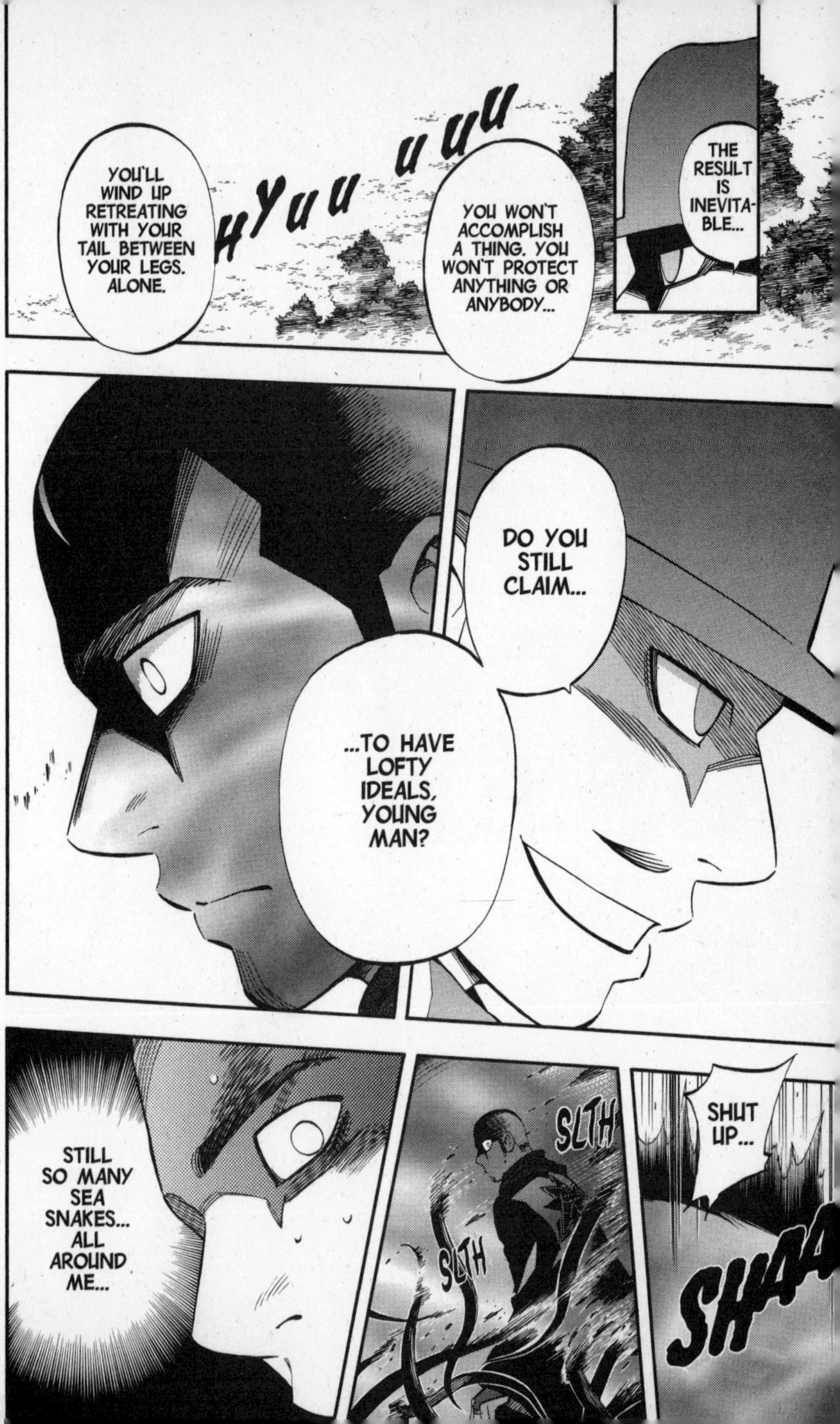

THE RESULT IS INEVITA-BLE...
YOU WON'T ACCOMPLISH A THING. YOU WON'T PROTECT ANYTHING OR ANYBODY...
HYUU UUU
YOU'LL WIND UP RETREATING WITH YOUR TAIL BETWEEN YOUR LEGS. ALONE.
DO YOU STILL CLAIM...
...TO HAVE LOFTY IDEALS, YOUNG MAN?
SHUT UP...
SHAA
SLTH
SLTH
STILL SO MANY SEA SNAKES... ALL AROUND ME...

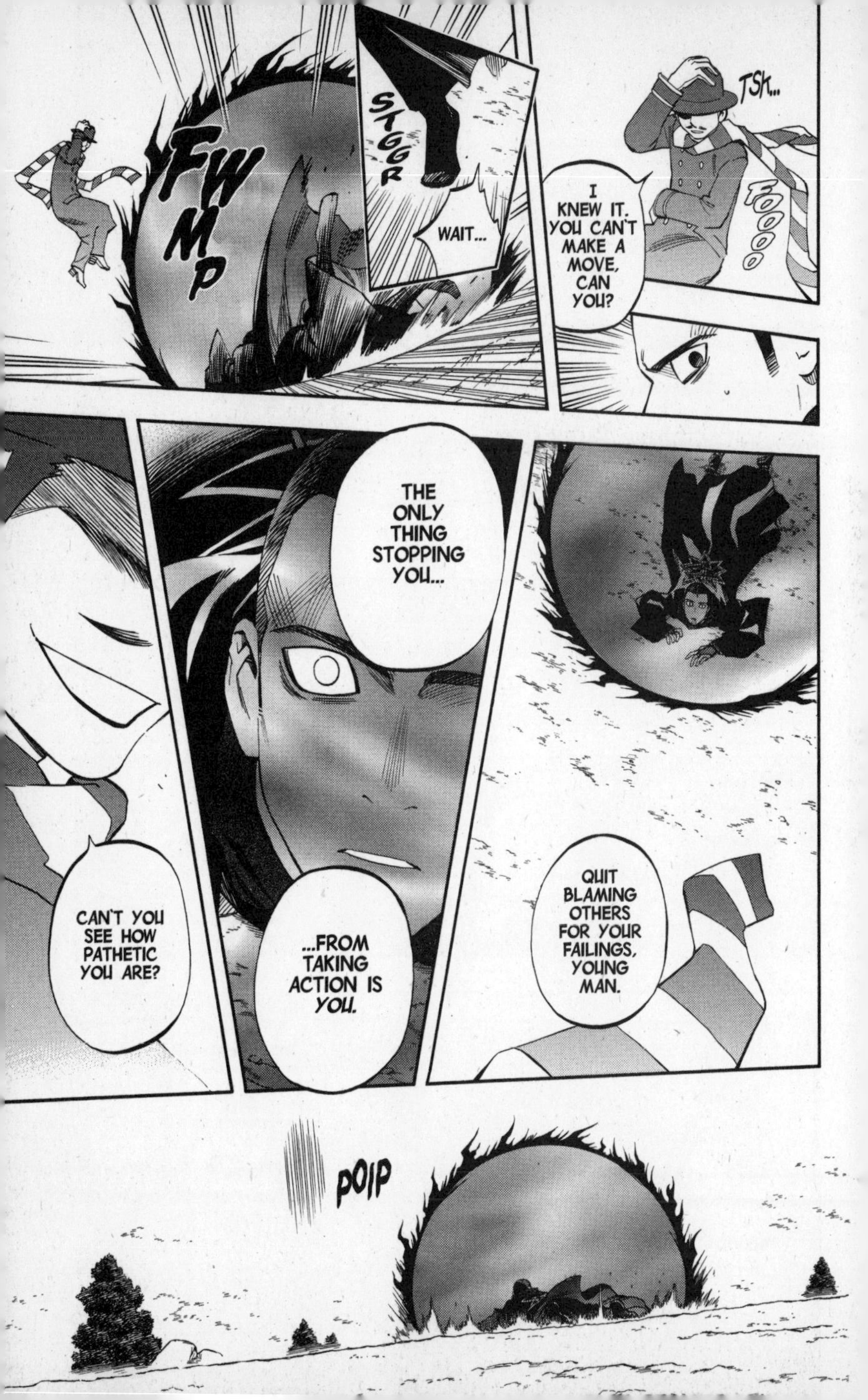
TSK...
FOOOO
I KNEW IT. YOU CAN'T MAKE A MOVE, CAN YOU?
STGGR
WAIT...
FWMP
QUIT BLAMING OTHERS FOR YOUR FAILINGS, YOUNG MAN.
THE ONLY THING STOPPING YOU...
...FROM TAKING ACTION IS YOU.
CAN'T YOU SEE HOW PATHETIC YOU ARE?
POIP

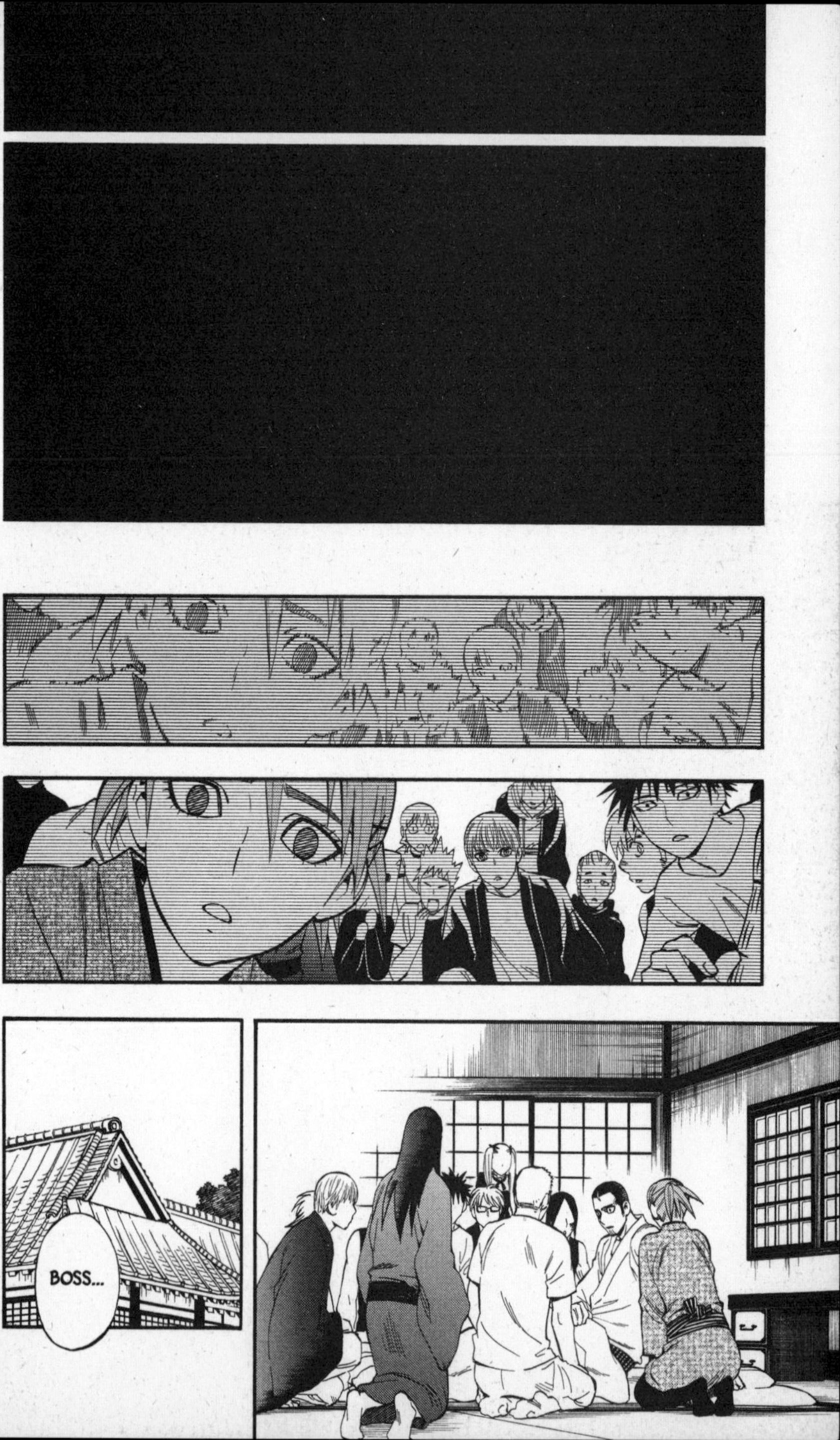
BOSS...

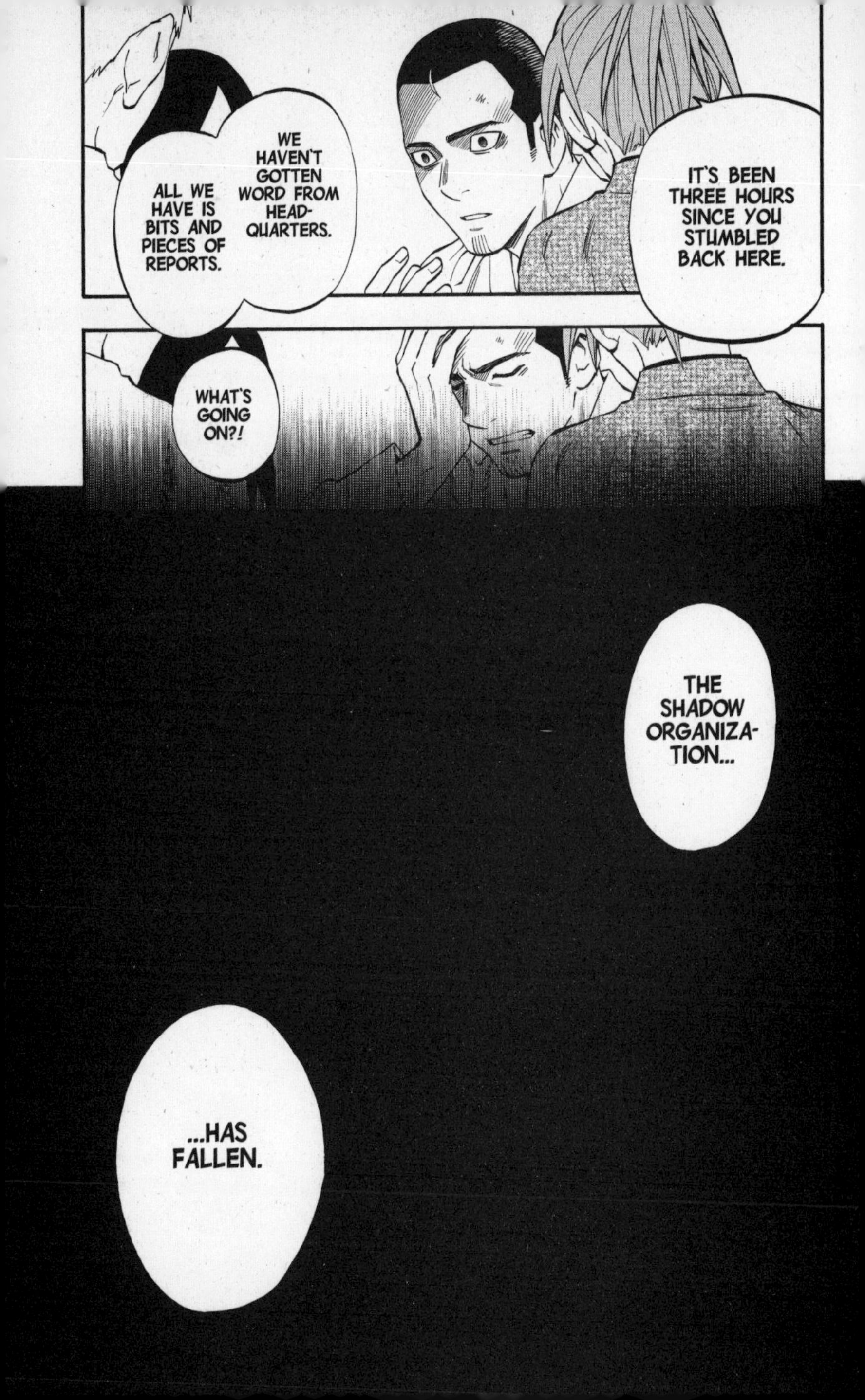
IT'S BEEN THREE HOURS SINCE YOU STUMBLED BACK HERE.
WE HAVEN'T GOTTEN WORD FROM HEAD-QUARTERS.
ALL WE HAVE IS BITS AND PIECES OF REPORTS.
WHAT'S GOING ON?!
THE SHADOW ORGANIZA-TION...
...HAS FALLEN.

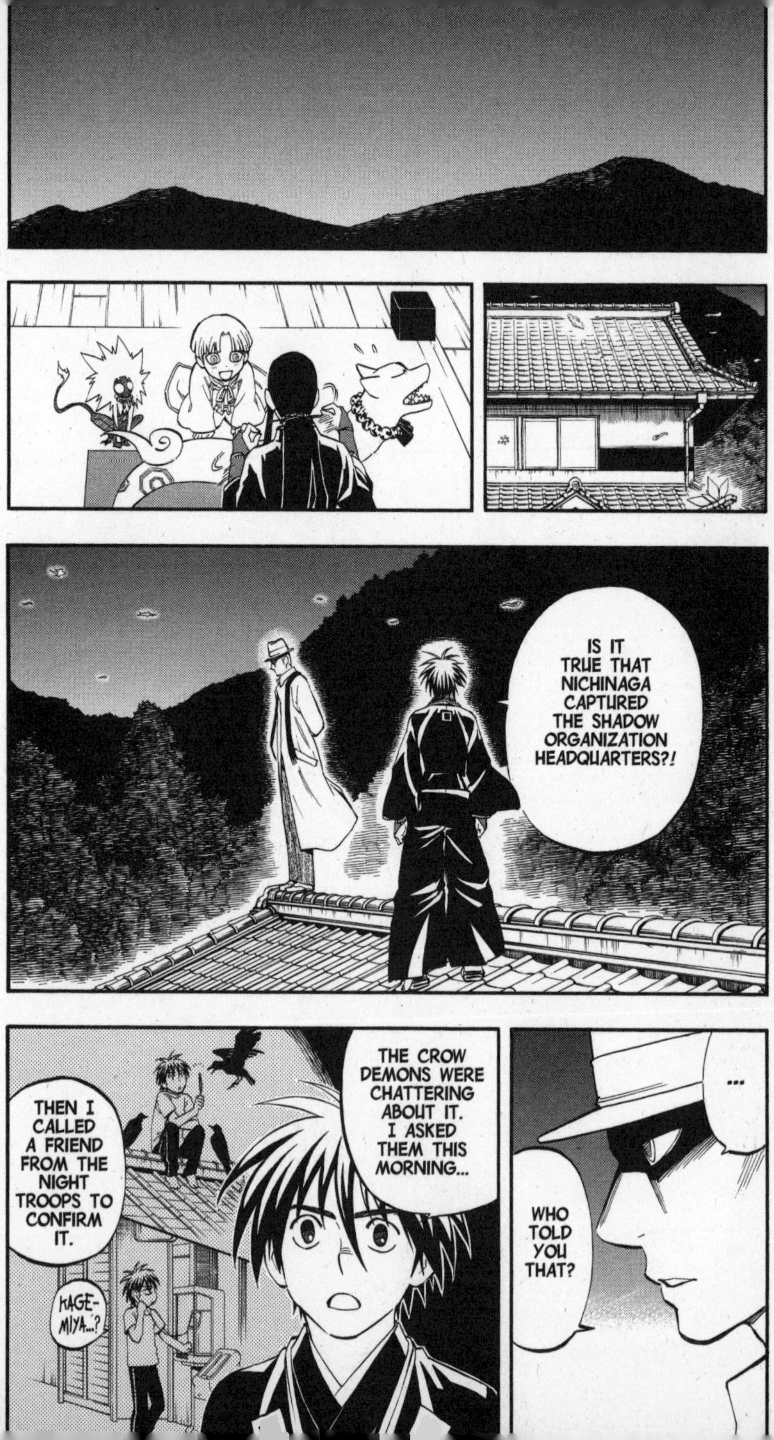
IS IT TRUE THAT NICHINAGA CAPTURED THE SHADOW ORGANIZATION HEADQUARTERS?!
...
WHO TOLD YOU THAT?
THE CROW DEMONS WERE CHATTERING ABOUT IT. I ASKED THEM THIS MORNING...
THEN I CALLED A FRIEND FROM THE NIGHT TROOPS TO CONFIRM IT.
KAGE-MIYA...?

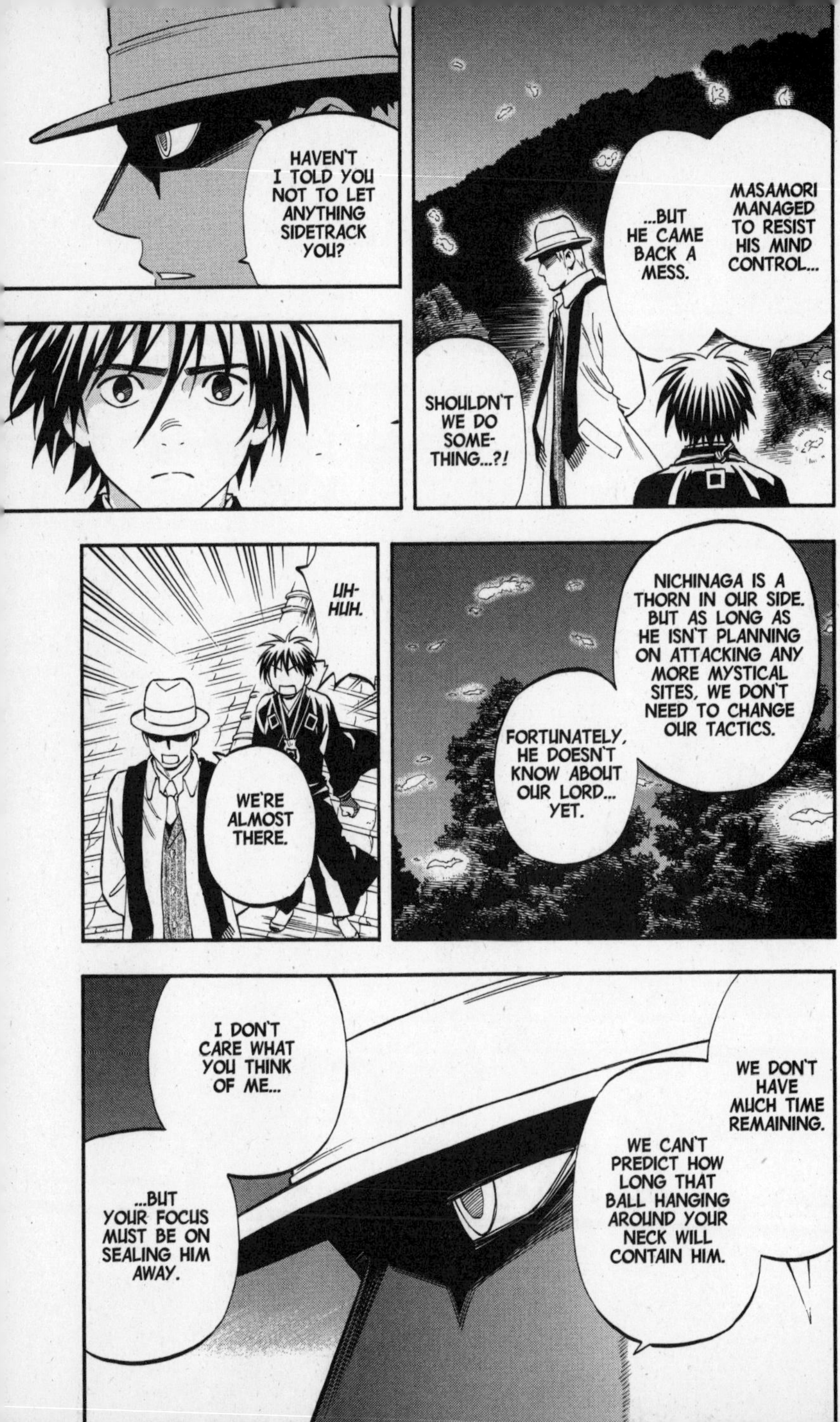
MASAMORI MANAGED TO RESIST HIS MIND CONTROL...
...BUT HE CAME BACK A MESS.
SHOULDN'T WE DO SOME-THING...?!
HAVEN'T I TOLD YOU NOT TO LET ANYTHING SIDETRACK YOU?
NICHINAGA IS A THORN IN OUR SIDE. BUT AS LONG AS HE ISN'T PLANNING ON ATTACKING ANY MORE MYSTICAL SITES, WE DON'T NEED TO CHANGE OUR TACTICS.
FORTUNATELY, HE DOESN'T KNOW ABOUT OUR LORD... YET.
UH-HUH.
WE'RE ALMOST THERE.
WE DON'T HAVE MUCH TIME REMAINING.
WE CAN'T PREDICT HOW LONG THAT BALL HANGING AROUND YOUR NECK WILL CONTAIN HIM.
I DON'T CARE WHAT YOU THINK OF ME...
...BUT YOUR FOCUS MUST BE ON SEALING HIM AWAY.

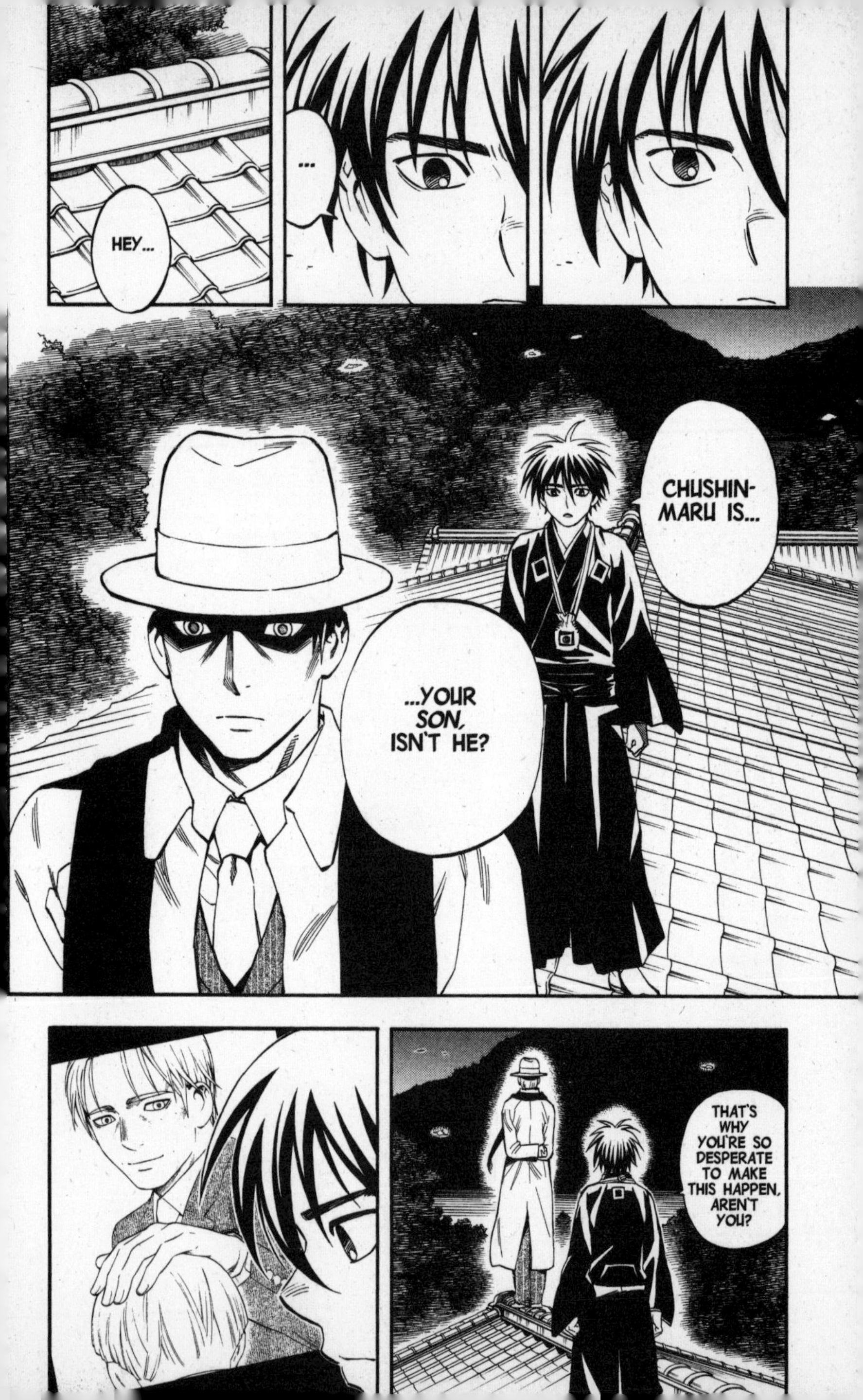
...
HEY...
CHUSHIN-MARU IS...
...YOUR SON, ISN'T HE?
THAT'S WHY YOU'RE SO DESPERATE TO MAKE THIS HAPPEN, AREN'T YOU?

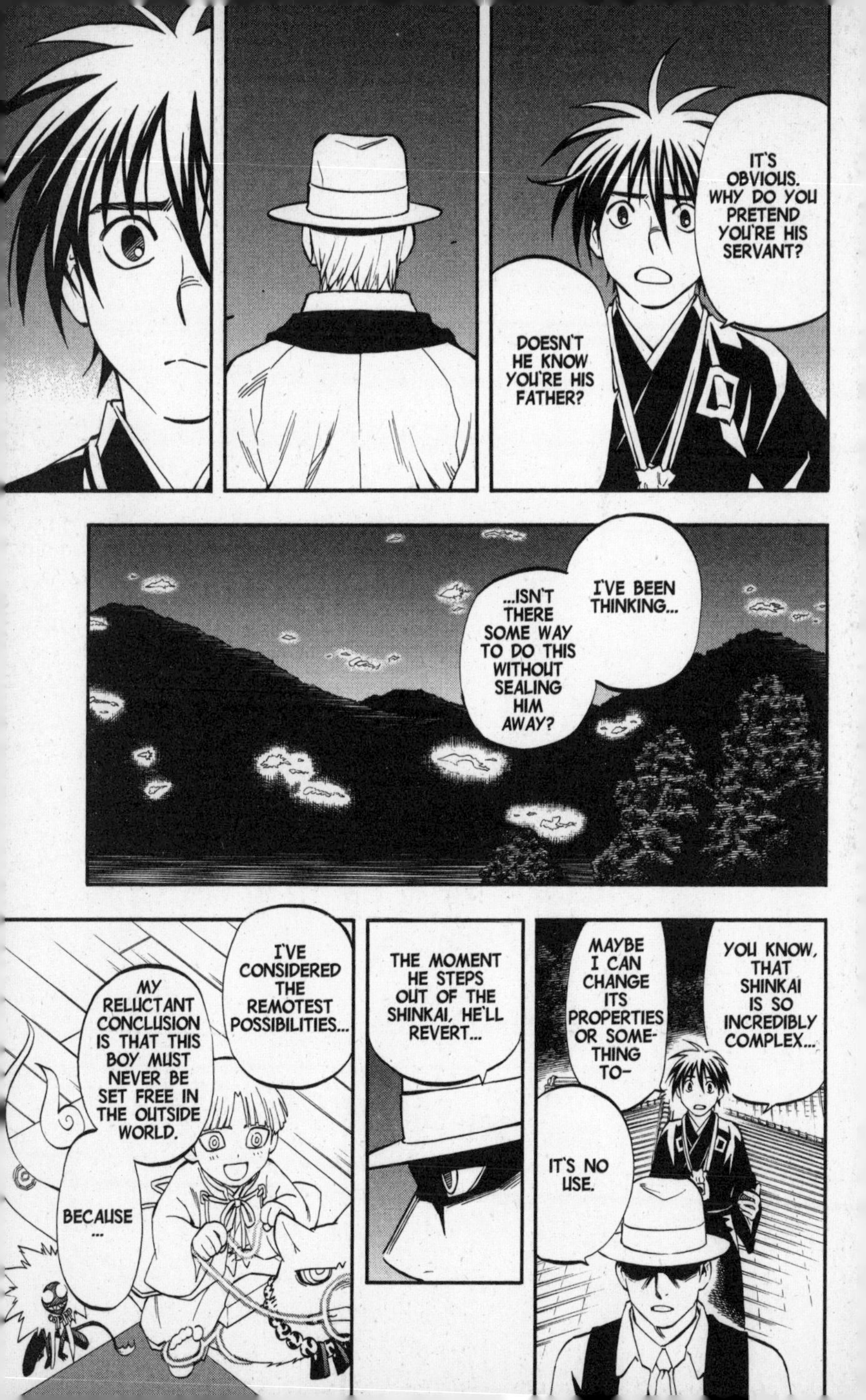

IT'S OBVIOUS. WHY DO YOU PRETEND YOU'RE HIS SERVANT?
DOESN'T HE KNOW YOU'RE HIS FATHER?
I'VE BEEN THINKING...
...ISN'T THERE SOME WAY TO DO THIS WITHOUT SEALING HIM AWAY?
YOU KNOW, THAT SHINKAI IS SO INCREDIBLY COMPLEX...
MAYBE I CAN CHANGE ITS PROPERTIES OR SOME-THING TO-
IT'S NO USE.
THE MOMENT HE STEPS OUT OF THE SHINKAI, HE'LL REVERT...
I'VE CONSIDERED THE REMOTEST POSSIBILITIES...
MY RELUCTANT CONCLUSION IS THAT THIS BOY MUST NEVER BE SET FREE IN THE OUTSIDE WORLD.
BECAUSE ...

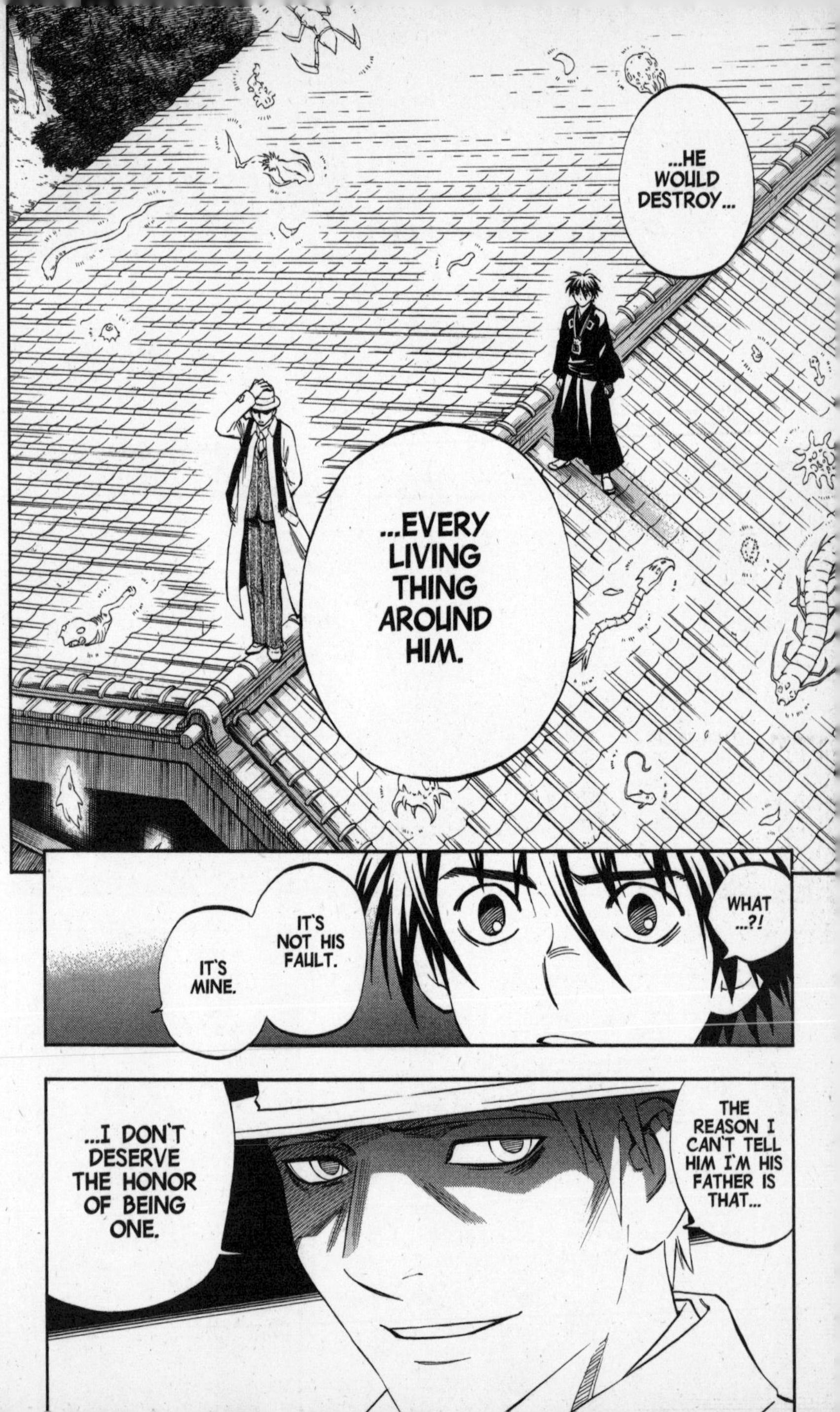
...HE WOULD DESTROY...
...EVERY LIVING THING AROUND HIM.
WHAT ...?!
IT'S NOT HIS FAULT.
IT'S MINE.
THE REASON I CAN'T TELL HIM I'M HIS FATHER IS THAT...
...I DON'T DESERVE THE HONOR OF BEING ONE.

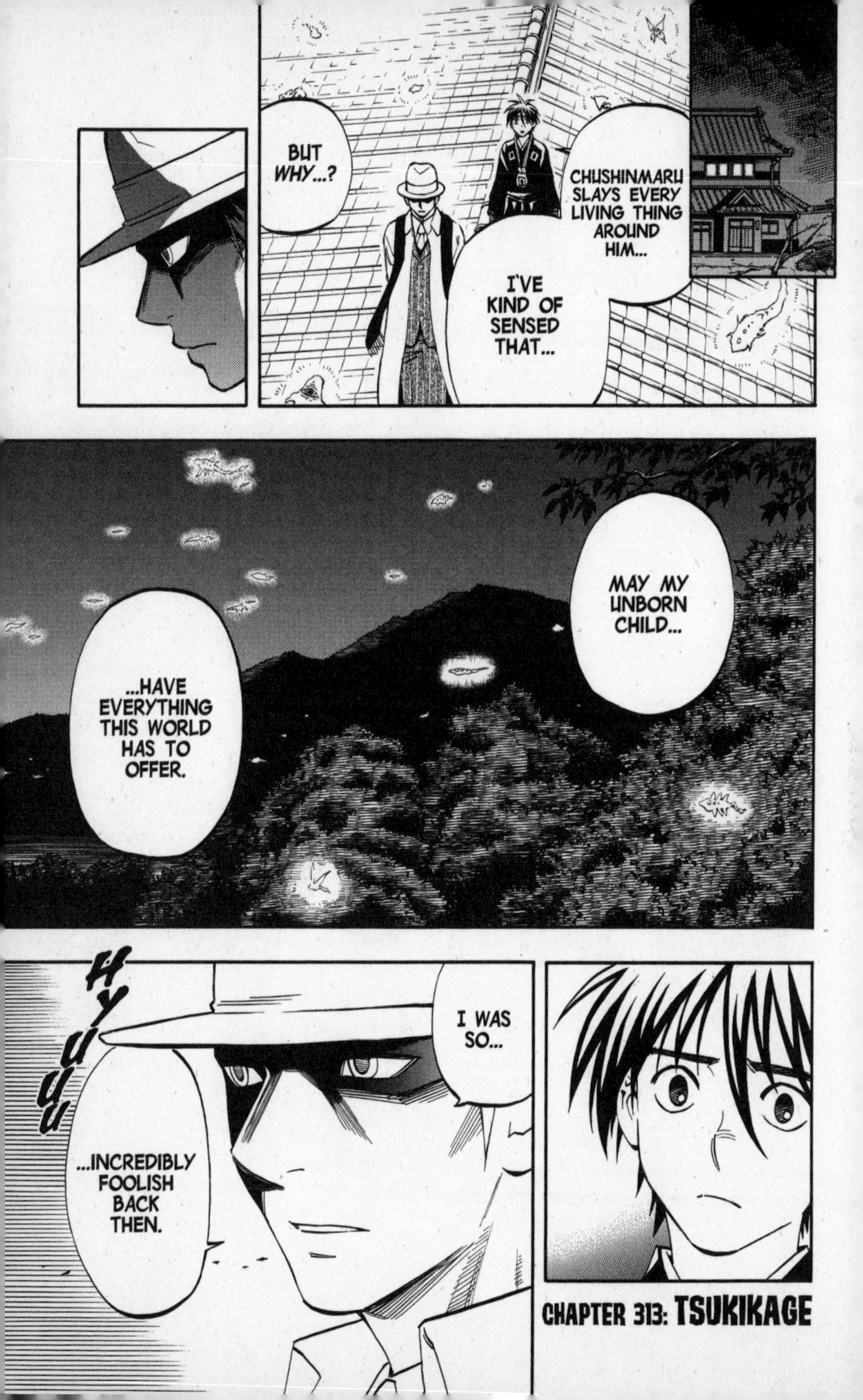
CHUSHINMARU SLAYS EVERY LIVING THING AROUND HIM...
I'VE KIND OF SENSED THAT...
BUT WHY...?
MAY MY UNBORN CHILD...
...HAVE EVERYTHING THIS WORLD HAS TO OFFER.
I WAS SO...
...INCREDIBLY FOOLISH BACK THEN.
HYUUUU

CHAPTER 313: TSUKIKAGE

Tsukikage

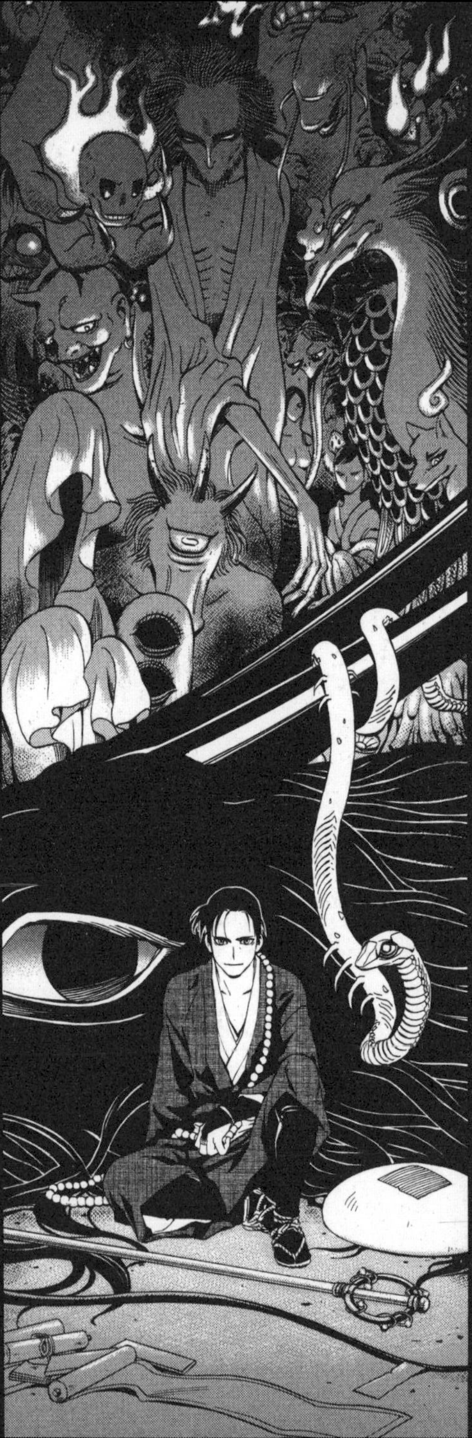

Chapter 313

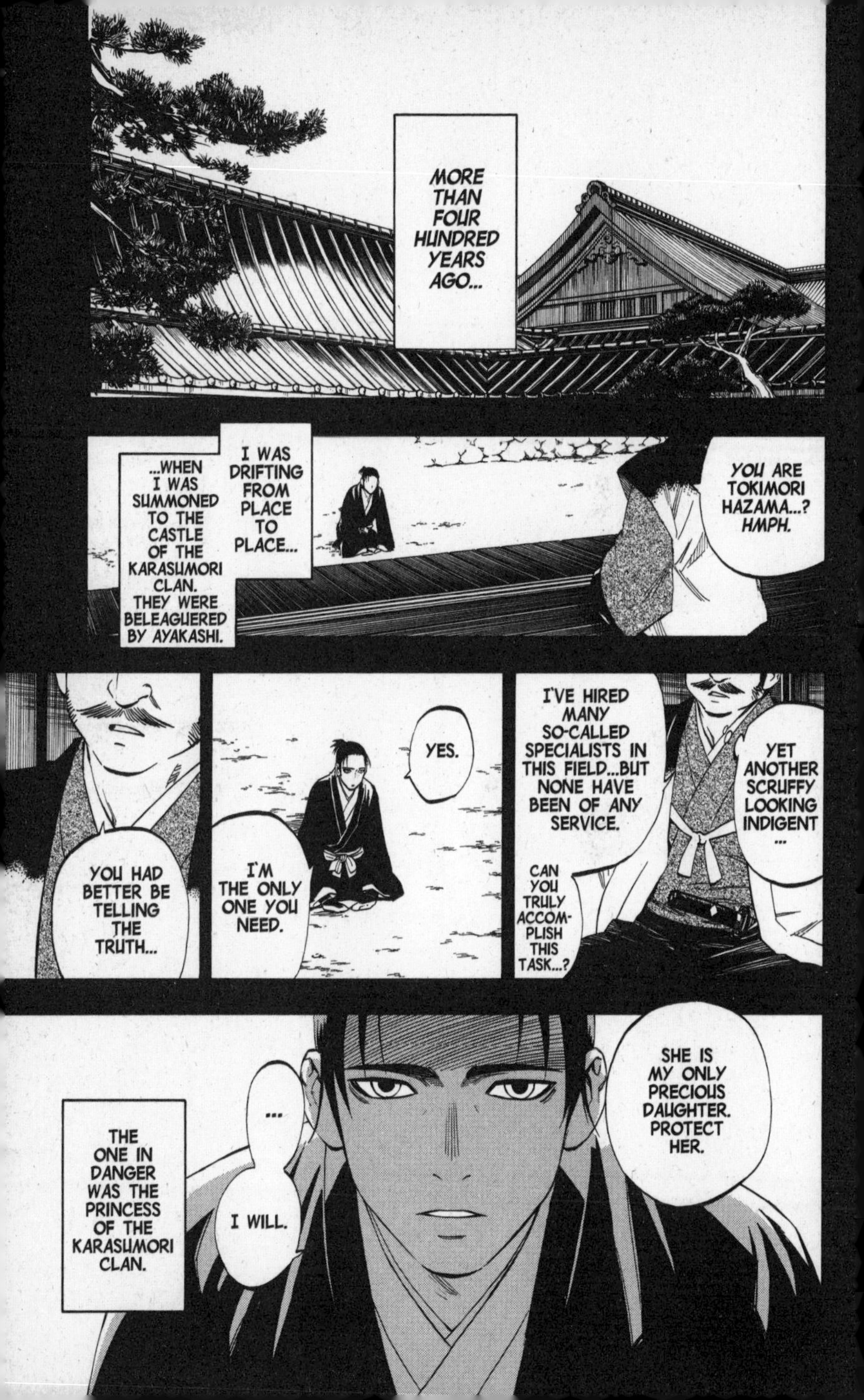
MORE THAN FOUR HUNDRED YEARS AGO...
YOU ARE TOKIMORI HAZAMA...? HMPH.
I WAS DRIFTING FROM PLACE TO PLACE...
...WHEN I WAS SUMMONED TO THE CASTLE OF THE KARASUMORI CLAN. THEY WERE BELEAGUERED BY AYAKASHI.
YET ANOTHER SCRUFFY LOOKING INDIGENT ...
I'VE HIRED MANY SO-CALLED SPECIALISTS IN THIS FIELD...BUT NONE HAVE BEEN OF ANY SERVICE.
CAN YOU TRULY ACCOMPLISH THIS TASK...?
YES.
I'M THE ONLY ONE YOU NEED.
YOU HAD BETTER BE TELLING THE TRUTH...
SHE IS MY ONLY PRECIOUS DAUGHTER. PROTECT HER.
...
I WILL.
THE ONE IN DANGER WAS THE PRINCESS OF THE KARASUMORI CLAN.

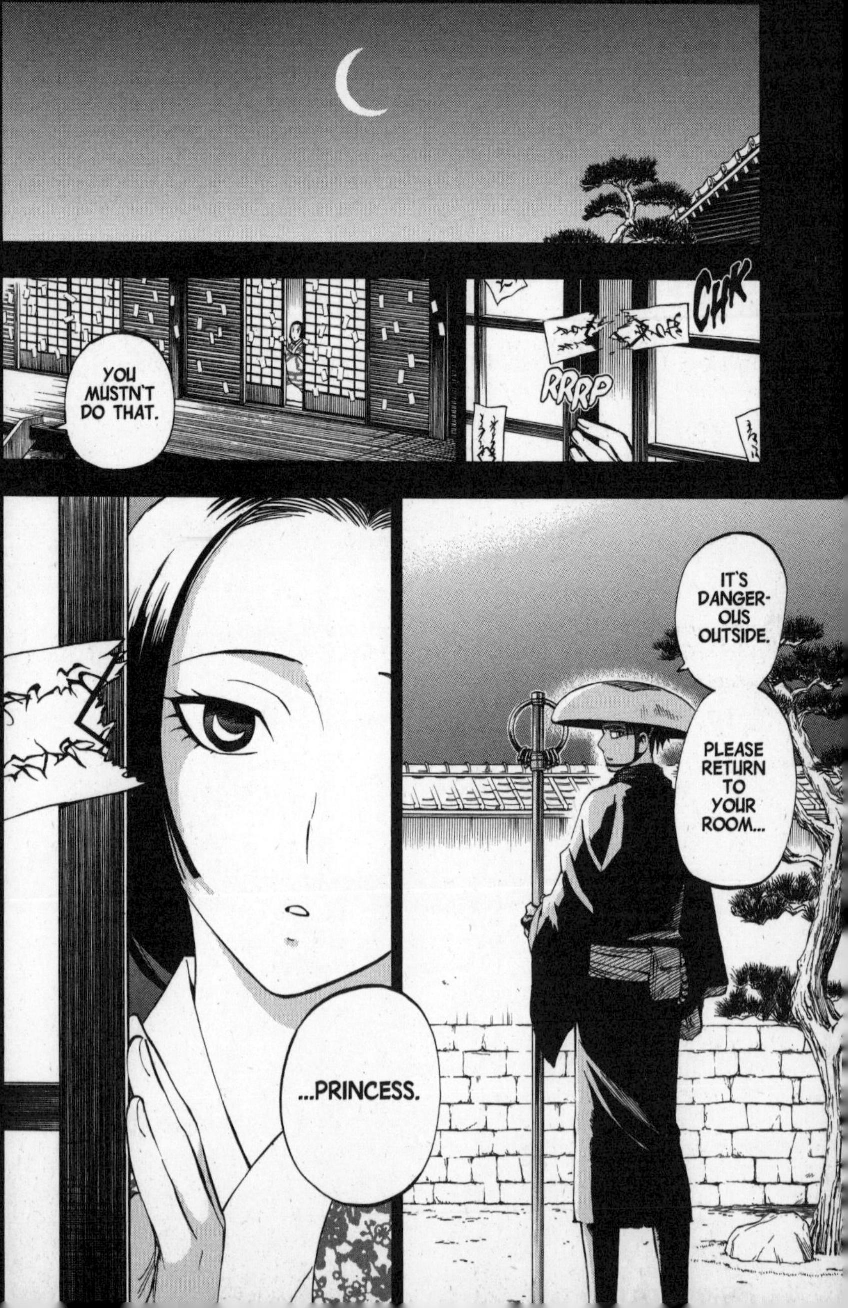
CHK
RRRP
YOU MUSTN'T DO THAT.
IT'S DANGER-OUS OUTSIDE.
PLEASE RETURN TO YOUR ROOM...
...PRINCESS.

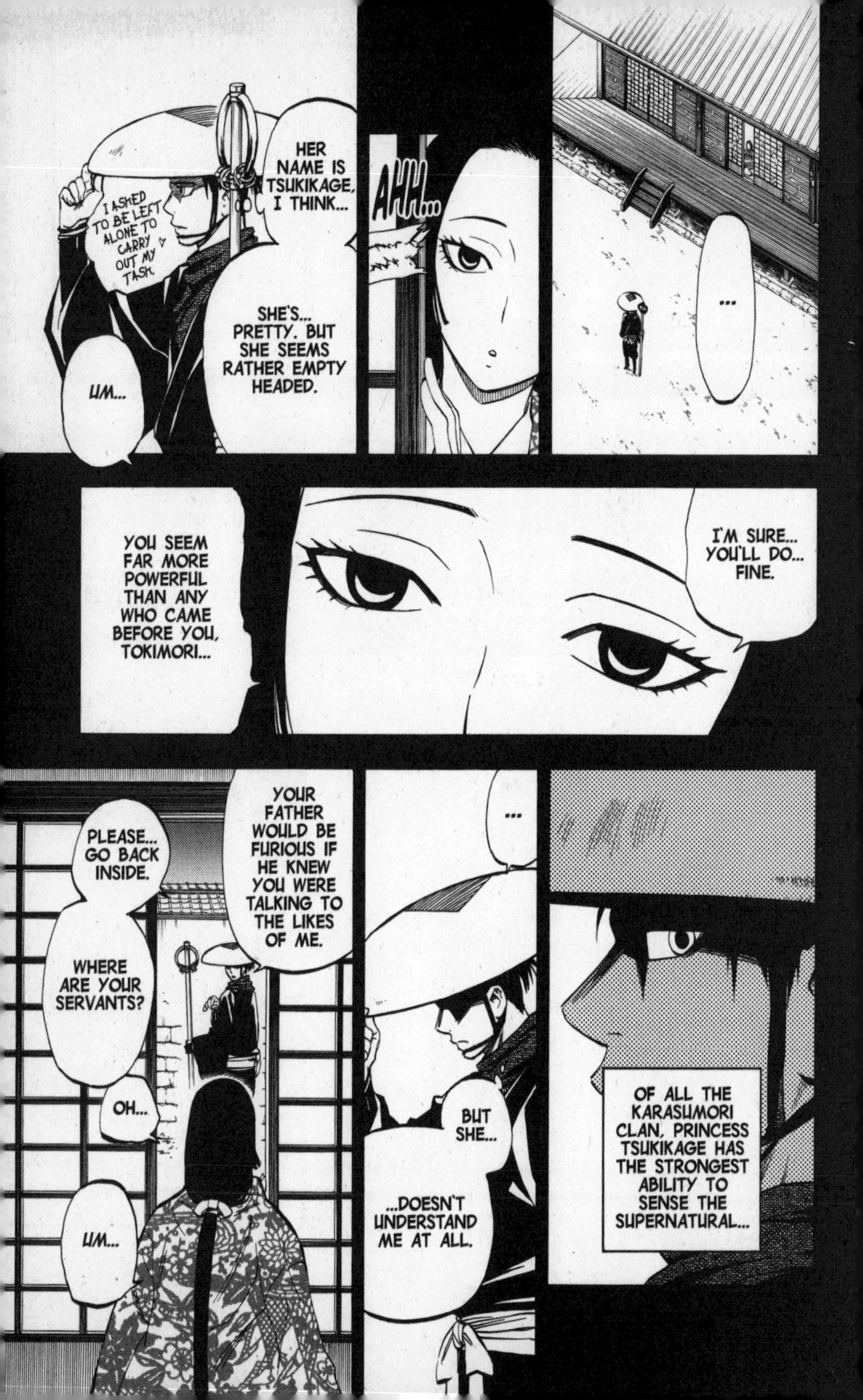
...
AHH...
HER NAME IS TSUKIKAGE, I THINK...
I ASKED TO BE LEFT ALONE TO CARRY OUT MY TASK.
SHE'S... PRETTY. BUT SHE SEEMS RATHER EMPTY HEADED.
UM...
I'M SURE... YOU'LL DO... FINE.
YOU SEEM FAR MORE POWERFUL THAN ANY WHO CAME BEFORE YOU, TOKIMORI...
OF ALL THE KARASUMORI CLAN, PRINCESS TSUKIKAGE HAS THE STRONGEST ABILITY TO SENSE THE SUPERNATURAL...
...
BUT SHE...
...DOESN'T UNDERSTAND ME AT ALL.
YOUR FATHER WOULD BE FURIOUS IF HE KNEW YOU WERE TALKING TO THE LIKES OF ME.
PLEASE... GO BACK INSIDE.
WHERE ARE YOUR SERVANTS?
OH...
UM...

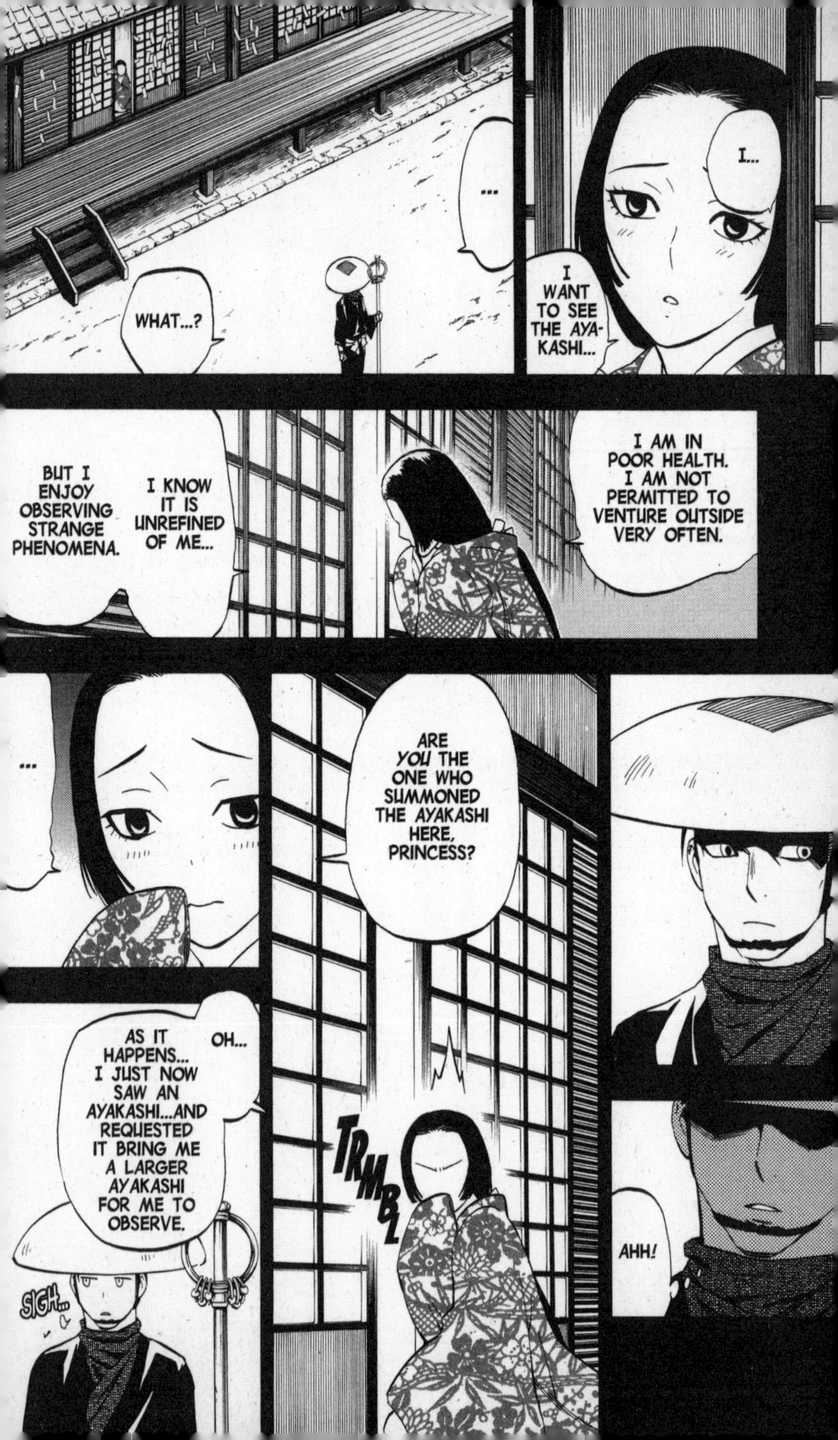
I...
I WANT TO SEE THE AYA-KASHI...
...
WHAT...?
I AM IN POOR HEALTH. I AM NOT PERMITTED TO VENTURE OUTSIDE VERY OFTEN.
I KNOW IT IS UNREFINED OF ME...
BUT I ENJOY OBSERVING STRANGE PHENOMENA.
AHH!
ARE YOU THE ONE WHO SUMMONED THE AYAKASHI HERE, PRINCESS?
TRMBL
...
OH...
AS IT HAPPENS... I JUST NOW SAW AN AYAKASHI...AND REQUESTED IT BRING ME A LARGER AYAKASHI FOR ME TO OBSERVE.
SIGH...

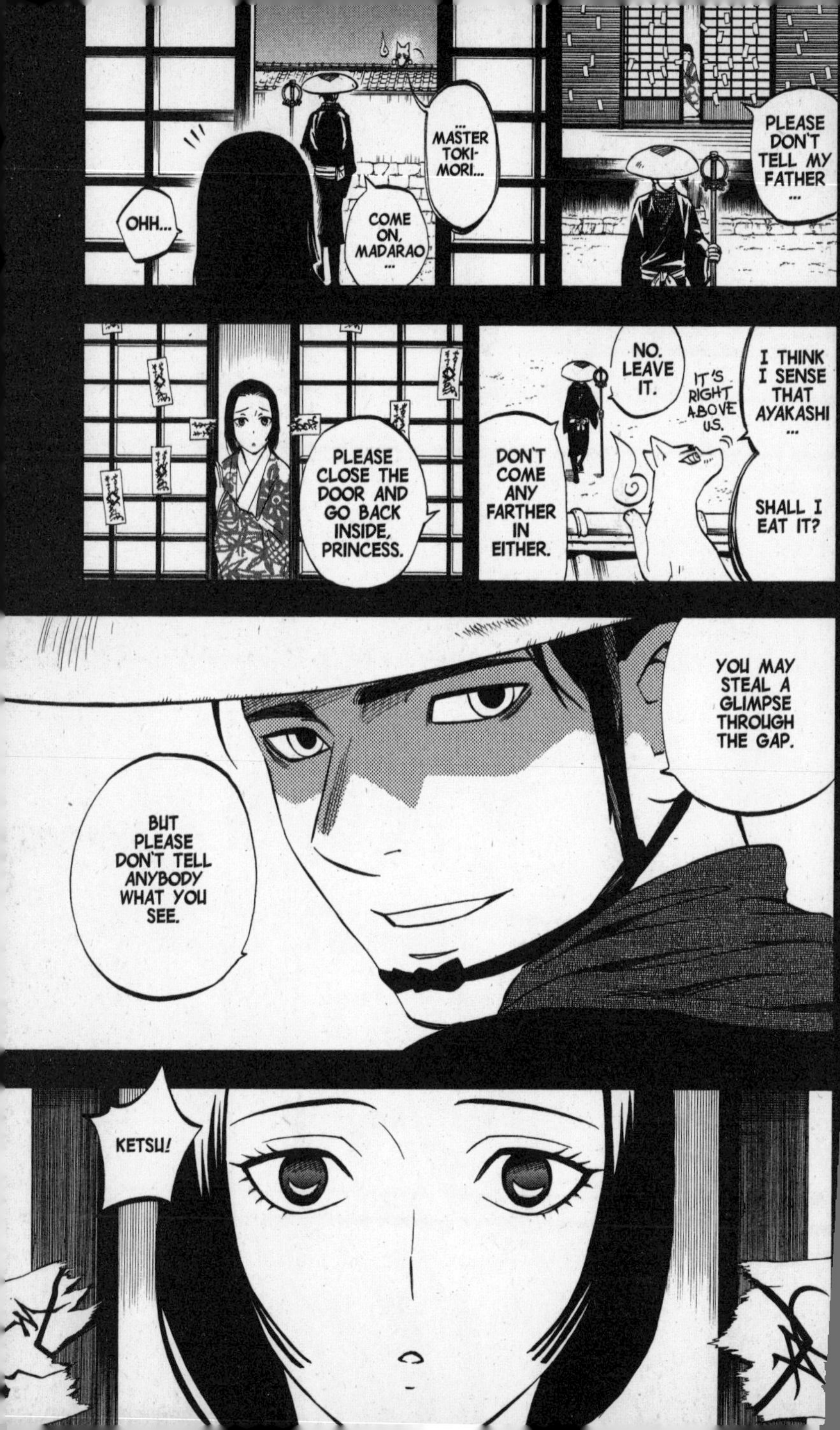
PLEASE DON'T TELL MY FATHER ...
... MASTER TOKI-MORI...
COME ON, MADARAO ...
OHH...
I THINK I SENSE THAT AYAKASHI ...
SHALL I EAT IT?
IT'S RIGHT ABOVE US.
NO. LEAVE IT.
DON'T COME ANY FARTHER IN EITHER.
PLEASE CLOSE THE DOOR AND GO BACK INSIDE, PRINCESS.
YOU MAY STEAL A GLIMPSE THROUGH THE GAP.
BUT PLEASE DON'T TELL ANYBODY WHAT YOU SEE.
KETSU!

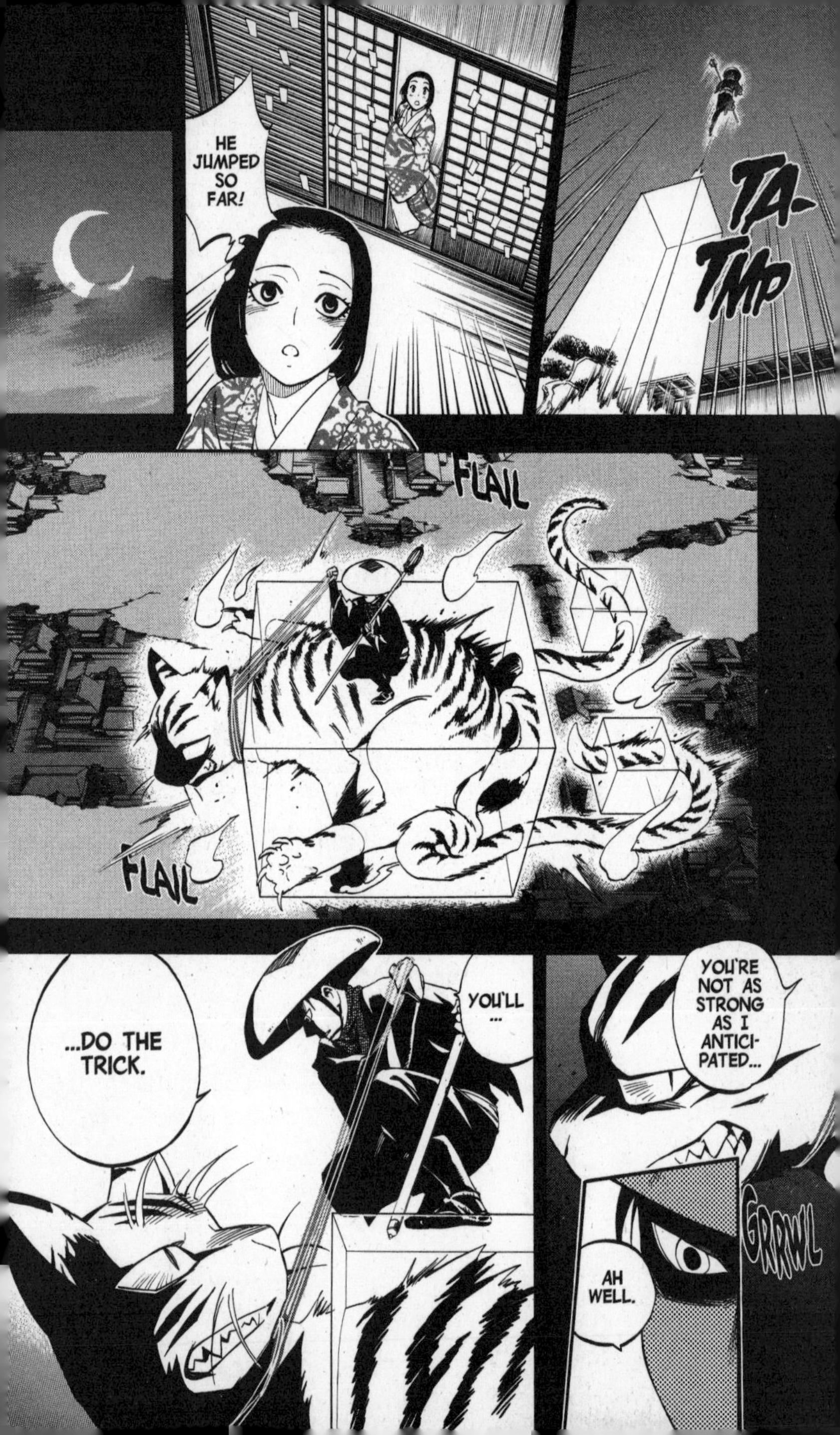
TA-TMP
HE JUMPED SO FAR!
FLAIL
FLAIL
YOU'RE NOT AS STRONG AS I ANTICI-PATED...
GRRWL
AH WELL.
YOU'LL...
...DO THE TRICK.

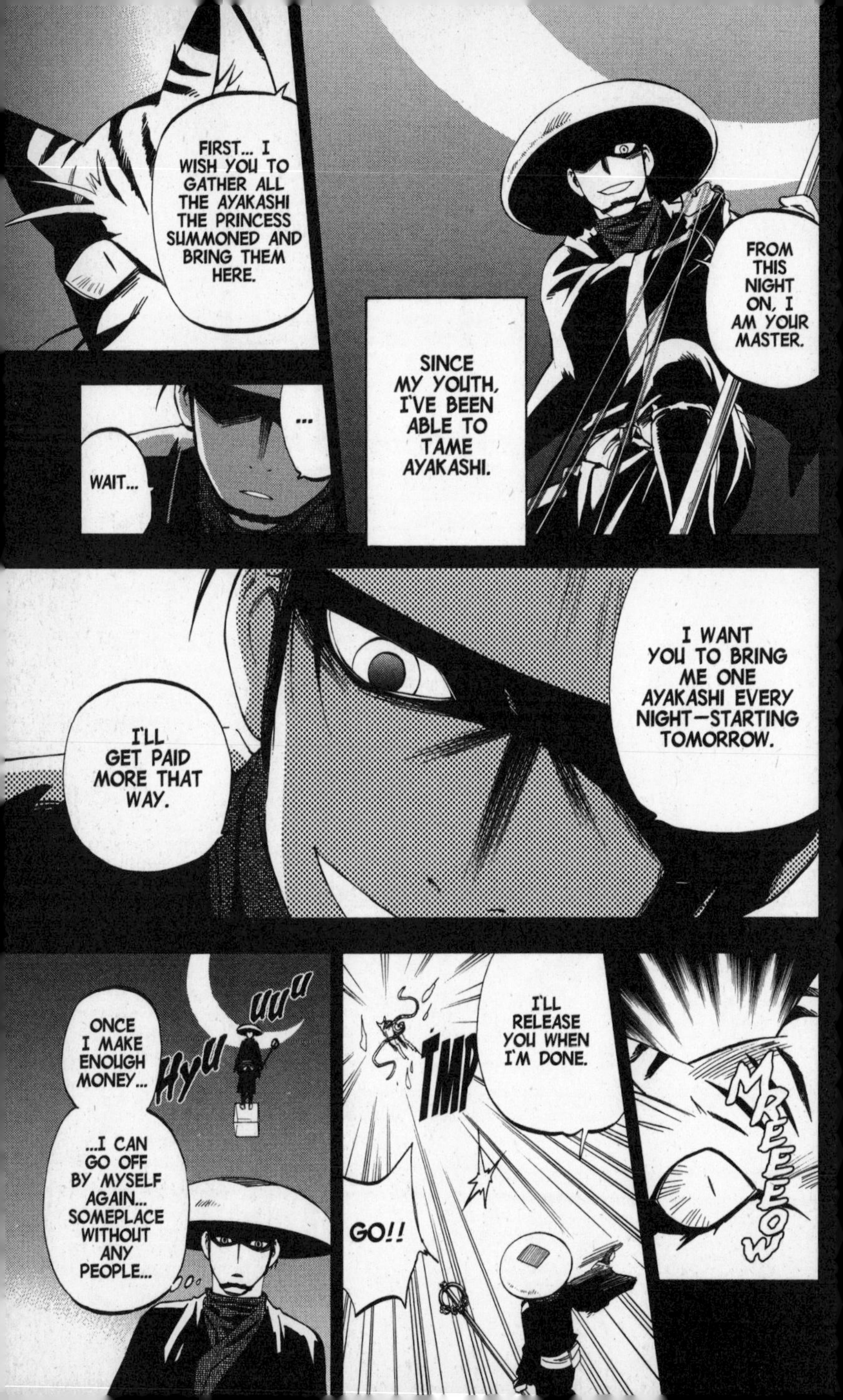
FROM THIS NIGHT ON, I AM YOUR MASTER.
SINCE MY YOUTH, I'VE BEEN ABLE TO TAME AYAKASHI.
FIRST... I WISH YOU TO GATHER ALL THE AYAKASHI THE PRINCESS SUMMONED AND BRING THEM HERE.
...
WAIT...
I WANT YOU TO BRING ME ONE AYAKASHI EVERY NIGHT—STARTING TOMORROW.
I'LL GET PAID MORE THAT WAY.
MREEEOW
I'LL RELEASE YOU WHEN I'M DONE.
TMP
GO!!
HYUUU
ONCE I MAKE ENOUGH MONEY...
...I CAN GO OFF BY MYSELF AGAIN... SOMEPLACE WITHOUT ANY PEOPLE...

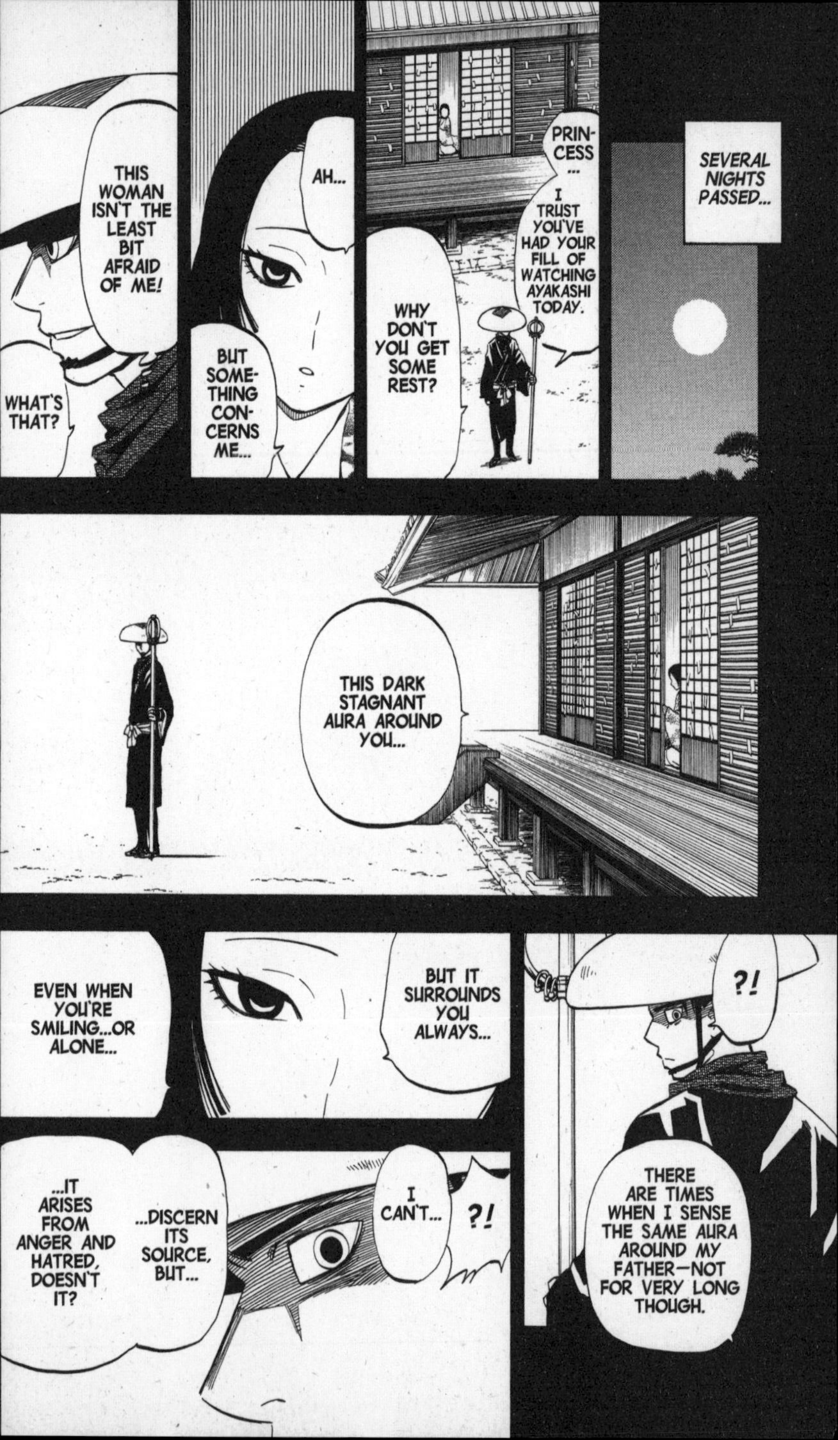
SEVERAL NIGHTS PASSED...
PRIN-CESS... I TRUST YOU'VE HAD YOUR FILL OF WATCHING AYAKASHI TODAY.
WHY DON'T YOU GET SOME REST?
AH...
BUT SOME-THING CON-CERNS ME...
THIS WOMAN ISN'T THE LEAST BIT AFRAID OF ME!
WHAT'S THAT?
THIS DARK STAGNANT AURA AROUND YOU...
?!
THERE ARE TIMES WHEN I SENSE THE SAME AURA AROUND MY FATHER—NOT FOR VERY LONG THOUGH.
BUT IT SURROUNDS YOU ALWAYS...
EVEN WHEN YOU'RE SMILING...OR ALONE...
I CAN'T...
?!
...DISCERN ITS SOURCE, BUT...
...IT ARISES FROM ANGER AND HATRED, DOESN'T IT?

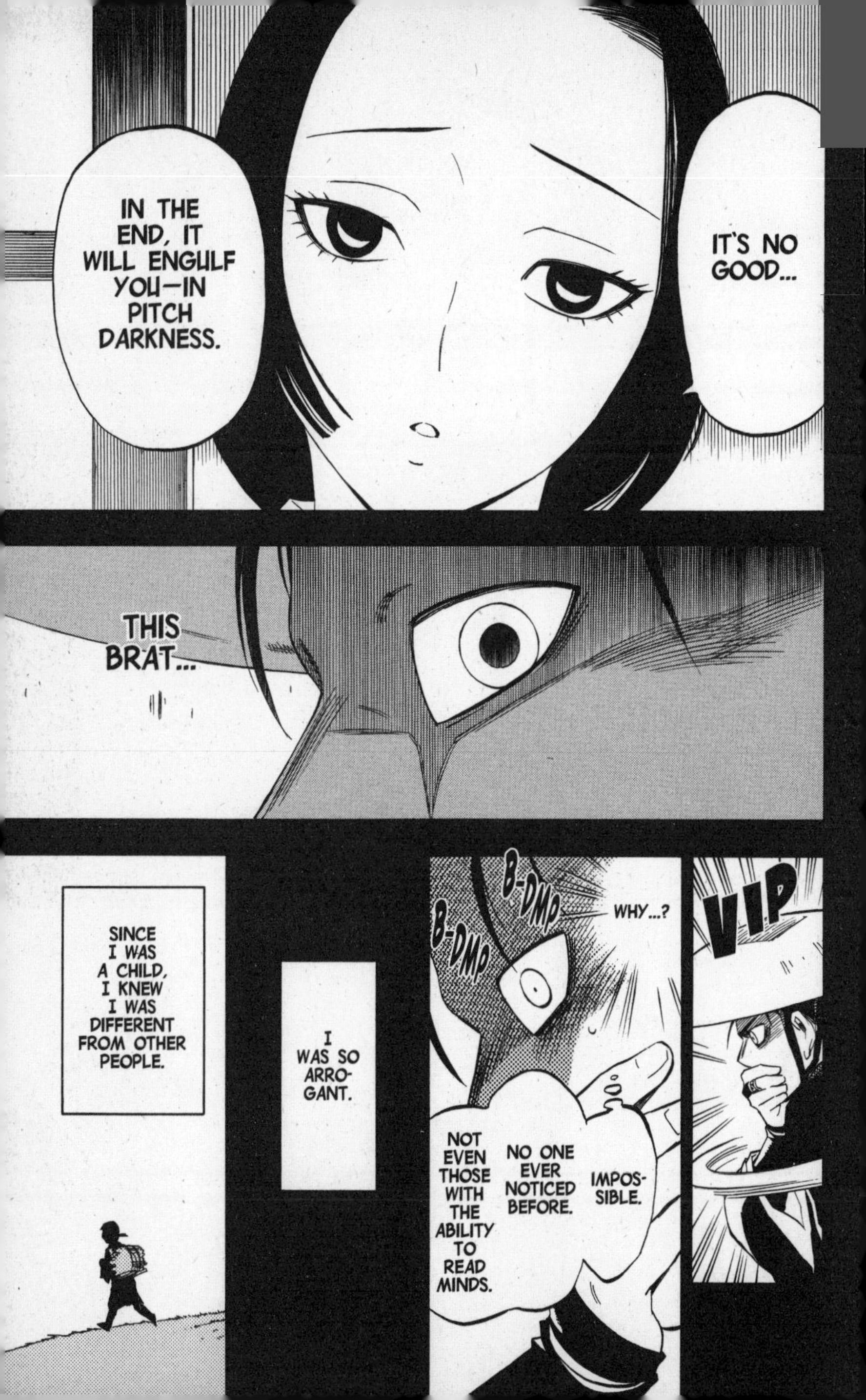
IT'S NO GOOD...
IN THE END, IT WILL ENGULF YOU—IN PITCH DARKNESS.
THIS BRAT...
VIP
B-DMP
B-DMP
WHY...?
IMPOSSIBLE.
NO ONE EVER NOTICED BEFORE.
NOT EVEN THOSE WITH THE ABILITY TO READ MINDS.
I WAS SO ARROGANT.
SINCE I WAS A CHILD, I KNEW I WAS DIFFERENT FROM OTHER PEOPLE.

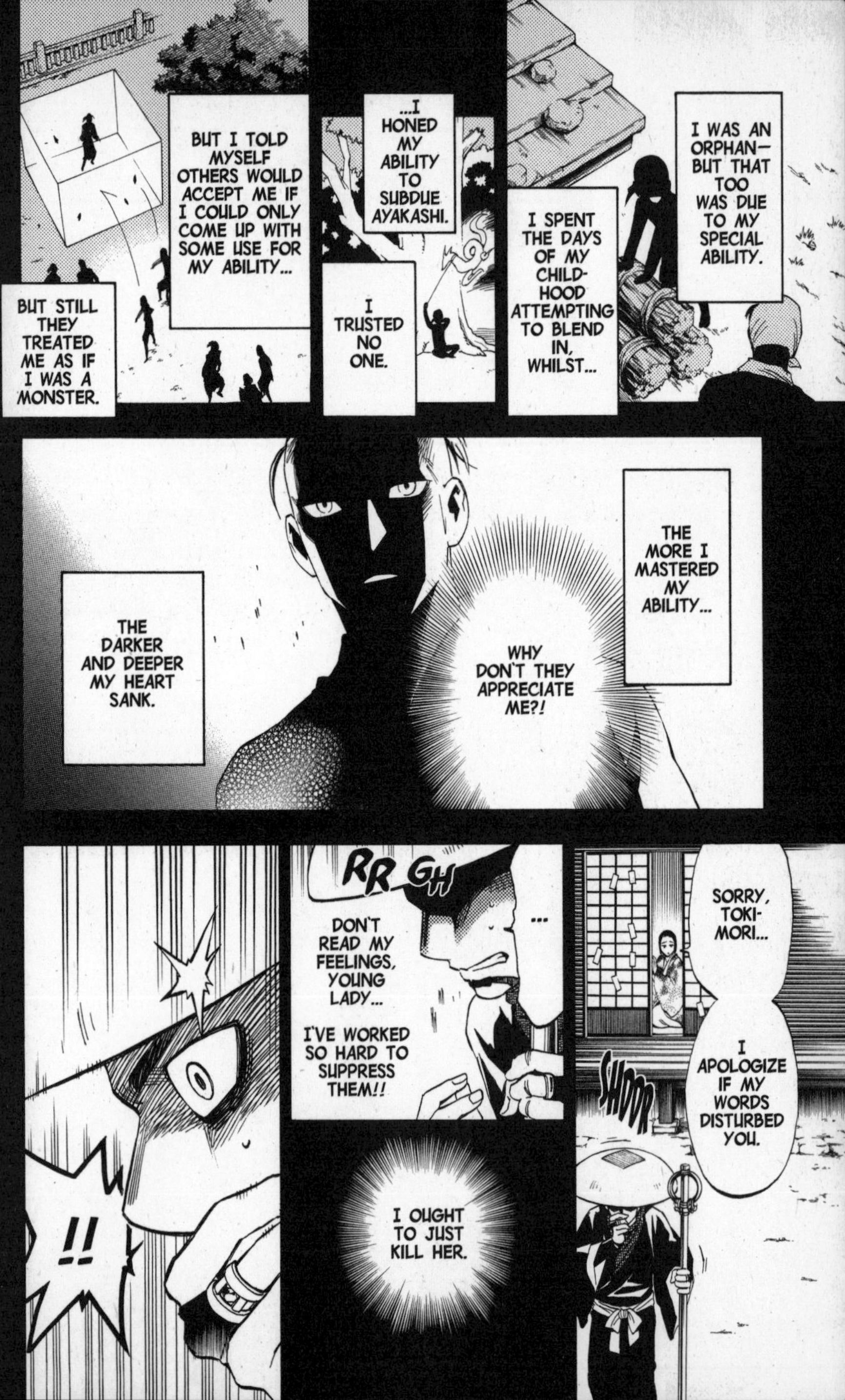
I WAS AN ORPHAN—BUT THAT TOO WAS DUE TO MY SPECIAL ABILITY.
I SPENT THE DAYS OF MY CHILDHOOD ATTEMPTING TO BLEND IN, WHILST...
...I HONED MY ABILITY TO SUBDUE AYAKASHI.
I TRUSTED NO ONE.
BUT I TOLD MYSELF OTHERS WOULD ACCEPT ME IF I COULD ONLY COME UP WITH SOME USE FOR MY ABILITY...
BUT STILL THEY TREATED ME AS IF I WAS A MONSTER.
THE MORE I MASTERED MY ABILITY...
WHY DON'T THEY APPRECIATE ME?!
THE DARKER AND DEEPER MY HEART SANK.
SORRY, TOKI-MORI...
I APOLOGIZE IF MY WORDS DISTURBED YOU.
SHOOM
RRGH
...
DON'T READ MY FEELINGS, YOUNG LADY...
I'VE WORKED SO HARD TO SUPPRESS THEM!!
I OUGHT TO JUST KILL HER.
!!

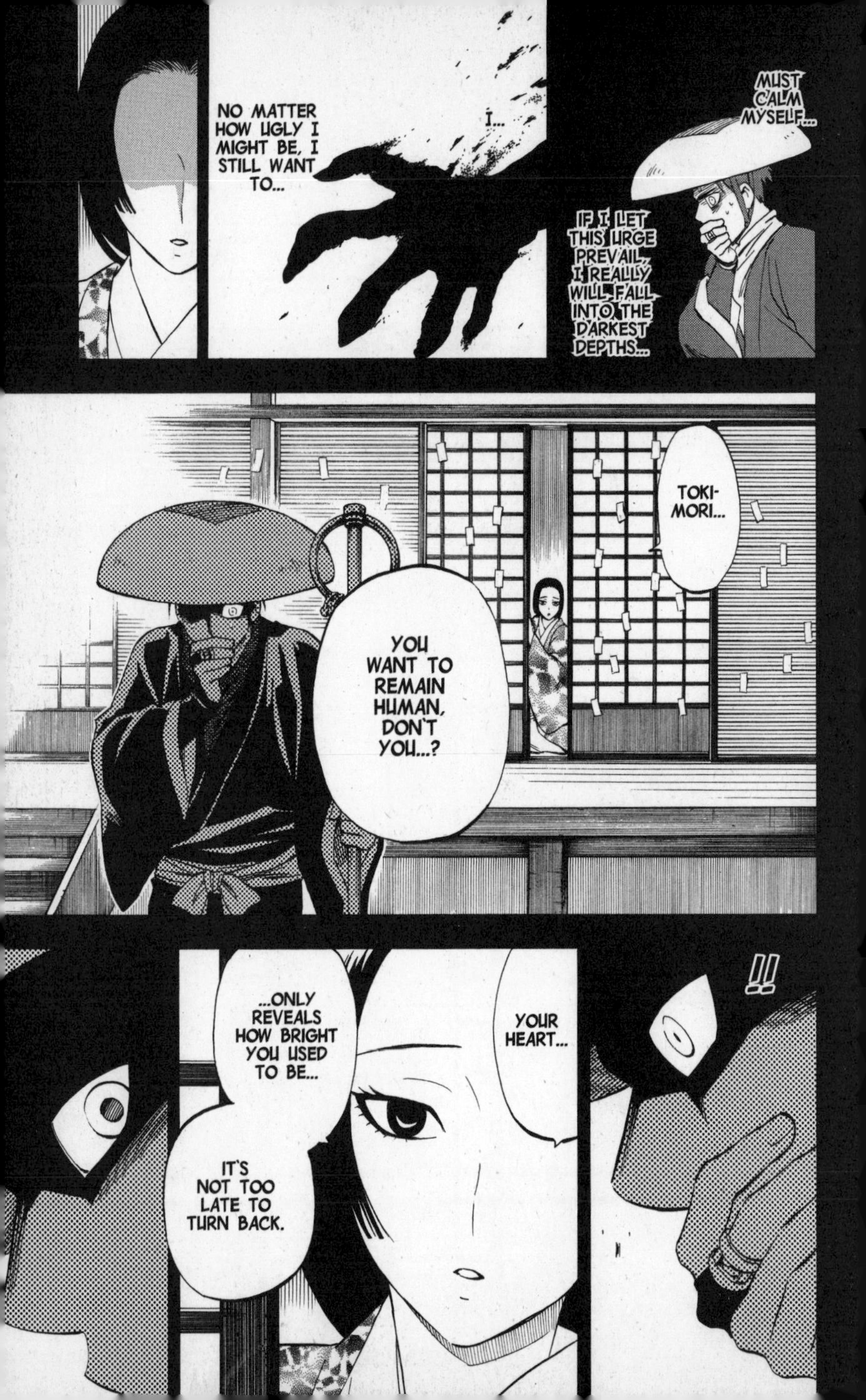
MUST CALM MYSELF...
IF I LET THIS URGE PREVAIL, I REALLY WILL FALL INTO THE DARKEST DEPTHS...
I...
NO MATTER HOW UGLY I MIGHT BE, I STILL WANT TO...
TOKI-MORI...
YOU WANT TO REMAIN HUMAN, DON'T YOU...?
!!
YOUR HEART...
...ONLY REVEALS HOW BRIGHT YOU USED TO BE...
IT'S NOT TOO LATE TO TURN BACK.

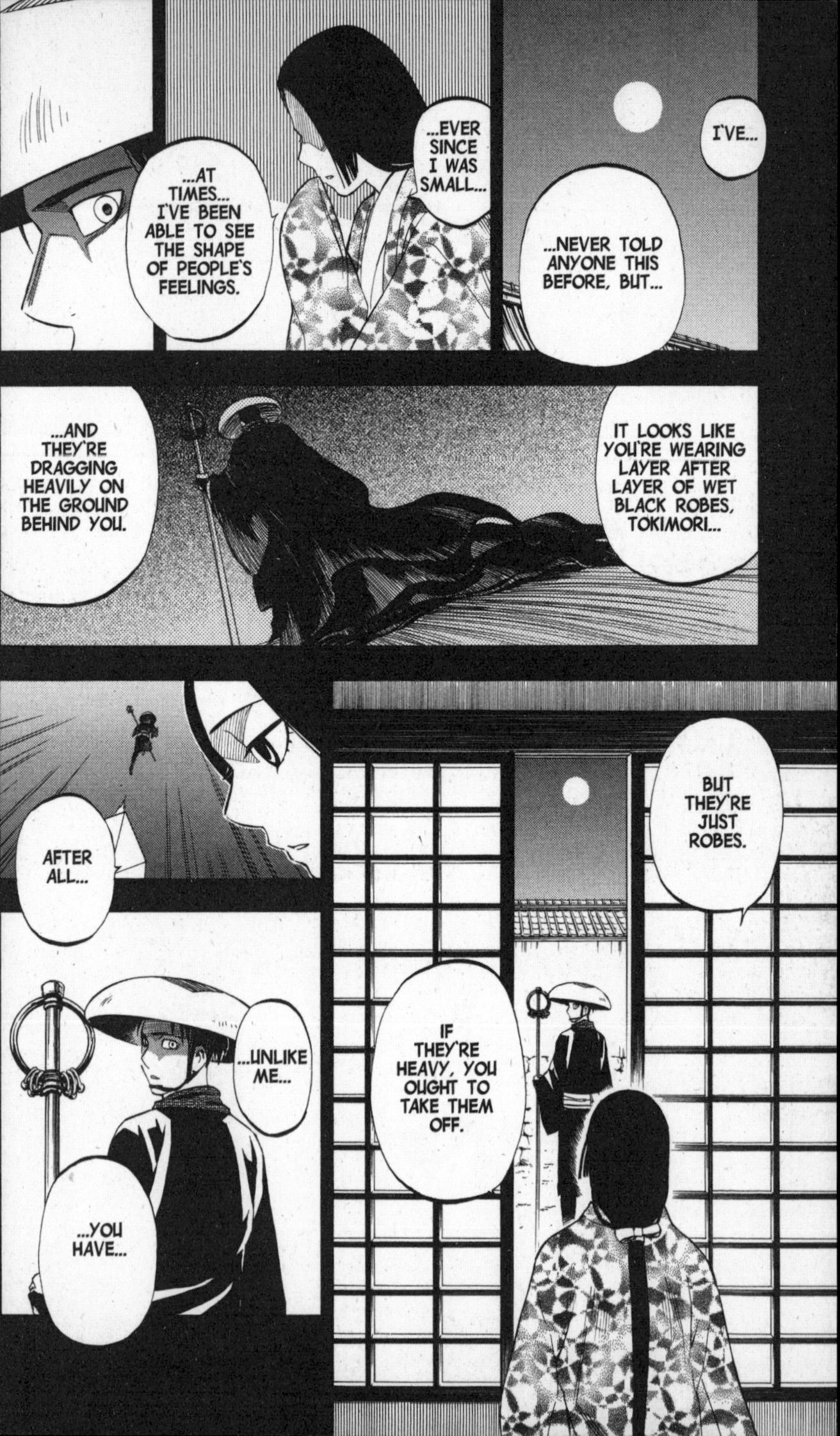
I'VE...
...NEVER TOLD ANYONE THIS BEFORE, BUT...
...EVER SINCE I WAS SMALL...
...AT TIMES... I'VE BEEN ABLE TO SEE THE SHAPE OF PEOPLE'S FEELINGS.
IT LOOKS LIKE YOU'RE WEARING LAYER AFTER LAYER OF WET BLACK ROBES, TOKIMORI...
...AND THEY'RE DRAGGING HEAVILY ON THE GROUND BEHIND YOU.
BUT THEY'RE JUST ROBES.
IF THEY'RE HEAVY, YOU OUGHT TO TAKE THEM OFF.
AFTER ALL...
...UNLIKE ME...
...YOU HAVE...

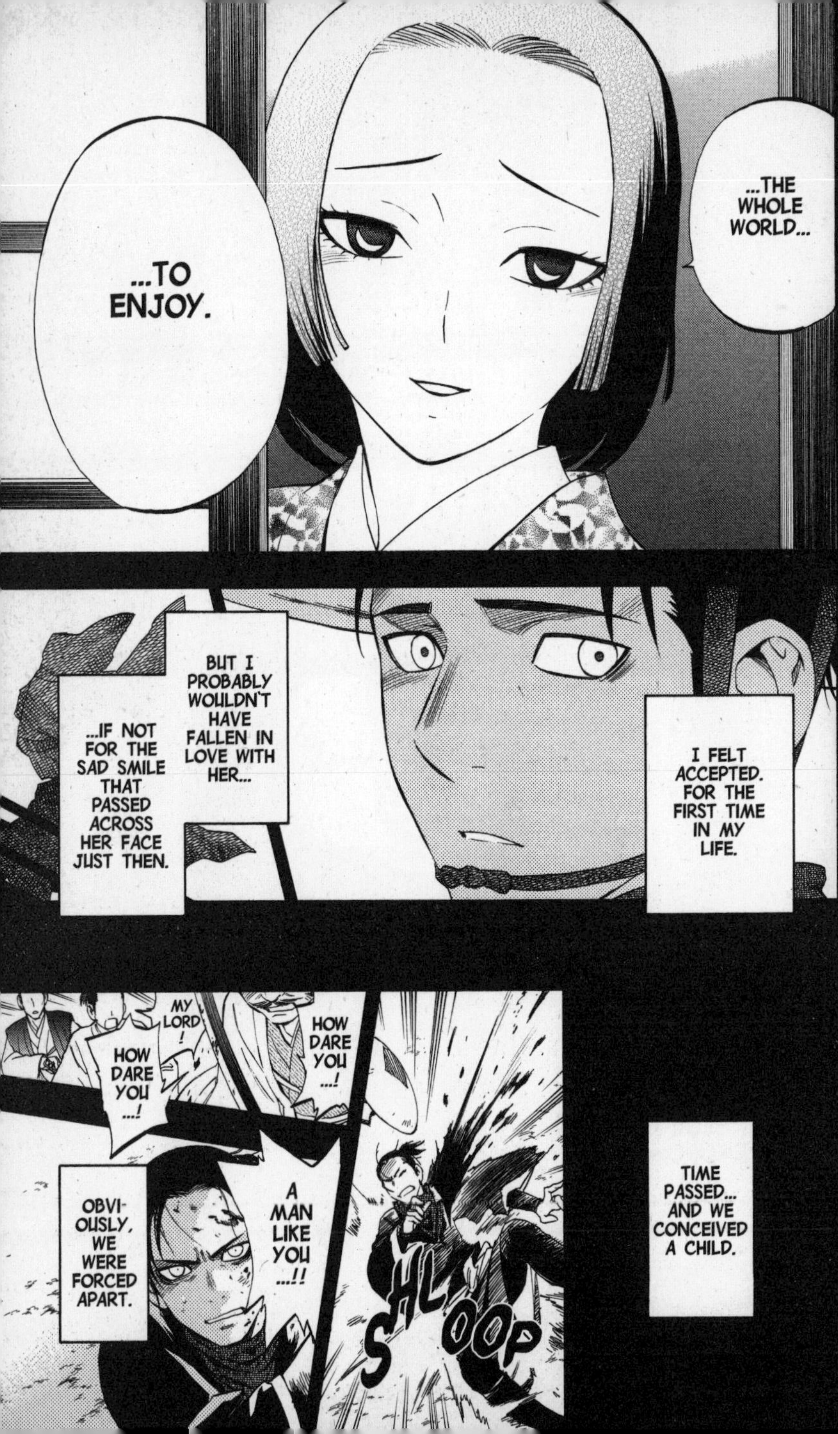
...THE WHOLE WORLD...
...TO ENJOY.
I FELT ACCEPTED. FOR THE FIRST TIME IN MY LIFE.
BUT I PROBABLY WOULDN'T HAVE FALLEN IN LOVE WITH HER...
...IF NOT FOR THE SAD SMILE THAT PASSED ACROSS HER FACE JUST THEN.
TIME PASSED... AND WE CONCEIVED A CHILD.
HOW DARE YOU ...!
MY LORD!
HOW DARE YOU ...!
A MAN LIKE YOU ...!!
SHLOOP
OBVIOUSLY, WE WERE FORCED APART.

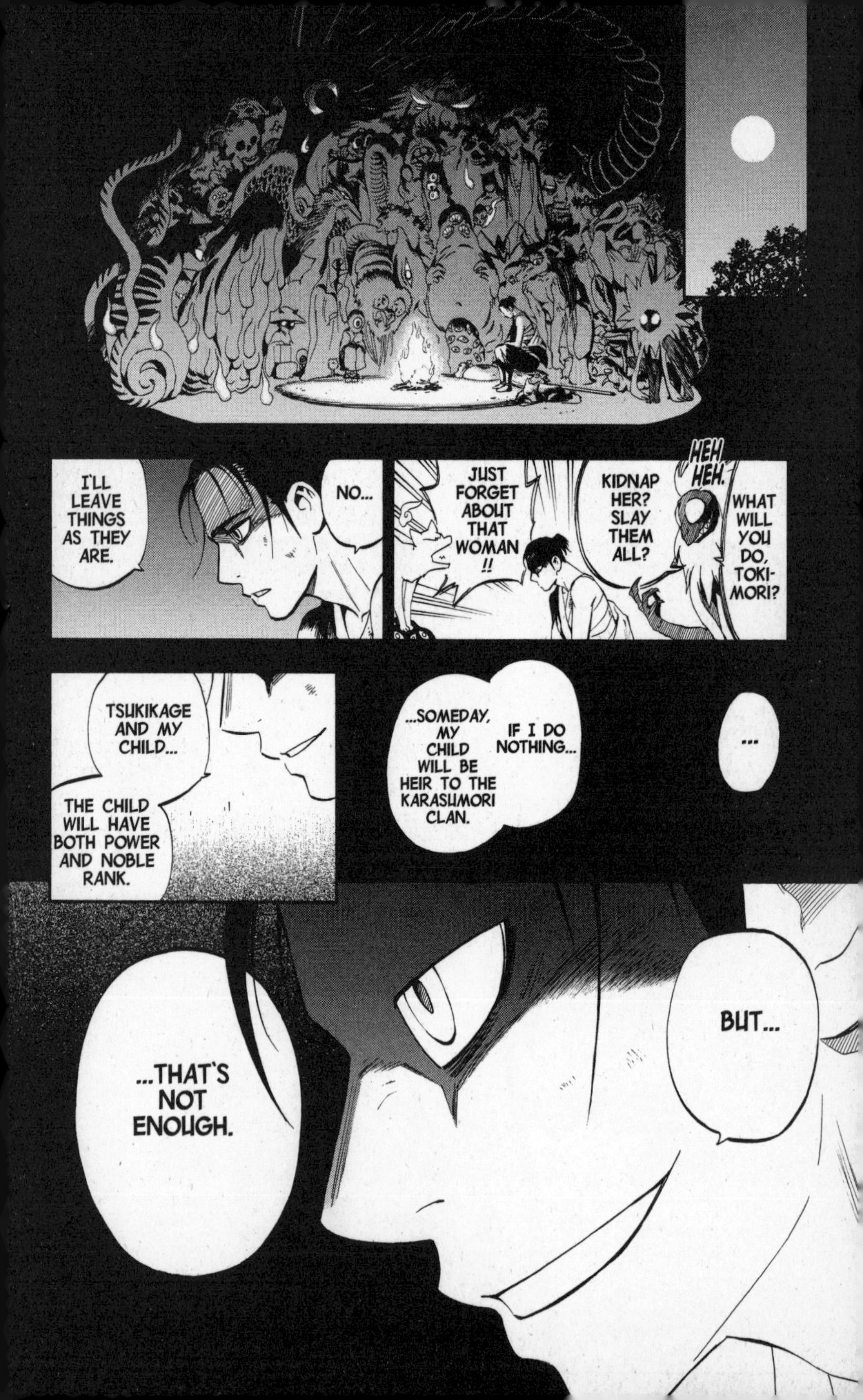
HEH HEH.
WHAT WILL YOU DO, TOKIMORI?
KIDNAP HER? SLAY THEM ALL?
JUST FORGET ABOUT THAT WOMAN !!
NO...
I'LL LEAVE THINGS AS THEY ARE.
...
IF I DO NOTHING...
...SOMEDAY, MY CHILD WILL BE HEIR TO THE KARASUMORI CLAN.
TSUKIKAGE AND MY CHILD...
THE CHILD WILL HAVE BOTH POWER AND NOBLE RANK.
BUT...
...THAT'S NOT ENOUGH.

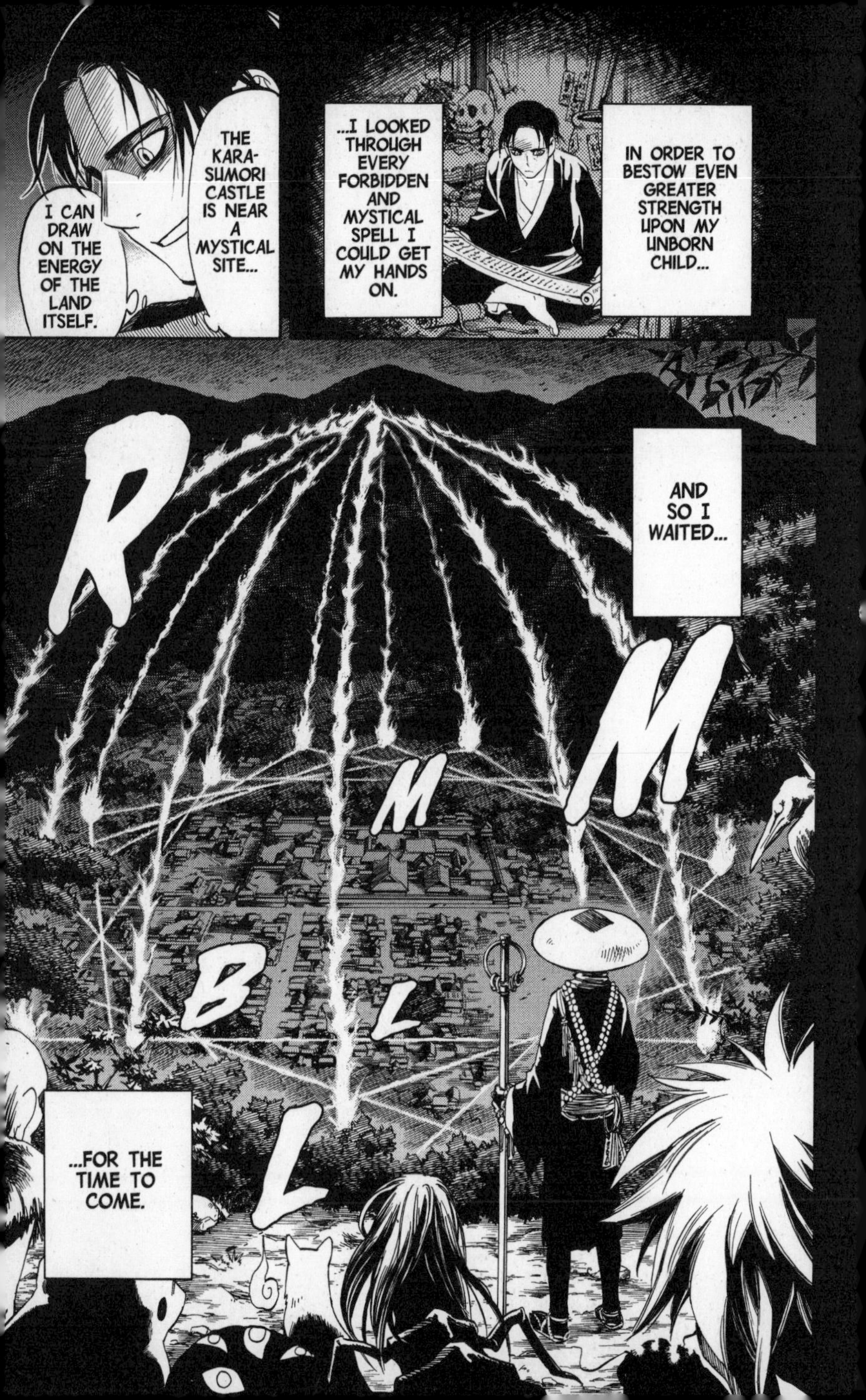
IN ORDER TO BESTOW EVEN GREATER STRENGTH UPON MY UNBORN CHILD...
...I LOOKED THROUGH EVERY FORBIDDEN AND MYSTICAL SPELL I COULD GET MY HANDS ON.
THE KARA-SUMORI CASTLE IS NEAR A MYSTICAL SITE...
I CAN DRAW ON THE ENERGY OF THE LAND ITSELF.
AND SO I WAITED...
RMMBLL
...FOR THE TIME TO COME.

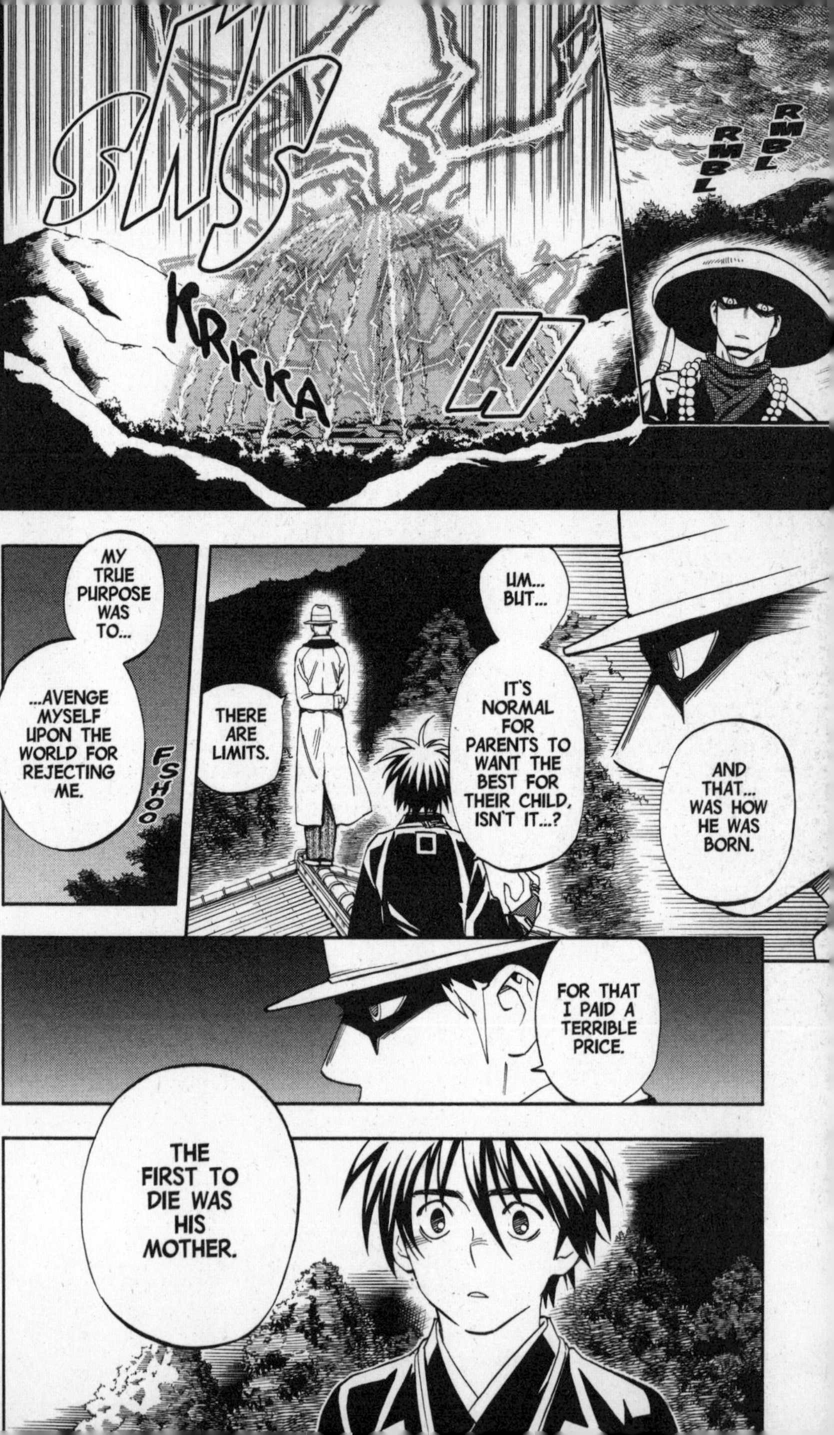
RMBL
RMBL
KRKKA
AND THAT... WAS HOW HE WAS BORN.
UM... BUT...
IT'S NORMAL FOR PARENTS TO WANT THE BEST FOR THEIR CHILD, ISN'T IT...?
THERE ARE LIMITS.
MY TRUE PURPOSE WAS TO...
...AVENGE MYSELF UPON THE WORLD FOR REJECTING ME.
FSHOO
FOR THAT I PAID A TERRIBLE PRICE.
THE FIRST TO DIE WAS HIS MOTHER.

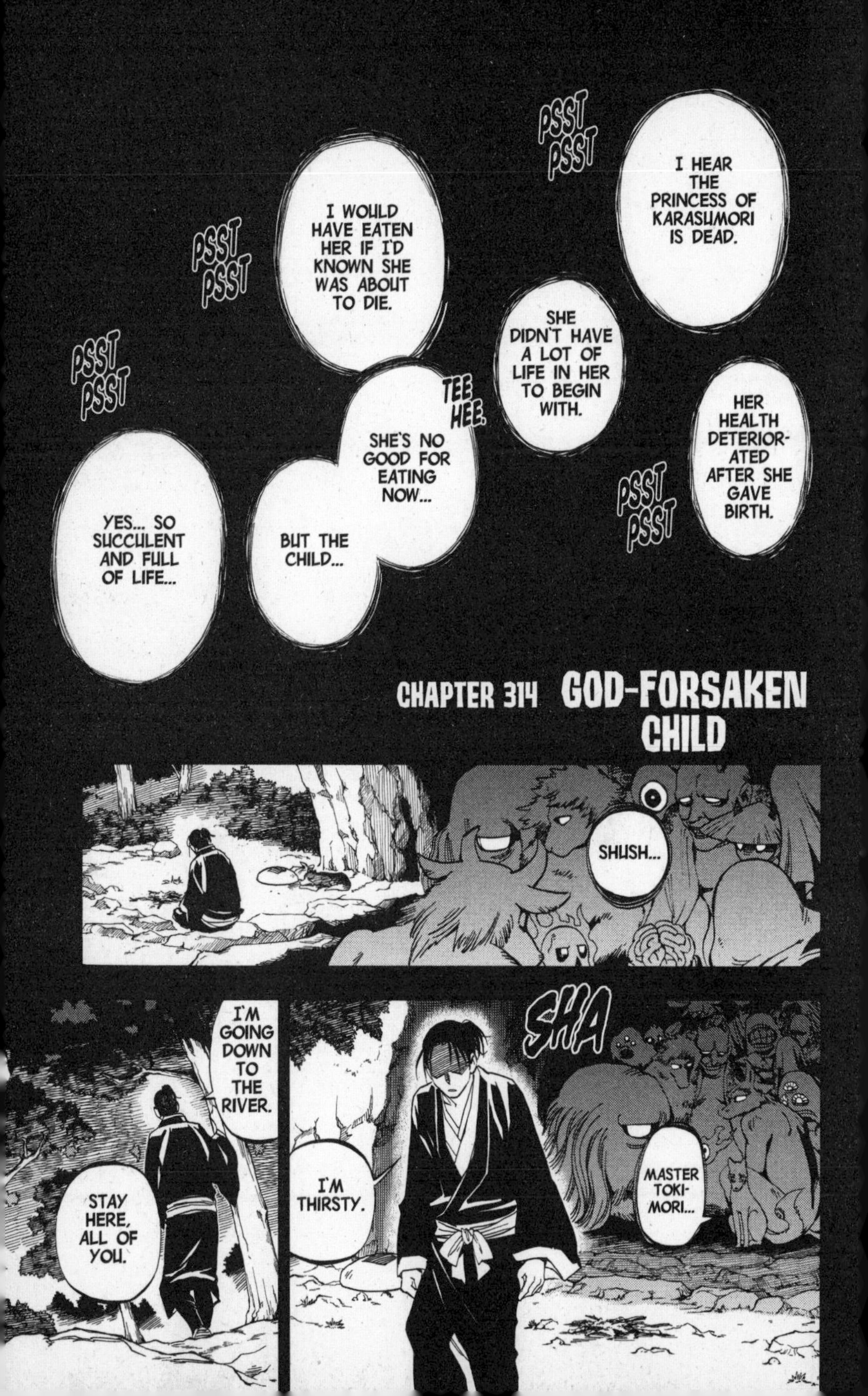
PSST PSST
I HEAR THE PRINCESS OF KARASUMORI IS DEAD.
PSST PSST
HER HEALTH DETERIOR-ATED AFTER SHE GAVE BIRTH.
SHE DIDN'T HAVE A LOT OF LIFE IN HER TO BEGIN WITH.
PSST PSST
I WOULD HAVE EATEN HER IF I'D KNOWN SHE WAS ABOUT TO DIE.
TEE HEE.
SHE'S NO GOOD FOR EATING NOW...
BUT THE CHILD...
PSST PSST
YES... SO SUCCULENT AND FULL OF LIFE...
CHAPTER 314 GOD-FORSAKEN CHILD
SHUSH...
SHA
MASTER TOKI-MORI...
I'M THIRSTY.
I'M GOING DOWN TO THE RIVER.
STAY HERE, ALL OF YOU.

Chapter 314 God-Forsaken Child

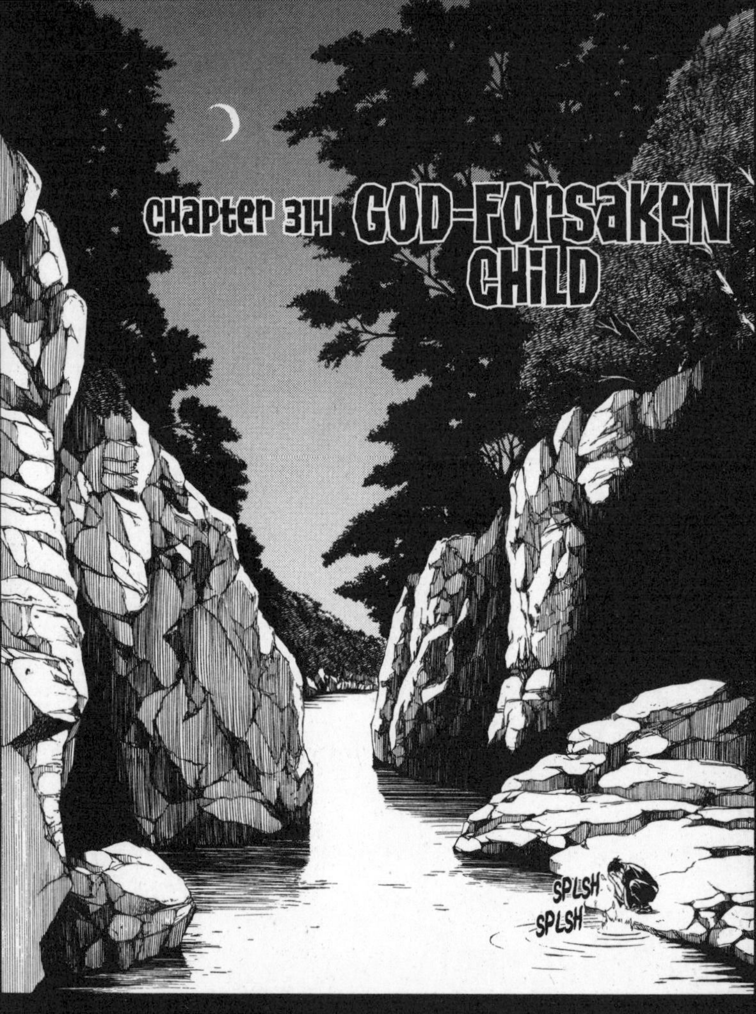
SPLSH
SPLSH

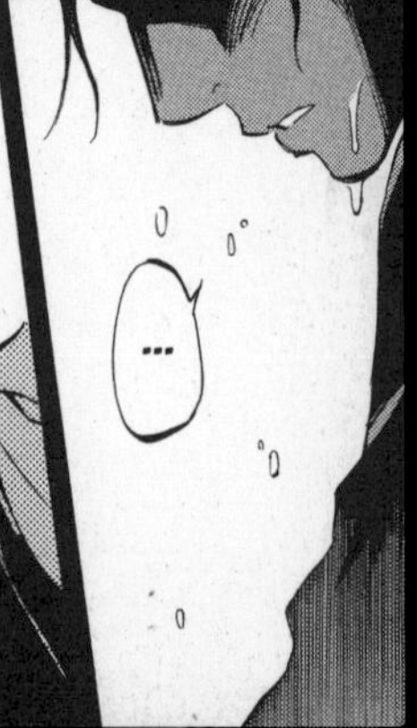
...

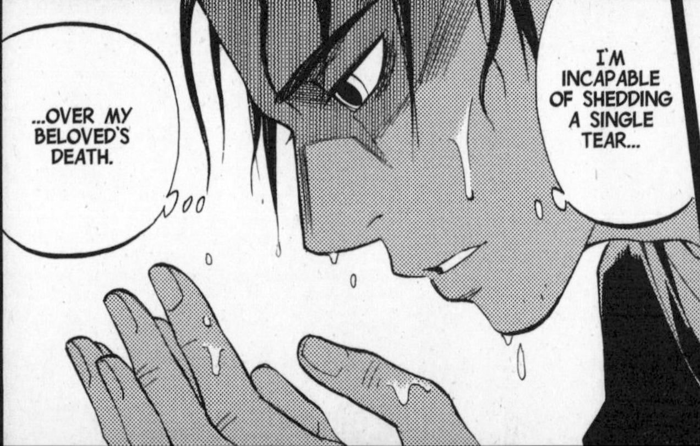
I'M INCAPABLE OF SHEDDING A SINGLE TEAR...
...OVER MY BELOVED'S DEATH.

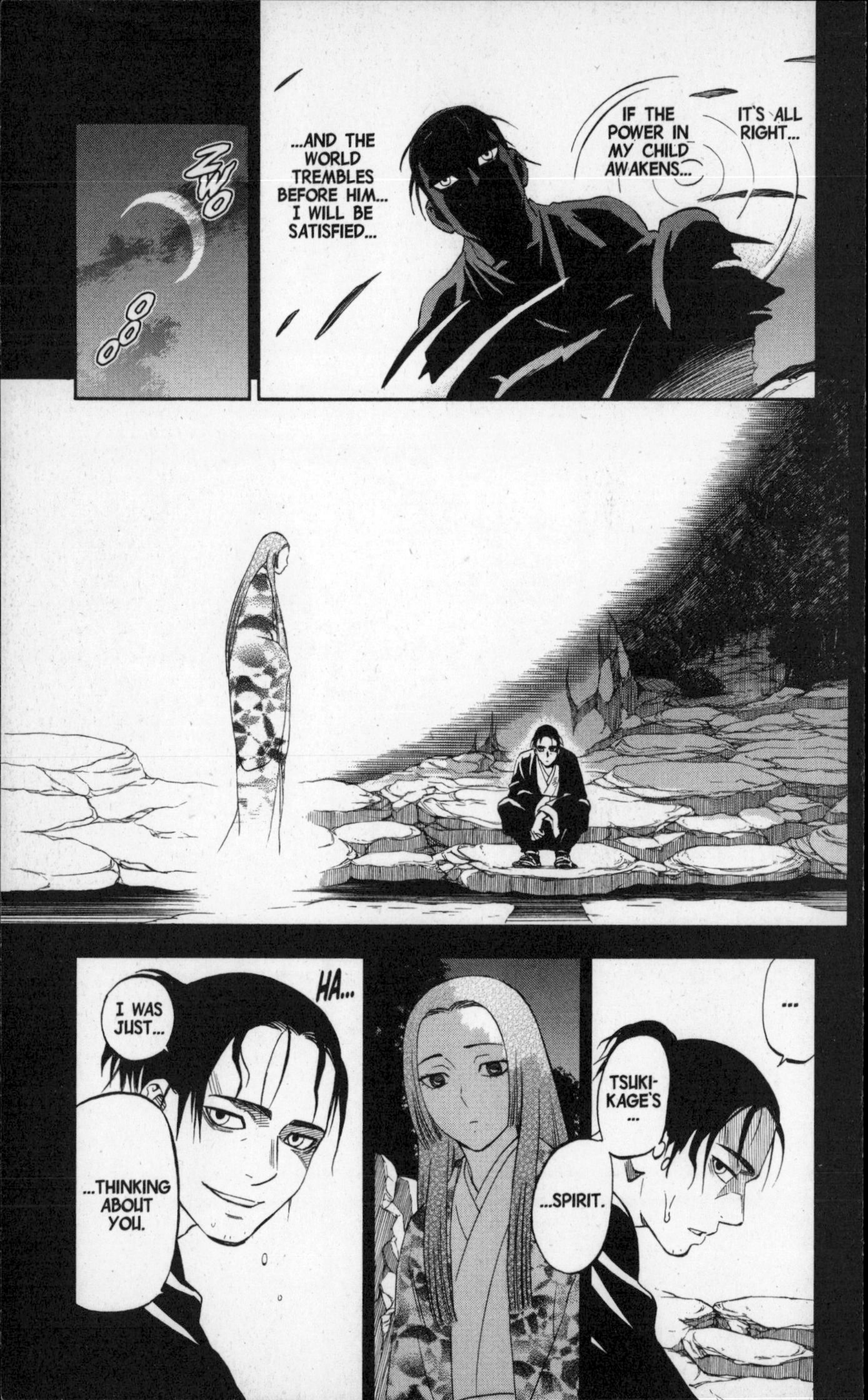
IT'S ALL RIGHT...
IF THE POWER IN MY CHILD AWAKENS...
...AND THE WORLD TREMBLES BEFORE HIM... I WILL BE SATISFIED...
ZWOOOOO
...
TSUKI-KAGE'S...
...SPIRIT.
HA...
I WAS JUST...
...THINKING ABOUT YOU.

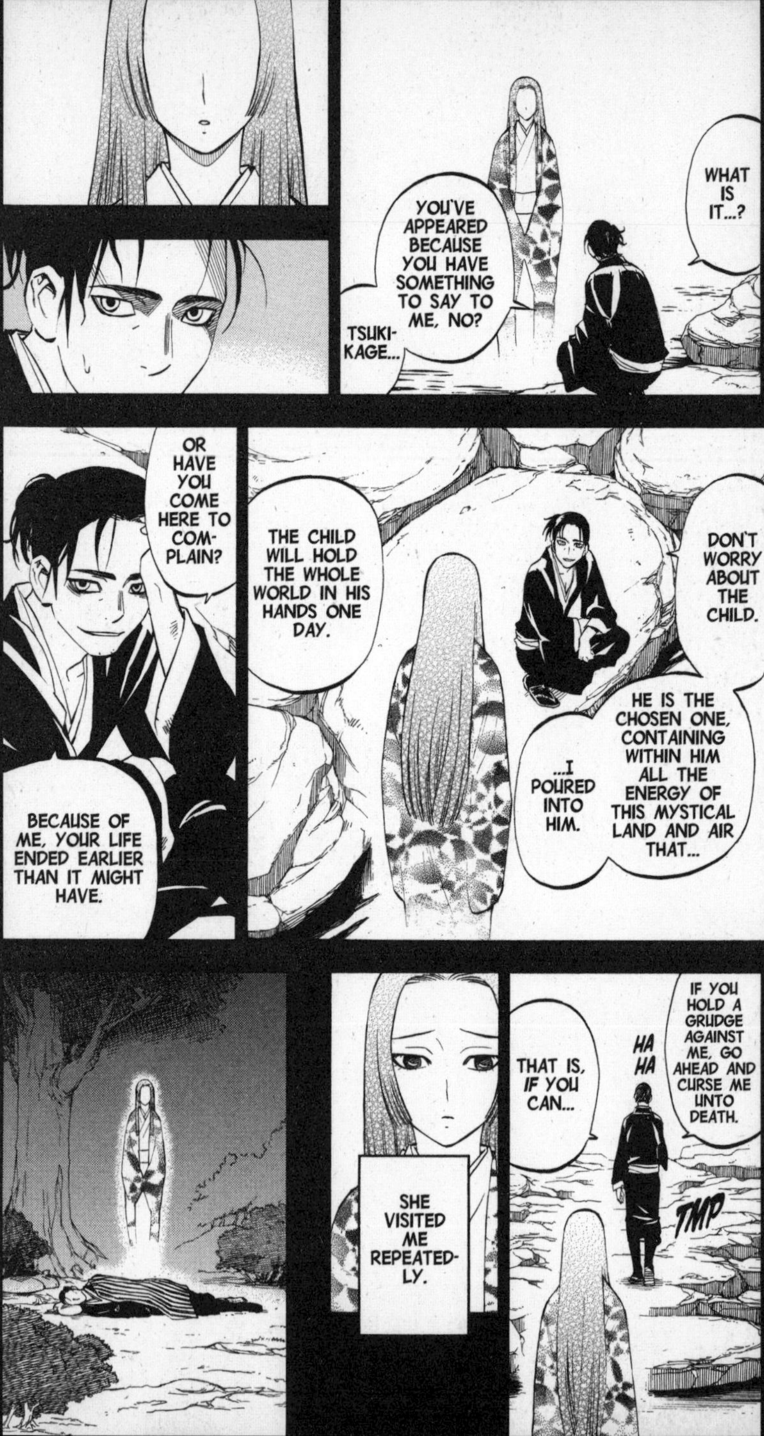

WHAT IS IT...?
YOU'VE APPEARED BECAUSE YOU HAVE SOMETHING TO SAY TO ME, NO?
TSUKI-KAGE...
DON'T WORRY ABOUT THE CHILD.
THE CHILD WILL HOLD THE WHOLE WORLD IN HIS HANDS ONE DAY.
HE IS THE CHOSEN ONE, CONTAINING WITHIN HIM ALL THE ENERGY OF THIS MYSTICAL LAND AND AIR THAT...
...I POURED INTO HIM.
OR HAVE YOU COME HERE TO COM-PLAIN?
BECAUSE OF ME, YOUR LIFE ENDED EARLIER THAN IT MIGHT HAVE.
IF YOU HOLD A GRUDGE AGAINST ME, GO AHEAD AND CURSE ME UNTO DEATH.
HA HA
THAT IS, *IF* YOU CAN...
TMP
SHE VISITED ME REPEATED-LY.

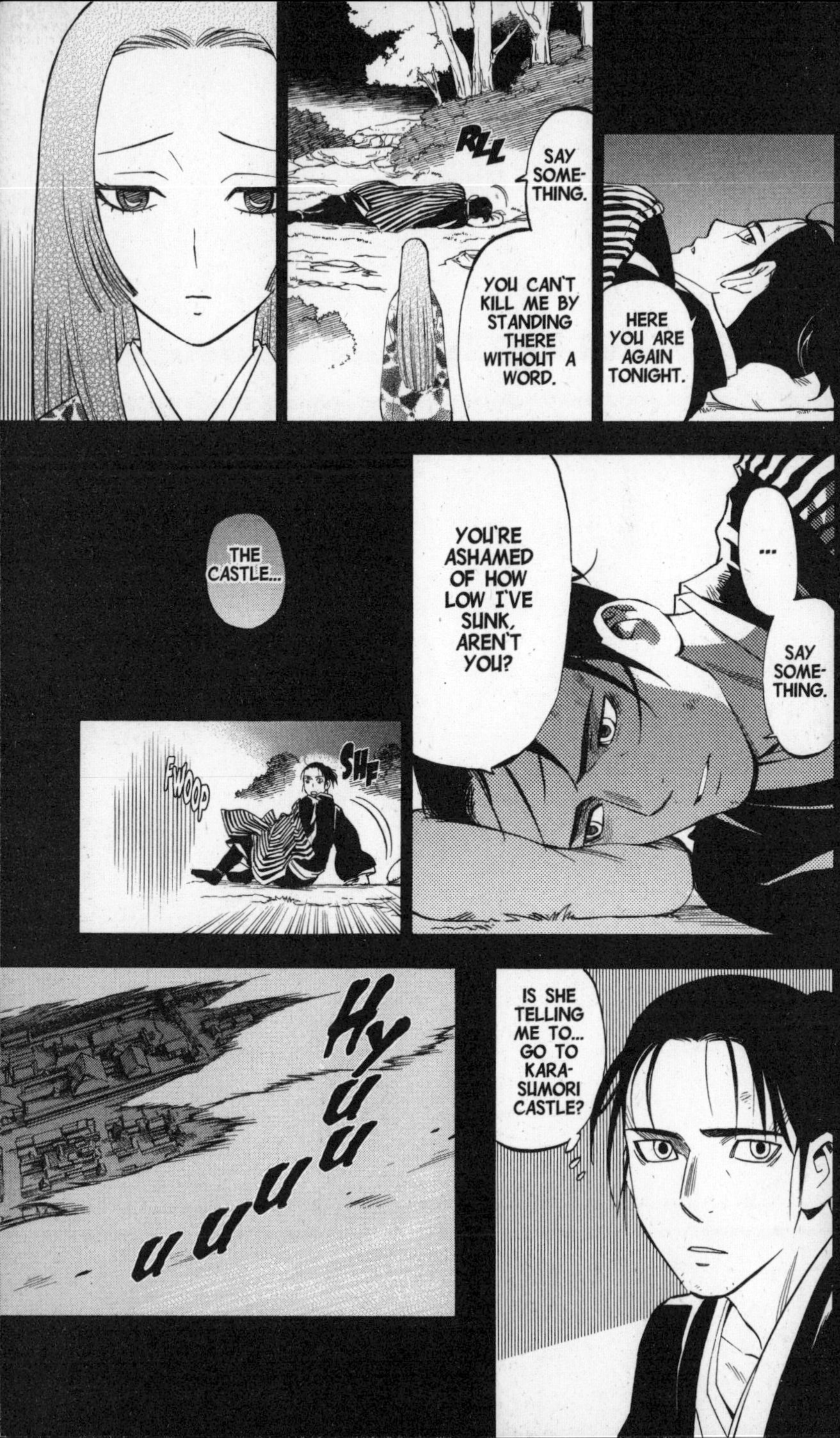
HERE YOU ARE AGAIN TONIGHT.
SAY SOME-THING.
RLL
YOU CAN'T KILL ME BY STANDING THERE WITHOUT A WORD.
...
SAY SOME-THING.
YOU'RE ASHAMED OF HOW LOW I'VE SUNK, AREN'T YOU?
THE CASTLE...
SHF
FWOOP
IS SHE TELLING ME TO... GO TO KARA-SUMORI CASTLE?
HYUUUUUUU

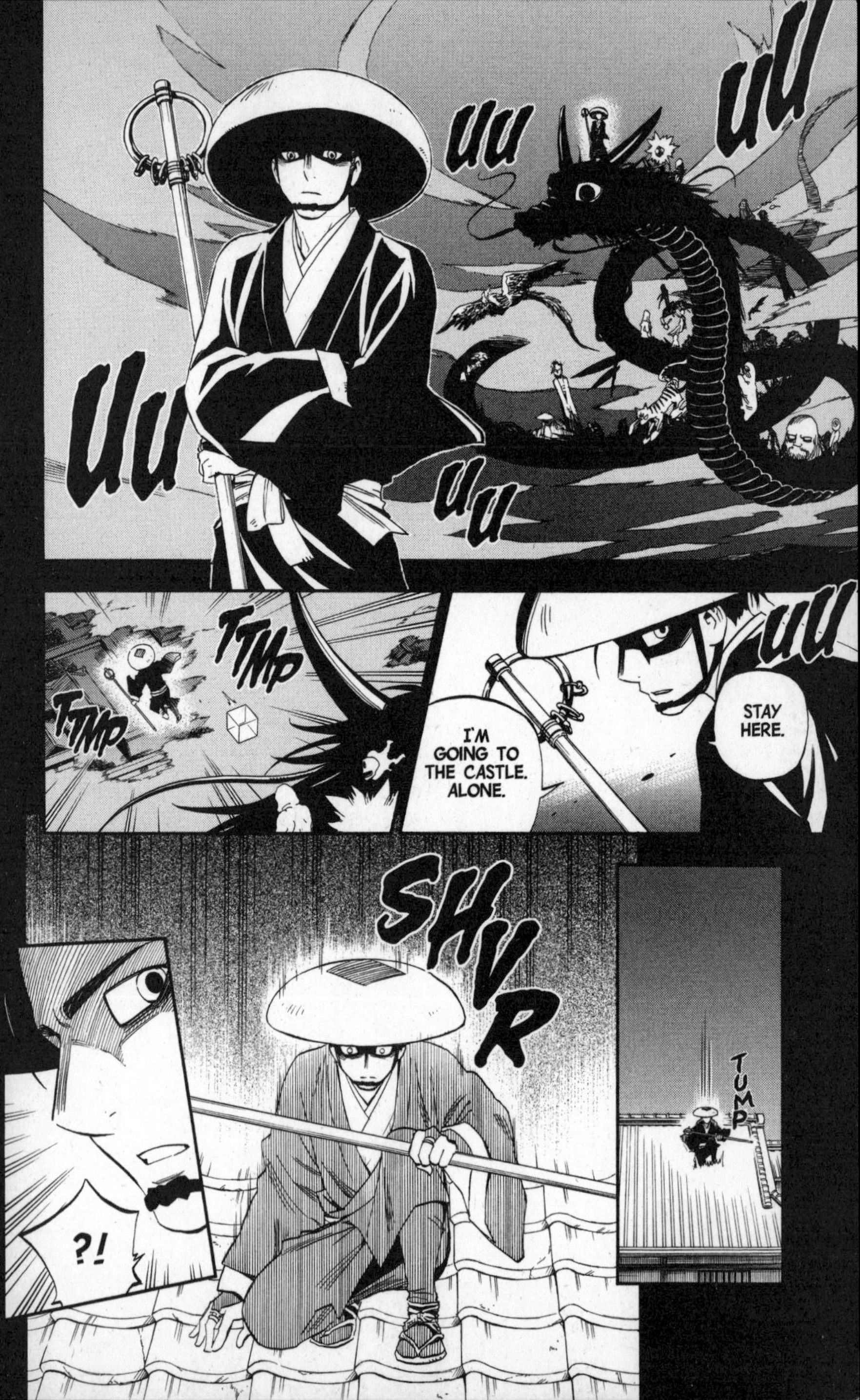
UU
UU
UU
UU
UU
STAY HERE.
I'M GOING TO THE CASTLE. ALONE.
TTMP
TTMP
TUMP
SHVR
?!

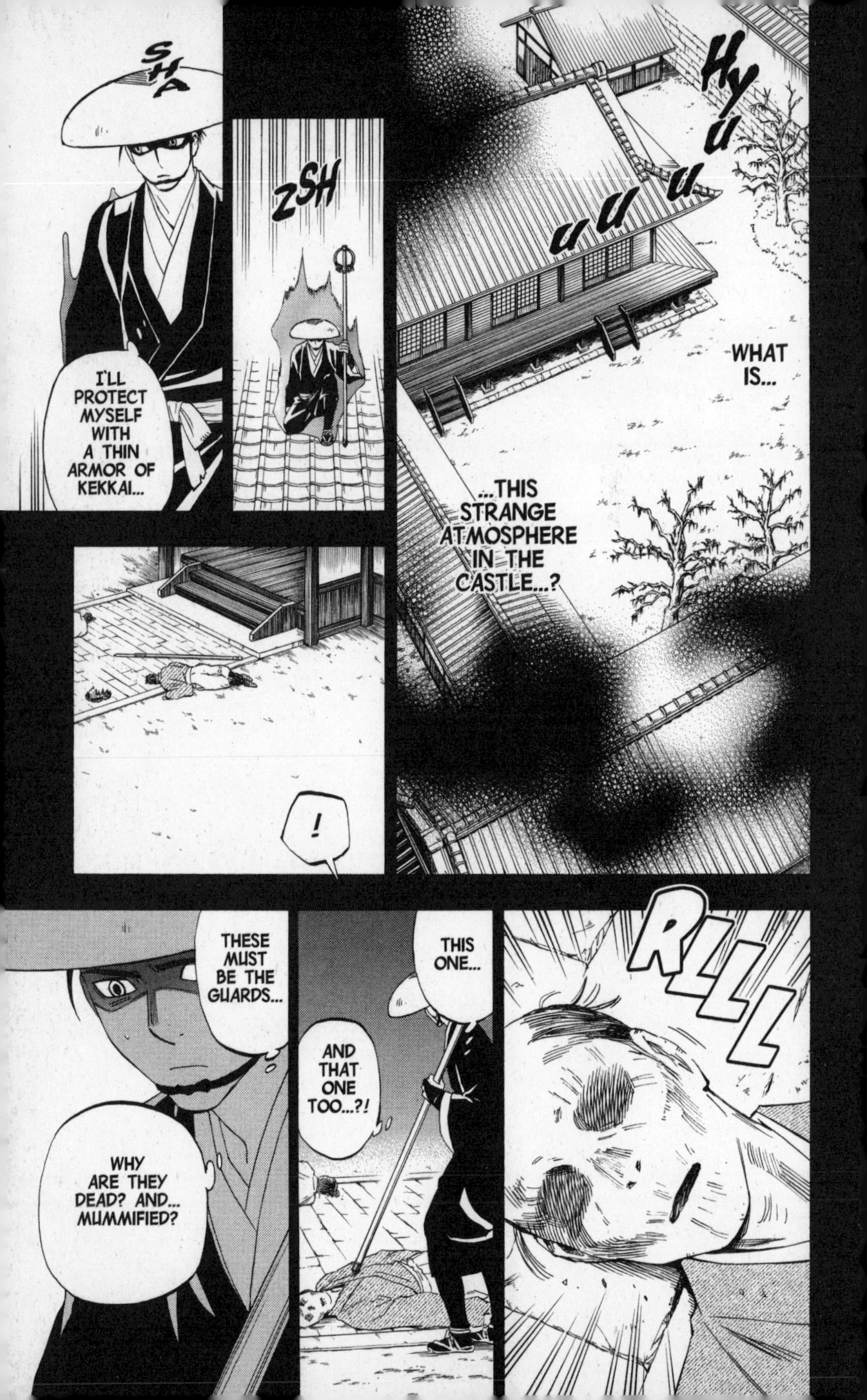
HYUUUUUU
WHAT IS...
...THIS STRANGE ATMOSPHERE IN THE CASTLE...?
ZSH
SHA
I'LL PROTECT MYSELF WITH A THIN ARMOR OF KEKKAI...
!
RLLL
THIS ONE...
AND THAT ONE TOO...?!
THESE MUST BE THE GUARDS...
WHY ARE THEY DEAD? AND... MUMMIFIED?

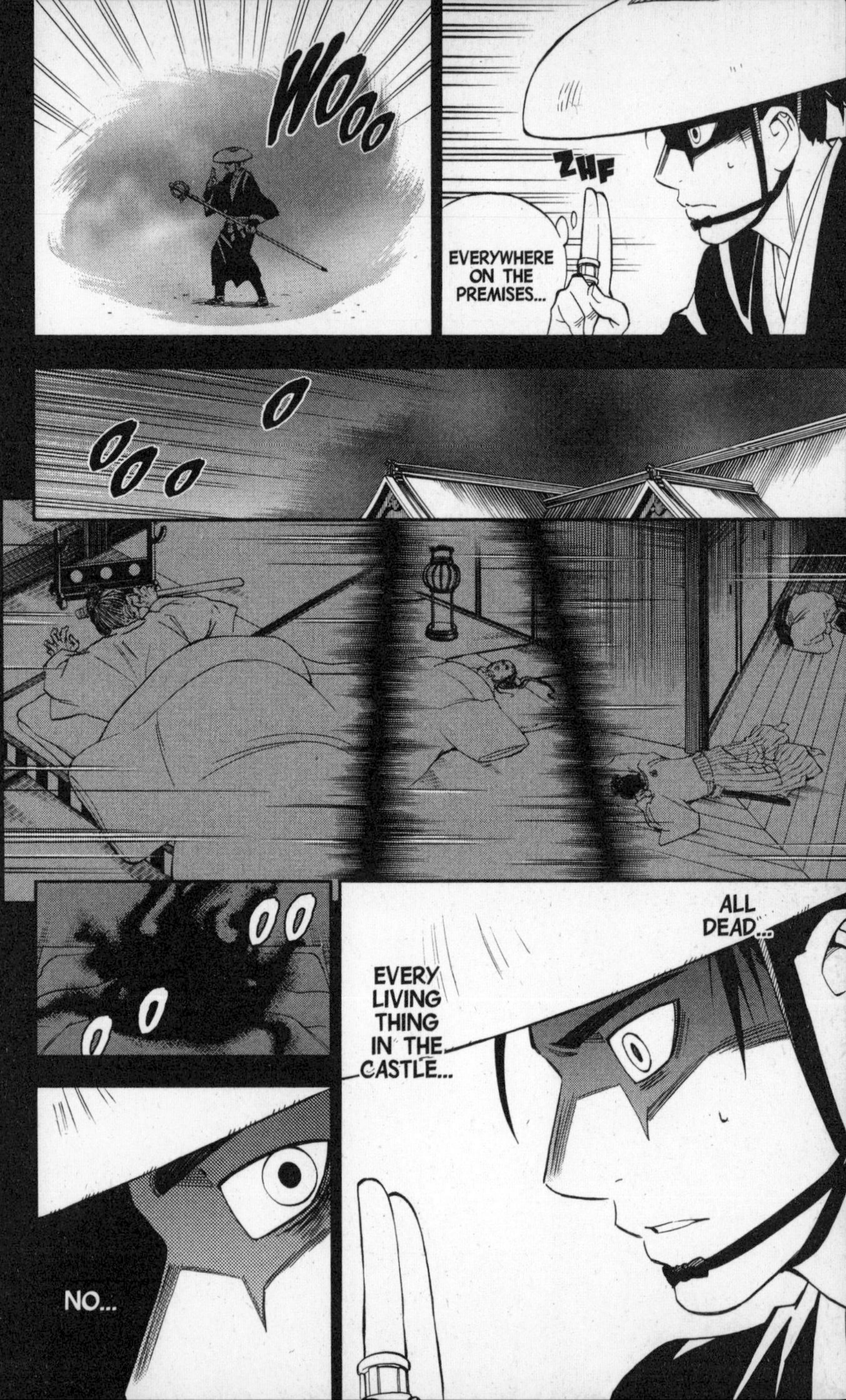
ZHF
EVERYWHERE ON THE PREMISES...
WOOO
OOOO
OOOO
ALL DEAD...
EVERY LIVING THING IN THE CASTLE...
NO...

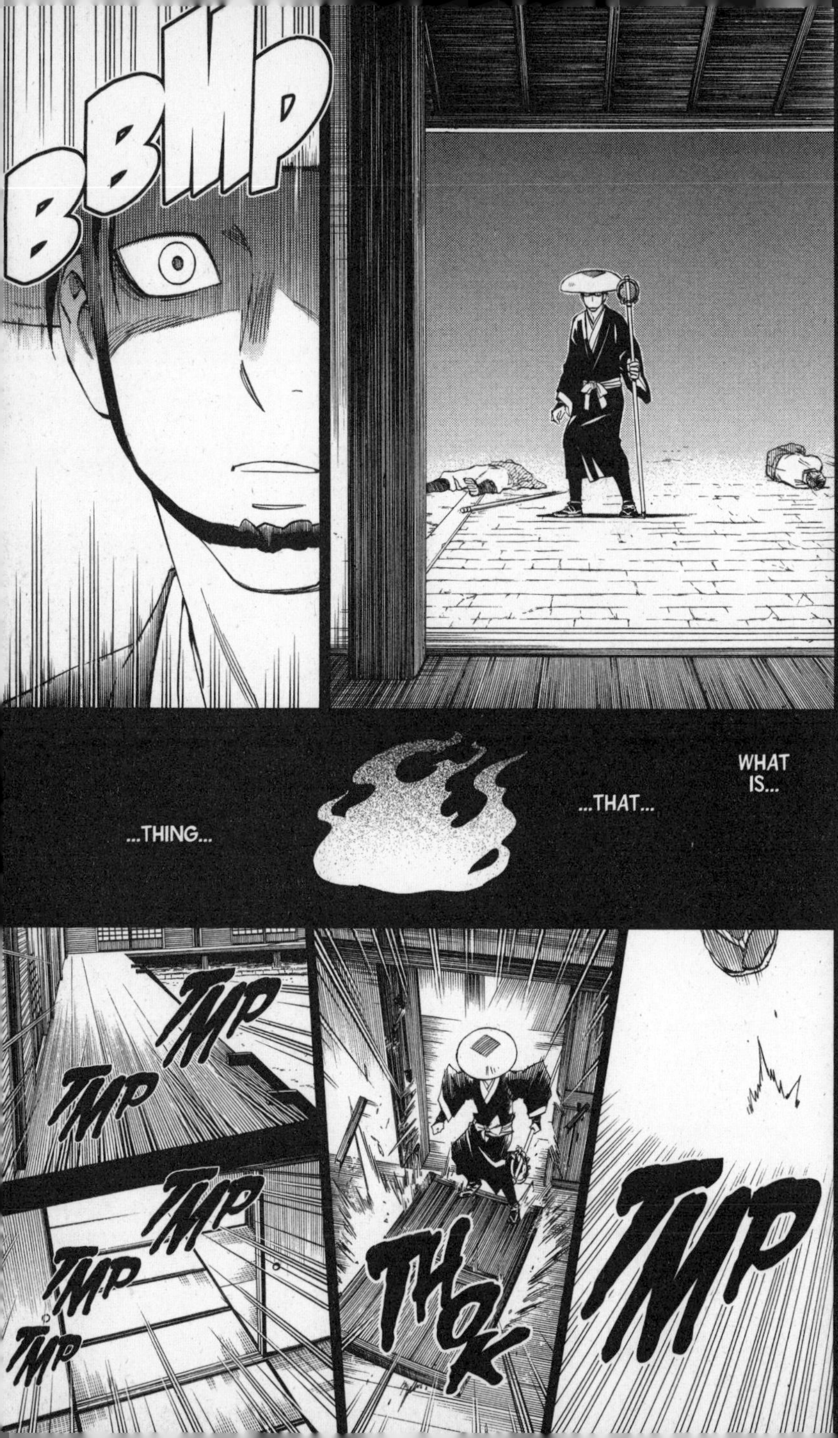
BBMP
WHAT IS...
...THAT...
...THING...
TMP
THK
TMP
TMP
TMP
TMP
TMP

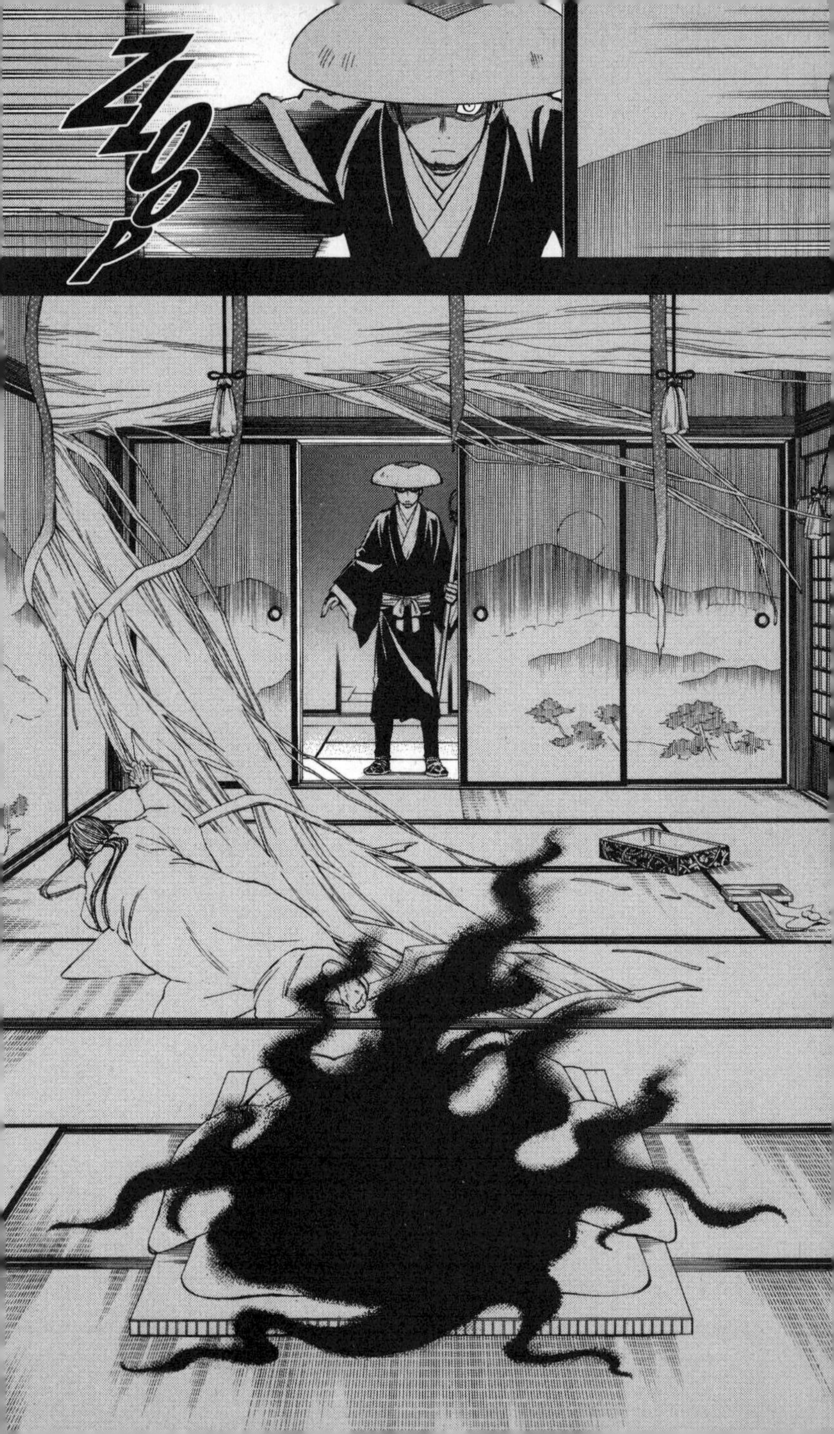
ZLOOP

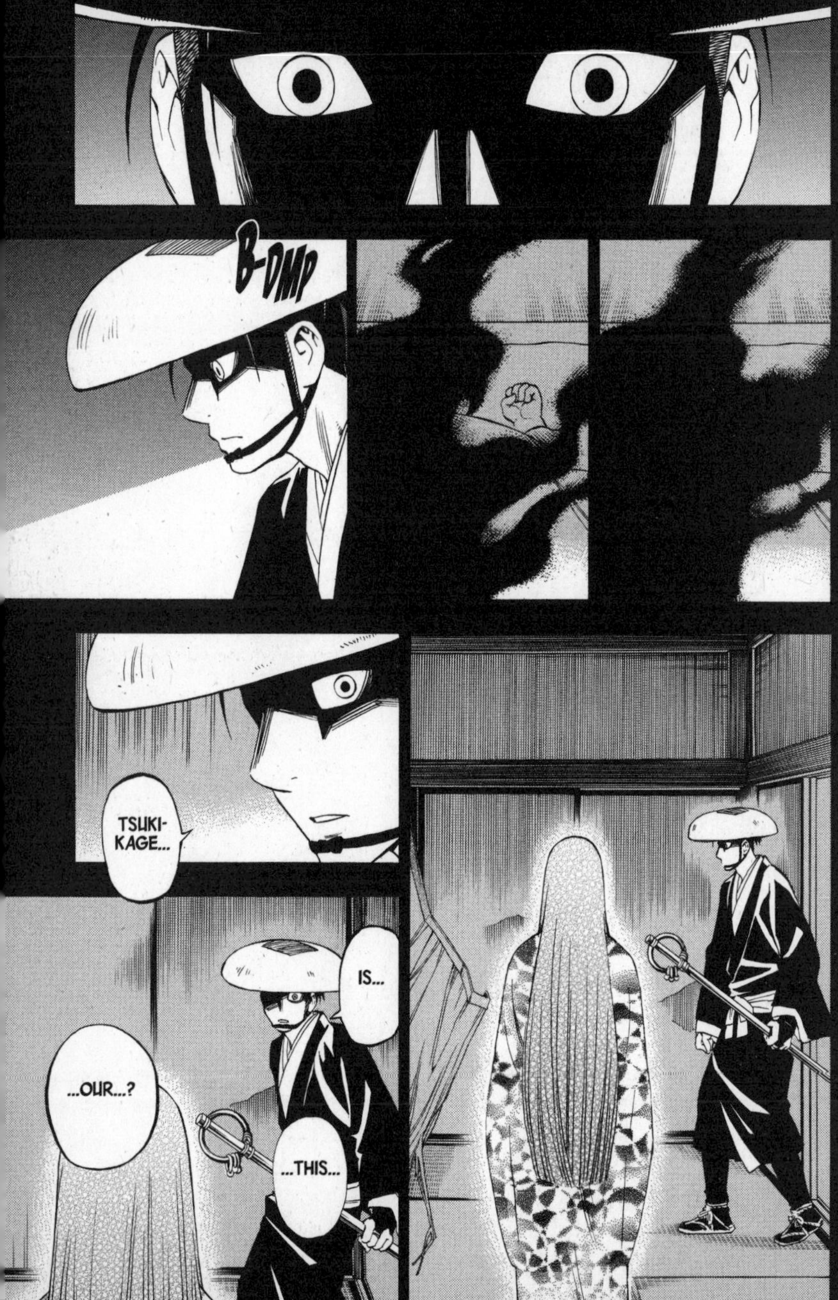
B-DMP
TSUKI-KAGE...
IS...
...THIS...
...OUR...?

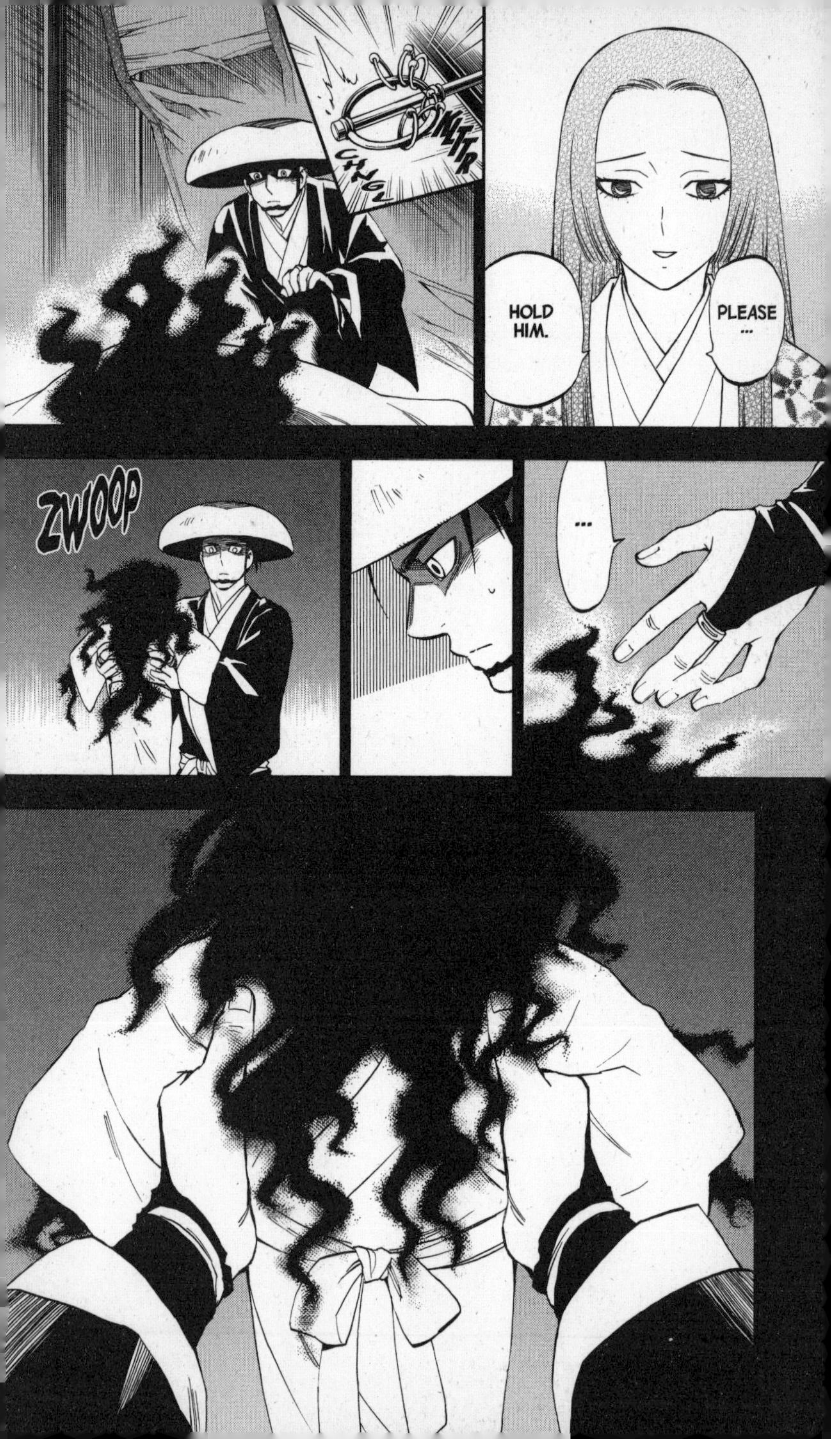
PLEASE ...
HOLD HIM.
KLTTR
CHNG
...
ZWOOP

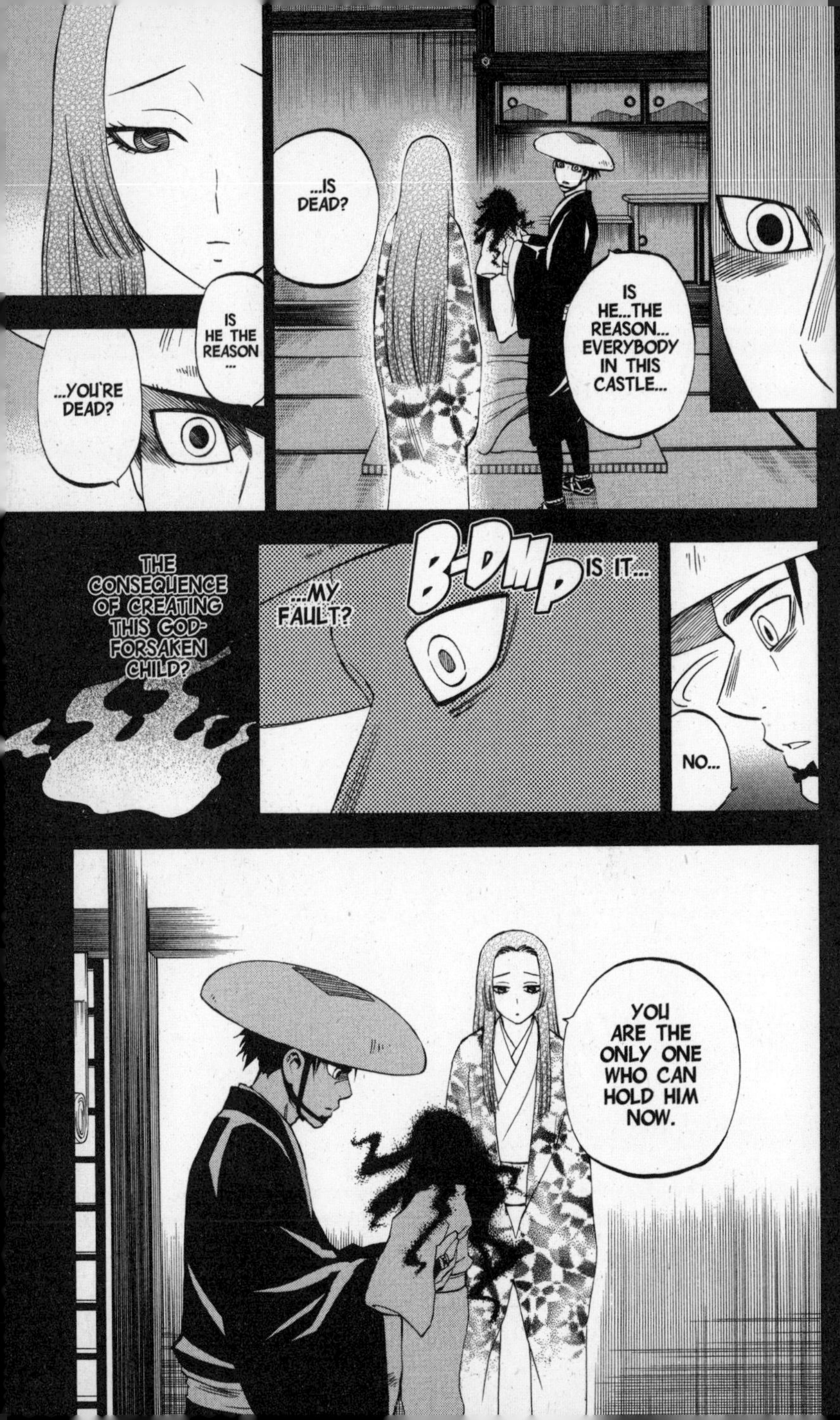
IS HE...THE REASON... EVERYBODY IN THIS CASTLE...
...IS DEAD?
IS HE THE REASON ...
...YOU'RE DEAD?
NO...
B-DMP
IS IT...
...MY FAULT?
THE CONSEQUENCE OF CREATING THIS GOD-FORSAKEN CHILD?
YOU ARE THE ONLY ONE WHO CAN HOLD HIM NOW.

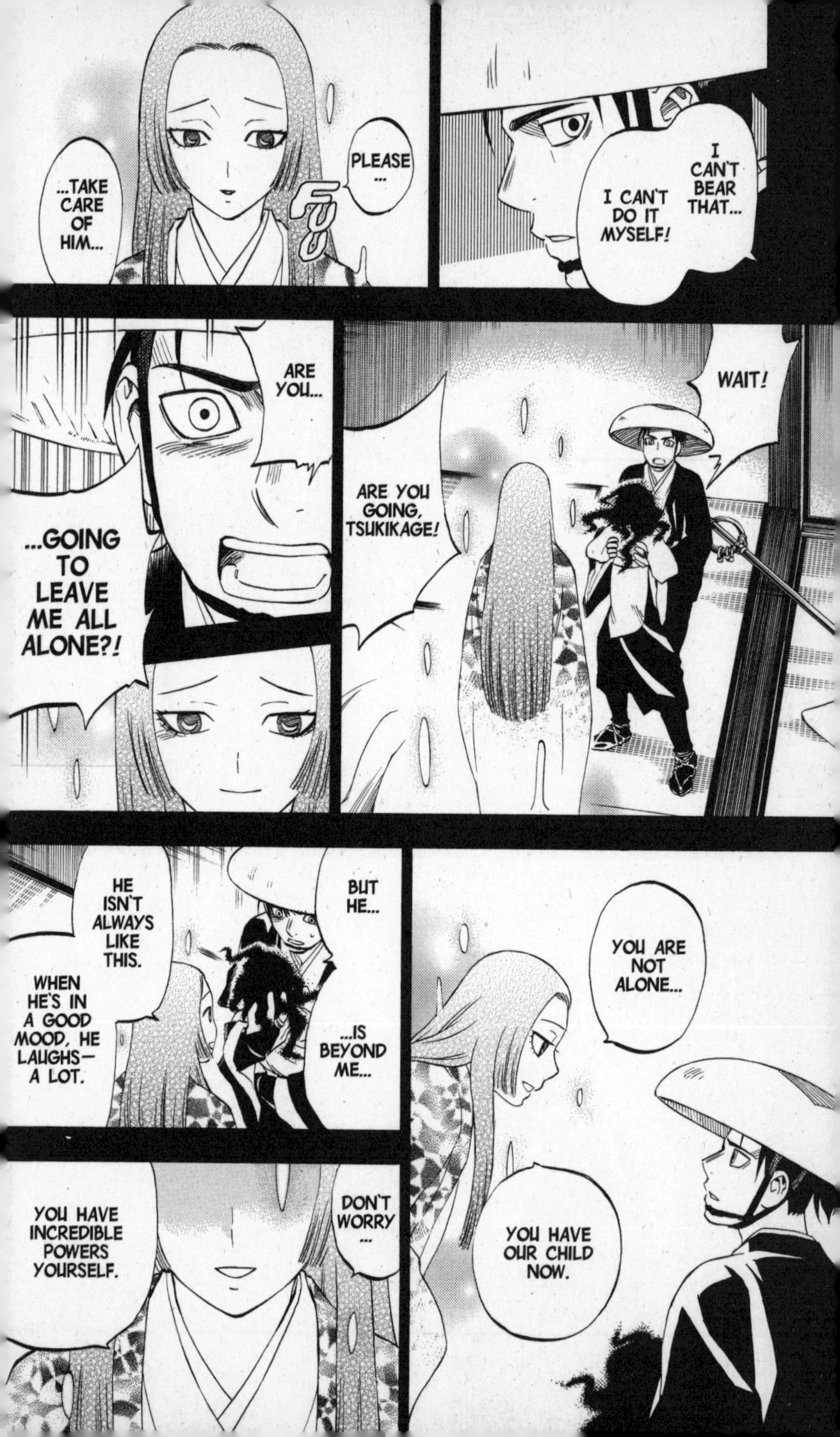
I CAN'T BEAR THAT...
I CAN'T DO IT MYSELF!
PLEASE ...
...TAKE CARE OF HIM...
WAIT!
ARE YOU GOING, TSUKIKAGE!
ARE YOU...
...GOING TO LEAVE ME ALL ALONE?!
YOU ARE NOT ALONE...
YOU HAVE OUR CHILD NOW.
BUT HE...
...IS BEYOND ME...
HE ISN'T ALWAYS LIKE THIS.
WHEN HE'S IN A GOOD MOOD, HE LAUGHS— A LOT.
DON'T WORRY ...
YOU HAVE INCREDIBLE POWERS YOURSELF.

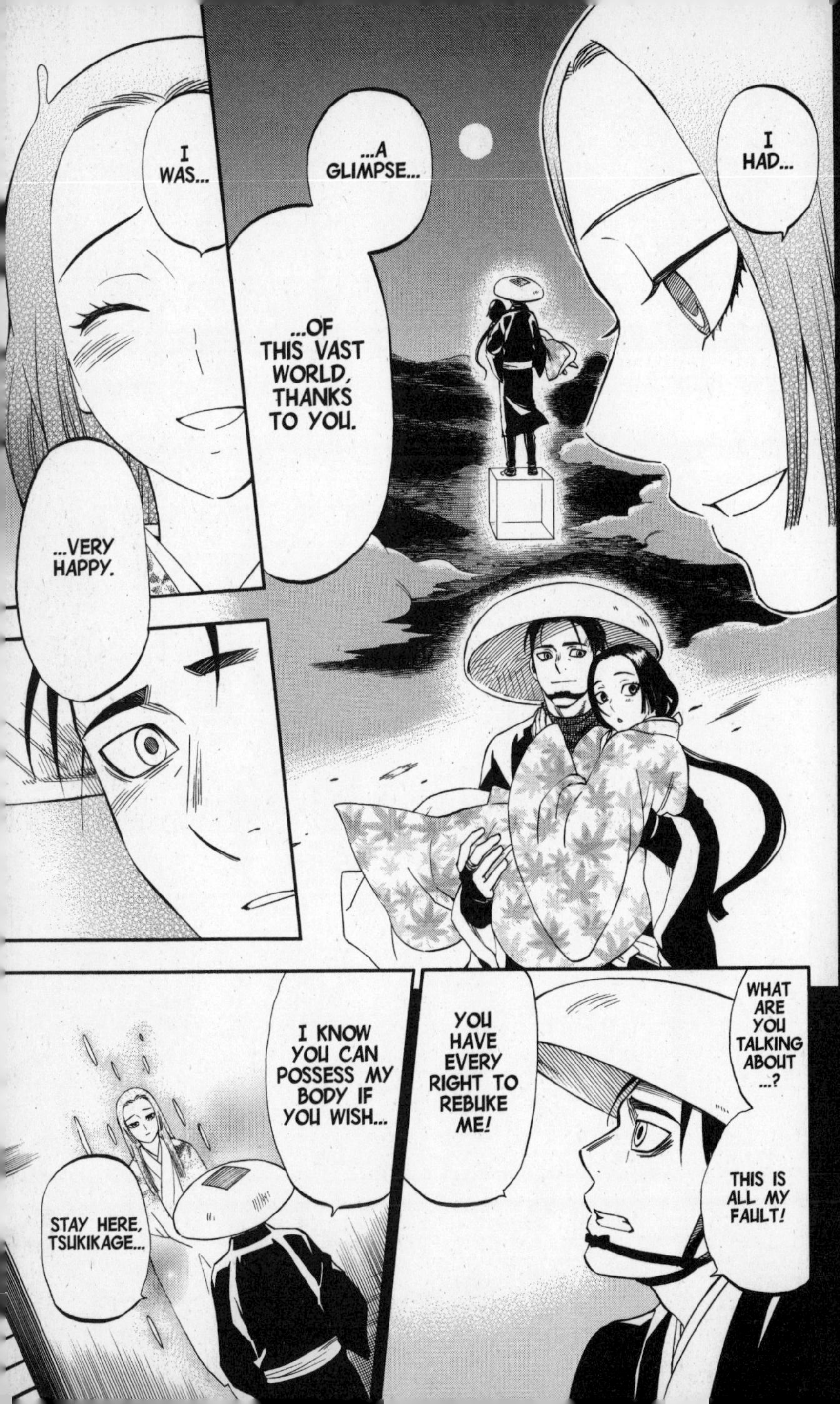
I HAD...
...A GLIMPSE...
...OF THIS VAST WORLD, THANKS TO YOU.
I WAS...
...VERY HAPPY.
WHAT ARE YOU TALKING ABOUT ...?
THIS IS ALL MY FAULT!
YOU HAVE EVERY RIGHT TO REBUKE ME!
I KNOW YOU CAN POSSESS MY BODY IF YOU WISH...
STAY HERE, TSUKIKAGE...

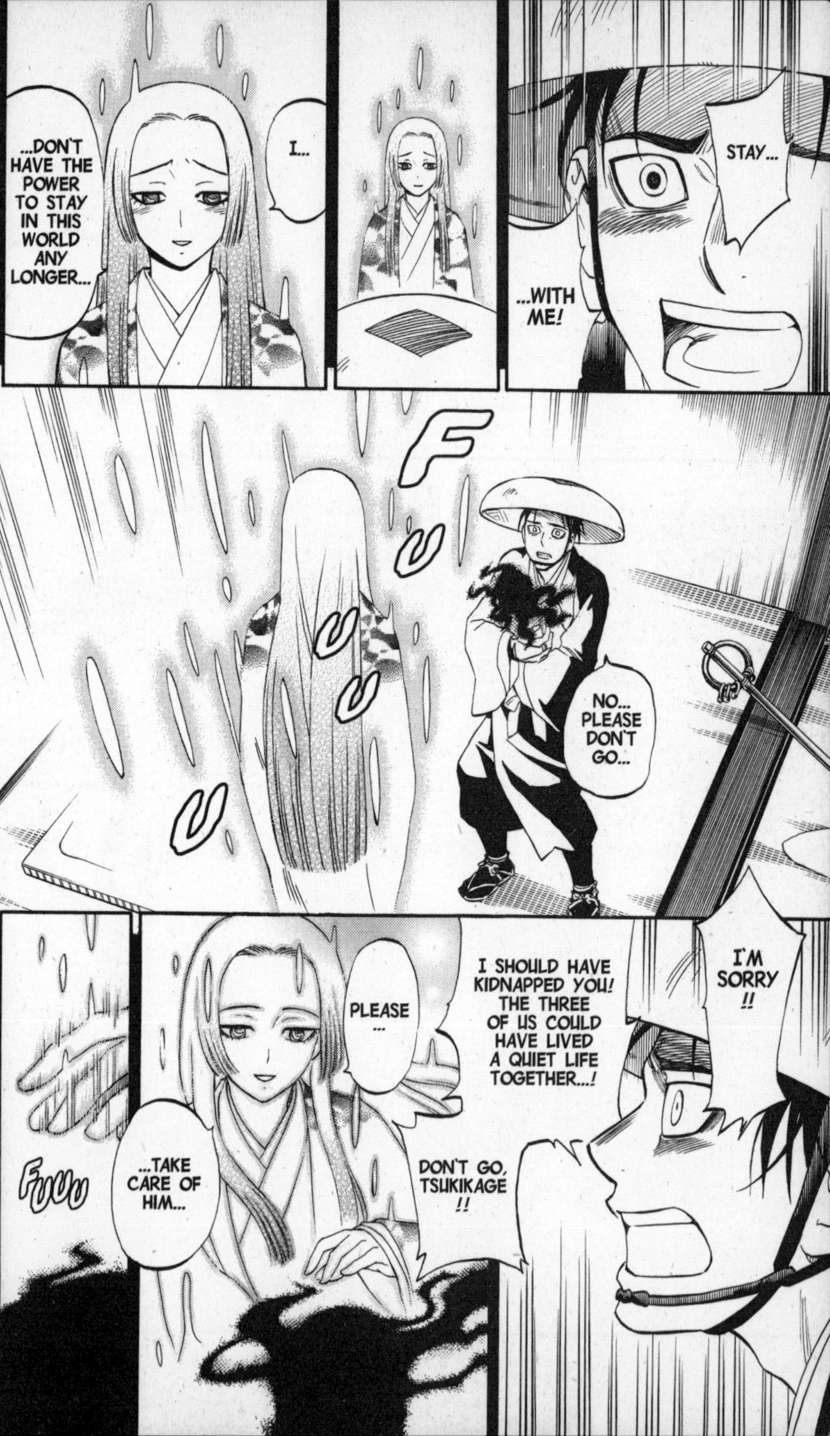
STAY...
...WITH ME!
I...
...DON'T HAVE THE POWER TO STAY IN THIS WORLD ANY LONGER...
NO... PLEASE DON'T GO...
FUUUUU
I'M SORRY!!
I SHOULD HAVE KIDNAPPED YOU! THE THREE OF US COULD HAVE LIVED A QUIET LIFE TOGETHER...!
DON'T GO, TSUKIKAGE!!
PLEASE ...
...TAKE CARE OF HIM...
FUUU

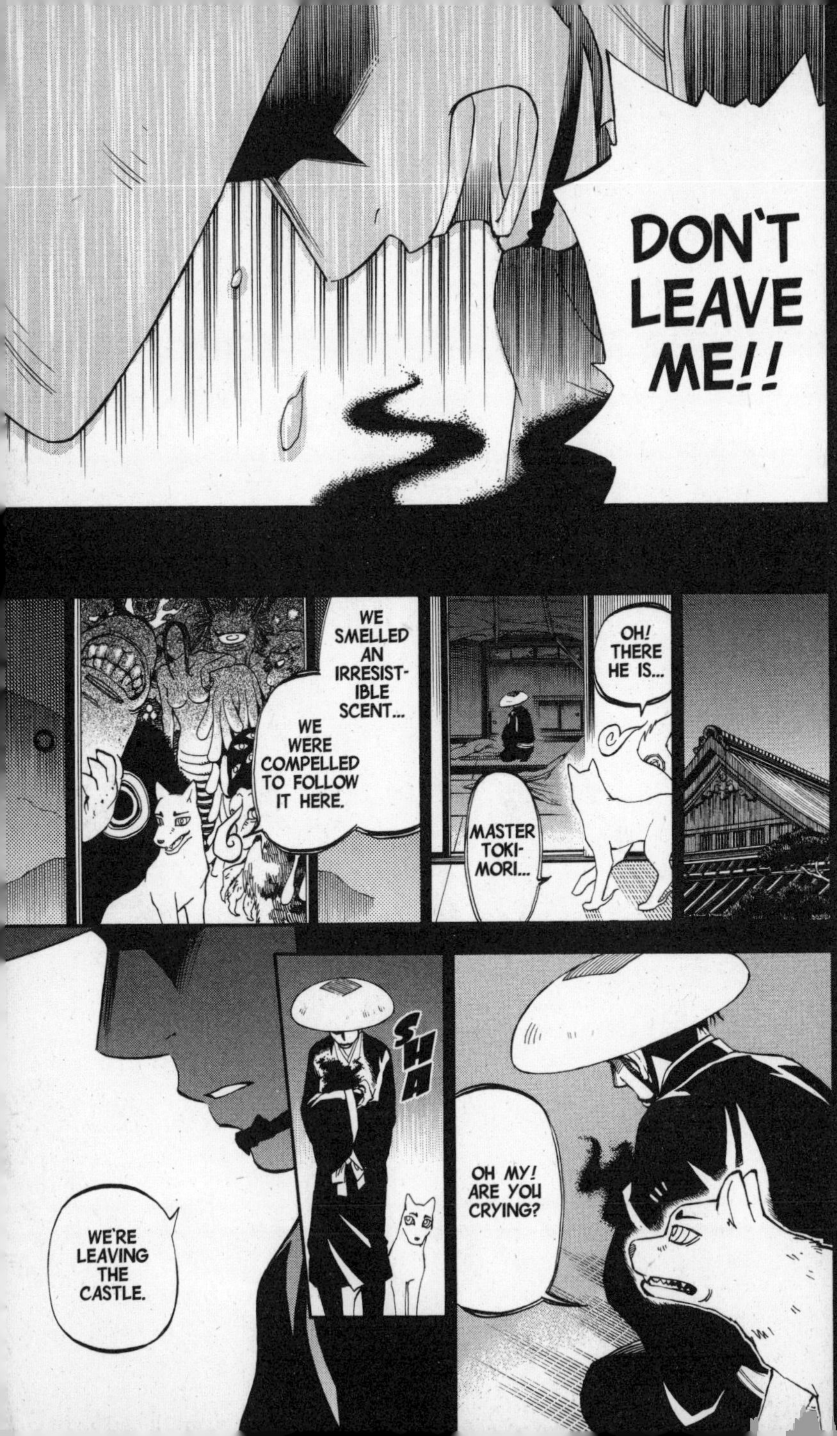
DON'T LEAVE ME!!
OH! THERE HE IS...
MASTER TOKI-MORI...
WE SMELLED AN IRRESIST-IBLE SCENT...
WE WERE COMPELLED TO FOLLOW IT HERE.
OH MY! ARE YOU CRYING?
SHA
WE'RE LEAVING THE CASTLE.

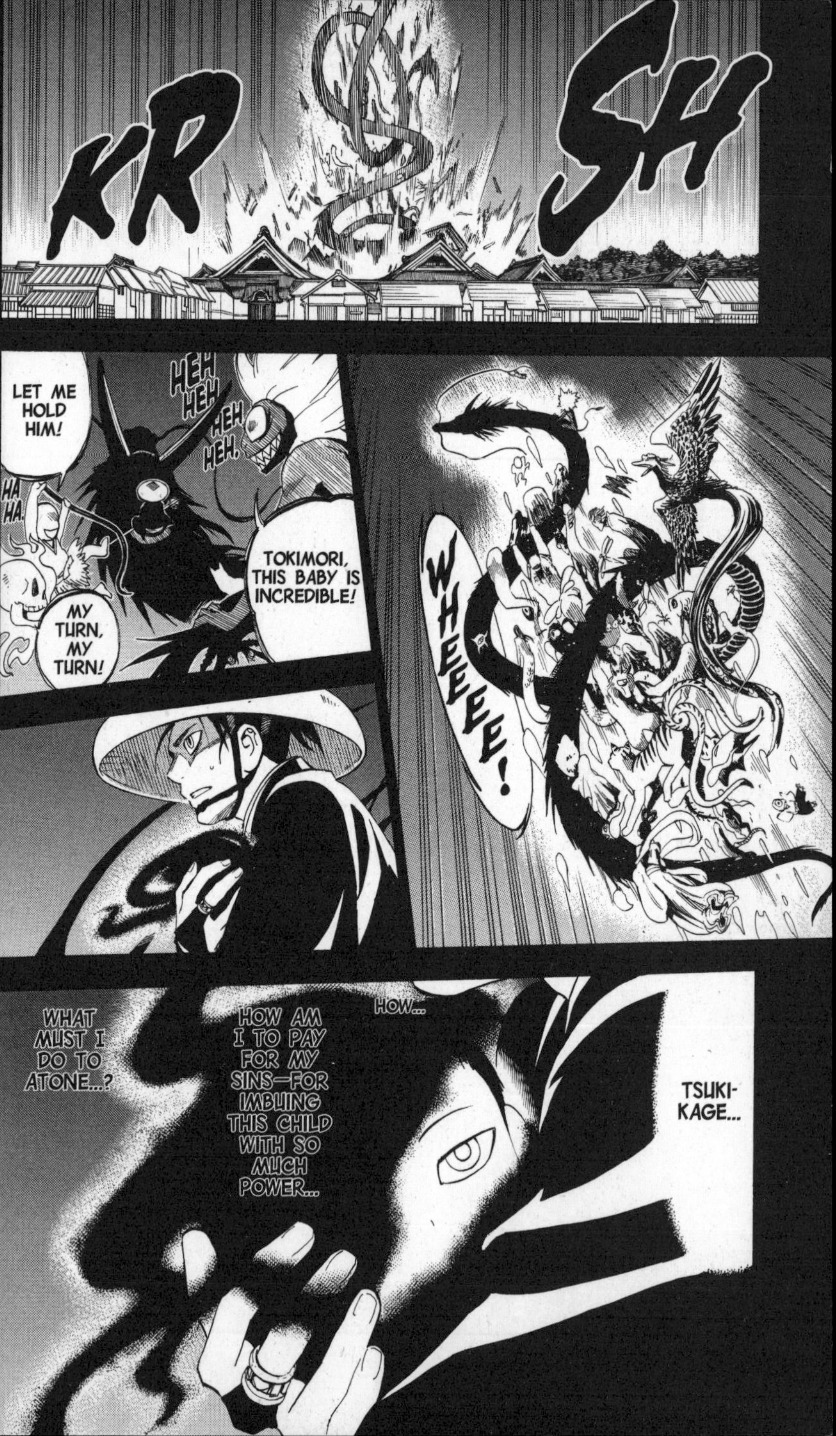
KR
SH
WHEEEE!
HEH HEH
HEH HEH.
TOKIMORI, THIS BABY IS INCREDIBLE!
LET ME HOLD HIM!
HA HA!
MY TURN, MY TURN!
TSUKI-KAGE...
HOW...
HOW AM I TO PAY FOR MY SINS—FOR IMBUING THIS CHILD WITH SO MUCH POWER...
WHAT MUST I DO TO ATONE...?

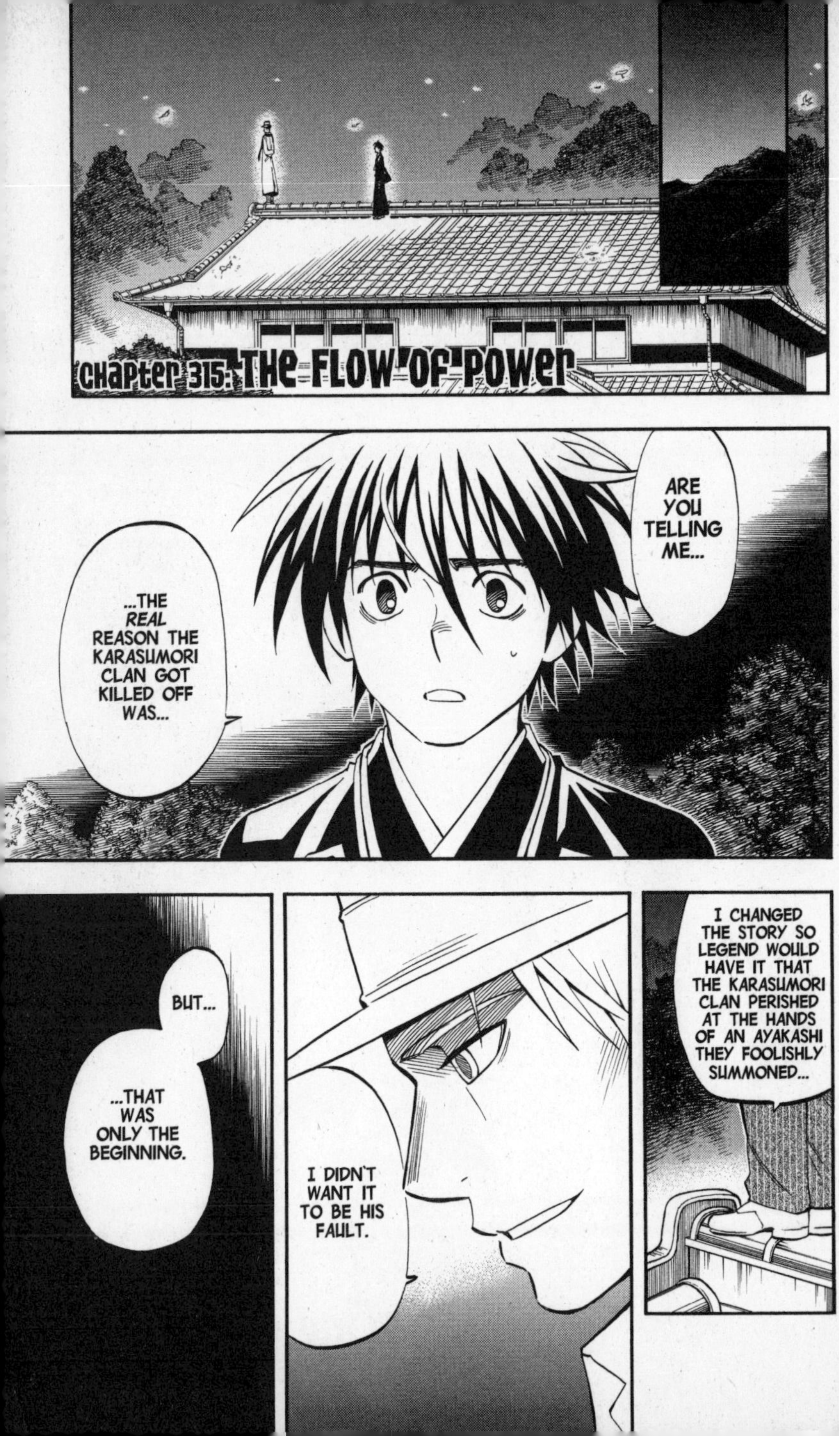
Chapter 315: The Flow of Power
ARE YOU TELLING ME...
...THE *REAL* REASON THE KARASUMORI CLAN GOT KILLED OFF WAS...
I CHANGED THE STORY SO LEGEND WOULD HAVE IT THAT THE KARASUMORI CLAN PERISHED AT THE HANDS OF AN AYAKASHI THEY FOOLISHLY SUMMONED...
I DIDN'T WANT IT TO BE HIS FAULT.
BUT...
...THAT WAS ONLY THE BEGINNING.

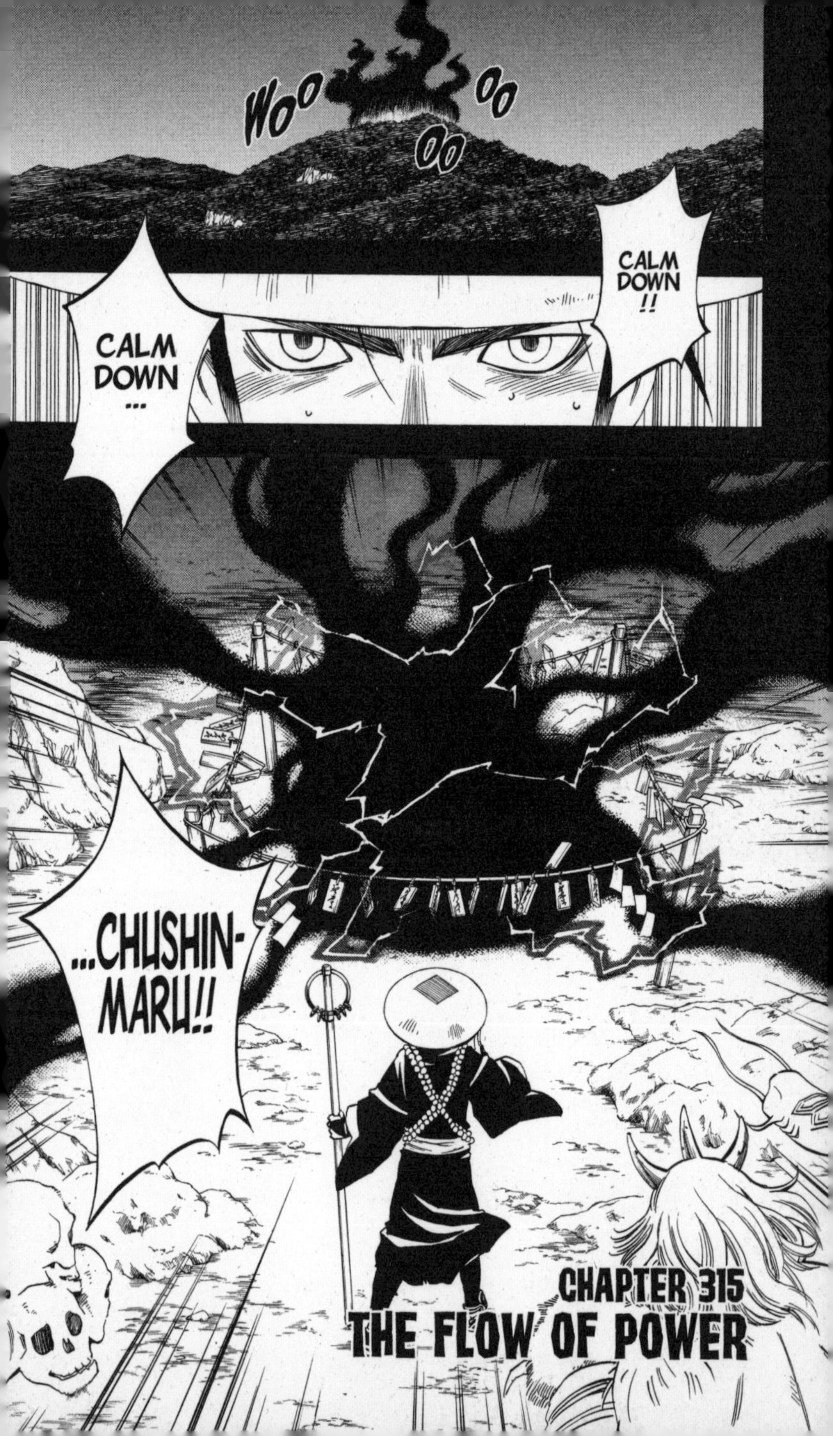
WOOOOOO
CALM DOWN!!
CALM DOWN...
...CHUSHIN-MARU!!
CHAPTER 315
THE FLOW OF POWER

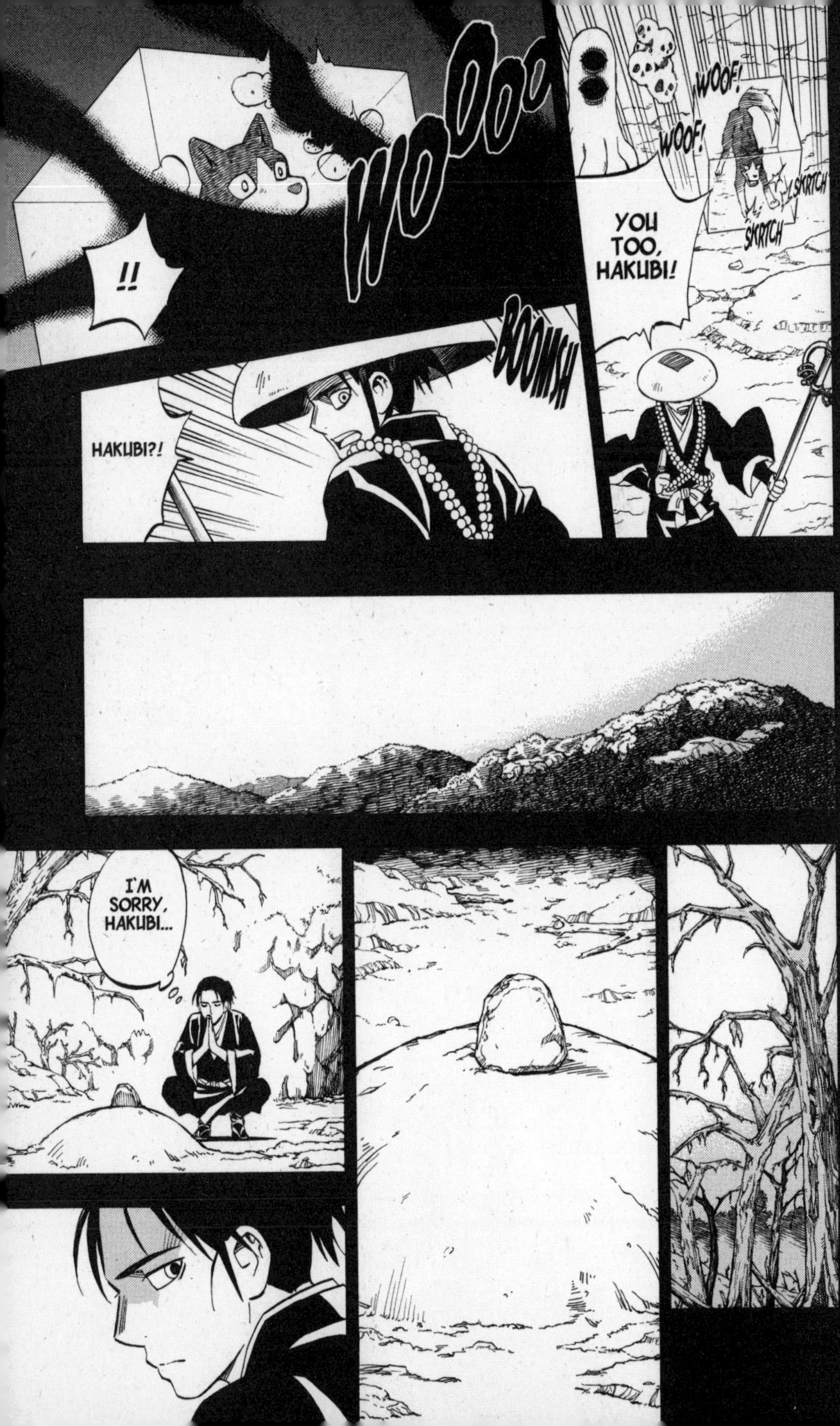
WOOF!
WOOF!
SKRTCH
SKRTCH
YOU TOO, HAKUBI!
!!
WOOOOO
BOOMSH
HAKUBI?!
I'M SORRY, HAKUBI...

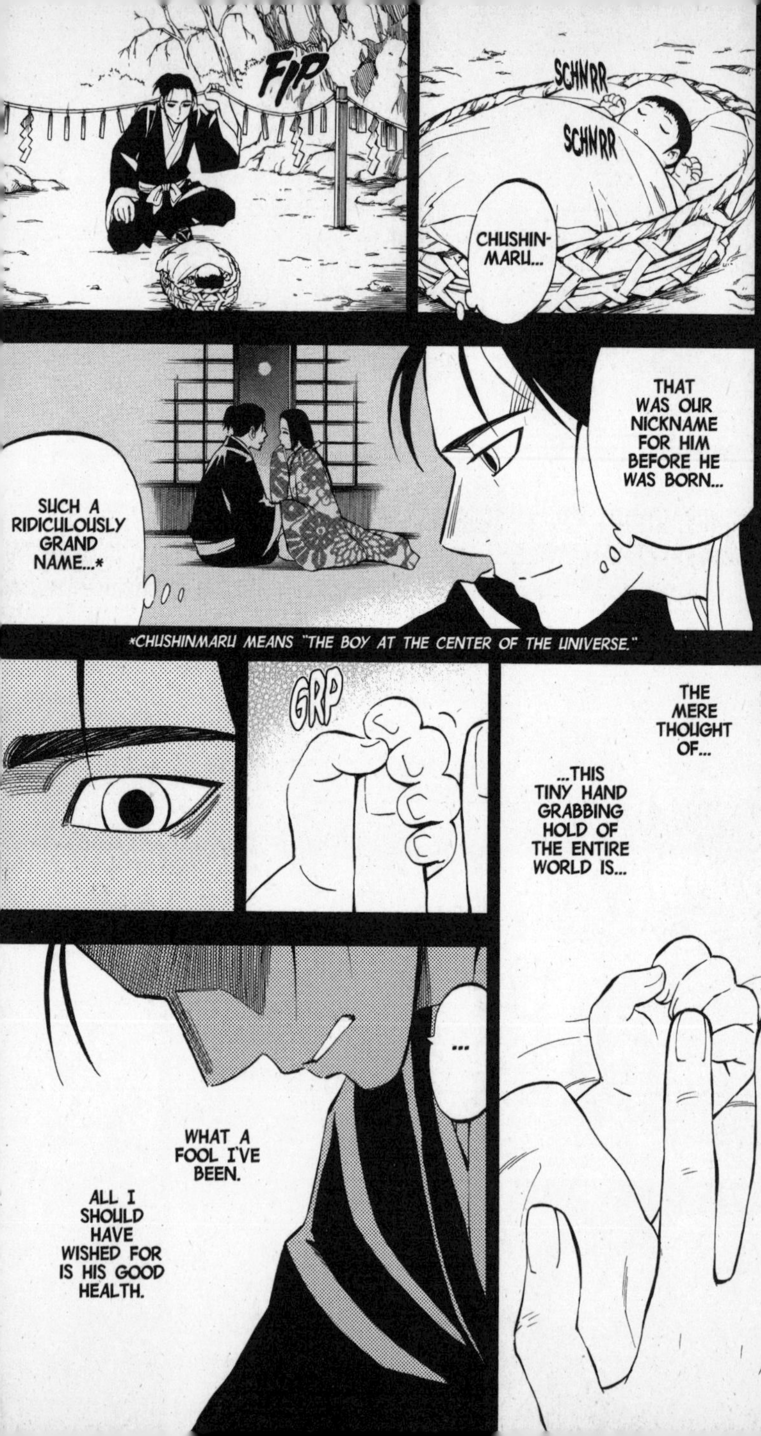
SCHNRR
SCHNRR
CHUSHIN-MARU...
FIP
THAT WAS OUR NICKNAME FOR HIM BEFORE HE WAS BORN...
SUCH A RIDICULOUSLY GRAND NAME...*
THE MERE THOUGHT OF...
...THIS TINY HAND GRABBING HOLD OF THE ENTIRE WORLD IS...
GRP
...
WHAT A FOOL I'VE BEEN.
ALL I SHOULD HAVE WISHED FOR IS HIS GOOD HEALTH.

*CHUSHINMARU MEANS "THE BOY AT THE CENTER OF THE UNIVERSE."

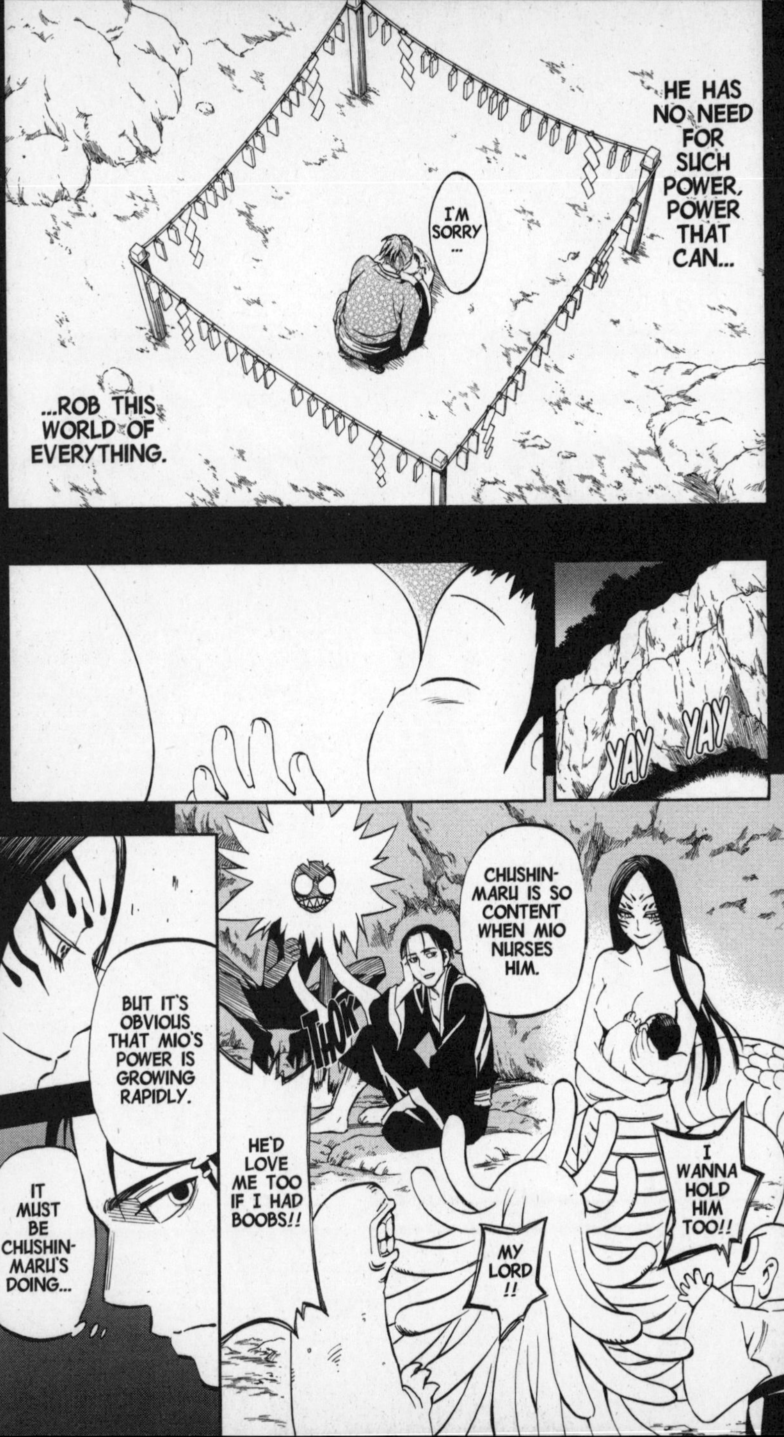
HE HAS NO NEED FOR SUCH POWER, POWER THAT CAN...
I'M SORRY...
...ROB THIS WORLD OF EVERYTHING.
YAY YAY
CHUSHIN-MARU IS SO CONTENT WHEN MIO NURSES HIM.
THOK
I WANNA HOLD HIM TOO!!
MY LORD!!
HE'D LOVE ME TOO IF I HAD BOOBS!!
BUT IT'S OBVIOUS THAT MIO'S POWER IS GROWING RAPIDLY.
IT MUST BE CHUSHIN-MARU'S DOING...

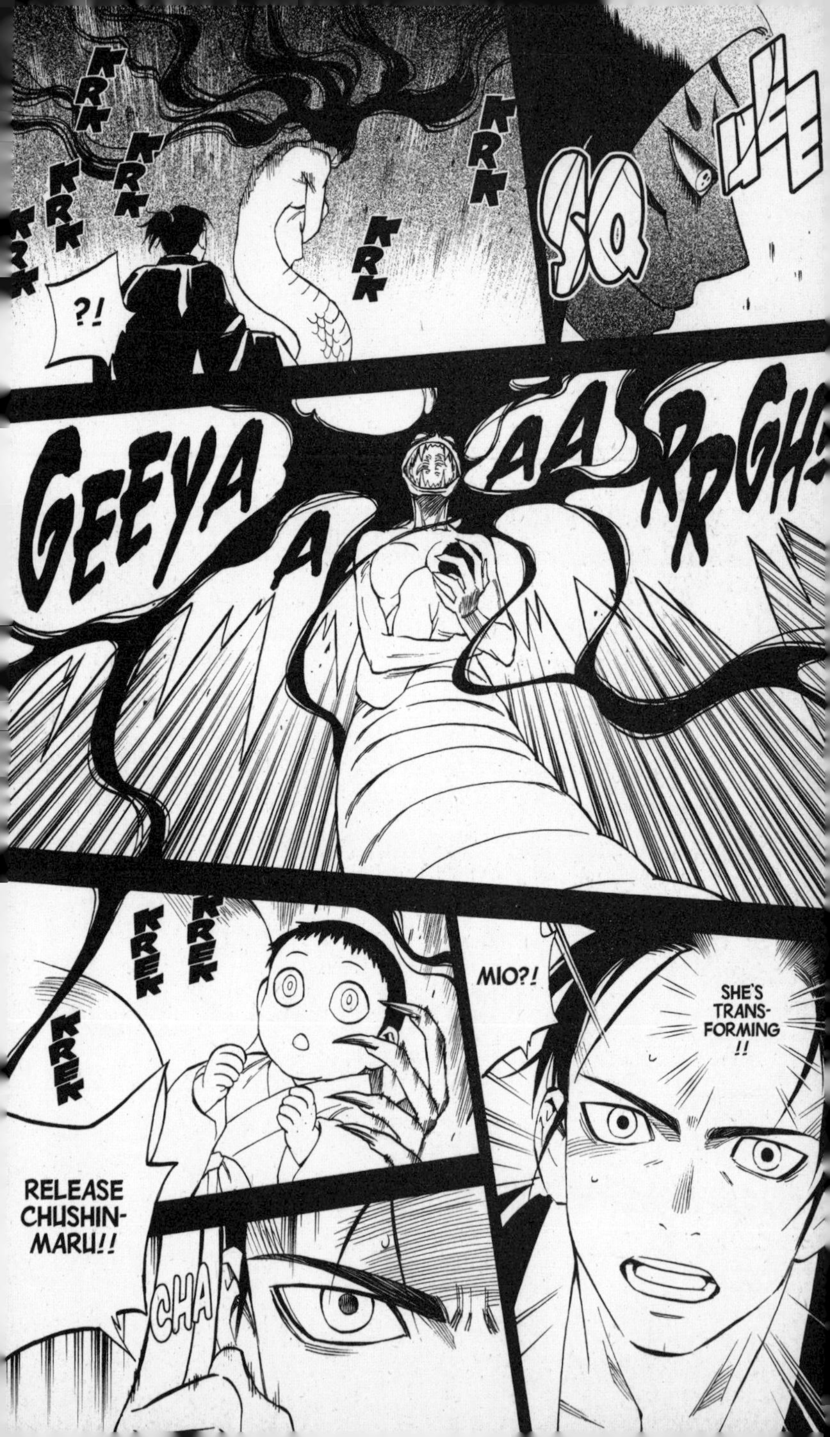
SQUEE
KRK KRK KRK KRK KRK KRK
?!
GEEYAAAAARRGH
MIO?!
SHE'S TRANS- FORMING!!
KREK KREK KREK
RELEASE CHUSHIN- MARU!!
CHA

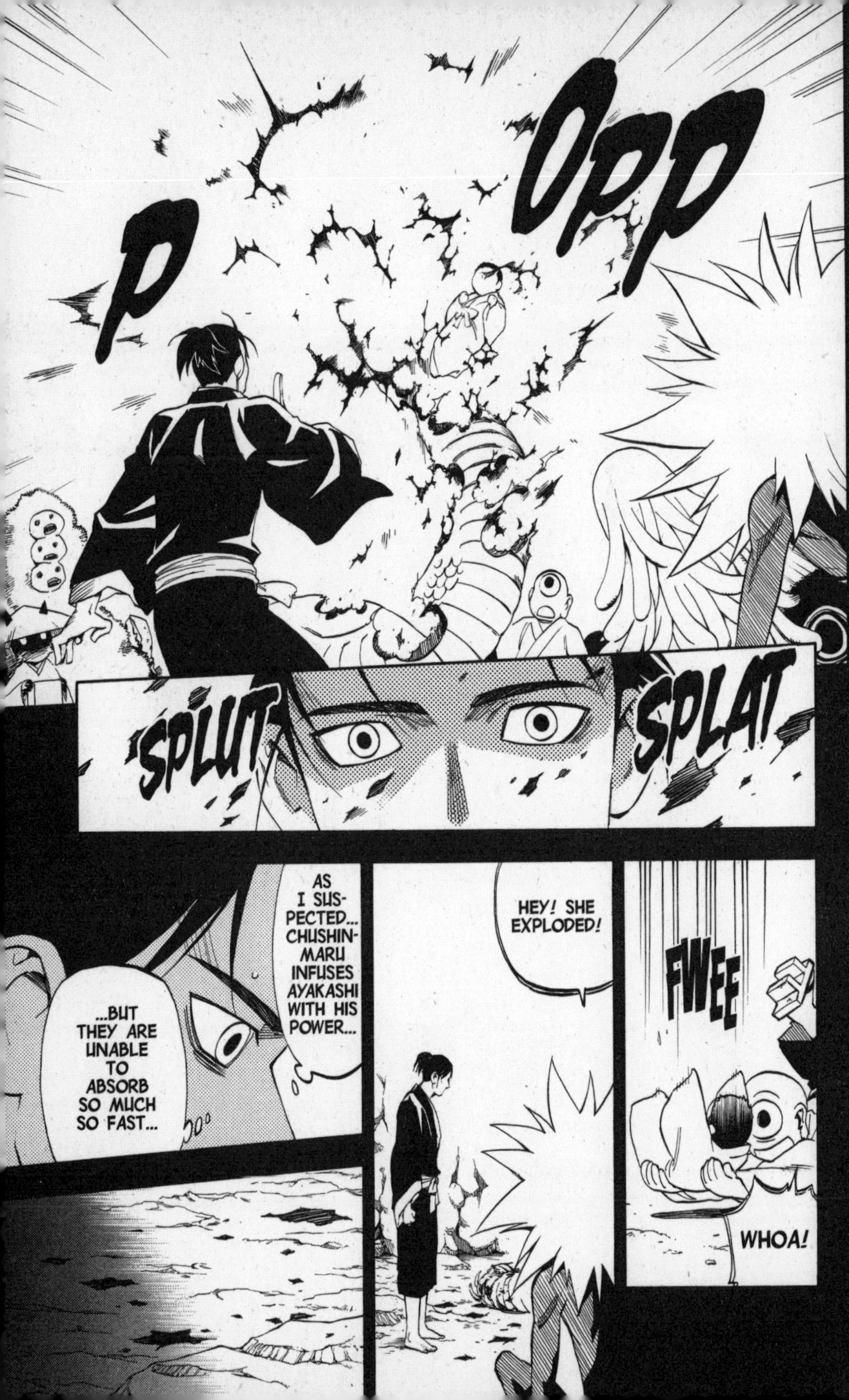

POPP
SPLAT
SPLUT
FWEE
WHOA!
HEY! SHE EXPLODED!
AS I SUSPECTED... CHUSHINMARU INFUSES AYAKASHI WITH HIS POWER...
...BUT THEY ARE UNABLE TO ABSORB SO MUCH SO FAST...

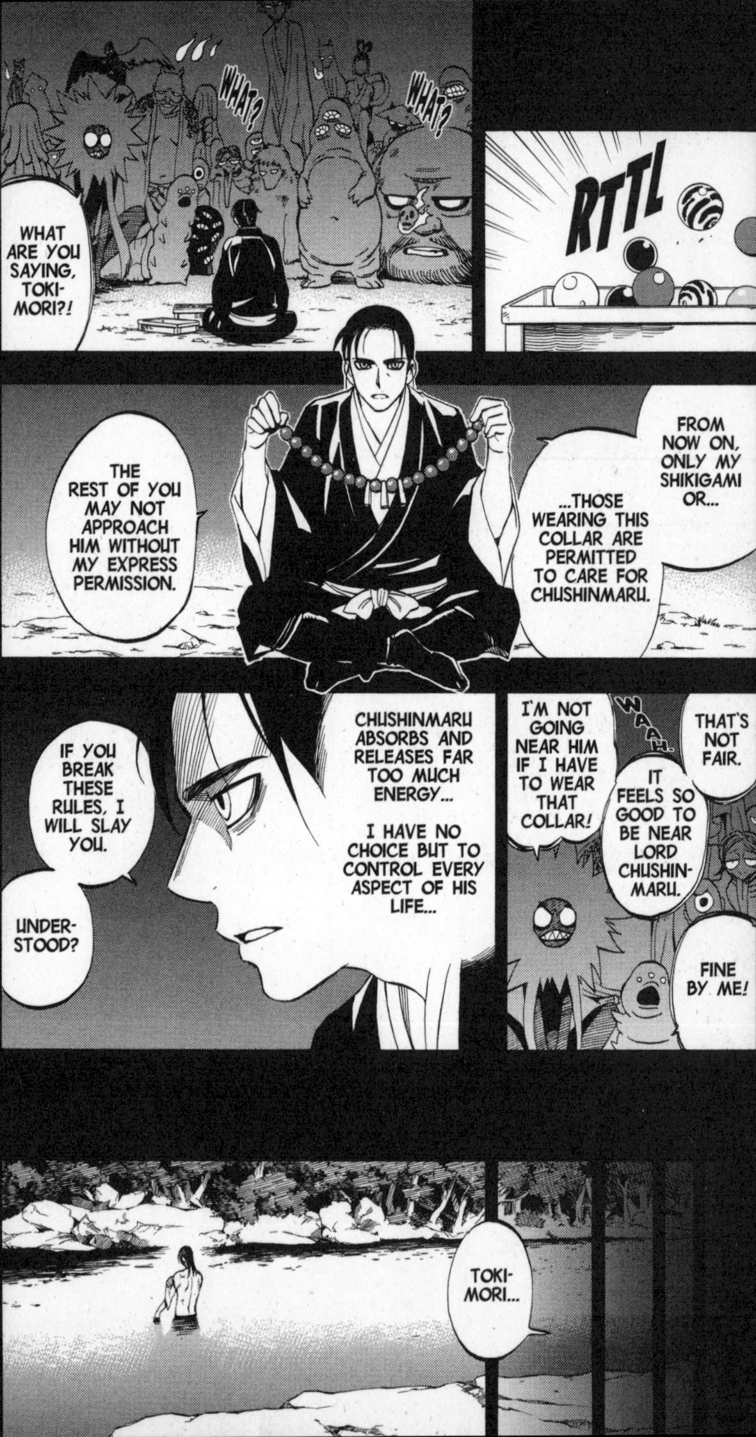
RTTL
WHAT?
WHAT?
WHAT ARE YOU SAYING, TOKI-MORI?!
FROM NOW ON, ONLY MY SHIKIGAMI OR...
...THOSE WEARING THIS COLLAR ARE PERMITTED TO CARE FOR CHUSHINMARU.
THE REST OF YOU MAY NOT APPROACH HIM WITHOUT MY EXPRESS PERMISSION.
THAT'S NOT FAIR.
WAAAH.
I'M NOT GOING NEAR HIM IF I HAVE TO WEAR THAT COLLAR!
IT FEELS SO GOOD TO BE NEAR LORD CHUSHIN-MARU.
FINE BY ME!
CHUSHINMARU ABSORBS AND RELEASES FAR TOO MUCH ENERGY...
I HAVE NO CHOICE BUT TO CONTROL EVERY ASPECT OF HIS LIFE...
IF YOU BREAK THESE RULES, I WILL SLAY YOU.
UNDER-STOOD?
TOKI-MORI...

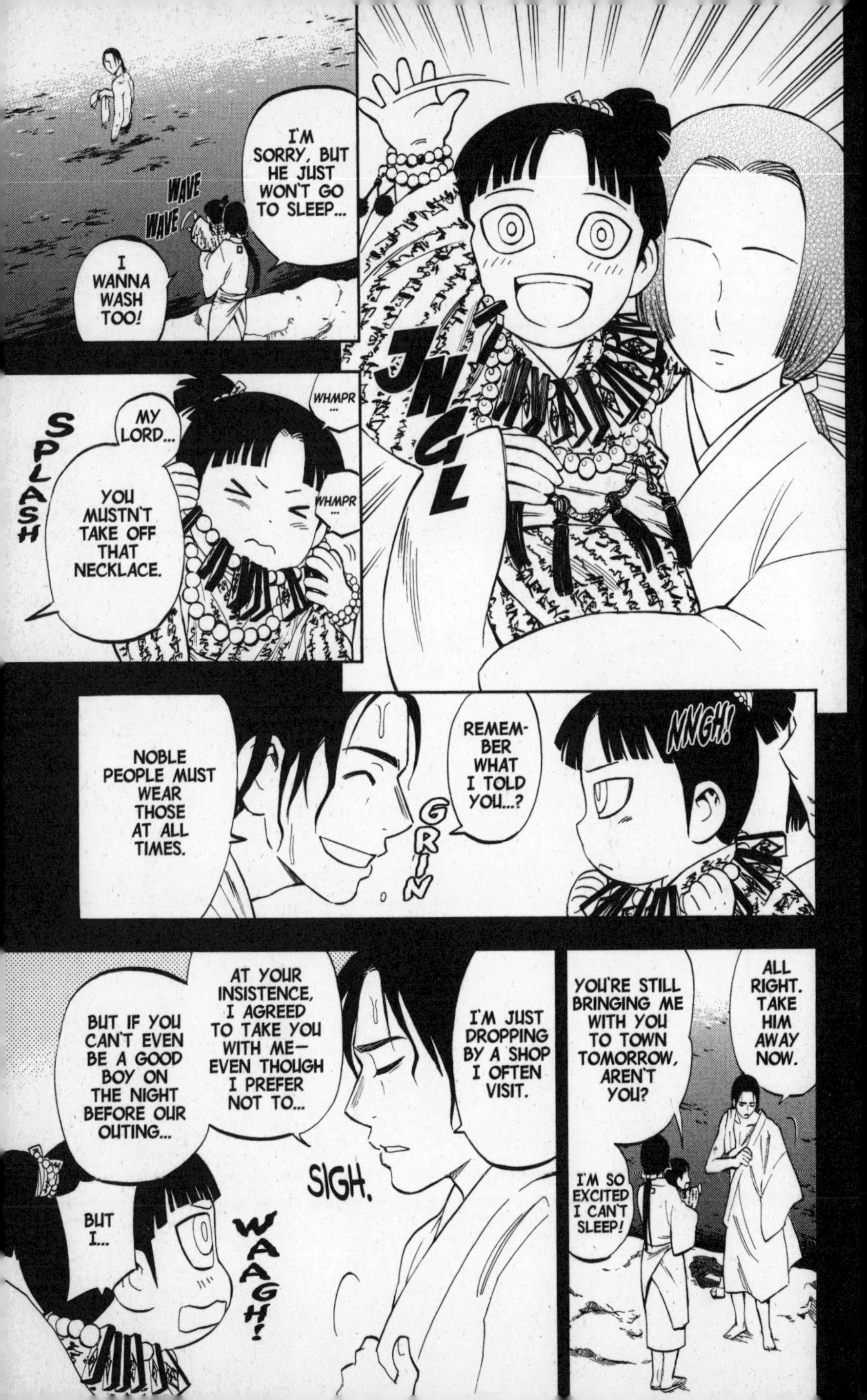
JNGL
I'M SORRY, BUT HE JUST WON'T GO TO SLEEP...
WAVE WAVE
I WANNA WASH TOO!
WHMPR...
MY LORD...
WHMPR...
YOU MUSTN'T TAKE OFF THAT NECKLACE.
SPLASH
NNGH!
REMEM-BER WHAT I TOLD YOU...?
GRIN
NOBLE PEOPLE MUST WEAR THOSE AT ALL TIMES.
ALL RIGHT. TAKE HIM AWAY NOW.
YOU'RE STILL BRINGING ME WITH YOU TO TOWN TOMORROW, AREN'T YOU?
I'M SO EXCITED I CAN'T SLEEP!
I'M JUST DROPPING BY A SHOP I OFTEN VISIT.
AT YOUR INSISTENCE, I AGREED TO TAKE YOU WITH ME— EVEN THOUGH I PREFER NOT TO...
BUT IF YOU CAN'T EVEN BE A GOOD BOY ON THE NIGHT BEFORE OUR OUTING...
SIGH.
WAAGH!
BUT I...

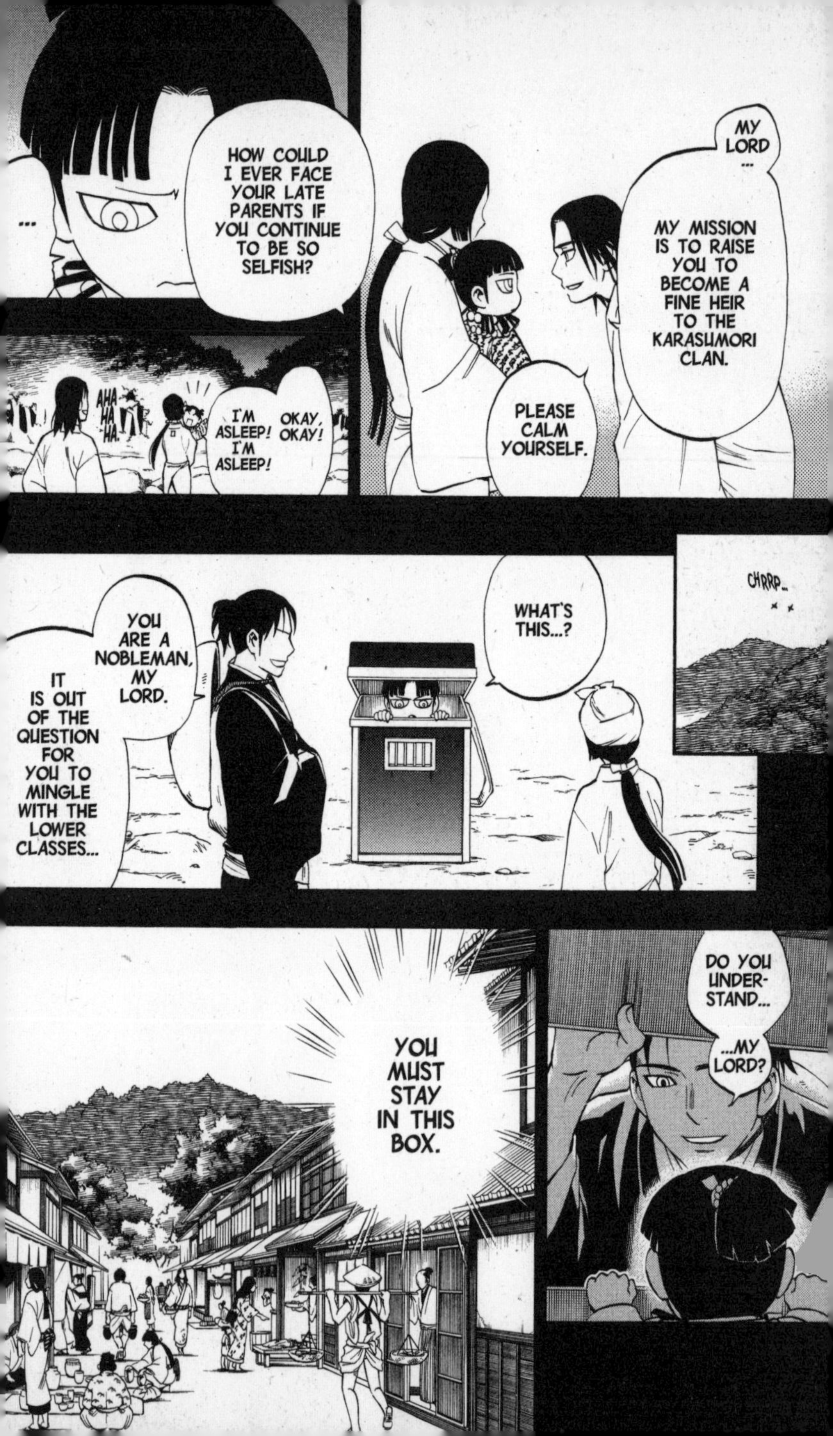
MY LORD...
MY MISSION IS TO RAISE YOU TO BECOME A FINE HEIR TO THE KARASUMORI CLAN.
PLEASE CALM YOURSELF.
HOW COULD I EVER FACE YOUR LATE PARENTS IF YOU CONTINUE TO BE SO SELFISH?
...
OKAY, OKAY!
I'M ASLEEP! I'M ASLEEP!
AHAHAHA.
CHRRP...
WHAT'S THIS...?
YOU ARE A NOBLEMAN, MY LORD.
IT IS OUT OF THE QUESTION FOR YOU TO MINGLE WITH THE LOWER CLASSES...
DO YOU UNDERSTAND...
...MY LORD?
YOU MUST STAY IN THIS BOX.

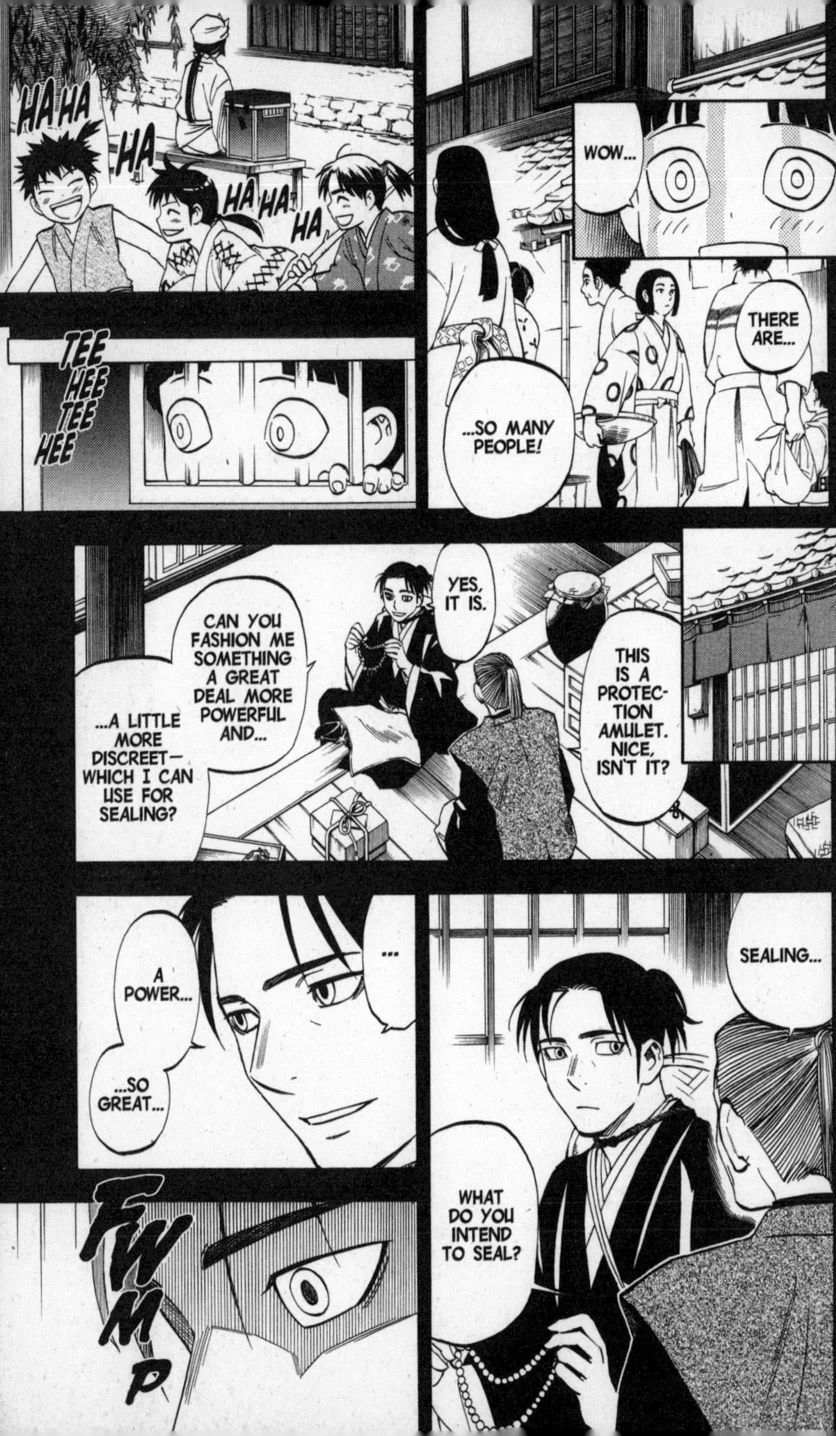
WOW...
THERE ARE...
...SO MANY PEOPLE!
HAHA HA HA HA HA HA
TEE HEE TEE HEE
THIS IS A PROTECTION AMULET. NICE, ISN'T IT?
YES, IT IS.
CAN YOU FASHION ME SOMETHING A GREAT DEAL MORE POWERFUL AND...
...A LITTLE MORE DISCREET—WHICH I CAN USE FOR SEALING?
SEALING...
WHAT DO YOU INTEND TO SEAL?
...
A POWER...
...SO GREAT...
FWMP

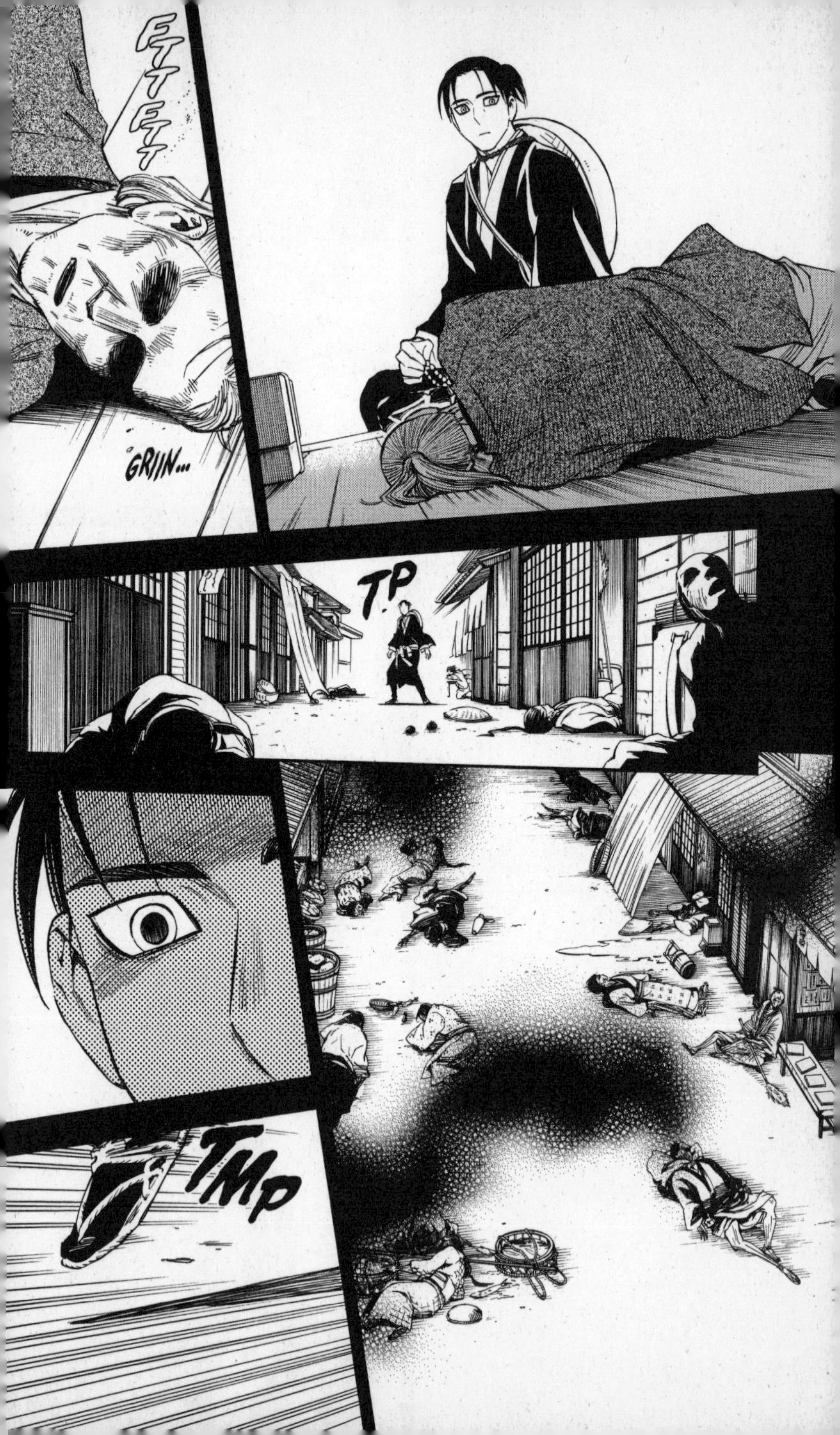
FTTFTT
GRIIN...
TP
TMP

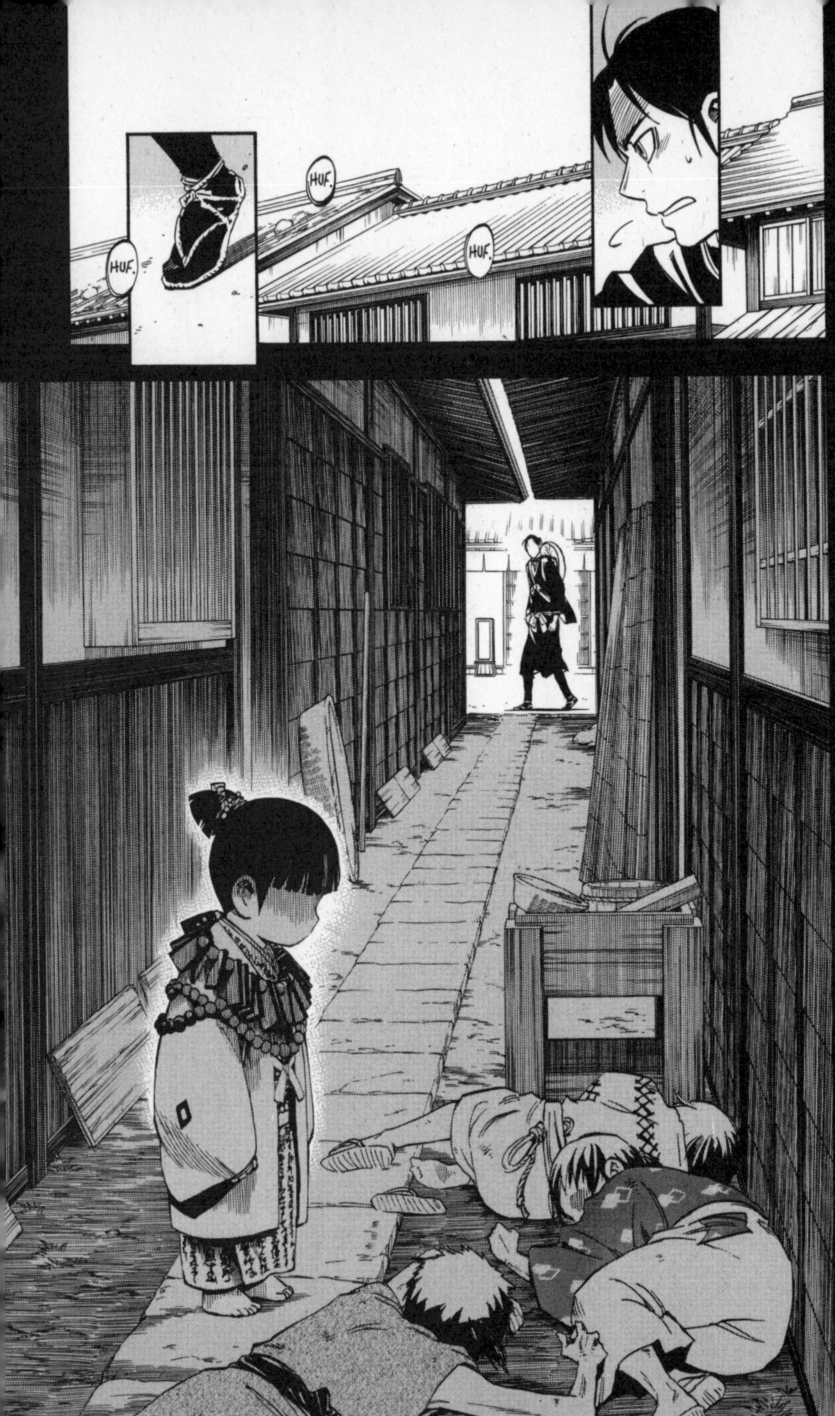
HUF.
HUF.
HUF.

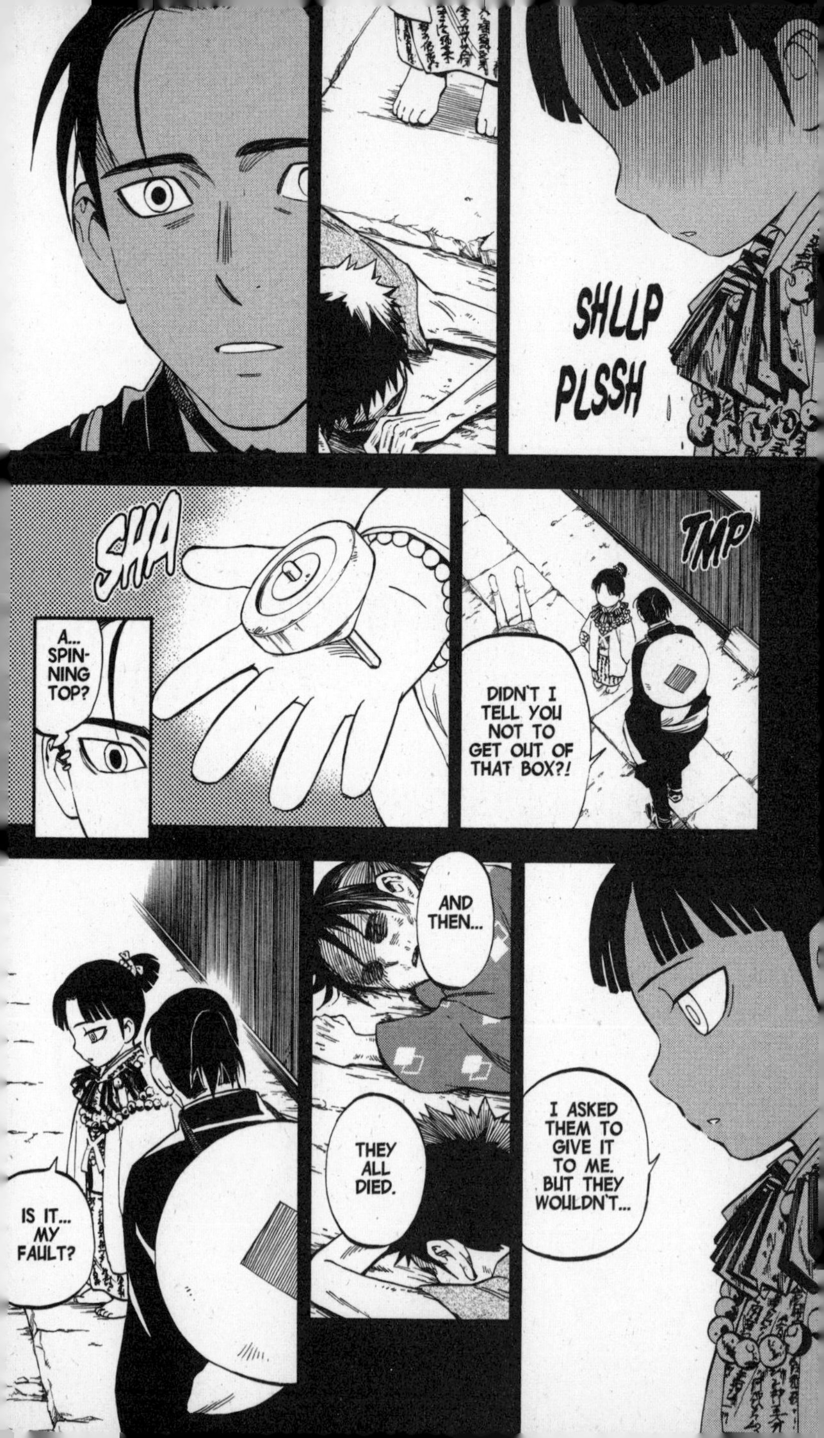
SHLLP
PLSSH
TMP
DIDN'T I TELL YOU NOT TO GET OUT OF THAT BOX?!
SHA
A... SPIN-NING TOP?
I ASKED THEM TO GIVE IT TO ME. BUT THEY WOULDN'T...
AND THEN...
THEY ALL DIED.
IS IT... MY FAULT?

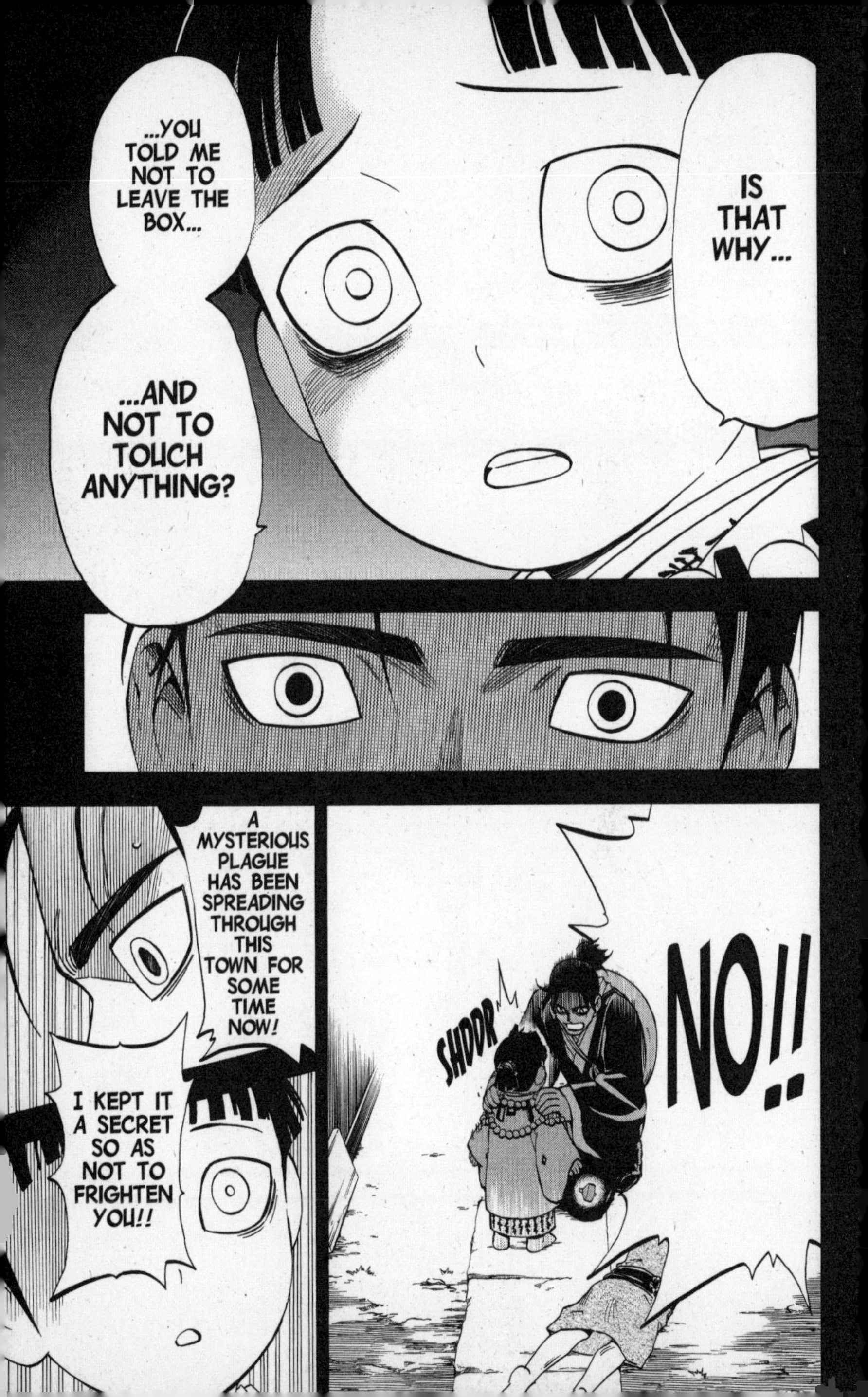
IS THAT WHY...
...YOU TOLD ME NOT TO LEAVE THE BOX...
...AND NOT TO TOUCH ANYTHING?
NO!!
SHDDR
A MYSTERIOUS PLAGUE HAS BEEN SPREADING THROUGH THIS TOWN FOR SOME TIME NOW!
I KEPT IT A SECRET SO AS NOT TO FRIGHTEN YOU!!

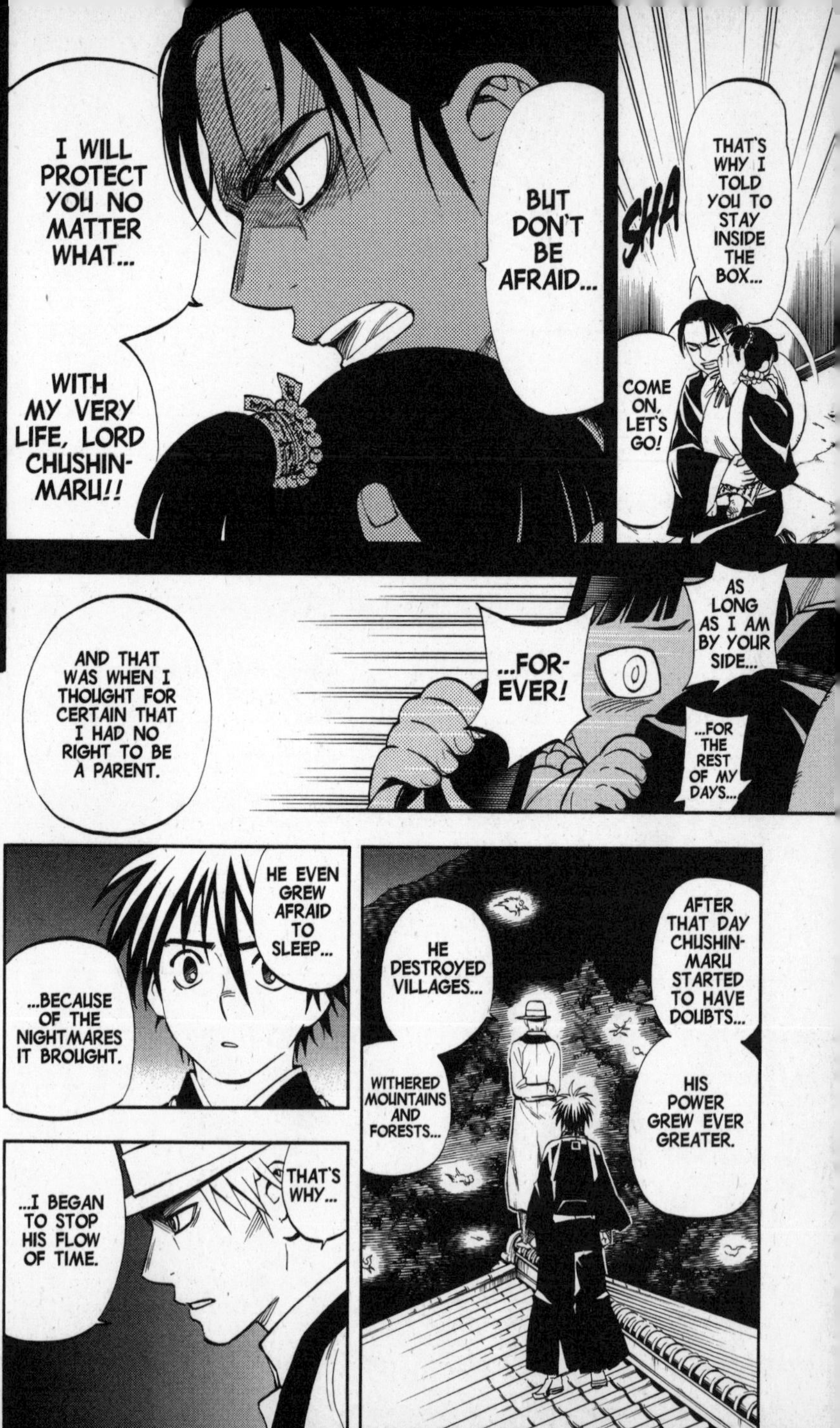
THAT'S WHY I TOLD YOU TO STAY INSIDE THE BOX...
SHA
COME ON, LET'S GO!
BUT DON'T BE AFRAID...
I WILL PROTECT YOU NO MATTER WHAT...
WITH MY VERY LIFE, LORD CHUSHIN-MARU!!
AS LONG AS I AM BY YOUR SIDE...
...FOR THE REST OF MY DAYS...
...FOR-EVER!
AND THAT WAS WHEN I THOUGHT FOR CERTAIN THAT I HAD NO RIGHT TO BE A PARENT.
AFTER THAT DAY CHUSHIN-MARU STARTED TO HAVE DOUBTS...
HIS POWER GREW EVER GREATER.
HE DESTROYED VILLAGES...
WITHERED MOUNTAINS AND FORESTS...
HE EVEN GREW AFRAID TO SLEEP...
...BECAUSE OF THE NIGHTMARES IT BROUGHT.
THAT'S WHY...
...I BEGAN TO STOP HIS FLOW OF TIME.

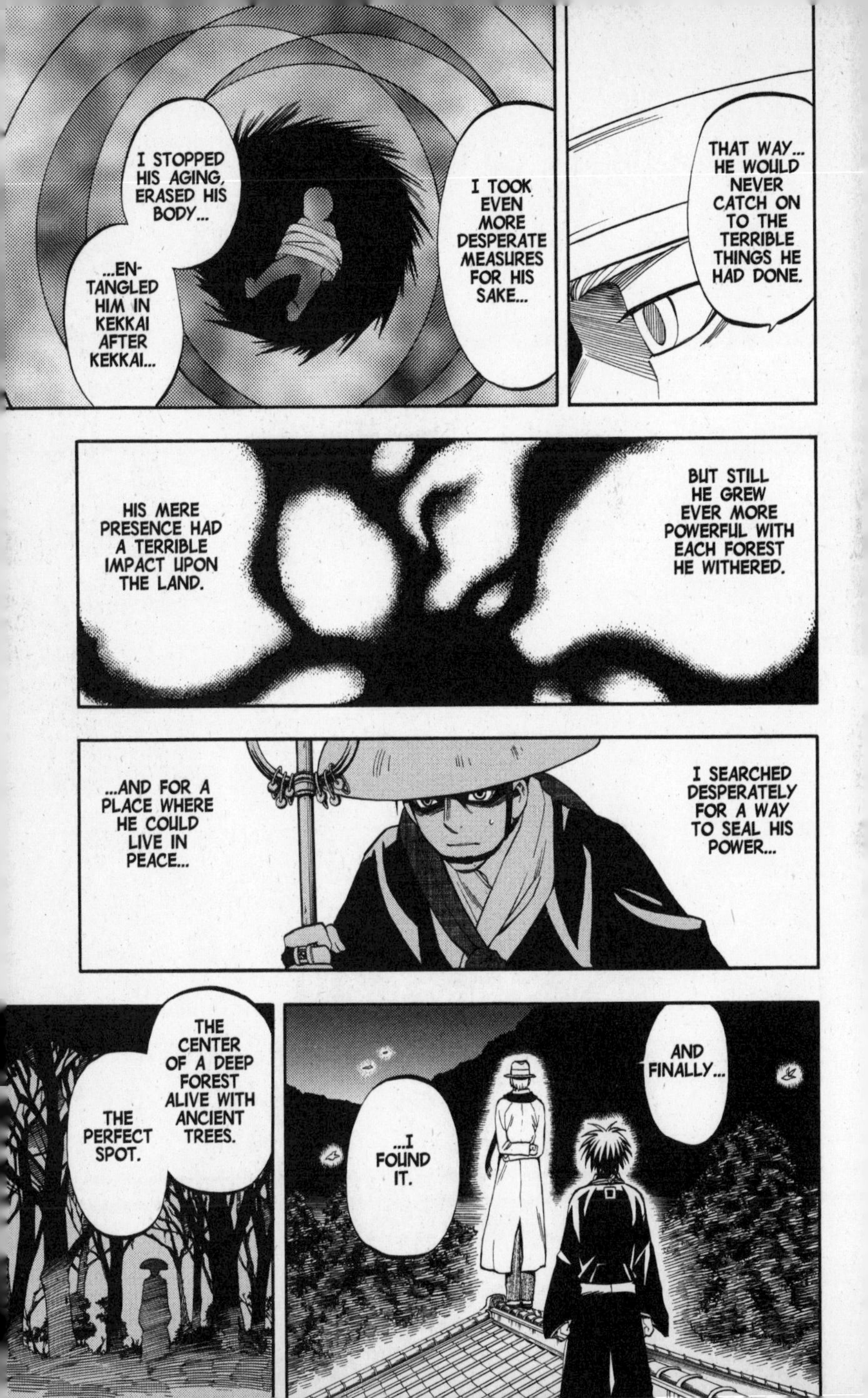
THAT WAY... HE WOULD NEVER CATCH ON TO THE TERRIBLE THINGS HE HAD DONE.
I TOOK EVEN MORE DESPERATE MEASURES FOR HIS SAKE...
I STOPPED HIS AGING, ERASED HIS BODY...
...EN-TANGLED HIM IN KEKKAI AFTER KEKKAI...
BUT STILL HE GREW EVER MORE POWERFUL WITH EACH FOREST HE WITHERED.
HIS MERE PRESENCE HAD A TERRIBLE IMPACT UPON THE LAND.
I SEARCHED DESPERATELY FOR A WAY TO SEAL HIS POWER...
...AND FOR A PLACE WHERE HE COULD LIVE IN PEACE...
AND FINALLY...
...I FOUND IT.
THE CENTER OF A DEEP FOREST ALIVE WITH ANCIENT TREES.
THE PERFECT SPOT.

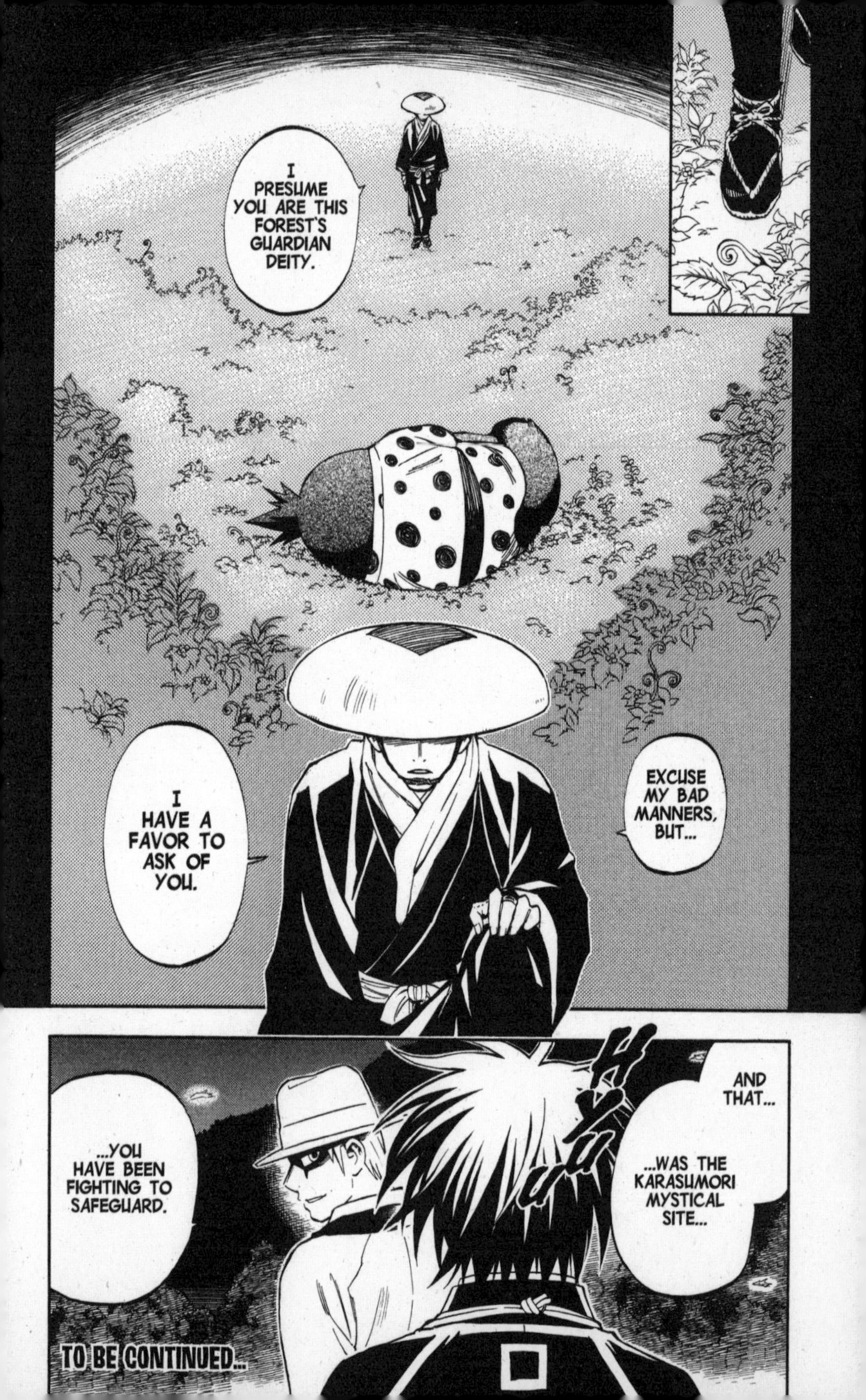
I PRESUME YOU ARE THIS FOREST'S GUARDIAN DEITY.
EXCUSE MY BAD MANNERS, BUT...
I HAVE A FAVOR TO ASK OF YOU.
AND THAT...
...WAS THE KARASUMORI MYSTICAL SITE...
...YOU HAVE BEEN FIGHTING TO SAFEGUARD.
TO BE CONTINUED...

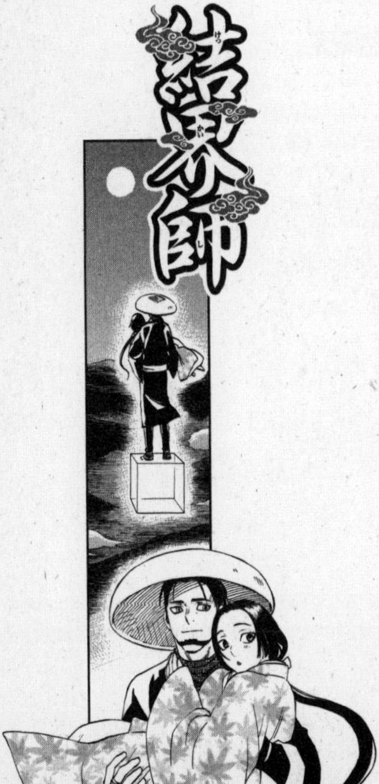
結界師

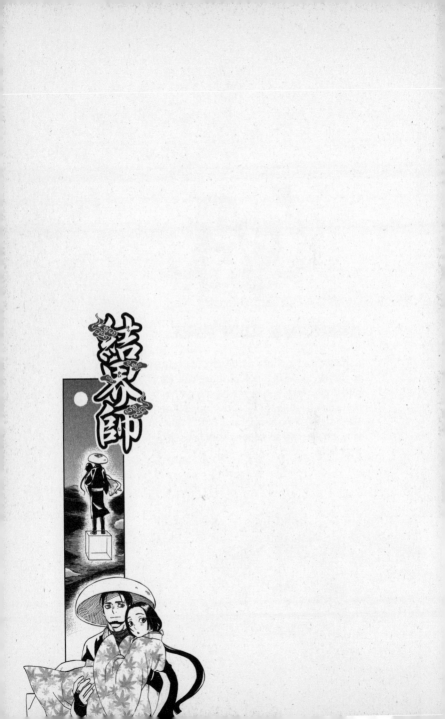

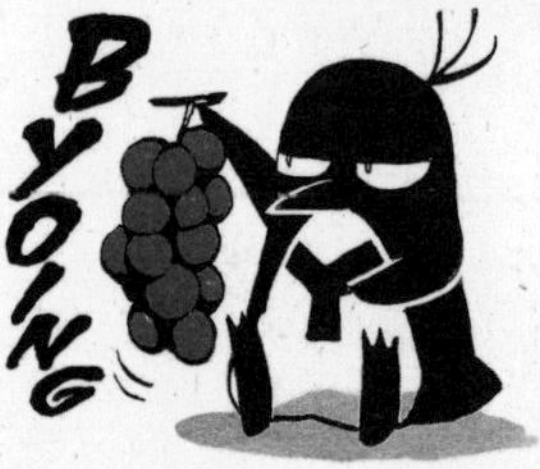
BYOING

MESSAGE FROM YELLOW TANABE

Sometimes, I get into a fruit fad. My current fad is grapes. I love the look of those clumps of big juicy fruits. By the way, I think the name for this particular large grape, "Kyoho," suits it perfectly. The sound of the word, the kanji... I don't know why, but there's something very tempting about it. It's lovely.

KEKKAISHI

VOLUME 32
SHONEN SUNDAY EDITION

STORY AND ART BY YELLOW TANABE

© 2004 Yellow TANABE/Shogakukan
All rights reserved.
Original Japanese edition "KEKKAISHI" published by SHOGAKUKAN Inc.

Translation/Yuko Sawada
Touch-up Art & Lettering/Stephen Dutro
Cover Design & Graphic Layout/Ronnie Casson
Editor/Annette Roman

The rights of the author(s) of the work(s) in this publication to be
so identified have been asserted in accordance with the Copyright,
Designs and Patents Act 1988. A CIP catalogue record for this book is
available from the British Library.

The stories, characters and incidents mentioned in this publication are
entirely fictional.

Printed in the U.S.A.

Published by VIZ Media, LLC
P.O. Box 77010
San Francisco, CA 94107

10 9 8 7 6 5 4 3 2 1
First printing, June 2012

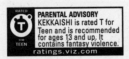

PARENTAL ADVISORY
KEKKAISHI is rated T for
Teen and is recommended
for ages 13 and up. It
contains fantasy violence.
ratings.viz.com

www.viz.com

WWW.SHONENSUNDAY.COM

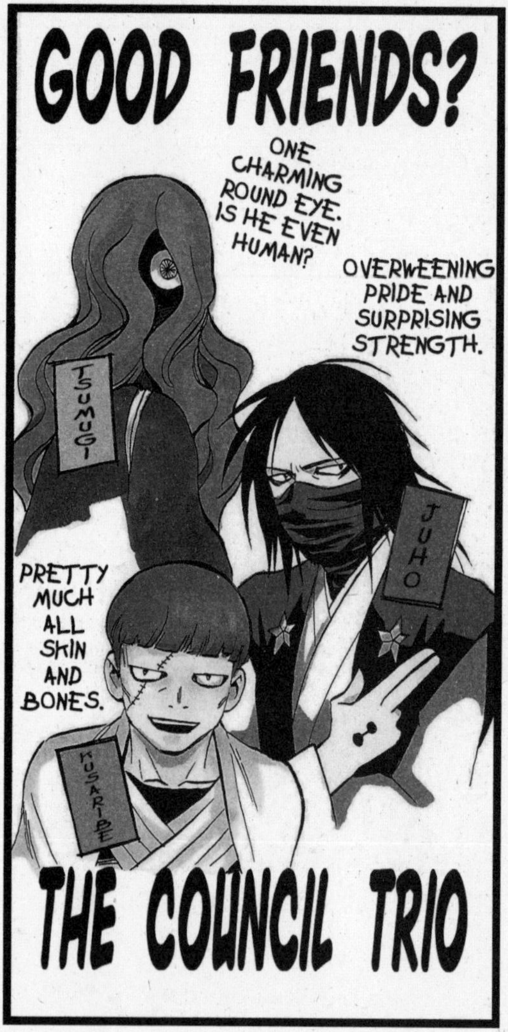
GOOD FRIENDS?
ONE CHARMING ROUND EYE. IS HE EVEN HUMAN?
OVERWEENING PRIDE AND SURPRISING STRENGTH.
JUHO
TSUMUGI
PRETTY MUCH ALL SKIN AND BONES.
KUSARIBE
THE COUNCIL TRIO